BIOGRAPHICAL
ENCYCLOPEDIA
of
SCIENTISTS

BIOGRAPHICAL ENCYCLOPEDIA of SCIENTISTS

Volume 3
Helmholtz – McCormick

Editor
RICHARD OLSON

Associate Editor
ROGER SMITH

Marshall Cavendish
New York • London • Toronto

Project Editor: Tracy Irons-Georges
Research Supervisor: Jeffry Jensen
Acquisitions Editor: Mark Rehn
Photograph Editor: Karrie Hyatt
Production Editor: Cynthia Breslin Beres
Proofreading Supervisor: Yasmine A. Cordoba
Layout: James Hutson

Photograph Researcher: Susan Hormuth, Washington, D.C.

Published By
Marshall Cavendish Corporation
99 White Plains Road
Tarrytown, New York 10591-9001
United States of America

Library of Congress Cataloging-in-Publication Data

Biographical encyclopedia of scientists / editor Richard Olson, associate editor Roger
    Smith.
        p.   cm.
    Complete in 5 v.
    Includes bibliographical references and index.
    1. Scientists—Biography—Encyclopedias. 2. Science—Encyclopedias. 3. Science—
Dictionaries. I. Olson, Richard, 1940-   . II. Smith, Roger, 1953 Apr. 19-   .
    ISBN 0-7614-7064-6 (set)
    ISBN 0-7614-7067-0 (vol. 3)
    Q141.B532   1998
    509'.2'2—dc21   97-23877
                                                                              CIP

First Printing

Contents

Key to Pronunciation

As an aid to users of the *Biographical Encyclopedia of Scientists*, guides to pronunciation for profiled scientists with foreign names have been provided with the first mention of the name in each entry. These guides are rendered in an easy-to-use phonetic manner. Stressed syllables are indicated by capital letters.

Letters of the English language, particularly vowels, are pronounced in different ways depending on the context. Below are letters and combinations of letters used in the phonetic guides to represent various sounds, along with examples of words in which those sounds appear and corresponding guides for their pronunciation.

Symbols	Pronounced As In	Spelled Phonetically
a	answer, laugh	AN-sihr, laf
ah	father, hospital	FAH-thur, HAHS-pih-tul
aw	awful, caught	AW-ful, kawt
ay	blaze, fade, waiter	blayz, fayd, WAYT-ur
ch	beach, chimp	beech, chihmp
eh	bed, head, said	behd, hehd, sehd
ee	believe, leader	bee-LEEV, LEED-ur
ew	boot, loose	bewt, lews
g	beg, disguise, get	behg, dihs-GIZ, geht
i	buy, height, surprise	bi, hit, sur-PRIZ
ih	bitter, pill	bih-TUR, pihl
j	digit, edge, jet	DIH-jiht, ehj, jeht
k	cat, kitten, hex	kat, KIH-tehn, hehks
o	cotton, hot	CO-tuhn, hot
oh	below, coat, note	bee-LOH, coht, noht
oo	good, look	good, look
ow	couch, how	kowch, how
oy	boy, coin	boy, koyn
s	cellar, save, scent	SEL-ur, sayv, sehnt
sh	issue, shop	IH-shew, shop
uh	about, enough	uh-BOWT, ee-NUHF
ur	earth, letter	urth, LEH-tur
y	useful, young	YEWS-ful, yuhng
z	business, zest	BIHZ-ness, zest
zh	vision	VI-zhuhn

BIOGRAPHICAL ENCYCLOPEDIA of SCIENTISTS

Hermann von Helmholtz

Areas of Achievement: Invention, mathematics, physics, and physiology

Contribution: Helmholtz, one of the last great universalists of science, made fundamental contributions in the fields of physiology, optics, acoustics, mathematics, meteorology, and electrodynamics. His investigations of optics led to the invention of the ophthalmoscope and a theory of color vision.

Aug. 31, 1821	Born in Potsdam, Prussia (now Germany)
1838-1842	Studies medicine and physics at the Friedrich-Wilhelms Medical Institute in Berlin
1843-1848	Serves as a surgeon in the Prussian army
1847	Publishes the world's first treatise on the principle of energy conservation
1848-1849	Works as an instructor of anatomy at the Academy for Fine Arts, Berlin
1849-1855	Serves as an associate professor of physiology at the University of Königsberg
1850-1851	Invents the ophthalmoscope and the ophthalmometer
1855-1858	Appointed a professor of anatomy and physiology at the University of Bonn
1858-1871	Serves as a professor of physiology at the University of Heidelberg
1871-1894	Works as a professor of physics at the University of Berlin
1888-1894	Serves as director of the Physio-Technical Institute in Berlin
Sept. 8, 1894	Dies in Berlin, Germany

Early Life

The eldest of five children, Hermann Ludwig Ferdinand von Helmholtz was a sickly child confined to his home for the first seven years of his life. His father, a teacher of philosophy and literature, instilled in the boy a love of learning and an interest in the philosophy of nature. Thus, when Helmholtz entered school at the age of nine, he advanced rapidly enough to graduate at seventeen despite the late start.

Helmholtz wished to attend a university in order to study physics, but his father's large family made financial support impossible. Instead, he accepted a scholarship for a free medical education at the Friedrich-Wilhelms Medical Institute in Berlin under the stipulation that, on his graduation, he would spend the next eight years as a military physician.

During his four years at the institute, in addition to studying medicine, he attended physics lectures, plowed through mathematics texts, and learned to play the piano profi-

(Library of Congress)

ciently. His lifelong passion to combine physiology and physics surely stems from this period.

In 1843, the young military doctor was assigned to a regiment in Potsdam, where minimal duties allowed ample time for scientific research. Focusing his attention on the study of energy, he derived a persuasive proof of the law of the conservation of energy, which he presented to the Physical Society of Berlin in 1847. Recognition of his obvious scientific talents allowed him to relinquish his military duties three years early.

Academic Career

In 1848, Helmholtz assumed his first academic post, as instructor of anatomy at the Academy for Fine Arts in Berlin. This minor post did not

The Trichromatic Theory of Color Vision

Only three primary colors are necessary to reproduce light of any hue because only three color receptors, each responding to one wavelength, exist in the human eye.

Modern theories of color date from the work of Sir Isaac Newton, who performed detailed investigations of the physics of light and color. By the advent of the nineteenth century, experiments had verified that light is a spectrum consisting of visible undulations that travel from a source to a receptor. Each color of the spectrum can be associated with a specific wavelength of light. The mechanism by which invisible wavelengths of light are converted into the perception of color in the human brain remained a mystery until the detailed investigations begun by Helmholtz.

Helmholtz reasoned that the eye's ability to perceive hundreds of different hues does not necessarily imply that a specific structure exists for each wavelength that can be discriminated. Although Thomas Young had speculated that all colors could be produced by mixing various amounts of three primary colors, no experimental verification of this had been provided. In fact, virtually no experimental investigations were conducted on color vision in the two hundred-year interim from Newton to Helmholtz.

Helmholtz resurrected Young's hypothesis and postulated that only three receptors, each sensitive to a different color of light, would be necessary for human color vision. He conducted experiments on color vision, eventually proving that any color of the spectrum could be matched by various amounts of three "physiological" primaries: red, green, and blue (as opposed to the spectral primaries of red, yellow, and blue). He also tied Young's hypothesis explicitly to possible physiological mechanisms and identified three color receptors. Helmholtz later extended his theory to account for color blindness, negative afterimages, and successive contrasts.

His theory, known today as the Young-Helmholtz trichromatic theory, contends that a wavelength of any hue can be matched exactly by different amounts of three primary colors (red, green, and blue). Light having a particular wavelength stimulates each of the three receptors differently. The pattern of nerve activity in the three receptors causes the perception of color; each wavelength of light is uniquely encoded in the human nervous system by a particular pattern of activity in the visual receptors. Two lights with different wavelength distributions will appear to be the same color, however, if they produce the same neural response in the receptors.

If the human eye had only a single receptor, the response to light of any color would depend only on the light's intensity. The presence of two or more receptors provides a crosspattern that signals which wavelength is present independent of the intensity—that is, the neural pattern remains constant as the brightness changes.

Although the Young-Helmholtz theory is no longer regarded as being true in every respect, it provided a firm experimental foundation for extensions and refinements in the twentieth century, as well as the first complete explanation of color vision.

Bibliography

Color Vision. J. Marvullo. New York: Watson-Guptill, 1989.

Color Vision. Leo M. Hurvich. Sunderland, Mass.: Sinauer Associates, 1981.

Sensation and Perception. E. B. Goldstein. 4th ed. Pacific Grove, Calif.: Brooks/Cole, 1996.

hold him long; commencing the next year, he successively accepted professorships at the Universities of Königsburg, Bonn, and Heidelberg.

These years, from 1849 to 1871, were professionally very productive ones. His investigations of the physiology and physics of the eye led to two important inventions, the ophthalmoscope in 1850, which is used to study the eye's interior, and the ophthalmometer in 1851, which is used to measure the eye's accommodation to changing conditions. During his tenure at Königsburg, he also measured the speed of nerve impulses in frogs' legs, and he began his studies of electromagnetism and acoustic vibration.

In 1856, while he was teaching at the University of Bonn, the first volume of Helmholtz's optical studies, *Handbuch der physiologischen Optik* (1856-1867; *Treatise on Physiological Optics*, 1924) was published. A preoccupation with acoustic matters led to a theory of combination tones and an embryonic understanding of musical harmony.

Helmholtz transferred to Heidelberg in 1858, and his research progressed rapidly. His definitive work on the analysis and perception of musical tones, *Die Lehre von den Tonempfindungen als physiologische Grundlage für die Theorie der Musik* (*On the Sensations of Tone as a Physiological Basis for the Theory of Music*, 1875), was published in 1863, and, in 1867, the next two volumes of *Handbuch der physiologischen Optik* were released. He continued his investigations of electrodynamics and hydrodynamics while broadening his interests to include non-Euclidean geometry and the theory of knowledge.

Later Life

In the spring of 1871, Helmholtz accepted the professorship of physics at the University of Berlin and began the last phase of his long and productive career. During the next twenty-three years, he continued his work in acoustics, investigated various meteorological problems, and made important contributions in thermodynamics and mathematics.

His main focus, however, was on the nascent science of electrodynamics. In 1888, his student Heinrich Hertz experimentally confirmed the existence of radio waves as predicted by James Clerk Maxwell twenty years earlier.

On July 12, 1894, Helmholtz, an aging but still active scientist, suffered a cerebral hemorrhage, from which he died on September 8.

Bibliography
By Helmholtz

Handbuch der physiologischen Optik, 1856-1867 (3 vols.; *Treatise on Physiological Optics*, 1924)

Die Lehre von den Tonempfindungen als physiologische Grundlage für die Theorie der Musik, 1863 (*On the Sensations of Tone as a Physiological Basis for the Theory of Music*, 1875)

Populare wissenschaftliche Vorträge, 1865-1876 (3 vols.; *Popular Scientific Lectures*, 1880)

Selected Writings of Hermann von Helmholtz, 1971 (Russell Kahl, ed.)

About Helmholtz

Hermann Ludwig Ferdinand von Helmholtz. John G. M'Kendrick. New York: Longmans, 1899.

"Hermann von Helmholtz." J. Beck. *International Encyclopedia of the Social Sciences*, edited by David L. Sills. Vol. 6. New York: Macmillan Free Press, 1968.

Hermann von Helmholtz. Leo Koenigsberger. Translated by Frances A. Welby. New York: Dover, 1906.

(George R. Plitnik)

Jan Baptista van Helmont

Areas of Achievement: Chemistry, medicine, and physiology

Contribution: Rejecting ancient medical authority, Helmont formulated reasonably accurate descriptions of chemical digestion, the physiological benefit of fever, and the cause of disease. His experiments led him to discover gas and the indestructibility of matter.

Jan. 12, 1580	Born in Brussels, Spanish Netherlands (now Belgium)
1599	Completes medical studies at the University of Louvain
1600-1605	Travels extensively throughout Europe
1609	Studied the medical ideas of Paracelsus
1616	Returns to Brussels and practices medicine
1621	Publishes *De magnetica vulnerum naturali et legitima curatione* (*Ternary of Paradoxes*, 1650)
1623	Denounced by the medical faculty of Louvain
1625	Twenty-four propositions from his text are condemned by the Spanish Inquisition
1628-1629	Many of his propositions are censored by the Universities of Louvain, Cologne, and Lyons
1634	Imprisoned at Brussels by Spanish authorities and then placed under house arrest until 1636
1642	Legal actions against him end
Dec. 30, 1644	Dies in Vilvoorde, near Spanish Netherlands (now Belgium)
1649	Acquitted posthumously of heresy

(Archive Photos)

Early Life

Jan (or Johannes) Baptista van Helmont was born on January 12, 1580 (1579 in the Old Style) in Brussels. An aristocrat, he took a degree in medicine at the University of Louvain in 1599.

Dissatisfied with traditional medical education, which stressed the biology of Aristotle and the anatomy of Galen, Helmont toured Europe between 1600 and 1605 hoping to learn something more useful. In 1609, he began seven years of research influenced by the iatrochemical method of the sixteenth century scientist Paracelsus (1493?-1541), which put chemistry in service to medicine.

Condemnations for Heresy

In 1621, Helmont wrote *De magnetica vulnerum naturali et legitima curatione contra* (*Ternary of Paradoxes*, 1650) in defense of the controversial practice of the weapon's salve, or the application of medicinal ointments to a weapon rather than to its victim's wounds. Arguing that the treatment depended on natural and divine power, he denied the accusation of its critics that it worked through the agency of Satan.

Subsequently, the medical faculty of Louvain denounced Helmont in 1623, and, two years later, the Spanish Inquisition condemned twenty-seven propositions from Helmont's pamphlet. Although protesting his innocence, he bowed to the judgment of the Inquisition. Nevertheless, new condemnations followed in 1627-1628 and in 1634.

Helmont was imprisoned briefly in Brussels before being released to house arrest, from which he was excused in 1636, only to endure further legal proceedings until 1642. A few years after Helmont's death in 1644, he was officially cleared of charges of heresy.

Helmont's son, Franciscus Mercurius van Helmont, published his father's manuscripts and previously released works as *Ortus medicinae* (1648; *Oriatrike: Or, Physick Refined*, 1662). The collection was published in five languages and went through twelve editions by the early eighteenth century.

Medical and Chemical Insights

In 1642, Helmont wrote a study of fever in which he concluded that it was the body's attempt to heal itself. Two years later, he compiled further medical observations.

Helmont denied that disease results from an imbalance of the "vital humors" and argued instead that it originates in the invasion of the body by distinctive pathological agents. Thus, he prescribed chemicals to treat specific diseases and, conversely, rejected purging and bloodletting as ineffective and possibly lethal.

While experimenting with chemical remedies for disease and exploring the chemistry of digestion, Helmont discovered gases. Moreover, upon dissolving metals in acid, he noticed that the original elements could be retrieved in their previous quantities, leading him to conclude that matter is indestructible.

Chemical Philosophy

Helmont's work was not strictly scientific, by that term's modern definition. Despite the brilliance of his discovery of gases and the accuracy of his description of their properties, Helmont's passion to understand the chemical composition of matter was not simply a rational investigation but a spiritual inquiry as well. Through chemical analysis, he sought to uncover a deeper mystical reality beneath tangible things; gas, he believed, was the spiritual essence of matter.

The Discovery of Gases

Helmont demonstrated that matter can exist in a rarified condition finer than steam but denser than air. He named this vaporous state of matter "gas."

To test the chemistry of matter, Helmont burned various substances and analyzed the resulting smoke. He noticed that each combusted material produced fumes that were chemically unique. He detected the same phenomenon when he fermented fruits and grains and when he dissolved metals in acid.

Helmont referred to these characteristics fumes and vapors as gases, a word that he probably derived from the Latin and Greek *chaos*. Using the balance and other devices, Helmont cataloged several gases (for example, sulfur dioxide, carbon monoxide, and carbon dioxide) and quantified some of their properties.

Conforming only to the shape of the vessels that contain them, gases have no inherent form or volume. Helmont also noted that contained gases distribute themselves equally throughout a vessel. Freed from a container, gases expand indefinitely and are the most elastic of all substances.

Thus, Helmont also began the study of the mechanical operations of gas. Prompted by these pioneering observations. Robert Boyle and Antoine-Laurent Lavoisier summarized the behavior of gas in mathematical laws and founded the modern science of pneumatics.

Bibliography

The Perfect Gas. J. S. Rowlinson. New York: Pergamon Press, 1963.

The Properties of Gases and Liquids. New York: McGraw-Hill, 1987.

Thermodynamics and Physics of Matter. Princeton, N.J.: Princeton University Press, 1955.

Bibliography

By Helmont

De magnetica vulnerum naturali et legitima curatione, 1641 (*Ternary of Paradoxes: The Magnetick Cure of Wounds, Nativity of Tartar of Wine, Image of God in Man*, 1650)

Ortus medicinae, 1648 (*Oriatrike: Or, Physick Refined*, 1662)

About Helmont

The Chemical Philosophy. Allen Debus. New York: Science History Publications, 1977.

"The Mysticism and Science of Johann Baptista Van Helmont (1579-1644)." Berthold Heinecke. *Ambix* 42 (1995).

Paracelsus: An Introduction to Philosophical Medicine in the Era of the Renaissance. Walter Pagel. Basel, Switzerland: S. Karger, 1982.

(David Allen Duncan)

Joseph Henry

Area of Achievement: Physics

Contribution: Henry was the leading American experimental physicist of his day. As secretary of the Smithsonian Institution, he nurtured America's scientific community and served as a spokesperson for the importance of basic research.

Dec. 17, 1797	Born in Albany, New York
1819-1822	Attends the Albany Academy
1826-1832	Teaches mathematics and physics at the Albany Academy
1829	Develops a powerful electromagnet
1831	Builds the first electric motor
1831	Devises the electromagnetic telegraph
1832	Independently of Michael Faraday, discovers mutual electromagnetic induction
1832	Discovers electromagnetic self-induction
1832-1846	Teaches physics at the College of New Jersey (later Princeton University)
1838	Discovers the transformer
1839-1844	Advises Samuel F. B. Morse concerning the telegraph
1842	Discovers the oscillatory nature of the discharge of a capacitor
1846-1878	Serves as the first secretary of the Smithsonian Institution
1868-1878	Serves as president of the National Academy of Sciences
May 13, 1878	Dies in Washington, D.C.

Early Life

Joseph Henry was born in Albany, New York, in 1797. His father was an alcoholic, and Henry was reared by an uncle and his maternal step-grandmother. At the age of eighteen, he read a popular introduction to science, which excited him about the subject. He decided to become a scientist.

From about 1815 to 1826, Henry worked as an actor, a country schoolteacher, a tutor, and a surveyor. He attended the Albany Academy as an older student from 1819 until 1822. In 1826, he was chosen as professor of mathematics and natural philosophy (physics) at the Albany Academy.

Studying Induction

While at the Albany Academy, Henry began his lifelong effort to understand the relationships between electricity, magnetism, light, and heat. During this period, he focused on the relationship between magnetism and electricity, especially the creation of an electric current by a changing magnetic field.

With a heavy teaching load, Henry had limited opportunities to experiment. Neverthe-

(National Portrait Gallery, Smithsonian Institution)

less, beginning in 1827, he published a number of papers. The most important are those in which he described the first electric motor, in 1831, and mutual electromagnetic induction and electromagnetic self-induction, in 1832. He demonstrated the electromagnetic telegraph to his students in 1831.

During these years, Henry often published in response to the announcement by European scientists of discoveries that parallelled or anticipated Henry's research. He was always in danger of losing his claim of priority or of being ignored by the European community. This was especially true of his work on induction, as Michael Faraday was working simultaneously on the same topic.

A Skilled Experimenter

Henry's growing national reputation led to his appointment in 1832 as professor of natural philosophy at the College of New Jersey (which later became Princeton University). He was frequently compared to Benjamin Franklin.

In 1837, Henry visited Europe and interacted with many of the leading scientists in England and France. He exchanged information on experimental techniques and purchased apparatuses.

While at Princeton, he continued to experiment on the nature of electricity and magnetism. In 1838, he discovered that by rearranging electrical coils, he could either step up or step down the voltage of a current, producing what is now known as the transformer. Four years later, he found that the discharge of a capacitor is oscillatory. That same year, he discovered that electrical induction could be detected over large distances, a finding that was the forerunner to radio transmission.

Henry also published on a wide variety of topics in other areas of physics, including capillarity (1839 and 1845), phosphorescence (1841), and molecular cohesion (1844). In 1845, he described his observations of the surface temperature of the sun using a thermoelectric apparatus, which was a major step in astrophysics. Henry also observed various terrestrial magnetic phenomena such as auroras.

A firm believer that science should benefit humankind, Henry was alert to the technological applications of his work. He provided technical assistance to Samuel F. B. Morse and an endorsement of Morse's telegraph. In contrast, he did not support efforts to develop the electric motor because he believed that steam power was much cheaper than batteries, the source of electric power at that time.

Secretary of the Smithsonian

Henry's many publications and status in international science led to his election in 1846 as the first secretary of the Smithsonian Institution. He used James Smithson's bequest to support research, scholarly publication, scientific cooperation, and international exchange. Dur-

ing his lifetime, the Smithsonian became the most important scientific institution in the United States.

As secretary, Henry served as a science adviser to the executive and legislative branches of the federal government. He also conducted research on behalf of the government, including studies of the acoustics of public buildings and investigations of fog signals. Henry was a founder in the United States of the field of applied acoustics.

One of the original members of the National Academy of Sciences when it was founded in 1863, Henry was elected its president in 1868

Mutual Induction and Self-Induction

Henry found that an electromotive force can be induced in a circuit by a changing magnetic field and that any circuit which has a varying current will induce in itself an electromotive force.

In 1820, Hans Christian Ørsted demonstrated that an electric current produced a magnetic field that surrounded the wire carrying the current. Scientists believed that electricity and magnetism had a fully reciprocal relationship, but efforts to produce electricity from a constant magnetic field had repeatedly failed.

Instead of using a constant magnetic field, Henry created a magnetic field that varied in intensity from zero to a maximum and back to zero again. He did so by varying the current in his circuit by alternately connecting or disconnecting the battery from the coil within which the current flowed. He found that while the magnetic field varied, an electromotive force was induced in a second coil. No current was generated in the second coil, however, when the magnetic field was constant.

Henry also found that any electrical circuit in which there is a varying current induces an electromotive force in itself. This electromotive force, caused by the variation in the current's own magnetic field, is in the direction opposite the original current. Henry's first discovery is known as mutual induction or mutual inductance; the second as self-induction or self-inductance.

At the same time that Henry was experiment-

ing in Albany, New York, Michael Faraday was conducting similar experiments in London, England. Faraday published his discovery of mutual induction first; Henry made the first announcement of self-induction.

The work of Henry and Faraday was fundamental to further understanding of electromagnetic phenomena. Their contemporaries, especially European scientists, were more aware of Faraday's publications and achievements than Henry's. Thus, it was through Faraday that later research was influenced. His work was one of the major sources on which James Clerk Maxwell drew, starting in 1853. Maxwell built on Faraday's concept of lines of force in developing his field theory, which is a mathematical explanation of electrodynamic phenomenon that is fundamental to further understanding of electricity and magnetism. There is no reference to Henry in *A Treatise on Electricity and Magnetism* (1873), Maxwell's most important publication.

Bibliography

Electromagnetic Induction Phenomena. David Schieber. New York: Springer-Verlag, 1986.

Lines and Waves: Faraday, Maxwell, and 150 Years of Electromagnetism. Robert D. Friedel. New York: Center for the History of Electrical Engineering, Institute of Electrical and Electronic Engineers, 1981.

A Treatise on Electricity and Magnetism. James Clerk Maxwell. 2 vols. Oxford, England: Clarendon Press, 1873.

and served in that office until his death. He transformed the academy into a honorific, impartial supporter of research and a voice of the American scientific community.

In recognition of his contributions to physics, the 1893 International Congress of Electricians named the international unit of inductance the "henry."

Bibliography

By Henry
Scientific Writings of Joseph Henry, 1886 (2 vols.)
The Papers of Joseph Henry, 1972-   (Nathan Reingold, ed. of vols. 1-5; Marc Rothenberg, ed. of vols. 6-)

About Henry
America's Castle: The Evolution of the Smithsonian Building and Its Institution, 1840-1878. Kenneth Hafertepe. Washington, D.C.: Smithsonian Institution Press, 1984.
Joseph Henry: His Life and Work. Thomas Coulson. Princeton, N.J.: Princeton University Press, 1950.
The Launching of Modern American Science: 1846-1876. Robert Bruce. New York: Alfred A. Knopf, 1987.

(Marc Rothenberg)

Herophilus

Areas of Achievement: Medicine and physiology

Contribution: Herophilus is known as the founder of scientific anatomy because he was the first to base his conclusions on dissection of the human body. He recognized that the brain is the center of the nervous system, distinguished the motor from the sensory nerves, and was the first to argue that the arteries contain blood, not air.

c. 330 B.C.E.	Born in Chalcedon, Bithynia
c. 260 B.C.E.	Dies, probably in Alexandria, Egypt

Early Life

Little is known about the life of Herophilus. He was born around 330 B.C.E. in Chalcedon (now Kadikoy, Turkey) and was trained as a physician by Praxagoras of Cos, from whom he developed a love of anatomy and physiology.

Herophilus became a successful teacher in Alexandria, the new capital of Egypt during this time, and published works entitled *Anatomika* (on anatomy) and *Peri Ophthalmon* (of the eyes), along with a handbook for midwives. None of his writings are preserved, except for a fragment describing the workings of the liver, but his achievements were recorded by later writers such as the Roman medical encyclopedist Celsus around the year 40 and the Christian writer Tertullian around 200.

Human Vivisection

With his younger contemporary Erasistratus of Cos, Herophilus may have been granted permission by the Ptolemaic rulers of Egypt to practice vivisection and perform medical experiments on the bodies of convicted murderers and criminals. By tradition, these events took place in the great museum of Alexandria which, along with the library there, was one of the greatest treasures of the city.

The museum was a publicly funded research institute and included an observatory,

Anatomical Studies

Herophilus carefully dissected the human brain, eye, liver, the spermatic duct, and the ovaries. He made distinctions, on anatomical grounds, between nerves, veins, and arteries.

Herophilus discovered that the brain is the central organ of the nervous system; he regarded it as the primary seat of intelligence and therefore the most important organ in the body. This finding disagreed with Aristotle, who had argued that the heart was the chief organ of the body. Through dissection, Herophilus described the meninges (membranous layers) and the torcular Herophili, which is named after him. In uncovering the various parts of the brain, Herophilus distinguished the cerebrum (the largest part of the brain) from the cerebellum (a part of the hindbrain) and discovered the fourth ventricle, naming part of it the calamus scriptorius ("the writing pen"). In animals, he discovered and named the rete mirabile (retiform plexus).

Herophilus divided the bundles of fibers, or nerves, that carry feeling and impulses to action toward and away from the brain, into sensory and motor, and he showed that all the peripheral nerves are connected to the central nervous system. He incorrectly concluded that the nerves were separate from the special senses of vision, smell, taste, touch, and hearing.

Herophilus also investigated the nature of the blood vessels in the human body. He was the first to claim that arteries and veins are different because only the arteries have "pulsations." Herophilus believed that these pulsations could be used to diagnose various diseases and tried to classify different types. After describing the pulse in terms of strength, rate, rhythm, and size, he tried to measure the rate of the pulse using a portable water clock designed by himself and fellow Alexandrian scientists.

Unlike his teacher, Praxagoras of Cos, Herophilus rejected the theory that the arteries carried only *pneuma*, or the spirit of sensation. Instead, he argued that the arteries contained both blood and pneuma. (The word "artery" originally meant "spirit or air carrier.") In other work on the blood vessels, he proved that the veins from the intestine end in the liver and discovered and named the duodenum and prostate. The term "duodenum" comes from the Greek for "twelve fingers," and Herophilus chose that name after measuring the size of the structure.

Overall, the major achievements of Herophilus were in establishing anatomy as a formal discipline and in detailing the structure of the nervous system, a field known today as neuroanatomy.

Bibliography

Anatomy: A Regional Atlas of the Human Body. C. D. Clemente. Baltimore: Urban & Schwarzenberg, 1987.

The Human Brain and Spinal Cord: A Historical Study Illustrated by Writings from Antiquity to the Twentieth Century. E. Clarke and C. D. O'Malley. Berkeley: University of California Press, 1968.

The Human Nervous System. M. L. Barr and J. A. Kiernan. Philadelphia: J. B. Lippincott, 1988.

zoological and botanical gardens, lecture halls, and rooms for research. Scholars such as Herophilus were reportedly provided with free meals in the great hall to encourage communal debates of ideas, and their salaries were tax exempt. Unfortunately, the museum was destroyed in 295 during a revolt against the rulers of Alexandria.

Herophilus and Agnodice

Herophilus is the first medical teacher recorded to have had a female student. By legend, Agnodice was from Athens and disguised herself as a man in order to be allowed to study medicine. When her disguise was discovered, she was prosecuted for breaking the laws that forbade women from studying and practicing medicine. Supposedly, her faithful paients rallied to her defense, warning the male judges that they would become the enemies of all women if they condemned their only female physician to death. Sadly, the end of the story is not recorded.

The "Best Physician"

Herophilus is credited with several sayings, or aphorisms, regarding health, including "Wisdom and art, strength and wealth, all are useless without health," and "The best physician is the one who is able to differentiate the possible from the impossible." Above all, he urged physicians to become familiar with the body through dissecting its parts and so to be prepared to intervene drastically with copious bloodletting and/or surgery in illness.

Herophilus is thought to have died around 260 B.C.E., probably in Alexandria.

Bibliography
By Herophilus
The following works, traditionally attributed to him, have been lost:
Anatomika (on anatomy)
Peri Ophthalmon (of the eyes)

About Herophilus
Herophilus: The Art of Medicine in Early Alexandria. Heinrich von Staden. Cambridge, England: Cambridge University Press, 1989.
A Short History of Anatomy and Physiology from the Greeks to Harvey. Charles Singer. Mineola, N.Y.: Dover, 1957.
The Western Medical Tradition: 800 B.C.-1800 A.C. Lawrence I. Conrad et al. Cambridge, England: Cambridge University Press, 1995.

(Lynda Stephenson Payne)

Caroline Lucretia Herschel

Area of Achievement: Astronomy
Contribution: Herschel was noted as an observer of comets and a locator of several new nebulas and star clusters, and for her transcription, reduction, and cataloging of astronomical data.

Mar. 16, 1750	Born in Hanover, Hanover (now Germany)
1772	Joins her brother William in Bath, England
1781	Moves to Windsor with her brother when he is appointed Royal Astronomer
1783	Discovers three new nebulas
1787	King George III gives her £50 per year as a salary to be an assistant to William
1798	Her Work *Catalogue of Stars Observed by Flamsteed* is published by the Royal Society of London
1822	After William's death, leaves England to return to Hanover
1828	Awarded the Gold Medal of the Royal Astronomical Society for *A Catalogue of Nebulae Which Have Been Observed by William Herschel in a Series of Sweeps*
1835	Given honorary membership in the Royal Astronomical Society
1838	Elected to membership in the Royal Irish Academy
1846	Receives the Gold Medal for Science from the king of Prussia on her ninety-sixth birthday
Jan. 9, 1848	Dies in Hanover, Hanover

Observations and Catalogs

Much of Herschel's contribution to astronomy was as an observer—locating comets, several new nebulas, and star clusters—and in the skilled and accurate transcription and reduction of astronomical data.

Herschel assisted her brother in the preparation of telescopes and in the making and recording of observations. She did difficult and tedious calculations. A major contribution was her preparation of catalogs of astronomical observations. The Herschels established sidereal astronomy, the study of stars and stellar systems. Between 1783 and 1802, they discovered 2,500 nebulas and star clusters. Caroline Herschel discovered several nebulas and comets.

After 1787, she began to catalog stars. She submitted to the Royal Society of London *Catalogue of Stars Observed by Flamsteed*; this work was published by the society in 1798. At the age of seventy-five, she finished her work on the positions of 2,500 nebulae—*A Catalogue of the Nebulae Which Have Been Observed by William Herschel in a Series of Sweeps*—and in 1828 was awarded the Gold Medal of the Royal Astronomical Society for this work, which was never published. The associated resolution of the society proclaimed that her catalog "may be considered as the completion of a series of exertions probably unparalleled either in magnitude or importance, in the annals of astronomical labor."

Bibliography

Hypatia's Heritage. Margaret Alic. Boston: Beacon Press, 1986.
Women in Science: Antiquity Through the Nineteenth Century. Marilyn Bailey Ogilvie. Cambridge, Mass.: MIT Press, 1986.

Early Life

Caroline Lucretia Herschel was born March 16, 1750 (according to the German calendar, and in 1751 by the British calendar) in Hanover. Her father, Isaac, was a military musician who thought that she should receive some education. Her mother, Anna, disagreed, holding that Caroline should learn to keep house and look after her brothers.

Although Caroline lacked a formal education, she had a great desire for self-improvement and was intelligent. Her father included her in his conversations with her brothers as far as possible and introduced her to astronomy. Her brothers trained as musicians, but Herschel's father informed her that because she was neither rich nor good-looking, she was unlikely to marry. She was not qualified to be a governess, as her knowledge of languages was inadequate.

After the French occupation of Hanover in 1757, Caroline's elder brother William escaped to England, where he was a musician and music teacher. Their father died in 1767, after which Caroline found life with her mother intolerable.

(Library of Congress)

Astronomical Work

In 1766, William became an organist at the Octagon Chapel in Bath, and, in 1772, Caroline joined him. There, she trained as a singer—a soprano—and was a successful soloist in oratorios. Apart from his interest in music, William was interested in astronomy, an interest that came to occupy an increasing amount of his time. In 1773, he started building and acquiring telescopes, and, in 1774, he began to devote all of his nights to astronomical observation. Caroline would sing only under William's direction, so she gave up singing and began to work as his assistant in astronomy.

William taught Caroline mathematics and astronomy. Their life consisted of making astronomical observations at night and doing tedious calculations and writing up their observations during the day. When William had made a number of telescopes and discovered the planet Uranus in 1781, he was appointed Royal Astronomer by King George III, with an annual allowance of £200. Brother and sister moved from Bath to Windsor in 1782.

In 1787, King George III gave Caroline a £50 per year salary as assistant to William. In 1788, William married Mary Pitt, the widow of one of his friends. Caroline was resentful but eventually reconciled herself to sharing her brother's affections and to her sister-in-law. When William was away, Caroline worked on her own. Only after his death did she again carry out an astronomical project independent (or semi-independent) of him.

William died in 1822, having discovered Uranus, the intrinsic motion of the sun, and the form of the Milky Way. Immediately after his death, Caroline Herschel left England, where she had lived for fifty years, to return to Hanover, where she lived for a further quarter century.

In 1835, Herschel and Mary Somerville were given honorary memberships in the Royal Society of London. In 1838, she was elected to membership in the Royal Irish Academy. Herschel died at the age of ninety-seven years and ten months, on January 9, 1848.

Bibliography

By Herschel

"An Account of a New Comet," *Philosophical Transactions*, 1787

"An Account of the Discovery of a Comet," *Philosophical Transactions*, 1794

Catalogue of Stars Observed by Flamsteed, 1798

Memoir and Correspondence, 1876 (Mary Herschel, ed.)

About Herschel

Dictionary of Scientific Biography. Charles Coulston Gillispie, ed. 16 vols. New York: Charles Scribner's Sons, 1970-1980.

Hypatia's Heritage. Margaret Alic. Boston: Beacon Press, 1986.

(Maureen H. O'Rafferty)

Sir John Herschel

Areas of Achievement: Astronomy, chemistry, mathematics, and technology
Contribution: Herschel, a noted astronomer, conducted extensive observations of stars and nebulas, making many discoveries and cataloging his findings.

Mar. 7, 1792	Born in Slough, Buckinghamshire, England
1813	Becomes a member of the Royal Society of London
1816	Graduated from Cambridge University with an M.A.
1819	Discovers hypo (sodium thiosulfate), a fixing agent for use in photography
1820	Completes the large reflector telescope needed for his observations
1821	Awarded the Copley Medal of the Royal Society of London
1826	Receives the gold medal of the Royal Astronomical Society
1827	Elected president of the Royal Astronomical Society
1831	Receives knighthood
1834	Moves to the Cape of Good Hope for southern sky research
1838	Returns to England
1845	Elected president of British Association for the Advancement of Science
1850	Receives a government position as master of the mint
1864	Publishes a catalog of 5,079 nebulas and stellar clusters
May 11, 1871	Dies in Hawkhurst, Kent, England

(Library of Congress)

Early Life

With prominent astronomers Sir William and Caroline Herschel as his father and aunt, John Frederick William Herschel was introduced to astronomy in childhood. At first a poor musician, William devoted his spare time and genius to becoming a self-educated astronomer of international fame. In sharp contrast, John's education at Eton and individual tutoring led to Cambridge University.

At Cambridge, John Herschel studied and excelled in mathematics. His fellow classmates George Peacock and Charles Babbage would become famous mathematicians. This trio initiated the Analytical Society, an association devoted to importing the analysis of continental mathematicians (such as Joseph-Louis Lagrange and Pierre-Simon Laplace) to English schools. Toward this end, Herschel and Peacock translated a calculus treatise. Next, Herschel published a book on finite difference calculus examples. Concurrently, he passed his examinations at the top of his class.

Herschel submitted several mathematical papers to the Royal Society of London and became a Fellow in 1813. He advanced in chemistry as well and even studied law. While there, Herschel's association with scientist William Wollaston and astronomer James South further motivated his decision to pursue astronomy.

Cataloging the Sky
Upon his graduation, Herschel directed his efforts toward his father's work, sidereal astronomy. This involved the design and construction of an improved reflective telescope, especially of the key component: a carefully ground and polished 18-inch mirror. His mathematical expertise proved significant in solving several optical problems. Along the way, he discovered the Herschel effect and created numerous measuring devices. With his new tool, Herschel launched his career as an observational astronomer. In collaboration with South, he began an award-winning reassessment and study of the binary stars from 1821 to 1823.

Herschel, who was knighted in 1831, refined and corrected his father's work, cataloging all nebulas and stellar systems of the northern sky by 1833. In an inspired move, he then ventured south. Packing his telescope, equipment, and texts, Herschel, his family, and mechanic John Stone journeyed to the Cape of Good Hope in South Africa, a British colony with an observatory that offered the best location for southern sky research. Herschel and Stone worked rapidly to set up his imported reflector. On March 4, 1834, the painstaking process of observation, charting, and drawing began.

At Cape Town, Herschel also conducted several botanical expeditions, introduced educational reforms, and contributed to the Cape Philosophical Society. Species of flora have received his name.

Later Life
After his triumphant return in 1838, he was made a baronet and published a large number of papers. He independently developed the medium of photography but was not given proportional credit. In 1839, Herschel produced the first glass photograph, twenty years

Mapping the Stars

Herschel recorded and charted the stellar and nebular objects in both hemispheres.

The term "monumental" best characterizes the extensive number of observations that Herschel conducted. The result was a succession of catalogs. In the final count, he had listed 5,079 nebulas and 10,300 double stars, a large portion being his own discoveries.

For the Southern Hemisphere, Herschel meticulously recorded the position and brightness of more than 2,100 binary stars, 1,707 nebulas, and 68,948 stellar objects. Most notable are his drawings of the Magellanic Clouds and the Eta Carinae nebula. In this nebula, he recorded a brief eruption, an increase in brightness, followed by a decline.

His observation of the Great Magellanic Cloud yielded the record "collection of detached or loosely connected Clusters and Nebulae." As with these "nebulae," Herschel did not realize the extragalactic nature of many of the objects that he saw. For example, the apparent "star cluster" that he observed southeast of the star alpha-Erdani is actually a major galaxy, NGC 782. He also named several of Saturn's and Uranus' moons.

In the process of observation, Herschel created tools for measuring characteristics of stars exactly. To measure brightness, he created the astrometer, which determined the relative intensity of light from a star in contrast to the full moon. These measurements set a standard for future astronomers to refine and interpret.

Bibliography
Astronomy: From the Earth to the Universe. Jay M. Pasachoff. 4th ed. Philadelphia: W. B. Saunders, 1995.
Burnham's Celestial Handbook. Robert Burnham, Jr. 3 vols. Mineola, N.Y.: Dover, 1978.
The John Herschel Bicentennial Symposium Proceedings. South Africa: Royal Society of South Africa, 1992.
Universe. W. J. Kaufmann. 4th ed. New York: W. H. Freeman, 1994.

after discovering sodium thiosulfate, a photographic fixing agent known as hypo.

Herschel was awarded a government position as master of the mint and recommended that Great Britain adopt a decimal currency system. His areas of interest, publications, and honors became innumerable. Sir John Herschel died on May 11, 1871, in Hawkhurst, Kent, and was buried at Westminster Abbey near Sir Isaac Newton.

Bibliography
By Herschel
A Collection of Examples of the Application of the Calculus of Finite Differences, 1820
Preliminary Discourse on the Study of Natural Philosophy, 1830
A Treatise on Astronomy, 1830
Results of Astronomical Observations, Made During the Years 1834-38 at the Cape of Good Hope, 1847
Outlines of Astronomy, 1849
Essays from the Edinburgh and Quarterly Reviews, with Addresses and Other Pieces, 1857
A General Catalog of Nebula and Clusters of Stars, 1864
Familiar Lectures on Scientific Subjects, 1866
Sir John Herschel: Scientific Papers, 1912 (2 vols.)
Herschel at the Cape: Diaries and Correspondence of Sir John Herschel, 1834-1838, 1969

About Herschel
The Herschels and Modern Astronomy. Agnes M. Clerke. London: Cassell, 1901.
"John Herschel (1792-1871)." C. A. Ronan. *Endeavor* 16 (1992).
The Shadow of the Telescope: A Biography of John Herschel. Gunther Buttman. New York: Charles Scribner's Sons, 1970.

(*John Panos Najarian*)

Sir William Herschel

Areas of Achievement: Astronomy and cosmology
Contribution: Herschel perfected reflecting telescopes, discovered Uranus, cataloged 800 double stars and 2,500 star clusters and nebulas, calculated the rotation time of Mars, and proved the universality of the law of gravity.

Nov. 15, 1738	Born in Hanover, Hanover (now Germany)
1757	Moves to England and works as a musician
1772	His sister Caroline joins him in England and becomes his partner in astronomical work
1773	Begins to construct telescopes
1779-1784	Conducts "sweeps" of the heavens and catalogs stars
Mar. 13, 1781	Discovers Uranus and becomes instantly famous
1781	Correctly calculates the rotation time of Mars
May, 1782	Named Royal Astronomer
1785-1789	Builds the world's largest telescope
1786	Moves to Observatory House, in Slough
1787	Discovers Mimas and Enceladus, moons of Saturn
1787	Discovers Titania and Oberon, moons of Uranus
1801	Proposes the term "asteroid" for bodies between Mars and Jupiter
1816	Knighted
1821	Publishes the last of his star catalogs
Aug. 25, 1822	Dies in Slough, Buckinghamshire, England

Early Life

Frederick William (originally Friedrich Wilhelm) Herschel was born on November 15, 1738, in Hanover as the third of six surviving children of Isaac Herschel. With little opportunity for formal education, William became an oboist with the Hanoverian Guards at the age of fourteen, touring England with the regiment in 1756. He learned English and made important contacts.

The French occupation of Hanover encouraged Herschel to seek refuge in Britain in 1757. For years, he supported himself by teaching, performing, conducting, and composing music in Leeds, Durham, Doncaster, and Halifax. Herschel secured employment as an organist at the Octagon Chapel and settled in Bath. His professional interest in music caused him to read Robert Smith's *Harmonics* (1749), and he next became acquainted with Smith's *A Compleat System of Opticks in Four Books* (1738), which changed his life.

Building Better Telescopes

By reading Smith's work, Herschel learned how to build telescopes. Joined by his sister and collaborator, Caroline Lucretia Herschel-Lucretia], he began constructing reflecting telescopes in 1773. These instruments had considerable light-gathering power, and, by 1782, the Royal Observatory took note of the superiority of Herschel's telescopes. Between 1785 and 1789, with government support, Herschel built

(Library of Congress)

what was then the world's largest telescope. These powerful tools brought the heavens down to Earth.

Finding Uranus and Fame

With his great reflective telescopes, Herschel swept the heavens, producing detailed star catalogs, with a particular interest in double stars. From their power of mutual attraction, he inferred that Sir Isaac Newton's law of universal gravity applied outside this solar system.

On March 13, 1781, Herschel discovered a planet that he named "Georgium Sidus" in honor of King George III but which was renamed "Uranus" by Johann Bode of the Berlin Observatory. Herschel became instantly world-famous as the first recorded discoverer of a planet. He was given the Copley Medal, elected a Fellow of the Royal Society of London, received by King George III, named Royal Astronomer, and awarded an annual pension of two hundred pounds.

Now able to devote himself to science, Herschel settled at Observatory House in Slough in 1786. Assisted in his research by his sister, Herschel achieved a brilliant career in astronomy. Although self-taught and entering this occupation only in midlife, he made enormous contributions to both solar and astral astronomy.

Exploration of the Solar System

In solar astronomy, Herschel confirmed the existence of infrared rays, calculated correctly the rotation time of Mars, proposed the name "asteroid" for the bodies bound between Mars and Jupiter, and predicted the discovery of the minor planets Juno (1804) and Vesta (1807). Herschel formulated the "trade winds theory" to explain Jupiter's mysterious belts and discovered two satellites of Saturn (Mimas and Enceladus) and two moons of Uranus (Titania and Oberon).

Contributions to Sidereal Astronomy

While Herschel won popular acclaim for the discovery of Uranus, his enduring professional reputation rested on his contributions to sidereal astronomy ("sidereal" means "pertaining to the stars"). He is regarded as the founder of the science of galactic structure, pertaining to the origin, evolution, and behavior of star systems.

By December, 1781, Herschel had become fascinated by the milky patches in the night sky called nebulas, and he studied the work on that topic by Charles Messier, who had located one hundred of them. Through his three vast "sweeps" of the heavens, Herschel increased that number to more than 2,500.

Not only an observational astronomer, Her-

schel was a natural historian, and, in his later life, he gave much thought to cosmology (the science of the general structure and evolution of the universe).

Family Life

In May, 1788, at the age of fifty, Herschel married Mary Pitt, the wealthy widow of one of his

Sidereal Astronomy

Herschel's major contribution to his profession was in founding the science of sidereal astronomy, the study of the universe beyond the solar system.

To this discipline, Herschel brought three main components: a passion for technical competence (seen in the construction of ever better and larger telescopes); a method for the rigorous, detailed, and documented observations of the heavens (seen in his catalogs of the stars); and a model for understanding the data discovered through imaginative and bold theorizing (seen in his paradigm of how the universe originated and operates). These contributions made Herschel the founder of observational cosmology.

This scientific method enabled Herschel to solve the mystery of nebulas. Named from a Latin root meaning "mists," these cloudy patches in the night sky had long defied explanation. Some thought that they were "self-luminous fluids." Others suggested that they were star clusters. Using superior refractory telescopes, Herschel located more than 2,500 nebulas, and, with the improved clarity of his observations, he determined them to be star clusters.

Having decided on their nature, Herschel turned to their behavior. By focusing on double stars Herschel noted the power of attraction, which provided the first proof that the law of gravity propounded by Sir Isaac Newton applied outside the solar system. This was a major accomplishment, both for theoretical science and for astronomy.

Next, Herschel attempted to measure the distance of these star clusters from Earth and each other. The Italian astronomer Galileo had assumed that all stars were equal in luminosity, the sun being the norm for all. For him, this meant that the dimmer a star, the further it was from

Earth, and the brighter it was, the nearer it was.

Initially, Herschel shared this notion. By 1793, however, he abandoned all thought of any correlation between the dimness and the distance of a star. The universe was more complex than Galileo had imagined, with stars differing vastly in size, brightness, distance, and distribution. This insight enhanced a sense of the diversity inherent in galaxies.

Not content to merely find, map, and measure stars, nor simply to describe their appearance and behavior, Herschel turned fearlessly to trying to formulate the principles of cosmological evolution. As a cosmologist, one who studies the general structure and evolution of the universe, Herschel devised a paradigm to explain the origin and growth of the universe. When the world began, Herschel thought, stars tended to be solitary and widely distributed. As the law of gravity took effect, over a period of great time, these isolated stars were drawn closer together, creating those clusters called nebulas.

By his combination of dogged perseverance and brilliant analysis, Herschel laid the basis of not only the systematic observation of the world beyond the solar system but also its rational explanation. Although his achievements have been surpassed, his role as the founder of sidereal astronomy will never be eclipsed.

Bibliography
Galaxies: Structure and Evolution. Roger John Taylor. Cambridge, England: Cambridge University Press, 1993.
The Guide to the Galaxy. Nigel Henbest. Cambridge, England: Cambridge University Press, 1994.
William Herschel and the Construction of the Heavens. Michael A. Hoskin, with notes by D. W. Dewhirst. New York: W. W. Norton, 1963.

neighbors. Their son, John Frederick William Herschel, was as noted for mapping the skies of the Southern Hemisphere as his father had been for charting the heavens of the Northern Hemisphere. William Herschel's sister, Caroline, was the first notable female astronomer, discovering more than eight comets.

Knighted in 1816 and honored throughout the world, Sir William Herschel died peacefully at home in Slough on August 25, 1822.

Bibliography
By Herschel
"Account of a Comet," *Philosophical Transactions of the Royal Society of London*, 1782 (also as *The Discovery of Uranus*, 1782)

"On the Proper Motion of the Sun and the Solar System: With an Account of Several Changes That Have Happened Among the Fixed Stars Since the Time of Mr. Flamsteed," *Philosophical Transactions of the Royal Society of London*, 1783

"Account of Some Observations Tending to Investigate the Construction of the Heavens" and "On the Construction of the Heavens," *Philosophical Transactions of the Royal Society of London*, 1784 and 1785 (published together as *The Structure of the Universe*, 1784-1785)

"On the Georgian Planet and Its Satellites," *Philosophical Transactions of the Royal Society of London*, 1788

"Catalogue of a Second Thousand of New Nebulae and Clusters of Stars: With a Few Introductory Remarks on the Construction of the Heavens," *Philosophical Transactions of the Royal Society of London*, 1789

The Scientific Papers of Sir William Herschel, 1912 (2 vols.; J. L. E. Dreyer, ed.)

The Herschel Chronicle, 1933 (Constance A. Lubbock, ed.)

About Herschel
William Herschel. Angus Armitage. Garden City, N.Y.: Doubleday, 1963.

William Herschel: Explorer of the Heavens. J. B. Sidgwick. London: Faber & Faber, 1953.

William Herschel: Pioneer of Sidereal Astronomy. Michael A. Hoskin. New York: Sheed & Ward, 1959.

(C. George Fry)

Gustav Hertz

Area of Achievement: Physics
Contribution: Hertz and James Franck provided experimental evidence of the accuracy of Niels Bohr's theory of atomic structure. Hertz later invented and refined methods for separating isotopes that were essential to the advancement of nuclear power.

July 22, 1887	Born in Hamburg, Germany
1911	Earns a Ph.D. from the University of Berlin
1914	Enters the Germany army after the outbreak of World War I
1915	Is severely wounded
1917	Returns to the University of Berlin as a lecturer
1920	Accepts a research position at the Philips Incandescent Lamp Factory in the Netherlands
1925	Returns to Germany as director of the Physics Institute at the University of Halle
1925	Shares the Nobel Prize in Physics with James Franck
1934	Takes a job as chief physicist for Siemens Corporation in Berlin
1945	Goes to the Soviet Union
1949	Begins work on the first Soviet atomic bomb
1954	Returns to East Germany to direct the Physics Institute and teach at the University of Leipzig
1955	Receives the Lenin Prize of the Soviet Union
1961	Retires from teaching
Oct. 30, 1975	Dies in East Berlin, East Germany

Early Life

Gustav Ludwig Hertz was born in Hamburg, Germany, on July 22, 1887, as the son of lawyer Gustav Hertz and Auguste Arning. His uncle was the well-known physicist Heinrich Hertz.

After preparatory school in Hamburg, Gustav Hertz went to the University of Göttingen to study mathematics and physics in 1906 and from there to the University of Munich in 1907. He performed his military service and enrolled in the University of Berlin in 1908, completing his doctoral degree in 1911. At that time, he began collaborating with another Jewish physicist from Hamburg, James Franck, with whom he would share the Nobel Prize in Physics in 1925.

Scientific Collaboration

Franck and Hertz believed that much remained to be done in studying spectral line emissions, and their work concentrated on the electron bombardment of mercury and other gases and their resultant ionization (change in number of electrons orbiting the nucleus). They hoped to develop a kinetic theory of electrons in gases, but they inadvertently verified Max Planck's quantum theory and Niels Bohr's subsequent elaboration of atomic structure according to corresponding "energy states."

(The Nobel Foundation)

Quantum Theory and the Bohr Model of the Atom

Hertz and his colleague James Franck confirmed the correspondence of emitted light wavelengths of an element with that element's possible energy states at the atomic level.

Hertz and Franck confirmed what had been foreseen by Niels Bohr, who had used quantum theory to explain the structure of the atom. They won the 1925 Nobel Prize in Physics for their experiments showing that when an electron strikes an atom, it must possess a minimum amount of energy, depending on the element, in order to displace an electron. This energy is known as the ionization potential of the element.

Because of his experimentation with techniques of isotope separation using the diffusion cascade, his pioneering work with Germany's first "atom-smashing" cyclotron, his work on the Soviet Union's atomic bomb project, and his advancement of quantum theory, Hertz is considered one of the major figures in the history of atomic power.

Bibliography

The Genesis of Quantum Theory, 1889-1913. Armin Hermann. Translated by Claude W. Nash. Cambridge, Mass.: MIT Press, 1971.

"On the Recent Past of Physics." Gerald Holton. *American Journal of Physics* 29 (1961).

"A Personal Memoir." James Franck. In *Niels Bohr: A Centenary Volume*, edited by Anthony P. French and P. J. Kennedy, Cambridge, Mass.: Harvard University Press, 1985.

When they read Bohr's work at the conclusion of their research in 1914, it was clear that their electron bombardment experiments had confirmed Bohr's connection between energy levels within the atom and the wavelength of electrons emitted from or absorbed by the atom. Their achievement, which they did not fully appreciate at the time, came through meticulous study of the light spectrum of emissions from glowing gases.

After Hertz recovered from wounds received in World War I, he returned to studying the phenomenon of discrete energy exchanges at the atomic level. He also began to experiment with X-ray spectroscopy. Between 1920 and 1925, he worked in private industry, returning to academe the year that he received the Nobel Prize in Physics.

At the University of Berlin in the early 1930's, he developed a technique known as the diffusion cascade. His first use for this method was in the separation of gaseous isotopes of helium and neon, but he would later apply the method to other isotopes, including uranium 235, which would prove of supreme importance in the creation of nuclear energy. Hertz left his academic post after refusing to take a Nazi loyalty oath in 1934, but he continued his researches undisturbed at the Siemens Corporation in Berlin.

The Cold War

Hertz joined about two hundred other German scientists in leaving for the Soviet Union after the end of World War II in 1945. They were given houses and laboratories at Stochi on the Black Sea. From the beginning, Hertz was one of the prime leaders in the Soviet nuclear program, because of his work with uranium 235 and his participation on the team of experts that built Germany's first cyclotron, or "atom smasher."

By 1949, Soviet espionage had begun assembling the remaining technical information necessary for Hertz and others to complete their atomic bomb project. Hertz returned to East Germany in 1954 to become director of the Physics Institute in Leipzig. He retired in 1961 and died in 1975.

Bibliography
By Hertz
Grundlagen and Arbeitsmethoden der Kernphysik, 1957 (principles and techniques of nuclear physics)
Lehrbuch der Kernphysik, 1958-1962 (3 vols.; manual of nuclear physics)

About Hertz
"Gustav Hertz." Mark R. McCulloh. In *The Nobel Prize Winners: Physics*, edited by Frank N. Magill. Pasadena, Calif: Salem Press, 1989.
Stalin and the Bomb: The Soviet Union and Atomic Energy, 1939-1959. David Holloway. New Haven, Conn.: Yale University Press, 1994.

(Mark R. McCulloh)

Heinrich Hertz

Area of Achievement: Physics
Contribution: Hertz was the first to measure electromagnetic waves and their radiation as proposed by James Clerk Maxwell's theories.

Feb. 22, 1857	Born in Hamburg, Germany
1879	Receives the Philosophical Faculty Prize from the University of Berlin
1880	Earns a Ph.D. at Berlin
1880-1883	Serves as an assistant to Hermann von Helmholtz
1884	Begins studies into the work of English physicist James Clerk Maxwell
1885	Appointed professor of physics at the Technical University of Karlsruhe
1886-1889	Produces electromagnetic waves and measures them
1888	Awarded the Metteucci Medal by the Italian Scientific Society
1889	Appointed a professor of physics at the University of Bonn
1889	Awarded the Baumgartner Prize of the Vienna Academy of Sciences and the La Caze Prize by the Paris Académie des Sciences
1890	Awarded the Rumford Medal of the Royal Society of London
1891	Awarded the Bressa Prize by the Turin Royal Academy
Jan. 1, 1894	Dies in Bonn, Germany

Early Life

Heinrich Rudolf Hertz was born to a family that was both cultured and successful. His father, Gustav Hertz, was a lawyer and city senator; his mother, Anna Elisabeth Pfefforkorn, bore five children, of which Heinrich was the oldest. Young Heinrich demonstrated his fondness for practical things and at the age of twelve had woodworking tools and a workbench of his own. He attended the Johanneum high school, in preparation for an intended career in engineering and developed special gifts for Latin and more modern languages.

After completing high school, Hertz went to Frankfurt to obtain practical experience in engineering. He spent his free hours studying for the state examination in engineering, attended Dresden Polytechnic for a year, and served for a year in the military, in 1876. He then proceeded to Munich and planned to attend the Technische Hochschule, but he discovered his talent for the natural sciences. He had come to the conclusion that a career path in engineering would not engage him as much as a career of research and study.

Munich and Berlin

Hertz concentrated on his study of mathematics during his initial semester at the University

(Library of Congress)

The Propagation of Electric Waves

Hertz established a finite velocity for the propagation of electromagnetic waves and thereby provided confirmation of James Clerk Maxwell's theories. He showed that such waves were subject to the same properties as light waves, and he laid the foundation for what were to become radio transmissions.

Hertz began his studies of Maxwell's theories in 1884 and concluded that they shared the physical assumptions of competing electrodynamic theories and were preferable to those other theories. He did not yet, however, accept Maxwell's physical interpretation of those equations. He was inclined at first to believe the action-at-a-distance theory, in which it was held that the two forms of electric force, electrodynamic and electrostatic, operated at different velocities. This was the theory promulgated by Hertz's mentor, Hermann von Helmholtz. By 1890, Hertz had become a Maxwellian and had rejected those earlier beliefs.

Hertz arrived at the conclusion that the nucleus of Maxwell's theory was the notion that air-filled space or a vacuum behaved as any other substance or dielectric with regard to the electrodynamic forces acting upon it. Hertz proceeded to generate electric waves in 1887 by discharging an electrical current through a condenser and loop provided with a spark gap and detecting them with a similar circuit.

Hertz's condenser consisted of a pair of metal rods or wires, placed end to end but with a small gap for a spark between them. When these rods were given charges of the opposite polarity strong enough to spark, the current would oscillate back and forth across the gap and along the rods. By moving the receiving apparatus around the experimental field, he was able to measure the distance between waves. By coupling these measurements with his calculations of the oscillator frequency, he determined that the finite speed of radiation was the same for electric waves as for light. He thus was able to demonstrate what Maxwell had only implicitly theorized.

Hertz conducted additional experiments with this apparatus and firmly established the analogy between electric and light waves. For example, he passed electric waves through large, prism-shaped objects made of hard pitch and demonstrated that electric waves refract exactly as light waves do. Similarly, he polarized waves by sending them through a grating of parallel wires and diffracted them by means of a screen with a small hole it. By reflecting the waves off the walls of his laboratory, he was able to create interference between the original wave, prior to its being reflected, and the wave that was bounced off the wall. Finally, he had noticed, early in the course of his experiments, that the spark in the detector circuit was stronger when exposed to the light made by the oscillator circuit, thereby discovering the photoelectric effect.

Although Hertz did not think that much practical use would come from his discoveries, it was soon thereafter that Guglielmo Marconi, the inventor of radio, read of Hertz's experiments. The age of wireless communication was born. The unit of wavelength, the hertz, honors his contribution today.

Bibliography

The Creation of Scientific Effects: Heinrich Hertz and Electric Waves. Jed Z. Buchwald. Chicago: University of Chicago Press, 1994.

"Heinrich Rudolf Hertz." In *Dictionary of Scientific Biography*, edited by Charles Coulston Gillispie. Vol. 6. New York: Charles Scribner's Sons, 1972.

"Wave Motion." John N. Cooper and Apheus W. Smith. In *Elements of Physics*. New York: McGraw-Hill, 1964.

of Munich; he was especially fond of the historical development of the subject. He found that certain parts of more modern mathematics were rather arcane and thought that they would be of little use to a physicist. Nevertheless, his grounding in mathematics was thorough and extensive.

Traveling to Berlin in 1878, Hertz allied himself with Hermann von Helmholtz, the noted physicist, and quickly set about his original research, culminating in the awarding of the Philosophical Faculty Prize in 1879. Helmholtz proposed questioning the assumptions made by physicist James Clerk Maxwell on magnetism and electricity and designing an experimental apparatus by which such theories could be tested. Hertz declined, however, fearing that such a topic would take him many years of study with an uncertain outcome. Instead, his doctoral dissertation was a study of electromagnetic induction. It took him only three months to conclude and earned a rare magna cum laude.

Karlsruhe and Bonn

After holding a position at the University of Kiel, Hertz moved to Karlsruhe and took a position at the university there. In November, 1886, he started to conduct the experiments that Helmholtz had proposed seven years earlier, which were to make him world renowned. Indeed, by 1888, he had gone far beyond the questions asked by Helmholtz and had firmly established the existence of electric waves propagated through air.

In 1889, Hertz made a final move to Bonn and took up a position at the university. In Bonn, he published two classic papers on his continued study of Maxwell's theories and began researching the principles of mechanics in a purely theoretical way. He died on January 1, 1894, of blood poisoning.

Bibliography
By Hertz
Untersuchungen über die Ausbreitung der elektrischen Kraft, 1892 (*Electric Waves: Being Researches on the Propagation of Electric Action with Finite Velocity Through Space*, 1893)
Schriften Vermischten Inhalts, 1895 (*Miscellaneous Papers by Heinrich Hertz*, 1896)
Die Prinzipien der Mechanik, in neuem Zusammenhange dargestellt, 1894 (*The Principles of Mechanics Presented in a New Form*, 1899)
Heinrich Rudolph Hertz (1857-1894): A Collection of Articles and Addresses, 1994 (Joseph F. Mulligan, ed.)

About Hertz
The Creation of Scientific Effects: Heinrich Hertz and Electric Waves. Jed Z. Buchwald. Chicago: University of Chicago Press, 1994.
Hertz and the Maxwellians: A Study and Documentation of the Discovery of Electromagnetic Wave Radiation, 1873-1894. J. G. O'Hara and W. Pricha. London: P. Peregrinus, 1987.

(*Joseph T. Malloy*)

Ejnar Hertzsprung

Areas of Achievement: Astronomy and physics

Contribution: A pioneer in the detailed study of light from stars, Hertzsprung is most remembered for discovering the relationship between the brightness and temperature of stars. He also made the first measurement of the distance to another galaxy.

Oct. 8, 1873	Born in Frederiksberg, Denmark
1898	Graduated from the Polytechnical Institute in Copenhagen
1898	Moves to St. Petersburg, Russia, to begin work as a chemist
1901	Studies photochemistry in Leipzig, Germany
1902	Returns to Denmark as an astronomer at the University of Copenhagen
1909	Accepts a position in astrophysics at Göttingen University
1909	Moves to the Potsdam Astrophysical Observatory
1913	With Henry Norris Russell, recognized for inventing the diagram that bears their names
1919	Appointed associate director of Leiden Observatory, later becoming its director
1929	Awarded the gold medal of the Royal Astronomical Society for measuring the distance to the Small Magellanic Cloud
1937	Awarded the Bruce Gold Medal of the Astronomical Society of the Pacific
1944	Retires from Leiden Observatory
Oct. 21, 1967	Dies in Roskilde, Denmark

Early Life

Ejnar Hertzsprung was born in Frederiksberg, Denmark, in 1873. His father, Severin Hertzsprung, had studied astronomy at the University of Copenhagen but decided that he could not support his family well by pursuing science. Therefore, he took a position with the Danish government, rising rapidly to director of the state life insurance company. Severin retained his love for astronomy and mathematics, however, and Ejnar became interested in these sciences as well.

Although he studied chemical engineering and worked as a chemist after his graduation from college, Ejnar Hertzsprung decided to make astronomy his life's work. In 1902, he began work at the observatory of the University of Copenhagen and at the Urania Observatory in Frederiksberg.

Early Research

In 1905 and 1907, Hertzsprung published two papers that are now considered classics. The title for both was "Zur Strahlung der Sterne," which translates as "on the radiation of the stars." These papers dealt with spectroscopy, the study of which colors (or wavelengths, in the language of physics) make up the light from glowing objects. Hertzsprung showed that stars that have a particular kind of light spectrum are more luminous than the rest. His research laid the foundation for methods of finding the distances to far-off stars and galaxies.

The Famous Diagram

Hertzsprung's extensive studies showed him that stars can be classified into two overall categories. He knew the absolute brightness of thousands of stars and from their spectra could determine the temperature of each.

In 1911, Hertzsprung made a plot to show the relation of the brightness (or magnitude, in the language of astronomers) to the temperature. On such a plot, stars fall into two overall categories. Most stars fall on what is called the main sequence area of the graph, but some, such as blue giant stars and red dwarf stars, fall on a much different part of the plot.

Both Hertzsprung and Henry Norris Russell are given credit for this important discovery, and the diagram has long been known as the Hertzsprung-Russell (or H-R) diagram.

Measuring Intergalactic Distance

After conducting research at several institutions and in many countries, Hertzsprung eventually settled at the Leiden Observatory in the Netherlands, where he remained for twenty-five years. It was during this time that he made a groundbreaking measurement of the distance to an object outside the Milky Way. Hertzsprung used a discovery by fellow astronomer Henrietta Swan Leavitt to estimate the distance to the Small Magellanic Cloud. His method became widely used for these long-distance measurements.

A Long and Fruitful Career

Hertzsprung was still doing astronomical measurements after his ninetieth birthday. In

---

The Measurement of Cosmic Distances

Hertzsprung made the first true measurement of a distance to an object beyond the Milky Way.

The only way to measure the distance to a star directly is the method of parallax. As the earth orbits the sun, stars that are far away do not appear to move, but the apparent position of an object nearby seems to move against the background of faraway stars. One observes the position of the star in relation to the very distant background, when the earth is at opposite sides of the sun (six months apart in time.) By measuring the angle θ and knowing the earth-sun distance (A), one can use trigonometry to find the distance to the star (L). This method works only for stars closer than 100 light-years away. (A light-year is the distance light travels in one year, or about $9.5 \times 1,012$ kilometers.) Other methods must be used for objects at greater distances.

Harvard College astronomer Henrietta Swan Leavitt studied a class of stars that grow brighter and dimmer with time. She found a relationship between the period of variation of these Cepheid variable stars and their average brightness.

Hertzsprung applied Leavitt's observation to some of the Cepheid stars in Earth's galaxy, the Milky Way, whose distance from Earth was known. When he compared these stars to similar stars in the Small Magellanic Cloud, outside the Galaxy, he was able to calculate that it was 32,600 light-years from Earth.

Hertzsprung's measurement was groundbreaking, but it did contain an error: He did not know that there are actually two classes of Cepheid variables, which act in different ways. With this correction, and accounting for intergalactic dust, the currently accepted distance is about 160,000 light-years away. By comparison, the Milky Way is 50,000 light-years in diameter.

Bibliography

The Dynamic Universe. Theodore P. Snow. 3d ed. New York: West, 1988.

Images of the Universe. Carole Stott, ed. Cambridge, England: Cambridge University Press, 1991.

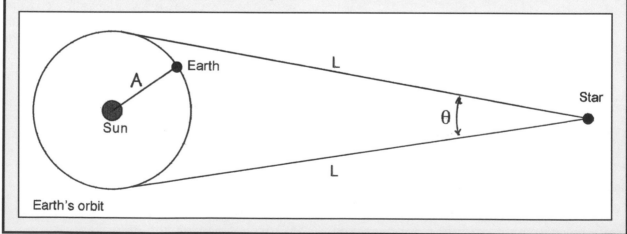

Earth's orbit

his long and productive career, he held both himself and his students to very high standards of accuracy and care in observation. He cared deeply about the education of young astronomers and thereby affected the direction of astronomy for decades. His contributions place him among the great astronomers of history. Hertzsprung died in 1967 at the age of ninety-four.

Bibliography
By Hertzsprung
"Zur Strahlung der Sterne," *Zeitschrift für wissenschaftliche Photographie*, 1905

"Zur Strahlung der Sterne," *Zeitschrift für wissenschaftliche Photographie*, 1907

"Effective Wave-Lengths of 184 Stars in the Cluster N.G.C. 1647," *Astrophysical Journal*, 1915

"On the Relation Between Mass and Absolute Brightness of Components of Double Stars," *Bulletin of the Astronomical Institutes of the Netherlands*, 1923

"The Pleiades," *Monthly Notices of the Royal Astronomical Society*, 1929

About Hertzsprung
Dictionary of Scientific Biography. Charles Coulston Gillispie, ed. Vol. 6. New York: Charles Scribner's Sons, 1972.

"Ejnar Hertzsprung—Measurer of Stars." Axel V. Neilsen. *Sky and Telescope* 35 (1968).

Notable Twentieth-Century Scientists. Emily J. McMurray, ed. New York: Gale Research, 1995.

(Tom R. Herrmann)

Harry Hammond Hess

Area of Achievement: Earth science
Contribution: Hess connected seemingly unrelated geologic phenomena into a comprehensive theory and proposed a new paradigm for interpreting the structure and mechanics of the earth.

May 24, 1906	Born in New York, New York
1927	Graduated with a B.S. from Yale University
1927-1928	Works in Rhodesia as an exploration geologist
1932	Awarded a Ph.D. in mineralogy from Princeton University
1932-1933	Teaches at Rutgers University
1934	Joins the Princeton geology department
1941	Called to active naval duty
1949-1950	Serves as a visiting professor at Capetown University, South Africa
1950-1966	Named department chair at Princeton
1952	Elected to the National Academy of Sciences
1960	Publishes his mobile seafloor theory
1963	His theory is confirmed experimentally
1964	Appointed to the Blair Professorship of Geology
1965	Serves as a visiting professor at Cambridge University
1966	Awarded the Penrose Medal from the Geological Society of America
1969	Given the Distinguished Public Service Award by NASA
Aug. 25, 1969	Dies in Woods Hole, Massachusetts

Early Life

Harry Hammond Hess grew up in a comfortable household with his mother, Elizabeth, and his stock broker father, Julian S. Hess. Although interested in things scientific, he appeared to be only an average student throughout his elementary and high school days.

Hess entered Yale University in 1923 as an electrical engineering major but soon discovered that his interest lay in another area, geology. After his graduation with a B.S. degree in 1927, his first job took him to Africa, where he worked as an exploration geologist.

Returning to the United States, he entered Princeton University, from which he was graduated with a Ph.D. in mineralogy in 1932. Hess then taught at Rutgers University, where he participated in a study of gravity anomalies in the Lesser Antilles with the U.S. Navy. With this study, he began to form the idea of mobile oceanic plates.

The War Years

Hess, a teenager during World War I, was greatly influenced by the heady patriotism of the era. Therefore, it was not surprising that he joined the naval reserves and became an officer. During his command, he took continuous recordings of the seafloor as he crisscrossed the Pacific.

His research led to the discovery of a new submerged geographical feature, flat-topped mountains, which he named "Guyots," in honor of the first professor of geology at Princeton, Arnold Guyot. These investigations steered him in the direction of unraveling the nature of the ocean basins.

Reinterpreting the Ocean Floors

At the end of World War II, aspects of submarine warfare convinced the military of the importance of understanding the oceans. The next decade featured a frenzy of oceanic re-

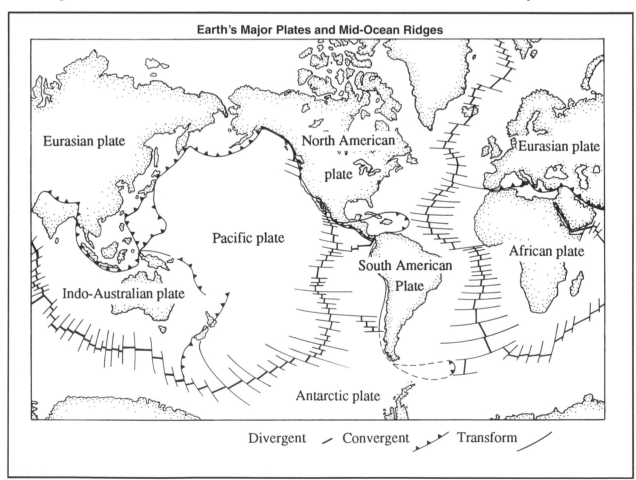

Earth's Major Plates and Mid-Ocean Ridges

Decoding the Nature of the Ocean Floors

Hess proposed that the ocean floor is a dynamic place where new crust is being created at the mid-oceanic ridges.

At the end of World War II, the U.S. military was interested in the oceans as the next strategic "high ground." A frenzy of oceanic research began, supported largely by the Office of Naval Research. Some of this research revealed a continuous mountain ridge running down the middle of the oceans; a tensional rift-valley in the middle of the ridge, which released more heat than the surrounding area; a strong correlation of earthquakes with this ridge; an absence of continental-type rocks in the oceans; and the age of the ocean, the youngest portion of the ocean floor being in the center and the oldest bordering the continents. Clearly, these and other discoveries did not fit any current model of the ocean.

This puzzle of information intrigued Hess, and he began to wonder if Alfred Lothar Wegener's idea of drifting continents might be correct. Wegener had proposed as early as 1912 that the present continents had once been a single supercontinent, Gondwanaland, which had subsequently broken apart and drifted to their present positions.

In 1928, the idea of plate tectonics was hotly debated and dismissed by most geologists, although it did have a small group of supporters from the Southern Hemisphere. Then, in 1956, Sam Warren Carey of the geology department of the University of Tasmania sponsored a symposium on plate tectonics known as the Hobart Symposium. In that same year, scientists at the Lamont Observatory reported the discovery of a submarine mountain range circling the globe that was 20 miles wide and 40,000 miles long. A year later, the International Geophysical Year would reveal even more details of the ocean floor.

In the late 1950's, Hess began to incorporate these divergent observations into a coherent model. The model was a refinement of Wegener's hypothesis, developed with the benefit of more than half a century's additional observations and technology. He suggested that new crust is continually created on the ocean floor. This action then pushes laterally, dragging the continental crust along with it. The idea was so radical that Hess knew his colleagues would have difficulty with it, and he suggested that his theory was a more poetic than scientific explantion of the observations of the ocean floor.

The decade of the 1950's was characterized by an avalanche of stunning new data about oceanic phenomena. The next decade, fueled by Hess's hypothesis, was one of testing and model modification rather than radical new discoveries. First came the confirmation of seafloor spreading by Frederick Vine and Drummond H. Matthews from 1961 to 1963, and then came the global phenomena of transform faults and magnetic symmetry along the oceanic ridges from 1965 to 1967.

These "fingerprints" of seafloor spreading set the stage for a series of symposia and professional meetings in 1967 and 1968 in which a coherent model was presented and debated before the scientific community. The 1970's was a decade of debate. A revolution in the fundamental interpretation of the earth's structure and mechanism was in full force, and geologists begin to reinterpret their data in light of the new model. While the details of continental drift and seafloor spreading are continually refined, the model remains the paradigm for the earth sciences.

Bibliography

Continents in Motion: The New Earth Debate. Walter Sullivan. New York: McGraw-Hill, 1974.

Drifting Continents and Shifting Theories. Homer E. LeGrand. New York: Cambridge University Press, 1988.

Drifting Continents, Shifting Seas. Patrick Young. New York: Impact Books, 1976.

The Ocean of Truth: A Personal History of Global Tectonics. H. W. Menard. Princeton, N.J.: Princeton University Press, 1986.

Hess (center) with astronauts Donald K. "Deke" Slayton (left) and Joseph P. Kerwin at a press conference in 1965. As head of the selection board of the National Academy of Sciences, Hess helped choose six scientist-astronauts out of hundreds of applicants. (AP/Wide World Photos)

search. The oceanic data intrigued Hess, and he began to wonder if Alfred Lothar Wegener's idea of drifting continents might be correct. By 1960, Hess had formulated a theory that allowed these data to mesh and support Wegener's theory.

He proposed that the mid-oceanic ridges were the surface expression of convection currents in the mantle of the earth's crust. These currents brought new material to the surface, forming ridges and radiating heat. The ridges then broke apart under tensional forces and moved laterally, pushing the continents along as the ocean floors were created.

Priority Conflict
This idea was so radical that Hess did not publish it in mainstream journals. Instead, he included it in a report for the Navy and circu-

lated reprints among his colleagues. This was unfortunate because another geologist and oceanographer, Robert S. Dietz, also working for the Navy, published virtually identical ideas in a 1961 *Nature* article, "Continent and Ocean Basin Evolution by Spreading of the Sea Floor."

Hess became aware of Dietz's ideas and published a full account of his theory in a collection of essays dedicated to his former teacher, *Petrologic Studies: A Volume in Honor of A. F. Buddington* (1962). Dietz acknowledged Hess's priority of the mobile seafloor theory, and Hess credited Dietz for coining the term "seafloor spreading." This theory began a revolution in the earth sciences, as geologists began to reinterpret their data in light of the new model.

Hess died in 1969 at the age of sixty-three.

Bibliography
By Hess
"An Appreciation" in *Petrologic Studies: A Volume in Honor of A. F. Buddington*, 1962
Evolution of Ocean Basins, 1960
"Mid-Oceanic Ridges and Tectonics of the Sea Floor" in *Submarine Geology and Geophysics*, 1965 (W. Whittard and R. Bradshaw, eds.)

About Hess
Dictionary of Scientific Biography: Supplement II. Frederick L. Homes, ed. New York: Charles Scribner's Sons, 1990.
"Harry Hammond Hess." H. L. James. *National Academy of Sciences Biographical Memoirs* 43 (1973).

(Richard C. Jones)

Victor Franz Hess

Area of Achievement: Physics
Contribution: Hess was a pioneer in establishing the extraterrestrial origin of cosmic rays. He also carried out important studies in radioactivity and atmospheric electricity.

June 24, 1883	Born in Schloss Waldstein, Styria, Austria
1906	Receives a Ph.D. from the University of Graz
1908	Becomes a privatdocent at the Vienna Veterinary Academy
1910	Becomes an assistant at the Institute for Radium Research
1919	Awarded the Lieben Prize of the Vienna Academy of Sciences
1920	Appointed an associate professor at Graz
1925	Promoted to full professor at Graz
1931	Appointed a professor of physics at the University of Innsbruck
1932	Awarded the Ernst Abbe Prize of the Carl Zeiss Foundation
1933	Elected to the Austrian Academy of Sciences
1936	Wins the Nobel Prize in Physics
1938	Flees Nazi-occupied Austria
1938	Joins the faculty of Fordham University in New York City
1944	Becomes a U.S. citizen
1946	Awarded an honorary Sc.D. from Fordham
1956	Retires from Fordham
1959	Awarded the Austrian Medal for Science and Arts
Dec. 17, 1964	Dies in Mount Vernon, New York

(The Nobel Foundation)

Early Life

Victor Franz Hess was the son of Serafine Grossbauer-Waldstätt and Vinzenz Hess, a forest warden for the Prince of Oettingen-Wallerstein. Beginning in 1901, Victor studied physics and mathematics at the University of Graz, where he received a Ph.D. in 1906. He then pursued additional study at the University of Vienna.

In 1908, Hess became privatdocent—a private teacher paid directly by the students—in physics at the Vienna Veterinary Academy. In 1910, he was named assistant to the director of the new Institute for Radium Research at the University of Vienna. He became an associate professor there in 1911.

Ionization in the Atmosphere

By 1900, it was known that atmospheric gases are continuously ionized to a slight extent, which one scientist suggested might be attributable to radiation from an extraterrestrial source. Several daring scientists tested this hypothesis by measuring the radiation higher up in the atmosphere.

Between 1911 and 1912, Hess himself made nine balloon ascents for this purpose, eventually reaching an altitude of 5,350 meters (17,550 feet). Although he did not initially believe that the radiation came from outer space, his findings caused him to change his mind. This research stopped, however, with the outbreak of World War I.

After the war, Hess married Mary Bertha Warner Breisky, who was from Hungary, and that same year he became associate professor of physics at the University of Graz. Beginning in 1921, Hess spent two years in the United States, where he was chief physicist and director of research at the U.S. Radium Corporation and a consultant to the U.S. Bureau of Mines.

Returning to Graz in 1923, Hess resumed his research on the radiation that the American physicist Robert Andrews Millikan named "cosmic rays" in 1926. Later, Hess and Millikan publicly debated their relative contributions to cosmic-ray research. They were both recognized by the 1936 Nobel Prize in Physics, which was awarded jointly to Hess and to Carl David Anderson, one of Millikan's students, for his discovery of the positron.

From Austria to America

In 1931, Hess became a professor of physics at Innsbruck and director of the Institute for Radiation Research. Despite his stature both at home and abroad, he was dismissed from his academic positions by Nazi officials in 1938. Although he was a Roman Catholic, his wife was Jewish, and a Gestapo officer warned them of their impending deportation to a detention camp. After fleeing to Switzerland, they emigrated to the United States, where Hess became professor of physics at Fordham University in New York City.

With the development of the atomic bomb, Hess grew increasingly concerned about the biological effects of radioactivity and radiation. Warning that the long-term effects were not understood, he urged a halt to nuclear weapons testing. In 1946, Hess participated in

The Discovery of Cosmic Rays

The radiation causing the ionization of atmospheric gases originates from extraterrestrial sources.

Scientists initially considered three possible sources for the radiation found in the atmosphere: radioactive elements in the earth's crust, unknown radioactive materials in the atmosphere, and some extraterrestrial source.

To decide among these possibilities, Hess developed an improved electrometer for measuring the radiation at high altitudes. At 1,070 meters (3,510 feet), he found the radiation to be nearly the same as at ground level, while at 5,000 meters (16,400 feet) it was about six times greater.

Despite his original skepticism about an extraterrestrial source, he wrote that his measurements were "more readily explained by the assumption that a radiation of very high penetrating powers enters our atmosphere from above" and that at least some of the radiation at the earth's surface was thus "of extraterrestrial origin."

Although Hess was correct, his conclusions were not immediately accepted. In the 1920's, unmanned balloon flights up to 15,500 meters (50,600 feet) and other experiments by Robert Andrews Millikan provided, according to an 1989 article in *Technology and Culture* by Charles A. Ziegler, "the first *unambiguous* evidence in support of the extraterrestrial hypothesis."

Initially, cosmic rays were thought to be high-energy electromagnetic waves, but they are now known to be high-energy particles. Originating in space far beyond the solar system, protons and heavier nuclei enter the earth's atmosphere, where they produce a secondary component of many different kinds of particles, including short-lived ones such as the positron and the mu-meson (or muon).

Bibliography

Electrons (+ and –), Protons, Photons, Neutrons, Mesotrons, and Cosmic Rays. Robert A. Millikan. 2d ed. Chicago: University of Chicago Press, 1947.
"Technology and the Process of Scientific Discovery: The Case of Cosmic Rays." Charles A. Ziegler. *Technology and Culture* 30 (1989).

A cosmic-ray measuring device from the 1950's. (California Institute of Technology)

the first study of radioactive fallout in the United States.

Hess retired from Fordham in 1956, the year after the death of his wife. A short time later, he married Elizabeth M. Hoenke. His own death occurred in 1964 halfway through his eighty-second year.

Bibliography
By Hess

Die Elektrische Leitfähigkeit der Atmosphäre und Ihre Ursachen, 1926 (*The Electrical Conductivity of the Atmosphere and Its Causes*, 1928)
"Die Jonisierungsbilanz der Atmosphäre," *Ergebnisse der Komischen Physik*, 1933
"The Discovery of Cosmic Radiation," *Thought*, 1940
Die Weltraumstrahlung und ihre biologischen Wirkungen, 1940 (with Jacob Eugster; *Cosmic Radiation and Its Biological Effects*, 1949)
"Ungelöste Probleme in der Physik" in *Les Prix Nobel en 1936*, 1937 ("Unsolved Problems in Physics" in *Nobel Lectures: Physics, 1922-1941*, 1965)

About Hess

"The Discovery of Cosmic Rays: Rivalries and Controversies Between Europe and the United States." M. De Maria, M. G. Ianniello, and A. Russo. *Historical Studies in the Physical and Biological Sciences* 22 (1991).
"Hess, Victor Franz (Francis)." Josef Mayerhöfer. In *Dictionary of Scientific Biography*, edited by Charles Coulston Gillispie. Vol. 6. New York: Charles Scribner's Sons, 1964.
Nobel Prize Winners in Physics, 1901-1950. Niels H. de V. Heathcote. Reprint. Freeport, N.Y.: Books for Libraries, 1971.

(*Richard E. Rice*)

Antony Hewish

Area of Achievement: Astronomy
Contribution: Hewish won the Nobel Prize in Physics, along with Sir Martin Ryle, for the development of new techniques in radio astronomy. His observations of pulsars provided evidence for the existence of neutron stars.

May 11, 1924	Born in Fowey, Cornwall, England
1935	Attends King's College
1942	Enters Cambridge University
1943-1946	Serves Britain's effort during World War II in radar development at Farmborough and Malvern
1948	Joins Ryle's team at the Cavendish Laboratory at Cambridge
1952	Completes his Ph.D. at Cambridge on ionospheric fluctuations
1961	Becomes a lecturer at Cambridge
1964	Discovers interplanetary scintillation of small radio sources
1965	Detects a radio source in the Crab nebula
1967	Discovers the first pulsar
1968	Elected a Fellow of the Royal Society of London
1971	Made a professor of radio astronomy at Cambridge
1974	Wins the Nobel Prize in Physics, along with Ryle
1989	Retires from Cambridge University

Early Life
Antony Hewish was born in Fowey, Cornwall, England, in 1924. He was the youngest of three sons, and his father was a banker. Hewish attended Cambridge University in 1942, but World War II interrupted his studies in 1943

and he spent the next three years engaged in the development of airborne radar counter-measure devices with Martin Ryle.

Interplanetary Scintillation

After the war, Hewish returned to Cambridge, graduating in 1948. Two distant stars had just been discovered through radio waves, and Hewish realized that they would scintillate, or twinkle, as a result of effects of the earth's upper atmosphere, as did visible stars as a result of effects of the lower atmosphere. This twinkling could be used to understand the size and electron density of clouds in the ionosphere, a significant achievement at a time before the development of spacecraft.

The planets do not twinkle because they appear larger than the stars from the earth. Hewish realized that by using an interferometer, consisting of two radio telescopes sepa-

(The Nobel Foundation)

rated by 90 kilometers, the apparent size of radio sources could be known. This technique, which can also determine the velocity of solar wind, is called interplanetary scintillation (IPS).

In 1965, using IPS, Hewish and S. E. Okoye discovered a compact source of radio brightness inside the Crab nebula. They hypothesized that this brightness is the remains of a star that was observed exploding by Chinese astronomers in 1054.

"Little Green Men" and Pulsars

One of Hewish's research students, Jocelyn Bell (later Bell Burnell), noted in 1967 during a routine sky survey that fluctuating signals were being received at regular intervals. Often, such signals would be detected by the observatory, but they would keep time with the rotation of the earth, not with the sidereal time of the heavens, which differs from the solar day as a result of the motion of the earth in its orbit. Ruling out interference from satellites and other observatories, Hewish and Bell concluded that the signals probably had a heavenly origin.

Initially, it was suspected that the source might be a lighthouse belonging to an interstellar civilization, warning spaceships of the location of some hazard to navigation. Hewish and Bell therefore named their first few sources LGM-1 through LGM-4, the "LGM" prefix standing for "Little Green Men." However, Hewish could not detect any Doppler shift in the signals, which would be expected if the signaling object were orbiting something else.

Instead, Hewish soon adopted Thomas Gold's hypothesis that a neutron star was causing the pulses. The resulting term "pulsar" for the source of such signals is not credited to any individual; it was first used in a publication a month after the first paper published by Hewish, Bell, and their colleagues on their discovery, in a 1968 volume of *Nature*. Over the next thirty years, more than seven hundred pulsars were discovered.

Later Life

Hewish was awarded the Nobel Prize in Physics in 1974, along with Sir Martin Ryle, who had pioneered the work in radio telescope in-

What Causes a Pulsar?

A rotating neutron star is the best explanation for clocklike pulsed radio sources in space.

After a star has run out of nuclear fuel, it collapses as a result of gravitational attraction. For some stars, this collapse can be halted by the Pauli exclusion force, which prevents some kinds of particles from being in identical states of motion. What remains after the collapse is a small object that consists largely of protons and electrons smashed together to make neutrons.

The rotational energy and the magnetic energy of the collapsed star are conserved. The neutron star therefore has a tremendous rate of rotation and a powerful magnetic field. Because of its immense density, the rapid rotation does not tear the star apart.

In order to explain the repetition of pulses detected in space, Hewish adopted Thomas Gold's lighthouse model. The region close to the pulsar is called its magnetosphere. As the star spins, the magnetic field spins along with the pulsar, and it induces a electrical field on the surface of the star, like a huge electrical generator. The electrical field pulls electrons from the crust, which are accelerated by the rotating field lines.

These electrons emit radio signals in a tight beam along the field lines. As the pulsar generates electromagnetic radiation, the torque of the accelerating particles acts as a brake on the rotation, decreasing the period between pulses. The discovery of pulsars confirmed the scientific account of the evolution of stars.

Bibliography

"Clocks in the Cosmos." Duncan Lorimer. *Physics World* (February, 1996).

Pulsar Astronomy. A. G. Lyne and F. G. Smith. Cambridge, England: Cambridge University Press, 1990.

"The World of Radio Astronomy, Parts I-III." Michael Dahlem and Elias Brinks. *Mercury*, January/February, March/April, and May/June, 1996.

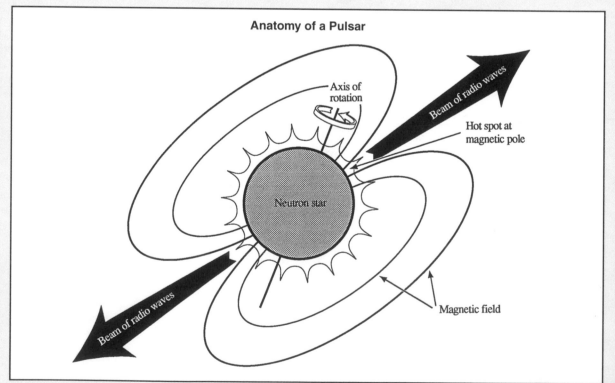

Anatomy of a Pulsar

Axis of rotation

Beam of radio waves

Hot spot at magnetic pole

Neutron star

Beam of radio waves

Magnetic field

A rapidly rotating neutron star generates a strong magnetic field that sends out radiation. The resulting radio waves can be detected on Earth.

terferometry. Hewish continued to be active in radio astronomy and retired from Cambridge University in 1989.

Bibliography
By Hewish
"Observation of a Rapidly Pulsating Source," *Nature*, 1968 (with S. J. Bell, J. D. H. Pilkington, P. F. Scott, and R. A. Collins)
"Pulsars," *Scientific American*, 1968
"Pulsars: Twenty Years After," *Mercury*, 1989

About Hewish
"Antony Hewish." In *The Nobel Prize Winners: Physics*, edited by Frank N. Magill. Pasadena, Calif.: Salem Press, 1989.
Frozen Star. George Greenstein. New York: Charles Scribner's Sons, 1989.
"Writing an Intellectual History of Scientific Development: The Use of Discovery Accounts." S. W. Woolgar. *Social Studies of Science* (1976).

(Drew L. Arrowood)

Hildegard of Bingen

Areas of Achievement: Botany, medicine, physiology, and zoology
Contribution: A Benedictine abbess, Hildegard wrote three major religious and philosophical treatises, composed music, and produced works on natural history and medicine.

1098	Born in Bermersheim, Rhineland-Palatinate (now Germany)
1106	Enters the nunnery of Jutta at nearby Disibodenberg
c. 1113	Takes the veil as a nun and begins to experience detailed visions
1136	Becomes head of the nunnery on Jutta's death
1140's	Begins to compose music
1141-1151	Writes *Scivias* (know the ways of the Lord)
1147-1150	Founds her own convent in Rupertsberg, near Bingen
1150	Begins to gain influence among the Church and the laity
1150-1160	Writes *Liber simplicis medicinae* (book of simple medicine), also called *Physica*
1158-1163	Writes *Liber vitae meritorum* (book of life's recompenses)
1163-1170	Writes *Liber divinorum operum* (book of the works of God), also called *Liber de operatione Dei*
1165	Establishes a cloister at Eibingen
1178	The interdict on Rupertsberg by prelates in Mainz is lifted by order of Archbishop Christian
Sept. 17, 1179	Dies at Rupertsberg, near Bingen, Rhineland-Palatinate

Early Life

The parents of Hildegard (pronounced "HIHL-duh-gahrt") of Bingen, Hildebert and Mechtild von Bermersheim, were members of the gentry, with connections to other landed families in the Rhineland-Palatinate (now Germany). Hildegard, the last of ten children, was evidently bright and precocious. In twelfth century Germany, however, only two courses were open to women: marriage and the Catholic Church. Therefore, her father arranged for Hildegard, at age eight, to enter the nunnery of Jutta, the daughter of a neighboring family who had established a hermitage on the grounds of the monastery at Disibodenberg.

There, Hildegard learned Christian liturgy, biblical doctrine, music, and domestic handwork. She was apparently a quick student, for she was soon teaching others. When she was fourteen or fifteen, she was ready to become a nun and received the veil from Otto, bishop of Bamberg and lord bishop of Mainz.

Middle Life and First Writings

For two decades, Hildegard's life was that of the nunnery. Biographical sources usually employ phrases such as "She grew in the grace of God" for this period. Two specifics, however, can be known or inferred. The first is the occurrence of her visions, which she describes as great suffusions of light during which understanding of the Bible, the universe, and the physical world was revealed to her by God. She stresses that she was fully conscious during these visions—that is, they were not mystic or out-of-body experiences.

The second inference is that she grew in authority, for when Jutta died in 1136, Hildegard was named head of the nunnery. Shortly afterward, she became abbess, and plans were made to build a cloister on the grounds. By 1143, the new church structure was consecrated and the cloister occupied.

In the meantime, Hildegard's visions, which she had kept secret from everyone except Jutta and her teacher, the monk Volmar, were brought into the open and formed the basis of her first work, *Scivias* (1141-1151), the title taken from a shortened form of the Latin phrase *Nosce vias Domini* (know the ways of the Lord). In twenty-six visions, she shows the complex interaction of Creator, universe, and humankind.

While Hildegard was composing *Scivias*, she was further advised by God to move to Rupertsberg, near Bingen, and to found a new cloister there. Against heavy opposition within and without the Church, she

In this drawing of Uomo al centro dell'Universo (man at the center of the universe), Hildegard is portrayed in the lower left-hand corner. (Art Resource)

accomplished this task, citing God's will, as expressed in her visions, as her justification. Although some commentators have regarded the visions as a convenient device, Hildegard's certainty that she was God's vessel was genuine and was accepted as such. In 1165, the Rupertsberg cloister established a new center at Eibingen. Today, Rupertsberg is gone, but Eibingen survives.

The decades from 1150 to 1170 saw Hildegard's production of two more philosophical works and one scientific one. *Liber simplicis medicinae* (1150-1160), or *Physica*, is a remarkable collection of observations of plants and animals, stones and minerals, usually with reference to their possible use in medicine. The descriptions are clear and straightforward; Hildegard's descriptions of the fishes of the Rhine and in the Palatinate tributaries have not been equaled. The observations in *Physica* came not from visions but from field work.

Liber vitae meritorum (1158-1163) is a reflection on Christian ethics, and *Liber divinorum operum* (1163-1170) considers the cosmos and its theological significance. Both were inspired by visions.

Hildegard's diagram of a year's cycle from Scivas. (Art Resource)

Other Works and Late Life

Hildegard produced a variety of undated works. *Liber compositae medicinae (causae et curae—de aegritudium causis, signis, et curis)*, commonly called *Causae et curae*, deals with the medicine that Hildegard practiced in her day-to-day healing. Her candid discussion of gender differences in this treatise shows that she regarded woman, although inferior by order and method of creation, as an entity separate from man, complementary and indispensable. This view was unusual at the time but hardly revolutionary.

Hildegard's music, which came into vogue in the 1990's, is gathered in the *Symphonia armonie celestium revelationum*, commonly shortened to *Symphonia*. The music is in an unusual type of chant, with a great melodic range and wide intervals designed specifically for women. The verses are of Hildegard's composition.

She also wrote a devotional play for her nuns to perform, as well as lives of St. Disibod and St. Rupert. Her extensive correspondence, directed to persons of every station in the Church and elsewhere, ranged from simple advice to admonishment about falling away from the faith to sharp criticism of Church leaders for fostering schism. Hildegard also toured the Rhineland, speaking to monastic groups.

In 1178, Hildegard brought interdiction (refusal to allow administration of the sacraments) upon her cloister in a dispute with the prelates of Mainz. The dispute was finally settled by Archbishop Christian of Mainz on his return from a meeting of the Lateran Council in Rome.

Only a few months later, Hildegard died at

Hildegard and the Science of the Middle Ages

Hildegard's scientific works covered most of what is now identified as science—that is, medicine and natural history.

Physical science in Hildegard's time was barely beginning to be rejuvenated by the recovery and translation of Greek and Arabic scientific works into Latin. As such, it was not speculative but immediate, descriptive, and directed toward use. These terms describe Hildegard's writings, such as *Physica* (written 1150-1160) and *Causae et curae* (written before 1158).

The observations behind her descriptions of plants, minerals, and medical procedures are not derivative but made at firsthand. Consequently, they are fresh and to the point. For example, Hildegard had this to say about the fish called the pike:

The pike prefers to stay in the middle depths in pure water. It likes daylight and is quick and fierce, like a wild beast. Wherever it stays it eats up fish and thus empties the water of other fish. [Its flesh] is beneficial for both infirm and healthy men.

Her other descriptions are of this same calmly informative nature.

Bibliography
"Hildegard of Bingen." Walter Pagel. In *Dictionary of Scientific Biography*, edited by Charles Coulston Gillispie. 16 vols. New York: Charles Scribner's Sons, 1970-1980.

"It Takes All Kinds: Sexuality and Gender Differences in Hildegard of Bingen's *Book of Compound Medicine*." Joan Cadden. *Traditio: Studies in Ancient and Medieval History, Thought, and Religion* 40 (1984).

The Medicine of Hildegard of Bingen: Her Twelfth-Century Theories and Their Twentieth-Century Appeal as a Form of Alternative Medicine. Sue Spencer Cannon. Thesis, University of California, Los Angeles. *Dissertation Abstracts* 54 (1993).

Rupertsberg. Two attempts were made to complete the process of canonization. Although neither succeeded, Hildegard is listed as a saint in the Roman martyrology.

Bibliography
By Hildegard
Scivias, wr. 1141-1151 (know the ways of the Lord; English trans., 1986)

Liber simplicis medicinae, wr. 1150-1160 (also called *Physica*; book of simple medicine)

Liber compositae medicinae (causae et curae—de aegritudium causis, signis, et curis), wr. before 1158 [commonly called *Causae et curae*; the book of composite medicine (causes and cures—cause, symptom, and cure)]

Symphonia armonie celestium revelationum, wr. before 1158 (commonly called *Symphonia*)

Liber vitae meritorum, wr. 1158-1163 (book of life's recompenses)

Liber divinorum operum, wr. 1163-1170 (also called *Liber de operatione Dei*; book of the works of God)

The Letters of Hildegard of Bingen, 1994

Selections: Writings of Hildegard of Bingen, 1996 (Sabina Flanagan, ed.)

About Hildegard
"The Flesh of the Voice: Embodiment and the Homoerotics of Devotion in the Music of Hildegard of Bingen (1098-1179)." Bruce Wood Holsinger. *Signs: Journal of Women in Culture and Society* 19 (Autumn, 1993).

"Hildegard of Bingen, St." Ernst H. Soudek. In *Dictionary of the Middle Ages*, edited by Joseph R. Strayer. 13 vols. New York: Charles Scribner's Sons, 1982-1989.

Introduction to *Scivias*, by Hildegard of Bingen. Barbara J. Newman. Translated by Mother Columba Hart and Jane Bishop. New York: Paulist Press, 1990.

"St. Hildegard, Virgin." In *Butler's Lives of the Saints*, edited by Herbert Thurston and Donald Attwater. Vol. 3. New York: P. J. Kenedy & Sons, 1956.

(Robert M. Hawthorne Jr.)

Sir Cyril Norman Hinshelwood

Area of Achievement: Chemistry
Contribution: Hinshelwood made important contributions in the area of chemical kinetics, including the discovery of the branching chain mechanism for explosive reactions.

June 19, 1897	Born in London, England
1916-1918	Works on explosives at the Royal Ordnance Factory
1920	Graduates from Balliol College, Oxford University
1921	Appointed a Fellow at Trinity College
1924	Obtains a doctorate from Oxford University
1927	Appointed a university lecturer in chemical dynamics at Trinity College
1928	Proposes the branching chain mechanism for explosions
1931	Appointed the head of the Balliol-Trinity laboratories
1937	Appointed a professor of chemistry at Oxford
1937	Begins work on the kinetics of reactions in bacteria
1948	Receives a knighthood
1955-1960	Serves as president of the Royal Society of London
1956	Shares the Nobel Prize in Chemistry with Nikolai Semenov
1964	Retires from Oxford to become a Senior Research Fellow at Imperial College
Oct. 9, 1967	Dies in London, England

Early Life

Cyril Norman Hinshelwood grew up in London as the only son of Norman Hinshelwood. During World War I, Cyril worked at the Royal Ordnance Factory, where his unique scientific abilities were quickly recognized. Hinshelwood's early work with explosives formed the basis for his later interest in chemical kinetics.

Following the end of the war, Hinshelwood completed an accelerated program of study at Oxford University, from which he was graduated in 1920. A year later, he was appointed a Fellow at Trinity College, a post that he would hold for sixteen years. Shortly thereafter, Hinshelwood entered the most productive period of his scientific career.

The Kinetics of Explosive Reactions

In the early 1920's, Hinshelwood began investigating the chemistry of explosives. Following work on the explosive decomposition of solids, he examined gas-phase decomposition reactions. He soon discovered that a correction to the Lindemann reaction theory was required to

(The Nobel Foundation)

account for the vibrational and rotational energy possessed by molecules in unimolecular chemical reactions.

Hinshelwood made other important discoveries concerning gas-phase reactions. He found that some reactions proceed by both molecular and free radical mechanisms. He also carried out extensive work on the effect of surfaces in catalyzing chemical reactions.

Hinshelwood's most important experiments, performed between 1927 and 1935, concerned explosive reactions in gases. Much of this work focused on the reaction of hydrogen with oxygen. He explained explosive reactions in terms of a branching chain reaction mechanism, in which the rate of reaction increased with increasing time. He also investigated the effect of surfaces on reaction rate and determined the limits for which hydrogen-oxygen mixtures were explosive.

Bacterial and Solution Reactions

In the early 1930's, Hinshelwood became interested in the kinetics of reactions in solutions. Many of his experiments paralleled his earlier work in gas-phase kinetics. An important series of measurements on the reaction of aromatic molecules served as a basis for theories relating molecular structure and reactivity.

In 1937, Hinshelwood initiated studies on the reactions of bacterial cells, which would remain a main area of his research for the rest of his life. Hinshelwood investigated the behavior of bacteria when they were exposed to new sources of nutrients and the reduction in bacterial growth in the presence of inhibiting agents. He developed a general theory for enzyme reactions in bacteria to account for his observations.

Scientific Recognition

In later years, Hinshelwood was recognized for his earlier accomplishments in gas-phase kinetics. In 1937, he was made a professor of chemistry at Oxford University. In 1948, he was awarded a knighthood. Eight years later, Hinshelwood shared the Nobel Prize in Chemistry with Nikolai Semenov.

Branching Chain Reactions

In his study of the oxygen-hydrogen reaction, Hinshelwood discovered the general conditions required for a branched chain reaction.

An unbranched chain reaction consists of one or more initiation, propagation, and termination steps. In such a reaction, new chain carriers, the chemical species involved in the propagation steps, are created only by initiation reactions. If initiation reactions cease to occur, the chain reaction gradually comes to a halt as termination reactions remove the chain carriers from the system.

In studies of the chemical reaction of mixtures of hydrogen and oxygen, Hinshelwood discovered a second general type of reaction, called a branching chain reaction. For example:

Initiation	$H_2 + O_2 \rightarrow 2\,OH$
Propagation	$OH + H_2 \rightarrow H + H_2O$
(Branching)	$H + O_2 \rightarrow OH + O$
	$O + H_2 \rightarrow OH + H$
Termination	$H + H \rightarrow H_2$

In a branched chain reaction, new chain carriers are created not only by the initiation reactions but also by the branching steps in the propagation reactions. In the absence of efficient termination steps, branched chain reactions will proceed at an accelerated rate with time, often leading to explosions.

One application of branching chain reactions is in nuclear fission. When a uranium 235 nucleus absorbs a neutron and falls apart, two or three neutrons are released. These neutrons can cause further fission to occur. In a nuclear power plant, control rods are used to enhance chain termination reactions and to prevent acceleration of the fission reaction.

Bibliography

Chemical Kinetics. 3d ed. Keith J. Laidler. New York: Harper & Row, 1987.

Chemical Kinetics and Reaction Mechanisms. James H. Espenson. New York: McGraw-Hill, 1981.

Foundations of Chemical Kinetics. Sidney W. Benson. New York: McGraw-Hill, 1960.

In 1964, Hinshelwood retired from Oxford and became a Senior Research Fellow at Imperial College in London. He died in London three years later at the age of seventy.

Bibliography
By Hinshelwood
The Kinetics of Chemical Change in Gaseous Systems, 1926
Thermodynamics for Students of Chemistry, 1926
The Reaction Between Hydrogen and Oxygen, 1934 (with A. T. Williamson)
The Chemical Kinetics of the Bacterial Cell, 1946
The Structure of Physical Chemistry, 1951
Growth, Function, and Regulation in Bacterial Cells, 1966 (with A. C. R. Dean)

About Hinshelwood
"Balliol-Trinity Laboratories, Oxford, 1853-1940." E. J. Bowen. *Notes and Records of the Royal Society* 25 227 (1958).
"Chemical Kinetics and the Oxford College Laboratories." K. J. Laidler. *Archives of the History of the Exact Sciences 38* 197 (1988).
"Cyril Norman Hinshelwood." H. W. Thompson. *Biographical Memoirs of Fellows of the Royal Society 19* 375 (1973).

(Jeffrey A. Joens)

Hippocrates

Area of Achievement: Medicine
Contribution: Hippocrates was reputedly the author of a collection of seventy works on medicine and ethics written in ancient Greece. His method, while not entirely original, emphasized the rational search for natural causes for disease.

c. 460 B.C.E.	Born on the island of Cos in Greece
431 B.C.E.	The Peloponnesian War begins
430-427 B.C.E.	Fights the plague in Athens
430-380 B.C.E.	Writes most of the *Corpus Hippocraticum* (Hippocratic collection)
404 B.C.E.	Athens surrenders to Sparta, ending the war
400-391 B.C.E.	Founds the school of medicine at Cos
390-381 B.C.E.	Plato refers to a physician named Hippocrates in the *Protagoras*
374 B.C.E.	The earliest accepted date for Hippocrates' death
c. 370 B.C.E.	Probably dies near Larissa, Thessaly
350 B.C.E.	The latest accepted date for Hippocrates' death

Early Life
Little is known about the historical Hippocrates (pronounced "hih-POK-ruh-teez"); the first source about his life that still exists is a half-mythical second century account by Soranus of Ephesus, although a physician Hippocrates is mentioned in passing by both Plato and Aristotle.

Born on the island of Cos, Hippocrates was said to be the son of Phainarete and the physician Heracleidas. Legend places him in the line of the hero Hercules (Heracles) and that of Asclepius (Asklepios), son of Apollo, the god of medicine, being twentieth in line of descent from the former and nineteenth from the latter.

Education

Hippocrates studied first with his father and then with the orator Gorgias of Leontini and the atomist-philosopher Democritus. After his parents died, Hippocrates left his homeland. In his lost work *On the Descent of Medicine*, Andreas, in order to appear as the originator of medical knowledge, spitefully claimed that Hippocrates left because he had burned the archives on Cos.

Curing Lovesickness and Madness

Hippocrates was summoned by Perdiccas, the king of the Macedonians, who was thought to have tuberculosis. Hippocrates interpreted by certain signs that the affliction was psychosomatic in origin. After the death of his father, Perdiccas had fallen in love with his father's

(Library of Congress)

mistress, Phila. Hippocrates explained the situation to Phila after he caught Perdiccas blushing when he looked at her. He then freed Perdiccas from his illness, but it is not reported how he did so.

Hippocrates was also summoned by the Abderites to cure Democritus, who was insane or perhaps believed to be insane because of some of the strange theories that the Greek philosopher propounded. Accounts portray Democritus as convincing Hippocrates of his sanity.

Teachings

It is believed that Hippocrates taught his students on the Greek island of Cos off the coast of Asia Minor under an old tree that still survives. His method stated that most disease was caused by an imbalance of the four humors: blood, phlegm, yellow bile, and black bile.

Hippocrates taught that proper diet and exercise should suffice to cure some ailments but that certain people who could not follow a regimen would need medicine. Some conditions such as dislocation of the hip could be cured by physical manipulation, as is presently done, and others were considered incurable. All diseases were caused by natural action, not the action of gods or spirits—even epilepsy, the so-called sacred disease.

Rational medicine, however, is not the same as scientific medicine. Hippocrates did not conduct experiments or consider the biological origins of humanity relevant to medicine.

The Hippocratic Oath

Hippocrates' oath, administered to his students and taken by many new physicians even today, was sworn to the god of medicine, Apollo. It provided for the free teaching of medicine to the offspring of one's teacher of medicine, abstention from the seduction of patients or members of a patient's household, and secrecy in what is learned from patients and teachers.

The part of the oath stipulating that the Hippocratic physician would not prescribe a pessary (a toxic suppository) to induce abortion has been historically misinterpreted as a moral prohibition against abortions provided by those who swear to the oath.

This interpretation is problematic, because

Could Hippocrates Cure Ebola Virus Infection?

Some scientists have theorized that the plague treated by Hippocrates in Athens in the fifth century B.C.E. was caused by the Ebola virus.

When a plague attacked the Illyrians and the Paeonians, the king of those regions begged Hippocrates to come to them. Hearing from their ambassadors what the winds were like there, however, he sent them away. After concluding that the plague would come to Greece, Hippocrates allegedly devised a cure.

The plague of Athens is one of the great medical mysteries of antiquity. This devastating three-year epidemic hastened the end of the Golden Age of Greece. Understood by Thucydides to have its origin in Ethiopia, the disease fell suddenly on Athens and ravaged the densely packed populace of citizens, allies, and refugees crowded together inside the city walls during the Peloponnesian War.

According to Thucydides, who himself survived the epidemic, sufferers were seized first with a strong fever and redness and burning of the eyes and the inside of the mouth, both throat and tongue, and they expelled an unusually foul breath. Following these symptoms were sneezing, hoarseness, a powerful cough, bilious vomiting, and, in most cases, an empty heaving that produced strong spasms. The flesh was livid and budding out in small blisters and ulcers. Victims suffered such high temperatures as to reject even the lightest coverings and had an awful thirst. Most perished between the seventh and ninth days or later died of weakness once the sickness passed into the bowels, where the ulceration became violent and extreme diarrhea simultaneously laid hold. Those who survived became immune, but those who vainly attended or even visited the sick fell victim.

The modern case definition of Ebola virus infection indicates a sudden onset, fever, and headache, followed by cough, vomiting, diarrhea, rash, and hemorrhage from the orifices of the body, with a fatality rate of 50 to 90 percent. Death typically occurs in the second week of the disease. Incidence of the disease among health care providers and caregivers has been a prominent problem. The Centers for Disease Control and Prevention report that in the best-studied outbreak, the most frequent initial symptoms were fever, diarrhea, and severe weakness, with clinical signs of bleeding also frequently present. Symptomatic hiccups are also reported in some patients. During the plague of Athens, Thucydides made the same unusual clinical observation of hiccups.

It has been suggested that polymerase chain reaction examination of genetic material present in ancient skeletal remains might test this hypothesis against the dozens of prior theories, which assigned blame for the plague of Athens to every disease from bubonic plague to tuberculosis. If the disease were caused by the Ebola virus, it is hard to see how setting bonfires—the method that Hippocrates purportedly used to cure the plague—could have cured anyone of the disease. Fire certainly could have been used as a public health measure, however, in order to destroy contaminated structures and corpses and to prevent the spread of the disease.

Bibliography

Diseases in the Ancient Greek World. Mirko D. Grmek. Baltimore: The Johns Hopkins University Press, 1989.

The Hippocratic Tradition. Wesley D. Smith. Cornell, N.Y.: Cornell University Press, 1979.

"The Thucydides Syndrome: Ebola Deja Vu? (or Ebola Reemergent?)" P. E. Olson et al. *Emerging Infectious Diseases* 2, no. 2 (April-June, 1996).

another part of the oath forbids the removal of gallstones but does not call the removal of gallstones immoral. Instead, the procedure is reserved for specialists in that art who had been trained in another tradition. Inducing abortion by means of the more toxic abortifacients would be the province of specialist midwives.

The Hippocratic physician could bring about miscarriage by the oral administration of the now-extinct silphium plant.

Another part of the oath interpreted by many to forbid euthanasia (mercy killing) might also be misinterpreted. It may only be a prohibition against homicide or assisting a homicide, since suicide was an accepted practice in antiquity.

Death

Hippocrates ended his days in Larissa. He lies buried between Gyrton and Larissa, but Soranus could not find his tomb. For a long time, there was a bee hive on it that produced honey. When infants were afflicted with thrush (a fungal infection of the mouth), wet nurses anointed their infants at the tomb to rid them of the disease.

When he died, Hippocrates left two sons, Thessalus and Dracon, and many students.

Bibliography

By Hippocrates

Epidemion (*The History of Epidemics*, 1780)
Peri Aeron Hydaton Topon ("Airs, Waters, Places" in *The Whole Course of Chirurgerie*, 1597)
Peri Agmon (*On Fractures*, 1928)
Peri Arthron (*On Joints*, 1928)
Peri Diaites Oxeon (*Regimen in Acute Diseases*, 1849)
Peri Ieres Noysoy (*On the Sacred Disease*, 1849)
Prognostikon ("Prognosis" in *The Whole Course of Chirurgerie*, 1597)

About Hippocrates

Hippocrates in a World of Pagans and Christians. Owsei Temkin. Baltimore: The Johns Hopkins University Press, 1991.
Hippocratic Lives and Legends. Jody Rubin Pinault. New York: E. J. Brill, 1992.
Methods and Problems in Greek Science. G. E. R. Lloyd. Cambridge, England: Cambridge University Press, 1991.

(*Drew L. Arrowood*)

George Herbert Hitchings, Jr.

Areas of Achievement: Biology, chemistry, medicine, and pharmacology
Contribution: Hitchings, one of the most successful twentieth century practitioners of chemotherapy, introduced rational drug design and numerous pharmaceuticals to medical use.

Apr. 18, 1905	Born in Hoquiam, Washington
1927	Receives a B.S. in chemistry at the University of Washington
1928	Earns an M.S. in chemistry from Washington
1933	Receives a Ph.D. in biological chemistry from Harvard University
1942	Hired by Burroughs Wellcome pharmaceutical company
1951	Develops the anticarcinogen 6-mercaptopurine
1957	Develops the drug azothioprine (Immuran), which is widely used as an immunosuppressant in organ transplantation
1967	Named vice president of research at Burroughs Wellcome
1971	Becomes president of the Burroughs Wellcome Fund
1975	Retires to become scientist emeritus for the company
1977	Develops the drug acyclovir (Zovirax)
1988	Awarded, with Gertrude Belle Elion and James Whyte Black, the Nobel Prize in Physiology or Medicine

Early Life

George Herbert Hitchings, Jr., was born on April 18, 1905. The slow death of his father, a naval architect, when Hitchings was twelve aimed him toward medicine. Another force in this direction was his awe for scientist and philanthropist Louis Pasteur, as described in Hitchings' high school salutatorian address.

Hitchings entered the University of Washington premedical track. He changed to chemistry, however, and received a B.S. and an M.S. in chemistry in 1927 and 1928, respectively. A well-rounded student, he also took courses in the arts and history.

From Harvard to Pharmaceuticals

Hitchings entered Harvard University's Ph.D. program in biological chemistry and worked with Cyrus J. Fiske on nucleic acids, before James D. Watson and Francis Crick showed that deoxyribonucleic acid (DNA) contains hereditary information. Hitchings' Ph.D. thesis, leading to a degree in 1933, concerned nucleic acid chemistry. That year, he married Beverly Reimer. They had two children, Laramie Ruth and Thomas Eldridge.

The Great Depression forced Hitchings to teach for the next nine years. In 1942, he was hired by the U.S. division of the British pharmaceutical company Burroughs Wellcome, started its biochemistry department, and soon hired Gertrude Belle Elion. He continued to study nucleic acids, which led him to a vice presidency in research in 1967. He held that job until retirement in 1975.

Rational Drug Design and a Nobel Prize

Hitchings' fame arose from work done with Elion. They pioneered pharmaceutical identification by rational drug design. The first stage of this process exposes the differences between abnormal (for example, infected or cancerous) tissue and normal tissue, and the second stage exploits those differences to kill abnormal cells and to affect normal ones only minimally. Rational drug design differs from screening, which tests available chemicals for useful drugs. Hitchings and his coworkers were prolific, earning approximately one hundred patents in a thirty-year association.

Many such drugs were synthetic bases, cousins of the bases in nucleic acids. Chemical alteration of natural prototypes yielded drugs that diminished or stopped the key steps of DNA synthesis and were excreted rapidly. These properties are useful in treating cancer, because cancer cells divide much more rapidly than normal cells. Hence, they are killed

Rational Drug Design

Rational drug design develops pharmaceuticals via the scientific study of life processes.

The use of rational drug design led Hitchings' group to the development of approximately one hundred pharmaceuticals, mostly modified nucleic acid bases. His premises were that suitable drugs kill abnormal cells or microbes with minimal harm to normal tissue and that every cell type has a unique biochemistry allowing attack at a point crucial to its survival and reproduction.

Hitchings' modified nucleic acid bases inhibited the synthesis of nucleic acid, especially deoxyribonucleic acid (DNA). They were chosen partly because of Hitchings' work with Cyrus Fiske on nucleic acid. Hitching also used modified bases because parasites live in hostile environments and utilize rapid nucleic acid synthesis for survival and because an understanding of the relationship between heredity and nucleic acid was emerging.

Hitchings' system of rational drug design produced chemotherapeutic bases, including immunosuppressants and drugs to fight leukemia, gout, virus, and acquired immunodeficiency syndrome (AIDS). It soon became the model for drug research.

Bibliography

"Presentation of Dr. George Herbert Hitchings for Passano Award." Paul Talalay. *Journal of the American Medical Association* 209 (September 1, 1969).

"Relevance of Basic Research to Pharmaceutical Inventions." George H. Hitchings. *Trends in Pharmacological Sciences* (1980).

quickly by DNA starvation, while slow-dividing normal cells are affected to a lesser degree before the drugs are excreted.

The first drug designed by Hitchings, in 1951, was the anticarcinogen 6-mercaptopurine, which is still in wide use. A second drug, azothioprine (Immuran), made in 1957, slows the division of white blood cells of the immune system. Immuran, a widely used immunosuppressant, enables high success rates in organ transplantation. A third drug, acyclovir (Zovirax), developed in 1977, was the first antiviral drug and treatment for acquired immunodeficiency syndrome (AIDS). The drugs designed by Hitchings' group treat diseases such as cancer, gout, malaria, and viral infections. It was no wonder that he, Elion, and British pharmacologist James Whyte Black won the 1988 Nobel Prize in Physiology or Medicine.

Hitchings won prizes, honorary degrees, and memberships to learned societies. In addition to the Nobel Prize, he was given the Passano Award, the Gregor Mendel Award of the

(The Nobel Foundation)

Czech Academy of Science, and the Papanicolaou Cancer Award. His honorary degrees included those from the University of Michigan, Emory and Duke Universities, and Mount Sinai Medical School. Hitchings was elected to the Royal Society of London, the National Academy of Science, and the American Society for Cancer Research.

After Retirement

Upon his retirement, Hitchings continued to conduct research and had more time for philanthropic work. One example is the Burroughs Wellcome Fund, a charitable organization for which he served as president from 1971 to 1990. Retirement also gave him the opportunity to travel extensively, a longtime hobby. After his wife died in 1985, Hitchings married Joyce Shave.

Bibliography
By Hitchings
"The Effect of Pyrimidines on the Growth of *Lactobacillus Caseii*," *Science*, 1945 (with E. A. Falco and M. B. Sherwood)
"A Quarter Century of Chemotherapy," *Journal of the American Medical Association*, 1969
"Indications for Control Mechanisms in Purine and Pyrimidine Biosynthesis as Revealed by Studies with Inhibitors," *Advances in Enzyme Regulation*, 1974
"Relevance of Basic Research to Pharmaceutical Invention," *Trends in Pharmacological Sciences*, 1980
"Rational Design of Anticancer Drugs: Here, Imminent, or Illusive?" in *Development of Target-Oriented Anticancer Drugs*, 1983 (Yung-Chi Cheng, Barry Goz, and Mimi Minkoff, eds.)

About Hitchings
"The Nobel Pair." Katherine Bouton. *New York Times Magazine*, January 29, 1989.
"Presentation of Dr. George Herbert Hitchings for Passano Award." Paul Talalay. *Journal of the American Medical Association* 209 (September 1, 1969).
"A Quarter Century of Chemotherapy." George H. Hitchings. *Journal of the American Medical Association* (1969).

(Sanford S. Singer)

Sir Alan Lloyd Hodgkin

Areas of Achievement: Cell biology and physiology

Contribution: Hodgkin discovered the chemical processes responsible for the passage of impulses along individual nerve fibers, for which he was given the Nobel Prize in Physiology or Medicine.

Feb. 5, 1914	Born in Banbury, Oxfordshire, England
1932-1935	Studies physiology at Trinity College, Cambridge University
1939-1945	Conducts radar research for the British Air Ministry during World War II
1945-1952	Delivers lectures at Cambridge
1952-1969	Works as a research professor for the Royal Society of London
1959-1963	Serves as a member of the Medical Research Council
1963	Shares the Nobel Prize in Physiology or Medicine with Andrew F. Huxley and Sir John Carew Eccles
1964	Publishes *Conduction of the Nerve Impulse*
1965	Awarded the Copley Medal of the Royal Society of London
1970-1981	Joins the faculty of Cambridge as professor of biophysics
1971-1984	Serves as chancellor of the University of Leicester
1978-1984	Appointed master of Trinity College, Cambridge
1988	Awarded the Helmerich Prize of the Retina Research Foundation
1992	Publishes *Chance and Design*

Early Life

Alan Lloyd Hodgkin was born in Banbury, England, in 1914. His father died when he was four years old. Hodgkin was reared by his mother, who took him and his two younger brothers around the pleasant country in Banbury and in Oxford where they later lived. He spent whole days walking, cycling, and canoeing, which brought him close to nature.

Action Potentials in Nerves

Action potential is an electrical signal of about 100 millivolts that is initiated at one end of a neuron and transmitted in an all-or-none fashion to its presynaptic terminal.

Neurons or nerve cells are one of the two major classes of cells in the nervous system. The other is the glial cell. The human brain contains about 10^{11} neurons, the basic signaling units of the nervous system. Three major types of neurons are found: sensory neurons, motor neurons, and interneurons. A typical neuron forms about a thousand synapses, specialized sites of communication between two neurons, and receives even more. Synapses can be categorized as chemical or electrical. Neurons have the unique ability to communicate rapidly with one another over great distances and with great accuracy.

Hodgkin's contribution to this knowledge of neurons relates to the conduction of nerve impulses. It was known that the activity of a nerve fiber depends on a large concentration of potassium ions inside the fiber and a large concentration of sodium ions in the surrounding solution. His discovery showed that the nerve membrane allows only potassium to enter the fiber during the resting phase but allows sodium to penetrate when the fiber is excited or depolarized.

Bibliography

Essentials of Neural Science and Behavior. Eric R. Kandel, James H. Schwartz, and Thomas M. Jessell. Norwalk, Conn.: Appleton & Lange, 1995.
Mind and Brain. Special Issue, *Scientific American* 267 no. 3 (1992).

(The Nobel Foundation)

England. They wanted to study the electrical impulses that occur on the surface membranes of nerve fibers. Together, they developed a technique to put small electrodes into giant nerve fibers of the squid *Loligo forbesi* without damaging the surface membrane.

Later, they found that a similar experiment had been done at about the same time by Kacy Cole and H. J. Curtis in the United States. Nevertheless, they were excited because the results proved that the nerve impulse does take place at the surface membrane and not, as some people thought, in long protein molecules in the protoplasm.

Hodgkin and Huxley's work also provided good evidence that the immediate source of energy for nervous impulse conduction comes from the movement of ions down their concentration gradients—an entry of sodium during the rising phase of the action potential, followed by an exit of potassium during the falling phase.

Also at Plymouth, Hodgkin worked with Peter Baker and Trevor Shaw. They showed that after the protoplasm had been squeezed out of a giant nerve fiber, the conduction of impulses could be restored by perfusing the remaining membrane with an appropriate solution. Eventually, this work contributed to the decision made by the Nobel Committee to recognize their ionic theory of nerve conduction.

Hodgkin enjoyed studying animals. When he was about fifteen years old, he began working with a professional ornithologist, a scientist who studies birds. Hodgkin's observations awakened an interest in zoology, and he started Trinity College at Cambridge University in 1932 with the intention of studying this field.

His attention, however, soon shifted to cell physiology. Hodgkin pursued this interest during an expedition to the Atlas Mountains in Morocco, where he studied flatworms found in high mountain lakes.

The Marine Biological Association
Hodgkin worked with Andrew F. Huxley at the Marine Biological Association in Plymouth,

A False Alarm and Recognition at Last
The Nobel Committee's acknowledgment of Hodgkin's work did not come easily. In 1961, Hodgkin was informed by some Swedish journalists that he, Huxley, and Sir John Carew Eccles were going to be awarded the Nobel

Prize in Physiology or Medicine. He was called for an interview in London. Later, he was told that the prize was actually being given to Georg von Békésy.

Two years later, Hodgkin, Huxley, and Eccles were honored with the Nobel Prize for their contribution to physiology.

Bibliography
By Hodgkin
The Conduction of the Nervous Impulse, 1964
"The Components of Membrane Conductance in the Giant Axon of Loligo," *Journal of Physiology*, 1952 (with Andrew F. Huxley)
"Beginning: Some Reminiscences of My Early Life (1914-1947)," *Annual Reviews in Physiology*, 1983
Chance and Design: Reminiscences of Science in Peace and War, 1992

About Hodgkin
"Alan Lloyd Hodgkin." In *The Nobel Prize Winners: Physiology or Medicine*, edited by Frank N. Magill. Pasadena, Calif.: Salem Press, 1991.
"Beginning: Some Reminiscences of My Early Life (1914-1947)." Alan L. Hodgkin. *Annual Reviews in Physiology* 45 (1983).
Chance and Design: Reminiscences of Science in Peace and War. Alan L. Hodgkin. Cambridge, England: Cambridge University Press, 1992.

(Sibel Erduran)

Dorothy Crowfoot Hodgkin

Areas of Achievement: Chemistry and physics
Contribution: Hodgkin used X-ray crystallography to determine the chemical structure of important substances such as penicillin, vitamin B_{12}, and insulin.

May 12, 1910	Born in Cairo, Egypt
1932	Earns a bachelor's degree from Oxford University
1934	Begins work at Oxford as a lecturer
1937	Earns a Ph.D. from Cambridge University
1945	Describes the structure of penicillin
1947	Made a Fellow of the Royal Society of London
1956	Determines the structure of vitamin B_{12}
1956	Awarded the Royal Medal of the Royal Society of London
1957	Promoted to full professor at Oxford
1960-1976	Serves as Wolfson Research Professor at Oxford
1964	Wins the Nobel Prize in Chemistry
1965	Named to the Order of Merit
1969	Determines the structure of insulin
1976	Awarded the Copley Medal
1976-1988	Presides over the Pugwash Conference on Science and World Affairs
1983	Given the Lomonosov Gold Medal by the Soviet Academy of Sciences
July 29, 1994	Dies in Shipston-on-Stour, Warwickshire, England

Early Life

Dorothy Crowfoot Hodgkin was born Dorothy Mary Crowfoot in Cairo, Egypt, on May 12, 1910. Her father, John Winter Crowfoot, was an educational administrator for the British government in the Sudan, a British colony at the time. Her mother, Grace Mary Hood Crowfoot, was a self-taught expert in botany and ancient textiles who would later publish the book *Flowering Plants of the Northern and Central Sudan* (1928).

When World War I started in 1914, Dorothy was sent to live in Great Britain. She developed an interest in chemistry at an early age. She read about X-ray crystallography, a method of determining the structure of chemical compounds by projecting X rays through crystals and observing the patterns they made on photographic film, in *Concerning the Nature of Things* (1925), by William Henry Bragg, a pioneer in the field.

Crowfoot earned a bachelor's degree at Oxford University in 1932. She then began work at Cambridge University with John Desmond Bernal, who was using X-ray crystallography to study proteins and other complex molecules. In 1934, while continuing her doctoral research with Bernal, she returned to Oxford as a lecturer. She was promoted to tutor at Oxford in 1936 and earned her Ph.D. from Cambridge in 1937. That same year, she married Thomas Hodgkin, a teacher and historian.

Penicillin

Dorothy Crowfoot Hodgkin continued her studies of complex molecules, despite the first signs of the rheumatoid arthritis that would eventually cause severe disability in her hands and feet. She worked at first on sterols, a group of chemicals that includes cholesterol.

During World War II, Hodgkin studied penicillin, a reently drug that was far more effective than any previously known antibiotic. Although penicillin is not a particularly complex molecule, it crystallizes in many different ways, making the determination of its structure a very difficult problem.

After making thousands of calculations, some with a very early version of a computer, Hodgkin determined the structure of penicillin. She found that it contains an unusual component known as a beta-lactam ring, which other chemists thought was impossible. It was determined that

Equipment in an X-ray crystallography laboratory. (California Institute of Technology)

X-Ray Crystallography

The chemical structure of crystals can be determined by studying the way in which their molecules diffract beams of X rays.

X rays are a form of electromagnetic radiation similar to light and radio, which means that X rays travel in waves. X rays are distinguished from other forms of electromagnetic radiation by having wavelengths that are roughly the same as the distances between atoms in molecules.

When electromagnetic radiation of a larger wavelength is directed at a substance, it simply bounces off and does not interact with the substance; this is what happens when light hits an object and is reflected. X rays, on the other hand, have a much smaller wavelength. When X rays are directed toward a substance, they pass through and are diffracted. Diffraction occurs when waves are bent around objects. X rays bend around the atoms within molecules in such a way that the waves interact with one another. This interaction may increase the strength of the X rays (constructive interference) or decrease it (destructive interference).

To perform X-ray crystallography, a crystal of the desired substance must be formed. The crystal must be an uncontaminated sample of the substance, free from impurities that would change the way in which it diffracts X rays. The next step is to direct X rays at the crystal, which pass through and then strike a piece of photographic film. Constructive and destructive interference show up on the film as a pattern of dots, which can then be studied to determine where the atoms are located within the molecule.

The pattern of dots on the film is analyzed by measuring the distances and angles between them. From a two-dimensional image, a three-dimensional structure must be determined. Scientists use advanced calculus to calculate where the electrons that orbit the atoms are located and then determine where each atom is located by using maps of these electrons.

The entire process requires thousands of calculations. Hodgkin, working in the days before high-speed computers were common, did her calculations by hand, aided only by shortcuts such as tables of logarithms and later by primitive computers. To determine the structure of molecules as large as the ones that Hodgkin chose to study took several years.

X-ray crystallography is a useful tool that allows chemists to understand the structure of complex substances, as long as these substances can be studied in crystalline form. This technique began with the study of simple crystals. During Hodgkin's time, the emphasis was on studying complex organic molecules composed of dozens or hundreds of atoms.

Hodgkin's pioneering work in X-ray crystallography aided chemists in synthesizing important substances such as penicillin and vitamin B_{12}. Crystallographers have continued to study increasingly complex molecules vital to understanding the chemistry of living organisms.

Bibliography
Crystal Structure Analysis: A Primer. Jenny Glusker. New York: Oxford University Press, 1985.
Elements of X-Ray Crystallography. Leonid V. Azaroff. New York: McGraw-Hill, 1968.
X-Ray Crystallography: An Introduction to the Theory and Practice of Single-Crystal Structure Analysis. G. H. W. Milburn. London: Butterworths, 1973.

penicillin obtains its antibiotic activity from the beta-lactam ring. Hodgkin's discovery, announced in 1945, allowed drug companies to manufacture many new antibiotics similar to penicillin.

Vitamin B_{12} and Insulin
Hodgkin's next major project was vitamin B_{12}. This substance was first isolated in 1948 from liver extract and was known to be an effective treatment for pernicious anemia, an otherwise fatal disease that causes a decrease in red blood cells. Hodgkin and her coworkers took 2,500 X-ray photographs of vitamin B_{12} over six years. She mailed her data to the University of California, Los Angeles, to be analyzed by one of the world's first high-speed electronic computers. The structure of vitamin B_{12} was announced in 1956.

Since the 1930's, Hodgkin had been working

(Library of Congress)

on the structure of the complex molecule insulin. Her results were announced at last in 1969, when faster computers made possible the extremely difficult calculations made necessary by insulin's hundreds of atoms.

Awards and Honors

Hodgkin was elected a Fellow of the Royal Society of London in 1947 and was awarded the society's Royal Medal in 1957, the first of many major awards. She was promoted to full professor at Oxford that same year and from 1960 to 1976 held the post of Wolfson Research Professor. Her greatest triumph came when she was awarded the Nobel Prize in Chemistry in 1964.

In 1965, Hodgkin received the Order of Merit from Queen Elizabeth II. She was the second woman to be given the award, after the nursing pioneer Florence Nightingale, who received it from King George VII in 1907.

Hodgkin received the Copley Medal from the Royal Society of London in 1976. From 1976 to 1988, she presided over the Pugwash Conference on Science and World Affairs, an annual meeting of scientists working for world peace. In 1983, she was awarded the Lomonosov Gold Medal from the Soviet Academy of Sciences.

Hodgkin spent her last years confined to a wheelchair as a result of her advancing arthritis and a fractured pelvis. To the end of her life, she continued to be involved in science and peace conferences. She died of a stroke in her home in England on July 29, 1994.

Bibliography

By Hodgkin

"X-Ray Analysis of the Structure of Penicillin," *Advancement of Science*, 1949

"The Structure of Vitamin B_{12}," *Proceedings of the Royal Society of London*, 1957-1962 (in 5 parts; with others)

"The X-Ray Analysis of Complicated Molecules," *Science*, 1965

Structural Studies on Molecules of Biological Interest, 1981

About Hodgkin

"Dorothy Crowfoot Hodgkin." In *The Nobel Prize Winners: Chemistry*, edited by Frank N. Magill. Pasadena, Calif.: Salem Press, 1990.

Nobel Prize Women in Science. Sharon Bertsch McGrayne. New York: Carol, 1993.

A Passion for Science. Lewis Wolpert and Alison Richards. New York: Oxford University Press, 1988.

Winners: Women and the Nobel Prize. Barbara Shiel. Minneapolis: Dillon Press, 1985.

(Rose Secrest)

Roald Hoffmann

Area of Achievement: Chemistry
Contribution: Hoffmann, an authority on chemical physics and applied chemical theory, shared the Nobel Prize in Chemistry with Kenichi Fukui for his theories concerning chemical reactions.

July 18, 1937	Born in Zloczow, Poland (now Ukraine)
1943-1949	Lives as a refugee in Poland, Czechoslovakia, Austria, and West Germany before moving to the United States
1949-1955	Attends public schools in Brooklyn, including Stuyvesant High School, a select science school for boys
1955-1956	Works summers at the National Bureau of Standards
1957	Conducts research at the Brookhaven National Laboratory
1958	Earns a B.A. in chemistry from Columbia University
1959	Studies at Per-Olov Löwdin's summer school in Sweden
1960	Earns an M.A. in physics from Harvard University
1960-1961	Works with A. S. Davydov on exciton theory as a graduate exchange student at Lomonosov State University, Moscow
1962	Earns a Ph.D. in chemical physics from Harvard
1968	Appointed a professor of chemistry at Cornell University
1974	Made John A. Newman Professor of Physical Science at Cornell
1981	Awarded the Nobel Prize in Chemistry

Early Life

Roald Safran, whose father was a civil engineer killed during the Holocaust and whose mother was a schoolteacher, adopted the surname of his stepfather, Paul Hoffmann. In 1941, Roald and his mother were forced by Nazis into a Jewish ghetto and then into a labor camp. They were smuggled out of the camp in 1943 and lived with a friendly Ukranian before beginning a long period of travel in various countries as refugees.

Like many other Jewish refugee children, Roald Hoffmann attended a number of different schools and experienced a mixture of languages, learning Polish, Ukrainian, Yiddish, German, Hebrew, and eventually English after he, his mother, and his stepfather arrived in the United States in 1949.

In 1955, Hoffmann entered Columbia College as a premedical student. Entranced by his courses in the humanities, he would have

(AP/Wide World Photos)

Rules Governing the Course of Chemical Reactions

The concept of the conservation of orbital symmetry, a theoretical model of events on an atomic and molecular level, has had practical consequences in the design of reactions for the preparation of a variety of products.

In order to design chemical reactions to produce specific desired products, it is necessary to determine the laws that govern the transformations of the molecules. In reactions, molecules collide with one another and the orbitals (the paths of the electrons, which form the bonds between atoms) are changed. Some old bonds are broken, and new ones are formed.

One factor governing the sequence of events during the collisions are the energy changes of the molecular orbitals associated with the system. New products will be at lower energy levels than the starting materials, but generally an energy barrier must be overcome.

Kenichi Fukui discovered that only a few orbitals—those with the highest energy, called frontier orbitals—dominate this barrier. Hoffmann and Robert B. Woodward showed that the way in which the orbitals move in energy is strongly controlled by the symmetry properties of the reaction pathway.

Their idea of the conservation of orbital symmetry is a useful and general concept that has been applied by Hoffmann and others to the synthesis of a wide spectrum of seemingly unrelated products.

Bibliography
The Conservation of Orbital Symmetry. Robert B. Woodward and Roald Hoffmann. Weinheim, Germany: Verlag Chemie, 1970.
Robert Burns Woodward and the Art of Organic Synthesis. Mary Ellen Bowden and Theodor Benfey. Philadelphia: Beckman Center for the History of Chemistry, 1992.
"Stereochemistry of Electrocyclic Reactions." Robert B. Woodward and Roald Hoffmann. *Journal of the American Chemical Society* 87 (1965).

switched to art history had he not encountered two excellent chemistry professors. The primary reason for his choice of chemistry was his summer research experiences at the National Bureau of Standards and the Brookhaven National Laboratory.

The Harvard Years
In 1958, Hoffmann began graduate work at Harvard University on a theoretical project with Martin P. Gouterman. In 1961, he switched research advisers to work with future Nobel chemistry laureate William N. Lipscomb.

With L. L. Lohr, Jr., Hoffmann programmed what came to be known as the extended Hückel method, a molecular orbital scheme that gave reasonable predictions of molecular conformations and simple potential surfaces. He applied it to boron hydrides and polyhedral molecules in general. Discovering that this method yielded the approximately correct barrier to internal rotation in ethane, he began to carry out theoretical work on organic molecules.

On receiving his doctorate in 1962, he became a Junior Fellow at Harvard, switching his interests from theory to applied theory, specifically in organic chemistry. Beginning in the spring of 1965, he collaborated with Robert B. Woodward, who received the Nobel Prize in Chemistry that year. In what was Hoffmann's second major contribution and the basis for his 1981 Nobel Prize in Chemistry, he and Woodward devised what have become known as the Woodward-Hoffmann rules. (Woodward did not share this Nobel Prize with Hoffmann because he had died in 1979.)

The Cornell Years
In 1965, Hoffmann joined the faculty of Cornell University, where he continued his work on applied theoretical chemistry, the particular blend of computations stimulated by experiment and the construction of generalized models, frameworks for understanding, that is his contribution to chemistry. He also considered himself a teacher, especially to beginning students not in the sciences.

Hoffmann was elected a member of the U.S.

National Academy of Sciences in 1972, wrote hundreds of scientific articles, and received many honorary degrees and numerous awards, including the American Chemical Society's Priestley Medal, its highest award. He became the first person to receive awards from the society in three different subfields of chemistry—organic chemistry, inorganic chemistry, and chemical education.

Renaissance Man

Hoffmann wrote many popular articles on science emphasizing the esthetics of chemists' work. He was the narrator and presenter for "The World of Chemistry," a series of twenty-six half-hour programs, that aired on the Public Broadcasting System (PBS) in 1990 and was shown widely abroad. His poetry has appeared in various literary magazines and in such books as *The Metamict State* (1987), *Gaps and Verges* (1990), and *Memory Effects* (1997).

Bibliography

By Hoffmann

"Stereochemistry of Electrocyclic Reactions," *Journal of the American Chemical Society*, 1965 (with Robert B. Woodward)

The Conservation of Orbital Symmetry, 1970 (with Woodward)

"Theory in Chemistry," *Chemical & Engineering News*, 1974

"Bonding Capabilities of Transition Metal Carbonyl Fragments," *Inorganic Chemistry*, 1975 (with Mihai Elian)

"Transition Metal Pentacoordination," *Inorganic Chemistry*, 1975 (with Angelo R. Rossi)

"Building Bridges between Inorganic and Organic Chemistry," *Angewandte Chemie, International Edition in English*, 1982

The Metamict State, 1987

Solids and Surfaces: A Chemist's View of Bonding in Extended Structures, 1988

Gaps and Verges: Poems, 1990

Chemistry Imagined: Reflections on Science, 1993 (with Vivian Torrence)

The Same and Not the Same, 1995

Memory Effects, 1997

About Hoffmann

"Interview: Fukui and Hoffmann, Two Conversations." István Hargittai. *The Chemical Intelligencer* 1, no. 2 (April, 1995).

"Profile: Modest Maverick: Hoffmann's World of Chemistry, Poetry, and Pedagogy." Russell Ruthen. *Scientific American* 256 (July, 1990).

"Roald Hoffmann." Jeremy K. Burdett. In *Nobel Laureates in Chemistry, 1901-1992*, edited by Laylin K. James. Washington, D.C.: American Chemical Society, 1993.

(George B. Kauffman)

Robert Hooke

Areas of Achievement: Astronomy, biology, invention

Contribution: Famous as an experimenter, Hooke conducted detailed investigations with the microscope that were epoch-making. He coined the term "cell" to describe the structural unit of living material.

July 18, 1635	Born in Freshwater, on the Isle of Wight, England
1648	Briefly apprenticed to portrait painter Sir Peter Lely in London
1653	Goes to Oxford, where he meets leading British scientists
1655	Becomes an assistant in chemistry under Robert Boyle
c. 1658	Perfects Boyle's air pump
1661	Publishes his first work, on the capillary attraction of water
1662	Becomes curator of the Royal Society of London
1663	Receives a master of arts degree
1665	Becomes a professor of geometry at Gresham College
1665	Publishes his masterpiece, the *Micrographia*, containing the first description of a cell
1666	Presents a paper describing the movements of the planets in terms of an attractive force
1672-1680	Writes his diary
1677	Becomes secretary of the Royal Society of London
1691	Receives the degree of "Doctor of Physic"
1700	Invents the marine barometer
Mar. 3, 1703	Dies in London, England

Early Life

Robert Hooke was born in Freshwater on the Isle of Wight in 1635. His father, John, was a curate of the Church of All Saints in Freshwater. Robert was a sickly child, suffering from headaches and nausea, and formal attempts at education only worsened his condition. Left to himself, however, he showed an amazing mechanical aptitude, copying or improving on any mechanical device that came his way.

In 1648, at the age of thirteen, he was apprenticed to the portrait painter Sir Peter Lely in London. Hooke soon left and entered the Westminster School, where he became proficient in Latin and Greek and immersed himself in the study of mathematics.

Hooke was sent to Oxford in 1653 on a minor scholarship. He came into contact with prominent British scientists, most notably the chemist Robert Boyle. In 1658, Hooke perfected Boyle's air pump, the first such device suitable for creating vacuums and compressed air for laboratory research.

Hooke became curator of the newly founded Royal Society of London in 1662 and remained the society's chief scientist for forty years.

The *Micrographia* and Its Impact

Hooke's position at the Royal Society of London required that he present three or four original experiments to the membership at every weekly meeting. The inventive and hardworking Hooke met this demand, but the time involved also prevented him from pursuing his own interests and systematically investigating any one subject. In short, Hooke was full of brilliant ideas, suggestions, and insights but was seldom able to bring an invention or research project to completion.

One exception is Hooke's masterpiece, the *Micrographia*, which he published in 1665, three years after assuming his post with the Royal Society of London. The *Micrographia* was the first important work on microscopy in which the observations of living material were so detailed and graphically represented. Hooke worked with his own improved method of illumination and refined the accuracy of microscopic measurements and the recording of results. He became famous for his fine and striking drawings, such as a louse grasping a human hair, and for the first observation of cells, in a sliver of cork.

The readability and attractiveness of the *Micrographia*, combined with its being written in English at a time when great scientific works were in Latin, made it an immediate success. Its impact, however, dwindled over time. Many people came to believe that its plain and

The *Micrographia*

Hooke published the first treatise on microscopy by a major scientist. He described microscopic structures with the same kind of imaginative comprehension as that with which Galileo had revealed the structure of the universe.

The title of *Micrographia* (1665) suggests simply a book of microscopical observations, but it is a remarkable combination of practical experimentation and philosophy surrounding fifty-seven observations on living and nonliving objects viewed with the compound microscope, which Hooke devised.

Hooke's preface contains his philosophical account of the state and aims of contemporary science. He emphasizes the human "command over things"—scientists do not simply accept nature but work to alter and improve it.

In this book, Hooke calls for rigor in judging scientific observations, stating that the senses can be misleading. He argues that the senses must therefore be supplemented by scientific instruments. He discusses many of his inventions, including his microscopical improvements. He describes different methods for illuminating his specimens, such as with a lamp shining through a globe of brine and then through a convex lens at night or on cloudy days.

The *Micrographia* made four fundamental theoretical contributions to science. The first was in optics, in which Hooke described the nature of light, the generation of iridescence in thin plates such as mother of pearl, and the phenomenon of refraction. Next was Hooke's theory of combustion, in which he challenged the belief that fire is an element in itself, consisting of atoms. His theorized that fire is the result of some part of the air mixing with combustible material, that the combusting part of the air is quickly used up, and that without a further supply of air, combustion ceases.

Hooke's third contribution concerned the nature of fossils. At the time, these were thought to be exotic rock formations. Hooke determined microscopically that they were the remains of once-living creatures. Lastly, Hooke demonstrated the cellular nature of plants and coined the term "cell" to describe the pores that he observed in sections of cork.

The *Micrographia* also contains a score of observations, mostly on animal material. Among these are Hooke's description of the structure of a feather and his observations of the metamorphosis of a water gnat. His mechanical insights are revealed in his description of the muscles and joints of spiders and fleas. His microscopical analysis of sponge tissue led him to assert that sponges were animals, not plants as other scientists thought.

In addition to his insightful observations, Hooke influenced the method of science with his precise recording of results and painstakingly accurate drawings. He made a point of observing the same object over and over again, from different angles and with different types of illumination, so that he could obtain the best possible representation of the object. In these ways, he set new standards for microscopy.

Bibliography

The Evolution of the Microscope. S. Bradbury. Oxford, England: Pergamon Press, 1967.

The History of the Microscope, Compiled from Original Instruments and Documents, up to the Introduction of the Achromatic Microscope. R. S. Clay. London: C. Griffin, 1932.

Micrographia: Or, Some Physiological Descriptions of Minute Bodies Made by Magnifying Glasses, with Observations and Inquiries Thereupon. Robert Hooke. Facsimile ed. New York: Dover, 1961.

Theories of Light from Descartes to Newton. A. I. Sabra. London: Oldbourne, 1967.

Window on the Unknown: A History of the Microscope. C. Jacker. New York: Charles Scribner's Sons, 1966.

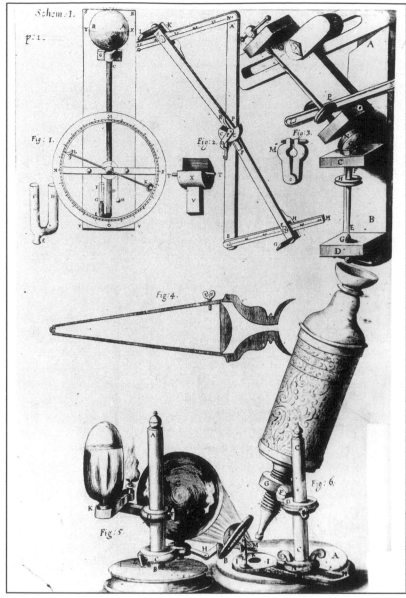

A diagram of the microscope used by Hooke. (National Library of Medicine)

He made fundamental contributions to the technology of his day, especially horology (the science of time-keeping), which was central to astronomy. He devised instruments with telescopic sights, the iris diaphragm for regulating light, and a clock mechanism enabling telescopes to be directed constantly at a particular part of the sky.

His other inventions were wide-ranging: more accurate thermometers, hygrometers, and rain and wind gauges; machines for gathering specimens from the seafloor; a spirit level for architects; and a wheel barometer for registering pressure on a dial. Hooke claimed to have solved the crucial problem of determining longitude at sea, but, because of a patent dispute, he never divulged his method.

Philosophy of Science

Hooke favored experiment over theory. He believed not only that practical research is beneficial to society but also that the act of discovery is gratifying to the senses. In this light, he worked furiously on most of his projects and made theoretical comments only in passing. For this reason, he was often looked on as a mere worker or mechanic, at a time when scientists were far more enamored of theory, as exemplified by the work of the mathematician Sir Isaac Newton, a contemporary of Hooke.

Hooke died in 1703 at the age of sixty-seven.

accessible language meant that it was superficial. It was centuries before its significance was fully appreciated.

The Mechanical Decade

Hooke's genius for mechanical devices, which had first manifested itself in his childhood, fueled his incessant inventiveness as an adult, especially in the period from 1670 to 1680. Basically, he commented on, or improved, any mechanical device that crossed his path. Other devices were his original inventions.

Bibliography

By Hooke

An Attempt for the Explication of the Phanomena, Observable in an Experiment Published by the Honourable Robert Boyle, Esq. . . . , 1661

Micrographia, 1665

The Diary of Robert Hooke, M.A., M.D., F.R.S., 1672-1680, 1935

Animadversions . . . , 1674
An Attempt to Prove the Motion of the Earth from Observations Made by Robert Hooke, 1674
A Description of Helioscopes and Some Other Instruments Made by Robert Hooke, 1676
Lampas: Or, Descriptions of Some Mechanical Improvements of Lamps and Waterpoises, 1677
Cometa, 1678
De Potentia Restitutiva, 1678
Microscopium, 1678
Philosophical Collections, 1679-1682 (7 vols.)

About Hooke

Founders of British Science. J. G. Crowther. London: Cresset Press, 1960.
Restless Genius: Robert Hooke and His Earthly Thoughts. Ellen Tan Grake. New York: Oxford University Press, 1996.
Robert Hooke. Margaret 'Espinasse. London: William Heinemann, 1956.
Robert Hooke: New Studies. Michael Hunter and Simon Schaffer, eds. Woodbridge England: Boydell Press, 1989.

(Robert T. Klose)

Sir Frederick Gowland Hopkins

Areas of Achievement: Cell biology, chemistry, medicine, and physiology
Contribution: The main figure in the establishment of biochemistry in Britain, Hopkins made important contributions to the understanding of the metabolism of living cells and to biochemical research methods.

June 20, 1861	Born in Eastbourne, Sussex, England
1894	Earns a medical degree from Guy's Hospital, London
1898-1910	Lectures in chemical physiology at Cambridge University
1905	Elected a Fellow of the Royal Society of London
1910	Named Fellow and Praelector in Biochemistry at Trinity College, Cambridge
1912	Publishes a paper demonstrating the need for vitamins in the diet
1914-1943	Named the first Professor of Biochemistry at Cambridge
1918	Awarded the Royal Medal of the Royal Society of London
1925	Knighted by King George V
1926	Awarded the Copley Medal of the Royal Society of London
1929	Wins the Nobel Prize in Physiology or Medicine
1930-1935	Elected president of the Royal Society of London
1933	Named president of the British Association for the Advancement of Science
1935	Awarded the Order of Merit
May 16, 1947	Dies in Cambridge, England

Early Life

Frederick Gowland Hopkins was born in the English seaside town of Eastbourne, in 1861. His father, a cousin of the poet Gerard Manley Hopkins, died when Frederick was a baby, but, at about age eight, Frederick began to play with his father's old microscope and was deeply impressed by what he saw.

In 1871, the family moved to north London. Hopkins attended the prestigious City of London School and did outstandingly in chemistry and English. Around age fourteen, however, bored with his classes, he began to play truant and spent several weeks walking alone in the countryside and exploring docks, museums, and the public library. For this, he was, effectively, expelled.

Working in London

At seventeen, Hopkins started work in an insurance office, but very soon he began to pursue his interest in science, publishing a paper in *The Entomologist* on the purple vapor ejected by the bombardier beetle and taking a job as an analyst in a commercial laboratory.

He studied for an associateship of the Institute of Chemistry, and his exceptional performance in the examination was noticed by Thomas Stevenson, who asked him to become an assistant in his forensic laboratory at Guy's Hospital. Hopkins' work there contributed to the conviction of several notorious murderers. In 1888, after inheriting some money, he began a medical degree at Guy's and, after qualifying, stayed on to teach and do research.

Cambridge University

In 1898, Hopkins married Jessie Anne Stevens. In addition, the professor of physiology at Cambridge University invited Hopkins to develop the almost moribund teaching and research program in "chemical physiology," as biochemistry was then known. The pay was poor, and, in order to support his new wife and family, Hopkins had to take on additional teaching work. In 1910, he became ill from overwork, but later that year Trinity College elected him as a Fellow and Praelector in Biochemistry, a position that gave him much more time for his research. By 1912, he had published his seminal paper demonstrating the importance of vitamins.

In 1914, Hopkins was appointed Cambridge's very first Professor of Biochemistry, a position that he held until his retirement in 1943. Under his leadership, both teaching and

Essential Amino Acids and Vitamins

Hopkins found that small quantities of specific complex chemicals in the diet are vital for health.

While teaching at Cambridge, Hopkins was surprised when a student's protein samples failed to turn blue in the standard Adamkiewicz test. This led him to the discovery of the amino acid tryptophan, present in many (but not all) proteins and necessary for the Adamkiewicz reaction. He found that mice fed a diet without tryptophan became sick and that certain other amino acids were also dietetically essential. The body needs these components in order to build its own proteins but cannot make them for itself.

Hopkins suspected that minute amounts of other, yet unknown chemicals were necessary in the diet. He fed mice solely on fat, starch, salts, and purified milk protein (containing all the essential amino acids). They became sick and ceased to grow. When also given a very small quantity of whole milk, however, they recovered.

This observation led to the isolation of vitamin C and what Hopkins called "fat-soluble A" (actually two vitamins, A and D). During World War I, butter, an important source of "fat-soluble A," was scarce, and Hopkins was asked to investigate margarine, finding that it lacked this vitamin complex. Consequently, vitamins A and D are now routinely added to margarines.

Bibliography

The Chemicals of Life. Isaac Asimov. New York: Abelard-Schuman, 1954.

The Vitamins. Gerald Combs. San Diego: Academic Press, 1992.

Vitamins. Wilhelm Friedrich. New York: De Gruyter, 1988.

research in biochemistry began to flourish and grow, both at Cambridge and later elsewhere in Britain and around the world. Although a mediocre teacher in introductory classes, Hopkins was inspiring at the advanced level, and, by the time that he died, seventy-five of his former students were professors of biochemistry throughout the world.

Although his 1929 Nobel Prize in Physiology or Medicine was "for his discovery of the growth-stimulating vitamins," for Hopkins, nutritional studies were secondary to his research on cellular metabolism: the very complex sequence of chemical reactions by which living cells extract energy from food molecules. This process was not fully understood during Hopkins' lifetime, but work done or inspired by him contributed enormously to the current understanding. His vision of the cell as a chemical machine was ahead of its time and provided an indispensable guiding framework not only for his own research but also for biochemical science as a whole.

Bibliography
By Hopkins
"Feeding Experiments Illustrating the Importance of Accessory Factors in Normal Dietaries," *The Journal of Physiology*, 1912

Report on the Present State of Knowledge Concerning Accessory Food Factors (Vitamines), 1919

Hopkins and Biochemistry, 1861-1947, 1949 (Joseph Needham and Ernest Baldwin, eds.)

About Hopkins
Gowland Hopkins. Ernest Baldwin. London: Van Den Berghs, 1961.

(The Nobel Foundation)

"Hopkins, Frederick Gowland." In *Dictionary of Scientific Biography*, edited by Charles Coulston Gillispie. New York: Charles Scribner's Sons, 1973.

"Hopkins, Sir Frederick Gowland." In *Dictionary of National Biography, 1941-1950*. Oxford, England: Oxford University Press, 1959.

(Nigel J. T. Thomas)

Grace Murray Hopper

Areas of Achievement: Mathematics and technology

Contribution: Hopper, one of the pioneers of the computer industry, developed the programming language FLOW-MATIC, which was the predecessor of COBOL.

Dec. 9, 1906	Born in New York, New York
1934	Earns a Ph.D. in mathematics from Yale
1943	Joins the U.S. naval reserves and is called to active duty
1944-1946	Programs computers at Harvard
1946	Publishes the first computer manual
1946	Presented with the Naval Ordnance Development Award
1949-1971	Works at Eckert-Mauchly as a senior mathematician
1952	Develops A-0, the first compiler
1957	Develops FLOW-MATIC
1959	Facilitates the development of the computer language COBOL
1966	Retires from the naval reserves
1969	Receives the first Data Processing Management Association's Man-of-the-Year Award
1970	Recalled to temporary active duty in the Navy
1985	Advances to rear admiral
1986	Retires as the oldest active Navy officer and becomes a senior consultant at Digital Equipment Company
1991	Receives the National Medal of Technology
Jan. 1, 1992	Dies in Arlington, Virginia

Early Life

Grace Murray Hopper was born in 1906 to a family that supported her interest in science and mathematics. Grace's two grandfathers played an important role in her early development: Her paternal grandfather was a rear admiral in the Navy, and her maternal grandfather, the chief civil engineer of New York City, fostered her interest in mathematics, particularly geometry.

Grace received a solid education, equal to that of her brother. She attended girls' schools in New Hampshire and New York City and was graduated Phi Beta Kappa from Vassar College in 1928, having studied engineering, mathematics, and physics. With a Vassar fellowship, she continued her studies at Yale University, earning a Ph.D. in 1934. Her early love of geometry was evident in her dissertation, "A New Criterion for Reducibility of Algebraic Equations." Hopper taught mathematics at Vassar for the next ten years.

The Navy and the World of Computers

World War II changed Hopper's life dramatically. Desiring to serve her country at this time of need, she chose the Navy, joining the naval reserves in 1943. She was commissioned a lieutenant, junior grade, in June, 1944, and ordered to report to the Bureau of Ships Computation Project at Harvard University. There, she became the third person to program the first large-scale computer, the Mark I.

In the early days of the 1940's, the machines had to be given instructions by the laborious method of hand-wiring circuits on plug boards. Hopper and her colleagues developed subroutines for various problems, such as developing the sine of an angle. Hopper wrote *A Manual of Operation for the Automatic Sequence Controlled Calculator* (1946), the first computer manual.

At the end of the war, Hopper petitioned to remain on active duty in the Navy, but she was considered too old. She had just turned forty, and naval regulations specified thirty-eight as the upper limit. Consequently, Hopper retired from active duty in the Navy for the first time. She remained in the reserves until 1966.

In 1946, Hopper received an appointment as a research associate at Harvard and continued to work on the Mark II and Mark III computers, and her interest in the business side of computers developed. Commodore Howard Aiken, the director of the Bureau of Ships Computation Project, encouraged the Prudential insurance company to use Mark I in its actuarial work. Hopper helped develop the program for this use.

Programming Languages

In 1949, Hopper joined the business world with the Eckert-Mauchly Company in Philadelphia. At that time, J. Prosper Eckert and John Mauchly, the inventors of the ENIAC, were developing BINAC and UNIVAC, the first commercial large-scale electronic computers. Hopper was involved in the development of the first compilers and of business languages.

Hopper's major contribution to data processing was her early recognition of the potential commercial importance of computers. She played an important role in the development of COBOL (*common business-oriented language*

Compilers and a Business Language

Hopper and her group at the Eckert-Mauchly Company developed the first computer compilers and the language FLOW-MATIC.

As early as 1944, programming was beginning at Harvard University. Subroutines for specific problems (such as the tangent of an angle) were being saved and passed from one individual to another. A generalized format was adopted for the Mark I computer.

Hopper realized that time was being lost and that many errors were being made as instructions were hand-copied. The A-O compiler translated the programmers' higher-level symbolic mathematical code into the computer's binary language or machine code. It also assigned call numbers to program routines stored on magnetic tape so that they could be brought over to do the calculations. Using these stored subroutines, application programs could be written much faster. The A-2 compiler added an easier way to input information and write programs. The directions to do the operation "x + y + z" were given by the 12 alpha-decimal word "[ADD 00X 00Y 00Z]." A number before the letter became the code to differentiate it.

In the early 1950's, Hopper supervised the development of the first compiler to use mathematical language, the AT-3, which was later marketed as MATH-MATIC. With this compiler, arithmetic and calculus could be done. A complex calculation that had previously taken six months to solve was completed in eighteen minutes. Hopper next began the development of the B-0 compiler, later known as FLOW-MATIC. It was designed to translate business terms such as those needed for inventory, billing, and payroll into a form acceptable to the computer. Hopper proposed to develop a programming language that would use variable-length English words, spaces, and periods. She knew that the commercial success of the computer industry was dependent on its understanding and use by nonmathematicians.

Hopper's group at UNIVAC wrote a small model program and invited management to a demonstration. The program read in part: "INPUT INVENTORY FILE A; PRICE FILE B; OUTPUT PRICED INVENTORY FILE C. COMPARE PRODUCT #A WITH PRODUCT #B. IF GREATER, GO TO OPERATION 10; IF EQUAL, GO TO OPERATION 5; OTHERWISE GO TO OPERATION 2." After showing the utility of the program, the team was given the necessary budget to finish the project. In 1956, the business community was given in FLOW-MATIC a computer language that it could understand. This achievement became an essential part of the development of the standardized COBOL, the common business-oriented language, that Hopper facilitated in 1959.

Bibliography

"The Early History of COBOL." In *History of Programming Languages*, edited by Richard Wexeblat. New York: Academic Press, 1987.

Women Inventors and Their Discoveries. Ethlie Ann Vare and Gary Ptacek. Minneapolis: Oliver Press, 1993.

Commodore Hopper speaks at the groundbreaking ceremony of the Grace M. Hopper Navy Regional Data Automation Center in 1985. Soon after, she was promoted to rear admiral. (Michael Flynn, U.S. Navy)

guage). She attended organizational meetings and served as an adviser to the Executive Committee of the Committee on Data Systems Languages (CODASYL). Her high-level programming language FLOW-MATIC was a part of the foundation of the new composite language.

Continuing a Naval Career
While working in industry, Hopper continued in the naval reserves from which she retired in December, 1966, at the mandatory age of sixty. Eight months later, she was recalled to the U.S. Naval Data Automation Control on "temporary" active duty. Her assignment was to standardize the Navy's computer languages and to urge the entire Navy to use them. She worked on this task for close to twenty more years. The work done by her group served as

the bases for government standards for the languages COBOL, FORTRAN, BASIC, and ADA.

On August 14, 1986, Rear Admiral Grace Murray Hopper, the oldest active Navy officer, retired in a ceremony on the oldest active Navy ship, the USS *Constitution*, called "Old Ironsides."

Spokesperson for the Computer Industry
At the age of seventy-nine, Hopper's long career with the Navy came to a close, but not her career with computers. In September, 1986, she became a full-time senior consultant at Digital Equipment Company. She gave two hundred talks each year to industry forums and to the educational community.

On September 16, 1991, President George Bush awarded Hopper the National Medal of Technology for spending a half century pushing America and its Navy to the leading edge of technology. Hopper died in 1992 at the age of eighty-five.

Bibliography
By Hopper
A Manual of Operation for the Automatic Sequence Controlled Calculator, 1946
"Keynote Address" in *The History of Programming Languages*, 1981 (Richard L. Wexelblat, ed.)
Understanding Computers, 1984 (with Steven L. Mandell)
"The Education of a Computer," *Annals of the History of Computing*, 1988

About Hopper
"Grace Hopper, Conscience of the Industry." P. Gillin. *Computerworld* 16, no. 37 (September 10, 1984).
"Pioneering Women in Computer Science." Denise Gurer. *Communications of the ACM* 38, no. 1 (January, 1995).
Portraits in Silicon. Robert Slater. Cambridge, Mass.: MIT Press, 1987.
"Through the Looking Glass with Grace Hopper." Marjorie Blair. *Electronic Education* 3, no. 4 (January, 1984).

(Helen M. Burke)

Bernardo Alberto Houssay

Area of Achievement: Physiology
Contribution: Houssay demonstrated the interconnection between pituitary and pancreatic hormones in carbohydrate metabolism and its bearing on diabetes.

Apr. 10, 1887	Born in Buenos Aires, Argentina
1907	Becomes a laboratory assistant and assistant pharmacist at the Hospital de Clinica
1910	Earns an M.D. with a thesis on pituitary function
1911	Named chief of clinical medicine at Alvear Hospital
1912	Becomes full professor in the faculty of veterinary science
1915	Named chief of experimental pathology at Alvear Hospital
1919	Named professor of physiology at the University of Buenos Aires and director of the Institute of Physiology
1920	Marries chemist María Catán
1943	Removed from his academic chair by the de facto government dominated by Juan Perón
1944	Founds the Institute of Biology and Experimental Medicine
1945	Reinstated but soon forced into retirement by the government
1947	Wins the Nobel Prize in Physiology or Medicine
1955	Reinstated again with the fall of the Perón government but resigns the next year to direct his institute
Sept. 21, 1971	Dies in Buenos Aires, Argentina

Early Life

Bernardo Alberto Houssay (pronounced "ew-SI") was born into an educated family of French extraction. He was bilingual in Spanish and French and showed an early interest in history, literature, and natural science. He plunged into the professional academic world by the age of seventeen and spent his entire life there.

DoHoussay's M.D. thesis was typical of his research throughout his lifetime—he elected to study the pituitary because no one else was, and he constructed his own research equipment and protocols because no such things existed in Argentina at the time.

Research Career

Houssay was extraordinarily self-motivated, and he almost single-handedly built a research tradition in physiology in his country. His thesis was published in book form as *Estudios sobre la acción de los extractos hipofisarios* (1911; studies of the action of pituitary extracts), but by the time that he was appointed to the University of Buenos Aires, he had published two other studies, of snake and spider venoms and of venous blood circulation, and had investi-

(The Nobel Foundation)

gated a number of other matters that appeared in shorter papers.

At the university, Houssay began a campaign of reforming the old-fashioned teaching methods to include real teaching, not simply memorization, and, above all, laboratory experience. Gradually, he succeeded, and the students who passed through the university began to take their places in his laboratory and in research facilities abroad.

When the antidiabetic hormone insulin became available in the mid-1920's, Houssay's group focused in on the complex interplay of organs and hormones that governs carbohydrate metabolism. After two decades, he had uncovered enough of the process to be recognized, along with Carl and Gerty Cori at Washington University in St. Louis, by the Nobel Committee in 1947.

Houssay continued to publish research results and direct his Institute of Biology and Experimental Medicine until his death in 1971.

Bibliography

By Houssay
Estudios sobre la acción de los extractos hipofisarios, 1911

La acción fisiológica de los extractos hipofisarios, 1918
Tiroides e inmunidad: Estudio crítico y experimental, 1924 (with A. Sordelli)
Collected Papers on Medical Subjects Including Physiology, 1924-1934
Functions of the Pituitary Gland, 1936
"The Hypophysis and Metabolism," *New England Journal of Medicine*, 1936
La acción diabetógena de la hipófisis, 1945
Fisiología humana, 1946 (*Human Physiology*, 1948)
"The Role of the Hypophysis in Carbohydrate Metabolism and in Diabetes" in *Les Prix Nobel en 1947*, 1948

About Houssay
"Bernardo Alberto Houssay, 1887-1971." Sir Frank Young and V. G. Foglia. *Biographical Memoirs of Fellows of the Royal Society* 20 (1974).
"Bernardo Alberto Houssay, 1947." Robert M. Hawthorne, Jr. In *The Nobel Prize Winners: Physiology or Medicine*, edited by Frank N. Magill. Pasadena, Calif.: Salem Press, 1991.
"Obituary: Bernardo Alberto Houssay." *The New York Times*, September 22, 1970.

(Robert M. Hawthorne, Jr.)

Carbohydrate Metabolism

Carbohydrate metabolism and other processes are maintained by a balance among the secretions of many endocrine glands, the pituitary being the center and most important of these.

The sugar glucose, obtained mostly from dietary carbohydrates, is the source of cell energy, and a constant level is maintained in the blood by an interactive regulation clarified by Houssay and his coworkers.

Lacking the methods of today's biochemistry, in which cells are reduced to a homogenate that can be used in test-tube quantities, with products separated and identified by micromethods, Houssay was restricted to whole-animal or whole-organ work. Organs were systematically removed from experimental animals to observe the effects on metabolism: Removal of the pituitary (or hypophysis) caused insulin sensitivity, which was abated by anterior pituitary extract.

Removal of both the pituitary and the pancreas produced no diabetes. Anterior pituitary given to whole animals induced diabetes and damaged the insulin-producing parts of the pancreas. The target organ in all of these effects is the liver, demonstrated by removing other organs (including the brain) without effect. The command compound from the pituitary is a protein of unknown structure. These results, together with Carl and Gerty Cori's contribution, gave the first picture, since much expanded, of a very complex metabolic system.

Bibliography
"Laboratory Styles in Argentine Physiology." Marcos Cueto. *Isis* 85 (1994).
"1947: Bernardo Alberto Houssay." Theodore L. Sourkes. In *Nobel Prize Winners in Medicine and Physiology, 1901-1965*. London: Abelard-Schuman, 1966.

Sir Fred Hoyle

Areas of Achievement: Astronomy, cosmology, and physics

Contribution: A controversial figure, Hoyle is best known as the coauthor of the steady state cosmological theory. He also made key contributions to astrophysics, especially in helping to explain how elements are made in stars and supernovas.

June 24, 1915	Born in Bingley, Yorkshire, England
1936	Receives a B.A. in mathematics from Cambridge University
1939	Earns an M.A. in physics from Cambridge
1940-1945	Helps develop radar for the British navy
1945-1956	Conducts lectures in mathematics at Cambridge
1950	Publishes *The Nature of the Universe*, a popular book on cosmology
1957	Elected a member of the Royal Society of London
1958-1972	Serves as Plumian Professor of Astronomy and as professor of experimental philosophy
1967	Founds the Institute of Theoretical Astronomy at Cambridge
1969	Named a foreign associate of the National Academy of Sciences
1969-1972	Acts as a professor of astronomy at the Royal Institution of Great Britain
1972	Knighted by Queen Elizabeth II
1974	Receives the Gold Medal from the Royal Society of London
1975-1985	Investigates the possibility that life exists in interstellar space

Early Life

Sir Fred Hoyle was born in Bingley, England, in 1915. His mother, a former schoolteacher, and his father, a cloth merchant, were determined that he receive a good education, an ambition that young Hoyle did not share. Frequent truancy from ages ten to twelve, he later claimed, allowed him to explore science on his own.

Nevertheless, Hoyle finished the English equivalent of high school and won a scholarship to Cambridge University in 1933, where he studied mathematics. He was graduated in 1936 and stayed at Cambridge to study physics with Rudolf Peierls and Paul A. M. Dirac, both leading theorists. He received a master's degree in 1939 and married Barbara Clark, with whom he had a son, Geoffrey, and a daughter, Elizabeth. Hoyle was about to begin a fellowship at St. John's College, Cambridge, when World War II started; instead, he helped modify radar to detect aircraft and submarines for the Royal Navy.

The Creation of Elements

Hoyle resumed his Cambridge fellowship as a lecturer in the mathematics faculty in 1945, where he quickly gained a reputation as an energetic, unconventional thinker. Despite a heavy teaching load, he developed a theory, begun during the war with Maurice Pryce, to explain the production of light elements in stars. He also predicted an energy state of carbon that had never been detected (experiments soon proved him correct) and pointed out that more helium existed in the universe than could be accounted for by theory.

During the late 1940's and 1950's, Hoyle spent several terms at the California Institute of Technology and at the Mount Wilson and Mount Palomar Observatories. He worked closely with Margaret Burbidge, Geoffrey Burbidge, and William A. Fowler to explain how supernovas form heavy elements. Their collaboration culminated in a landmark paper in astrophysics, "The Synthesis of Elements in Stars" (1957).

Cosmology

The prevailing cosmological theory in the 1940's held that the universe grew from an exploding primeval atom. During a radio lecture in 1949, Hoyle referred to the theory as the "big bang." The name stuck, even though Hoyle only intended it to be a picturesque description.

In fact, Hoyle thought the big bang theory to be seriously flawed. Beginning in 1946, he worked with Thomas Gold and Hermann Bondi on what became the chief rival theory of the big bang. Called the steady state cosmological theory, it proposes that the universe had no sudden beginning. Instead, matter is continuously created over trackless time. Hoyle's original version of the theory differed somewhat from that of Gold and Bondi, and he modified it significantly between 1960 and 1980.

The steady state theory has sparked continuous and harsh criticism, much to Hoyle's

Steady State Cosmology

The steady state cosmological theory proposes that matter in the universe is continuously created over time, rather than having arisen suddenly as suggested in the big bang model.

Serious problems troubled the early version of the big bang cosmological model: It proposed a universe three billion years old, younger than many stars in it, a clear contradiction; it could not account for the formation of galaxies; and it did not explain the distribution of elements well. Such difficulties led Hoyle, Thomas Gold, and Hermann Bondi to consider a universe without a finite age. Gold realized that such a theory requires that matter constantly be created in order to fill the empty space opened by the observed recession of galaxies as the universe expands.

Bondi and Gold rested their version of the theory on an axiom that they called the perfect cosmological principle, which assumes that the universe is uniform everywhere in space and time. As the universe expands and old matter drifts away, new particles materialize spontaneously to maintain the uniformity. They rejected Albert Einstein's treatment of mass in the general theory of relativity in favor of a version of Ernst Mach's principle that attributes the properties of mass to the influence of matter elsewhere in the universe.

In his version of the steady state model, Hoyle treated the cosmological principle not as an axiom but as a result of his calculations, which he based on the general theory of relativity. He did so by incorporating a new term into Einstein's field equations, which Hoyle called the C-field. This field produces new matter and fuels the expansion of the universe. He calculated that new matter, in the form of hydrogen, emerges slowly—about three atoms per cubic yard every million years. In an infinitely old universe, he argued, enough matter accumulates to produce new galaxies at a rate to replace old galaxies that have receded beyond observation. Using steady state principles, Hoyle and his colleagues were able to account for the abundance of helium in the universe and the existence of heavy elements and to explain why the laws of physics depend on a single direction of time.

Hoyle and Jayant Narlikar modified the steady state model in response to criticism from cosmologists and to new observational evidence. Their "quasi steady state" theory proposes an oscillating universe in which fields of negative pressure produce new particles in spurts rather than at a continuous rate. The oscillations last about forty billion years. Hoyle calculated that the Milky Way is about three hundred billion years old and that current observational instruments afford astronomers a look backward in time of about six hundred billion years.

The quasi steady state, according to Hoyle, accounts for the physical properties of the universe at least as well as the big bang model, but he did not claim that his theory settles all problems. He argued that future cosmological theories will make use of ideas from both the big bang and the steady state model.

Bibliography

Astronomy and Cosmology. John North. New York: W. W. Norton, 1995.

The Structure of the Universe. Jayant Narlikar. London: Oxford University Press, 1977.

The Universe at Large. Hermann Bondi. New York: Doubleday, 1960.

Nucleosynthesis of Elements

Hoyle and his colleagues tailored the modern theory of element building to explain the known abundance of elements in the universe. They concluded that element creation is part of the evolution of stars and that it varies with stellar age, type, and size.

Typically, a star converts hydrogen to helium during fusion as protons, which normally repel one another, are forced together. When the hydrogen is used up, the star's core contracts, and, in the increased heat and density, helium nuclei fuse into carbon, oxygen, and nitrogen nuclei. When the helium is exhausted, the core shrinks further and further, escalating temperatures and densities. In several processes of proton accumulation, carbon burns to form sodium, magnesium, neon, and oxygen and silicon burns to produce such heavier elements as sulfur, calcium, nickel, and iron.

In some stars, iron accumulating in the core damps the fusion reaction and a supernova follows. The star collapses inward under the pull of gravity, forming a neutron star, and a shock wave with a dense flux of neutrons spreads outward, forging the nuclei of such metals as gold, copper, mercury, lead, and uranium. Elements heavier than uranium also form but are unstable and decay into lighter elements.

Bibliography

Cauldrons of the Cosmos. Claus E. Rolfs and William S. Rodney. Chicago: University of Chicago Press, 1988.
Coming of Age in the Milky Way. Timothy Ferris. New York: William Morrow, 1988.
End in Fire: The Supernova in the Large Magellanic Cloud. Paul Murdin. New York: Cambridge University Press, 1990.

astonishment. Although early on Hoyle attracted important supporters, the discovery in 1965 that microwave radiation pervades the universe, as predicted by big bang theory cosmologist George Gamow, has been widely thought to invalidate the steady state theory.

Hoyle remained undeterred, however, and developed his modified "quasi steady state" theory with Jayant Narlikar. Hoyle insisted that this theory, in comparison to the big bang model, also accounts for the cosmic background radiation, is simpler in form, and has fewer untestable properties. In fact, he denounced big bang cosmology as metaphysics or a kind of religious fundamentalism.

The Origin of Life

In 1967, Hoyle was elected Plumian Professor of Astronomy at Cambridge, a prestigious position. He also brought a decade of effort to fruition by opening and heading the Institute of Theoretical Astronomy. Five years later, however, the academic politics connected with the institute and the building of new telescopes soured him on British academic science. He resigned his professorship in 1972.

The resignation freed time for writing and lecturing. Hoyle had already acquired renown

at both. He had published more than two dozen science fiction novels (some coauthored with his son) and popular astronomy books. He also lectured and wrote about overpopulation, Stonehenge, and nuclear energy.

In 1975, he began studying the possibility that life originated in interstellar space. With Chandra Wickramasinghe, he wrote a series of books theorizing not only that life came from outer space but also that disease-causing organisms continue to reach Earth ferried on comets and meteors. Long considered wildly speculative, this "panspermia" theory began to receive serious, if hesitant, attention from the scientific establishment in the mid-1990's.

Bibliography
By Hoyle
Some Recent Researches in Solar Physics, 1949
The Nature of the Universe, 1950
A Decade of Decision, 1953
Frontiers of Astronomy, 1955
Man and Materialism, 1956
The Black Cloud, 1957
Ossian's Ride, 1959
A for Andromeda: A Novel of Tomorrow, 1962 (with John Elliot)
Astronomy, 1962

A Contradiction in the Argument of Malthus, 1963

Fifth Planet, 1963 (with Geoffrey Hoyle)

Andromeda Breakthrough, 1964 (with Elliot)

Of Men and Galaxies, 1964

Encounter with the Future, 1965

Galaxies, Nuclei, and Quasars, 1965

Nucleosynthesis in Massive Stars and Supernovae, 1965 (with William A. Fowler)

Man in the Universe, 1966

October the First Is Too Late, 1966

Element 79, 1967

Rockets in Ursa Major, 1969 (with Geoffrey Hoyle)

Seven Steps to the Sun, 1970 (with Geoffrey Hoyle)

The Molecule Men, 1971 (with Geoffrey Hoyle)

The Monster of Loch Ness, 1971

The New Face of Science, 1971

From Stonehenge to Modern Cosmology, 1972

The Inferno, 1973 (with Geoffrey Hoyle)

Nicolaus Copernicus: An Essay on His Life and Work, 1973

Into Deepest Space, 1974 (with Geoffrey Hoyle)

Action at a Distance in Physics and Cosmology, 1974 (with Jayant Narlikar)

Astronomy Today, 1975

Highlights in Astronomy, 1975

Astronomy and Cosmology: A Modern Course, 1975

On Stonehenge, 1977

Ten Faces of the Universe, 1977

The Incandescent Ones, 1977 (with Geoffrey Hoyle; Barbara Hoyle, ed.)

Energy or Extinction?: The Case for Nuclear Energy, 1977

The Westminster Disaster, 1978 (with Geoffrey Hoyle; Barbara Hoyle, ed.)

The Cosmogony of the Solar System, 1978

Lifecloud, the Origin of Life in the Universe, 1978 (with Chandra Wickramasinghe)

(Archive Photos/Express News)

Diseases from Space, 1979 (with Wickramasinghe)

Commonsense in Nuclear Energy, 1980 (with Geoffrey Hoyle)

The Physics-Astronomy Frontier, 1980 (with Narlikar)

Steady-State Cosmology Re-visited, 1980

Space Travellers: The Bringers of Life, 1981 (with Wickramasinghe)

Ice, the Ultimate Human Catastrophe, 1981

The Quasar Controversy Resolved, 1981

Evolution from Space: A Theory of Cosmic Creationism, 1981 (with Wickramasinghe)

Proofs That Life Is Cosmic, 1982 (with Wick-

ramasinghe)
Facts and Dogmas in Cosmology and Elsewhere,
1982
The Intelligent Universe, 1983
From Grains to Bacteria, 1984 (with Wickramasinghe)
Comet Halley: A Novel in Two Parts, 1985
Living Comets, 1985 (with Wickramasinghe)
The Small World of Fred Hoyle: An Autobiography,
1986
Cosmic Life-Force, 1988 (with Wickramasinghe)
The Theory of Cosmic Grains, 1991 (with Wickramasinghe)
The Origin of the Universe and the Origin of Religion, 1993
Our Place in the Cosmos: The Unfinished Revolution, 1993 (with Wickramasinghe)
Home Is Where the Wind Blows: Chapters from a Cosmologist's Life, 1994
Lectures on Cosmology and Action at a Distance Electrodynamics, 1996 (with Narlikar)

About Hoyle
Lonely Hearts of the Cosmos. Dennis Overbye. New York: HarperCollins, 1991.
Origins: The Lives and Worlds of Modern Cosmologists. Alan Lightman and Roberta Brawer. Cambridge, Mass.: Harvard University Press, 1990.
"The Return of the Maverick." John Horgan. *Scientific American* 272 (March, 1995): 46-47.

(Roger Smith)

Alice S. Huang

Areas of Achievement: Genetics, medicine, and virology
Contribution: Huang's research on viral genetics aided in the discovery of the enzyme reverse transcriptase. She also studied how abnormal viruses interfere with the reproduction of normal viruses.

Mar. 22, 1939	Born in Nanchang, Jianxi, China
1949	Emigrates to the United States
1957-1959	Attends Wellesley College
1959-1966	Attends The Johns Hopkins University, earning bachelor's, master's, and Ph.D. degrees
1966	Employed as a visiting assistant professor at the National Taiwan University
1967	Serves a postdoctoral fellowship at the Salk Institute
1968-1969	Serves postdoctoral fellowship at the Massachusetts Institute of Technology (MIT)
1969-1970	Employed as a research associate at MIT
1970	Works as lecturer at the National Taiwan University
1971-1978	Serves as an assistant and then associate professor at Harvard University
1977	Receives the Eli Lilly Award
1979-1991	Employed as a professor at Harvard
1988-1989	Serves as president of the American Society for Microbiology
1991	Appointed the dean of science at New York University

654 Huang, Alice S.

Early Life

Alice Shih-hou Huang was born in Nanchang, China, on March 22, 1939. Her parents were Quentin K. Y. Huang, a bishop in the Anglican Episcopal Church, and Grace Betty Soong Huang, a nurse. In 1949, when the Communist Party took control of the government of China, Alice and her siblings were sent to live in the United States. She studied at an Episcopal boarding school in Burlington, New Jersey, and at the National Cathedral School in Washington, D.C. Huang became a citizen of the United States while a senior in high school.

Huang attended Wellesley College, in Massachusetts, from 1957 to 1959. She then enrolled at the School of Medicine at The Johns Hopkins University in Baltimore, Maryland, where she earned a bachelor's degree in 1961, a master's degree in 1963, and a Ph.D. in 1966. In 1966, she served as a visiting assistant professor at the National Taiwan University in Taipei, Taiwan.

Postdoctoral Research

After returning to the United States, Huang began working with David Baltimore as a postdoctoral fellow at the Salk Institute for Biological Studies in San Diego, California. The two

virologists were married in 1968. That same year, they took their research to the Massachusetts Institute of Technology (MIT), in Cambridge, Massachusetts, where Huang continued to serve as a postdoctoral fellow.

Huang's study of viral genetics enabled Baltimore to discover the enzyme reverse transcriptase, which is involved in the reproduction of viruses known as retroviruses. For this discovery, Baltimore shared the 1975 Nobel Prize for Physiology or Medicine with Renato Dulbecco and Howard M. Temin.

The Harvard Years

Huang worked as a research associate at MIT from 1969 to 1970, then returned to the National Taiwan University in 1970 as a lecturer. In 1971, she began her career at the Medical School of Harvard University in Cambridge, Massachusetts, as an assistant professor. She was promoted to associate professor in 1973 and to professor in 1979.

While working at Harvard, Huang also served as a scientific associate at Boston City Hospital, a visiting associate professor at Rockefeller University in New York, a visiting professor at the University of Mississippi, and a laboratory director at Children's Hospital in

Defective Interfering Particles

Defective interfering particles are abnormal viruses that interfere with the reproduction of normal viruses and that appear to be involved in determining the patterns of viral infections.

A normal virus consists of a chain of deoxyribonucleic acid (DNA) or ribonucleic acid (RNA) within a protein shell. Viruses must invade living cells within other organisms to reproduce. An invading virus uses the host cell's internal biological mechanisms to make copies of the viral DNA or RNA. These copies cause the host cell to produce the proteins that make up the viral shell. The DNA or RNA combines with the proteins to form new viruses.

Occasionally, an abnormal virus is produced during this process. This virus, known as a defective interfering particle, consists of a normal protein shell surrounding a small part of the viral

DNA or RNA. The particle is able to reproduce itself only when normal viruses are present.

As more defective interfering particles are produced, fewer normal viruses are produced. Eventually, the number of normal viruses is low enough that the number of defective interfering particles declines also. If the host is able to destroy the few remaining viruses, the disease is limited. If the remaining viruses survive to cause a new infection, the disease is recurrent.

Bibliography
A Dancing Matrix: Voyages Along the Viral Frontier. Robin Marantz Henig. New York: Alfred A. Knopf, 1993.
An Introduction to Virology. Clyde R. Goodheart. Philadelphia: W. B. Saunders, 1969.
Introduction to Virology. K. M. Smith and D. A. Ritchie. London: Chapman and Hall, 1980.

(New York University)

Boston. She also served as an associate editor of *Reviews of Infectious Diseases* and on the editorial boards of *Intervirology, Archive of Virology, Journal of Virology*, and *Microbial Pathogenesis*.

Huang's research at Harvard involved abnormal viruses known as defective interfering particles, which block the reproduction of normal viruses. For this research, she was granted the Eli Lilly Award in Microbiology and Immunology in 1977. From 1988 to 1989, she served as president of the American Society of Microbiology; she was the first Asian American to head a national scientific society in the United States. Huang left Harvard in 1991 to serve as dean of science at New York University.

Bibliography

By Huang

"Defective Viral Particles and Viral Disease Processes," *Nature*, 1970 (with David Baltimore)

"Status of Women Microbiologists," *Science*, 1974 (with Eva Ruth Kashket, Mary Louise Robbins, and Loretta Leive)

"Defective Interfering Particles as Antiviral Agents" (with Eduardo L. Palma) in *Perspectives in Virology*, 1975 (Morris Pollard, ed.)

"Defective Interfering Animal Viruses" (with Baltimore) in *Comprehensive Virology*, 1977 (H. Fraenkel-Conrat and R. R. Wagner, eds.)

"Virology" in *Highlights in Microbiology*, 1981 (R. L. Moon and D. D. Whitt, eds.)

"Modulation of Viral Diseases by Defective Interfering Particles" in *RNA Genetics: 3, Variability of RNA Genomes*, 1988 (Estaban Domingo, John J. Holland, and Paul Ahlquist, eds.)

"Science Education Shouldn't Be Restricted to Narrow Boxes," *Scientist*, 1992

"How Does Variation Count?," *Nature*, 1992 (with John M. Coffin)

About Huang

"Asian-Americans Bump Against Glass Ceilings." Susan Katz Miller. *Science* 258 (November 13, 1992).

Notable Twentieth-Century Scientists. Emily J. McMurray, ed. Detroit: Gale Research, 1995.

Who's Who in America. New Providence, N.J.: Marquis Who's Who, 1995.

(Rose Secrest)

Ruth Hubbard

Areas of Achievement: Biology, chemistry, and genetics

Contribution: A biochemist who studied chemicals involved in vision, Hubbard became a leading scientific critic of genetic research on gender-role differences and other human traits.

Mar. 3, 1924	Born in Vienna, Austria
1938	Leaves Austria with her family after the Nazi invasion
1942	Works in George Wald's laboratory at Harvard
1946	Begins graduate studies at Radcliffe College
1948	Receives a fellowship to study at the University College Medical School, London
1950	Earns a Ph.D. in biology from Harvard University
1952-53	Works at the Carlsberg Laboratory, in Copenhagen, Denmark, on a Guggenheim Fellowship
1954	Takes a position as a research fellow in Wald's laboratory
1958	Promoted to research associate
June 11, 1958	Marries George Wald
1967	Wald receives the Nobel Prize in Physiology or Medicine
1974	Becomes the first woman to receive tenure at Harvard in the natural sciences
1979	Edits *Women Look at Biology Looking at Women* and *Genes and Gender 2*
1990	Retires as professor emerita
1993	Publishes *Exploding the Gene Myth*

(Courtesy of Ruth Hubbard)

Early Life

Ruth Hubbard was born Ruth Hoffman in 1924. Her parents, Richard and Helene (Ehrlich) Hoffman, were physicians. They settled in Boston after fleeing Nazi persecution in Austria. Ruth entered Radcliffe College, the female branch of Harvard University, expecting to continue the family medical tradition. In her native country, women of her class usually entered a profession and left child care to servants.

Hoffman did not seriously consider a scientific career, even though she enjoyed science classes, because subtle messages constantly signaled that research science was not for women. During her senior year, however, she worked in the laboratory of George Wald, who was working on infrared vision. This experience turned her away from medicine and toward laboratory science.

Hoffman married Frank Twombly Hubbard on December 26, 1942. He was in the Army, and she moved to Chattanooga, Tennessee, where he was stationed, in 1945. Wanting to help in the war against the Nazis, Ruth Hubbard worked as a laboratory technician for the Tennessee Public Health Service. The marriage ended in divorce in 1951.

A Female Scientist at Harvard

Hubbard returned to Radcliffe in 1946 to begin a Ph.D. program in biology, resuming work in Wald's laboratory. After receiving her doctorate, she stayed on at Harvard for another forty years.

Like most women in science during the 1950's and 1960's, Hubbard held appointments that offered no prospects of a tenured faculty position. She was a research fellow, from 1950 to 1952 and from 1954 to 1958, and later served as a research associate and lecturer, from 1958 to 1974. Hubbard and George Wald were married on June 11, 1958.

Hubbard studied the biochemistry of vision, experimenting on frogs, cattle, and squid. She investigated the chemical structure of rhodopsin, which responds to light, and other pigments found in the eye.

She and her coworkers found that among the different forms of vitamin A, which is involved in vision, only one helps produce rhodopsin. They also discovered that light changes the shape of certain visual pigments, leading to the creation of electrical charges involved in nerve transmission.

Studying Science and Society

During the Vietnam War, Hubbard began questioning the role of laboratory science. She began to wonder why scientists do what they do. She asked herself whether it was worth killing squid, which she found beautiful, for the sake of her research.

Hubbard became interested in the politics of women's health care. The growing women's movement in the early 1970's led her to rethink her own career. She joined a group investigating the status of women at Harvard, where the only woman then holding a full professorship occupied a chair endowed specifically for a female.

After 1980, Hubbard's research focused on the history and sociology of medical genetics

Scientific and Social Ideas Are Intertwined

A scientific study of society requires an understanding of how social prejudices such as sexism and racism have been incorporated into biology, especially through genetic determinism.

Genetic determinism is an ideology that often guides biological research and sociological theorizing. It claims that individual traits (both social and medical) are inherited and can best be studied at the molecular level. Genetic determinism also claims that social institutions and public health trends can best be studied by investigating individual traits. Some argue, however, that genetic determinism is not scientifically valid.

Hubbard claimed that categories such as "race" and "sex" single out certain biological traits (such as skin color or genitalia) and use them to separate people who have far more biological traits in common. She sees them as social categories, not simple biological facts. Scientists should take this into account when designing research projects, or they run the risk of recycling

stereotypes instead of advancing scientific knowledge.

Genes and environments interact in very complex ways. The same gene expresses itself differently in different environments. Even within the same environment, organisms with identical genes often develop differently. Genetic determinism therefore limits the ability of medical science to understand and treat illnesses such as heart disease and cancer.

Bibliography

Biological Politics: Feminist and Anti-Feminist Perspectives. Janet Sayers. London: Tavistock, 1982.

Genes and Human Self-Knowledge: Historical and Philosophical Reflections on Modern Genetics. Robert F. Weir, Susan C. Lawrence, and Evan Fales, eds. Iowa City: University of Iowa Press, 1994.

Not in Our Genes: Biology, Ideology, and Human Nature. R. C. Lewontin, Steven Rose, and Leon J. Kamin. New York: Pantheon Books, 1984.

and human behavioral genetics. She wrote and lectured on the ways in which social ideas have influenced scientists' work, on the impact of science on society, and on the need for non-scientists to participate in public debates on science.

Bibliography
By Hubbard
Genes and Gender 2: Pitfalls in Research on Sex and Gender, 1979 (as editor, with Marian Lowe)

Women Look at Biology Looking at Women: A Collection of Feminist Critiques, 1979 (as editor, with Mary Sue Henifin and Barbara Fried)

Biological Woman—The Convenient Myth: A Collection of Feminist Essays and a Comprehensive Bibliography, 1982 (as editor, with Henifin and Fried)

Woman's Nature: Rationalizations of Inequality, 1983 (as editor)

The Shape of Red: Insider/Outsider Reflections, 1988 (as editor, with Margaret Randall)

The Politics of Women's Biology, 1990

Exploding the Gene Myth: How Genetic Information Is Produced and Manipulated by Scientists, Physicians, Employers, Insurance Companies, Educators, and Law Enforcers, 1993 (with Elijah Wald)

"Race and Sex as Biological Categories" in *Challenging Racism and Sexism: Alternatives to Genetic Explanations*, 1994 (Ethel Tobach and Betty Rosoff, eds.)

About Hubbard
"Turning the Inside Out." Marguerite Holloway. *Scientific American* 272 (June, 1995).

"'You've Got a Long Way to Go, Baby': A Conversation About the Women's Movement with Ruth Hubbard." M. Davidson. *USA Today* 116 (September, 1987).

(Bonnie Ellen Blustein)

Edwin Powell Hubble

Area of Achievement: Astronomy
Contribution: Hubble provided evidence that galaxies consist of ordinary stars and measured the distances of galaxies, showing that more distant ones have larger recession velocities.

Nov. 20, 1889	Born in Marshfield, Missouri
1900-1906	Attends public schools in Wheaton, Illinois, graduating at age sixteen
1910	Earns a B.S. in astronomy and mathematics at the University of Chicago
1913	Earns a B.A. in jurisprudence and Spanish at Oxford University on a Rhodes scholarship
1913-1914	Teaches high school Spanish and physics in New Albany, Indiana
1914-1917	Works at Yerkes Observatory and earns a Ph.D. from the University of Chicago
1917-1919	Serves in the U.S. Army, rising to the rank of major
1919	Begins his career as an astronomer at Mount Wilson Observatory, California
Feb. 26, 1924	Marries Grace Burke Leib, a widowed graduate of Stanford University
1942-1946	Works at the U.S. Army Ballistics Research Laboratory at Aberdeen, Maryland
1946-1953	Chairs the Research Committee for Mount Wilson and Palomar Observatories
1949	Becomes the first to use the 200-inch telescope at Mount Palomar Observatory, California
Sept. 28, 1953	Dies in San Marino, California

Early Life

Edwin Powell Hubble, the third of seven surviving children, was the son of an insurance agent. The Hubble family moved from Marshfield, Missouri, to Evanston, Illinois, in 1898, and two years later to Wheaton, west of Chicago.

Edwin's seventh-grade teacher was Harriet Grote, later to become the mother of Grote Reber, the radio astronomy pioneer who built in Wheaton the first true radio telescope. Edwin excelled in both academics and athletics at Wheaton High School, where he was a track star and was graduated at the age of sixteen.

Entering the University of Chicago, Hubble won letters in track and basketball and majored in astronomy and mathematics. After his graduation in 1910, he received a Rhodes scholarship and studied jurisprudence and Spanish at Oxford University. In 1913, he rejoined his family in Louisville and passed the Kentucky bar examination. Instead of practicing law, however, he spent a year teaching physics and Spanish and coaching basketball at New Albany High School in Indiana.

(AP/Wide World Photos)

Yerkes Observatory

After a year of teaching, Hubble enrolled in graduate astronomy studies at the University of Chicago and became an assistant at the Yerkes Observatory in Williams Bay, Wisconsin, which was operated by the university.

Before arriving at Yerkes, Hubble attended an American Astronomical Society meeting and heard Vesto Slipher present his discovery of the apparent shift of spectrum lines from faint patches of light called nebulas. All these lines were shifted toward the red end of the spectrum, and Slipher interpreted this redshift as the result of a recession velocity of the nebulas.

Although Yerkes had the largest refracting telescope in the world, with a 40-inch lens, Hubble began a program of nebular photography on a 24-inch reflecting telescope. Soon, he made his first discovery. By comparing his photographs with earlier ones, he found a nebula that had changed over a few years. He expanded this observation into his Ph.D. thesis, "Photographic Investigations of Faint Nebulae," in which he classified nebular types and suggested that spiral nebulas are probably outside the Milky Way.

After completing his thesis in 1917, Hubble volunteered for service in the U.S. Army, rising to the rank of major. His last assignment in the military was at Cambridge University, where he studied the statistical methods of the astronomer Arthur Eddington.

Mount Wilson Observatory

After his discharge in 1919, Hubble accepted an invitation to work at the Mount Wilson Observatory in California, where a new giant reflecting telescope was just being readied for service.

His first great discovery with this 100-inch telescope was the detection of a Cepheid variable star in the great spiral nebula in Andromeda on October 5, 1923. Ten years earlier, Henrietta Swan Leavitt had shown how such variables can be used to estimate distances. By the end of 1924, Hubble had found twelve Cepheids in the Andromeda nebula and derived a distance of about a million light-years, confirming that it was outside the Milky Way and thus a separate galaxy of stars.

In 1925, Hubble introduced the first significant classification system for galaxies in three main categories: irregulars, spirals, and ellipticals. He measured the distances of several other nearby galaxies from their Cepheids and then began to develop other methods of estimating the locations of more distant galaxies.

In 1929, he made his most important discovery by showing that the distances of these galaxies are proportional to their radial velocities as measured by his colleague, Milton Humason. This relationship was confirmed by Hubble and Humason between 1931 and 1936, out to about 100 million light-years. Hubble's law implies that the universe is uniformly expanding.

After 1936, Hubble attempted to measure the distribution of galaxies in order to deter-

Hubble's Law of the Expanding Universe

Hubble established the proportional relationship between the recession velocities of galaxies and their distances, showing that the universe is expanding and has a finite age.

Even before Hubble identified stars in nebulae in 1924 and showed that some are galaxies containing several hundred billions of stars, the recession velocities of these nebulas had been measured by Vesto Slipher in 1912. Slipher observed that the absorption lines in their spectra were shifted toward the longer wavelengths, a phenomenon called redshift. A similar effect with sound waves was observed by Christian Doppler in 1842, in which the pitch of a sound source is lowered as it moves away from an observer as a result of the stretching of waves in relation to the observer.

A Doppler interpretation of the redshift makes it possible to calculate the speed of recession of galaxies. All galaxies were found to have redshifts except for a few of the nearer ones, whose local motion within a cluster of galaxies gives them a small blueshift (a shift toward the blue end of the spectrum). Willem de Sitter used Albert Einstein's equations of general relativity to develop an idealized model of the universe in 1917 that predicts redshifts for distant light sources, suggesting an expanding universe.

When Hubble found Cepheid variables among the stars in galaxies, he was able to estimate their distances. Henrietta Swan Leavitt had shown that the luminosity of a Cepheid variable increased with the period of its pulsation. This period-luminosity law made it possible to estimate distances by comparing the apparent brightness of a star with its intrinsic luminosity, since brightness decreases with distance for a given luminosity. For distances out to about six million light-years, Hubble showed that recession velocity (V) is proportional to distance (D), giving Hubble's law ($V = HD$), with a constant ratio of V to D known as Hubble's constant (H).

Further confirmation of Hubble's law depended on greater distances and fainter galaxies whose stars could not be distinguished. Hubble developed other methods of estimating distances, such as the brightness of an entire galaxy compared to the brightness of a closer galaxy whose distance is known from its Cepheids. His colleague Milton Humason was able to measure redshifts for these more distant galaxies, and the velocity-distance relation was confirmed out to about one hundred million light-years.

Hubble's law implies that galaxies began expanding at the same time and place, but with different speeds, so that the faster ones are proportionally further away. The rates measured by Hubble imply that this expansion began about two billion years ago, contradicting estimates of more than four billion years for the age of the earth. Later corrections to the period-luminosity law suggest that the universe has been expanding for about ten to fifteen billion years. The expanding universe is the basis for all modern big bang cosmologies.

Bibliography
The Discovery of Our Galaxy. C. Whitney. New York: Alfred A. Knopf, 1971.
The Expanding Universe: Astronomy's "Great Debate," 1900-1931. Robert Smith. Cambridge, England: Cambridge University Press, 1982.
Man Discovers the Galaxies. Richard Berendzen, Richard Hart, and Daniel Seeley. New York: Columbia University Press, 1984.

mine the overall geometry of space. This work led him to some doubts about inferring radial velocities from redshifts, and he preferred to refer to "apparent velocities." In 1941, he used redshift data to determine the direction of the rotation of galaxies relative to their spiral arms.

During World War II, Hubble was chief of ballistics at the U.S. Army's Ballistics Research Laboratory at Aberdeen, Maryland. After the war, he helped to plan for the new 200-inch reflecting telescope at Mount Palomar Observatory and in 1949 became the first person to use it.

Hubble died following a cerebral thrombosis on September 28, 1953, in San Marino, California, at the age of sixty-three.

Bibliography
By Hubble
"Extra-Galactic Nebulae," *Astrophysical Journal*, 1926

"Distance and Radial Velocity Among Extra-Galactic Nebulae," *Proceedings of the National Academy of Sciences*, 1929

Red Shifts in the Spectra of Nebulae, 1934

The Realm of the Nebulae, 1936

The Observational Approach to Cosmology, 1937

"Explorations in Space: The Cosmological Program for the Palomar Telescopes," *Proceedings of the American Philosophical Society*, 1951

"The Law of Red-Shifts," *Monthly Notices of the Royal Astronomical Society*, 1953

About Hubble
"Edwin Hubble." M. L. Humason. *Monthly Notices of the Royal Astronomical Society* 114 (1954).

"Edwin Hubble and the Expanding Universe." Donald E. Osterbrock, Joel A. Gwinn, and Ronald S. Brashear. *Scientific American* 269 (July, 1993).

Evolution of the Universe of Galaxies: Edwin Hubble Centennial Symposium. Richard G. Kron, ed. San Francisco: Astronomical Society of the Pacific, 1990.

(Joseph L. Spradley)

David H. Hubel

Areas of Achievement: Biology, chemistry, and medicine
Contribution: Hubel, a pioneer in the science of vision, was the first to describe and map the visual cortex.

Feb. 27, 1926	Born in Windsor, Ontario, Canada
1947	Earns a B.Sc. from McGill University
1951	Earns an M.D. from McGill
1951-1952	Serves as an intern at Montreal General Hospital
1952-1953	Named a Fellow in the neurological sciences at The Johns Hopkins University
1959	Joins the faculty of Harvard University Medical School
1967-1968	Named George Packer Berry Professor of Neurobiology at Harvard
1972	Appointed James Arthur Lecturer at the American Museum of Natural History
1977	Wins the Karl Lashley Prize from the American Philosophical Society
1979	Given the Dickson Prize in Medicine by the University of Pittsburgh
1981	Awarded the Nobel Prize in Physiology or Medicine for his description of the visual cortex
1990	Given the Outstanding Science Leadership Award of the National Association for Biomedical Research

Early Life
David Hunter Hubel, the son of a chemist, grew up in the city of Montreal. From an early

age, he was fascinated by science. His first recorded experiment took place in his Montreal neighborhood. One day, young David created a mixture of potassium chlorate and sugar and placed it in the barrel of a toy brass cannon. Much to his neighbors' surprise, he proved the volatile characteristics of the mixture. Little did the Montreal police know that the source of their nuisance call would some day be awarded the Nobel Prize in Physiology or Medicine.

Hubel's academic success can be traced to his early days at high school, from which he was graduated with honors. All of his teachers predicted that Hubel would have a great college career, and their confidence was well founded.

The next stop on his academic journey was McGill University, where he was accepted to study in the selective physics department. During the latter half of his undergraduate career, he began to read about contemporary research in the field of medicine and decided to give up physics in order to attend medical school.

Success in Academia and Research

Upon his graduation, McGill accepted Hubel as a first-year medical student even though he had never taken a biology course in his life. He had never experienced the smell of formaldehyde or performed any laboratory work related to biology. Once again, he did outstanding work and was graduated among the top of his class.

Hubel was given a research appointment at the Walter Reed Army Institute of Research in Washington, D.C. From there, he went to The Johns Hopkins University and then to Harvard.

At Harvard, Hubel completed the work for which he won the Nobel Prize, his study of the visual cortex. The cortex is the outer shell of the brain. Each part of the cortex has a particular function. The part that interested Hubel was the area that dealt with vision. He wanted to know how the brain processes images of the world into recognizable objects. For example, he was interested in how the brain distinguishes the difference between a baseball and hockey skates. He recorded the reaction of various cells in the cortex to electrical stimulation in order to determine their function.

Hubel also conducted experiments which showed that a lack of visual stimulation hinders the growth and development of the visual centers of the brain. Studies suggest that all

The Processing of Visual Information

Hubel found that visual information is processed by hundreds of millions of cells known as neurons.

Hubel discovered that each cell has a particular job. Some deal with movement, others with distance, and still others with color. Each neuron performs its assembly line task again and again. He gathered this information by placing a tiny electrode in each cell of a certain part of the visual cortex. He then recorded its reaction to electrical stimulation. By carefully recording each reaction, he was able to describe both the function of each cell and its location.

Hubel took the experiment a step further by covering an eye of a newborn kitten for a short period of time. When the patch was removed, he discovered that the kitten had gone blind in the covered eye, even though the eye itself had not been injured. He concluded that the neurons in the covered eye were prevented from connecting with other neurons, which stopped them from becoming part of the visual cortex. The lack of visual stimulation hindered the growth and development of this part of the cat's brain.

This research led to important changes in how and when doctors deal with the problems of cross-eyes and cataracts in newborn babies. Hubel confirmed that the longer the wait, the greater the risk. Delay hinders the ability of the neurons to combine with other neurons, thus decreasing the operational level of the visual cortex.

Bibliography

Review of *Eye, Brain, and Vision*, by David H. Hubel. *BioScience* 39, no. 2 (February, 1989).

Review of *Eye, Brain, and Vision*, by David H. Hubel. Philip Morrison. *Scientific American* 258 (April, 1988).

areas of human brain development occur in this way. Scientists describe "critical periods" that are actually windows of opportunity for developing important intellectual and emotional skills. Holding a baby, speaking in a loving manner, and creating a visually stimulating environment affect the process of neuron connection.

Other Interests
Hubel became a modern-day Renaissance man who did not confine himself to the biological sciences. He became an accomplished flutist. He first developed an interest in the instrument when he was in his fifties. He became quite proficient and began to play regularly with his graduate students. When not playing his music, he could often be found at his loom, weaving a beautifully designed piece of cloth.

Bibliography
By Hubel
"Regular Patchy Distribution of Cytochrome Oxidase Staining in Primary Visual Cortex of Macaque Monkey," *Nature*, 1981 (with J. C. Horton)
"Evolution of Ideas on the Primary Visual Cortex, 1955-1978: A Biased Historical Account," *Bioscience Reports*, 1982
"Exploration of the Primary Visual Cortex, 1955-1978," *Nature*, 1982
"Specificity of Cortico-Cortical Connections in Monkey Visual System," *Nature*, 1983
"Colour-Generating Interactions Across the Corpus Callosum," *Nature*, 1983
"Spatial Relationship and Extrafoveal Vision," *Nature*, 1985
Eye, Brain, and Vision, 1988

(The Nobel Foundation)

About Hubel
"David H. Hubel." In *The Nobel Prize Winners: Physiology or Medicine*, edited by Frank N. Magill. Pasadena, Calif.: Salem Press, 1991.
"David Hubel." In *Larrouse Dictionary of Scientists*, edited by Hazel Muir. New York: Larousse, 1994.
"Hubel, David." In *The Grolier Library of Science Biographies*. 10 vols. Vol. 5. Danbury, Conn.: Grolier Educational, 1996.

(Richard D. Fitzgerald)

Robert Huber

Areas of Achievement: Biology, cell biology, and chemistry

Contribution: Huber crystallized the membrane proteins that take part in the chemical process known as photosynthesis.

Feb. 20, 1937	Born in Munich, Germany
1943	Enters school during World War II
1972	Obtains his Ph.D. from the Technical University of Munich
1972	Appointed a lecturer at the Technical University of Munich
1973	Becomes director of the Max Planck Institute for Biochemistry
1974	Studies the antibody structure proposed by Rodney Robert Porter
1978	Investigates the interaction between the digestive protease trypsin and pancreatic trypsin
1979	Studies the energetics of protein deoxyribonucleic acid (DNA) interactions
1982	Investigates the structure of the membrane-bound photosynthetic reaction center of the purple bacterium
1988	Awarded the Nobel Prize in Chemistry

Early Life

Robert Huber was born in Munich, Germany, on February 20, 1937. This was the most dramatic time in the nation's history. The economic and political chaos of the late Weimar Republic created the conditions that allowed Adolf Hitler and the Nazi Party to come to power. By the time of Huber's birth, Germany was completely dominated by the Nazis, who, by his second birthday, had invaded Poland and started World War II.

In 1943, Huber entered the German educational system. Within nine months, the Allies successfully invaded Western Europe at Normandy and the fate of Germany was sealed. The next eighteen months were terrible ones for the German people, especially the children. Instead of practicing fire drills, Huber and his classmates participated in real-life air raid drills. Hundreds of German children were killed during the most severe bombing in history. Huber woke up every morning not knowing if it would be the last for him or one of his beloved family members.

When the war ended in May, 1945, more than ten million German soldiers had been killed or wounded. With the help of the Marshall Plan, Huber's new country, the Federal Republic of Germany, was one of the first Western European nations to recover from the war. The German educational system recognized young Huber's talent and drive and placed him in the college-bound tract. When he was graduated from the Gymnasium, he studied at

(The Nobel Foundation)

Food and Population

The world faces what many people believe to be an almost-insurmountable problem: How will an ever-expanding population be fed?

By the end of the twentieth century, the world seemed to have reached a plateau in its ability to increase the food supply. Environmentalists warned of the damage inflicted on the planet by the continuing quest to produce more food. The terms "overplanting," "overgrazing," and "water depletion" became part of the vocabularies of many concerned citizens.

Most scientists state that if humans continue to plant and graze at current rates, the result will be a depletion of an unacceptable percentage of the earth's rich topsoil. The same holds true for the water supply. Some officials believe that water could replace oil as the world's most important resource in the twenty-first century.

By providing a better understanding of the pro-cess of photosynthesis, Huber's research could help the world find the key to alleviating some of the stress currently placed on its soil and water supply. If scientists can manipulate the process of photosynthesis, land that today is too cold, dry, or rocky could be used to produce food.

Huber's work has provided scientists with the opportunity to engineer greater crop yields. If they are successful, such programs could have an important impact on this major world problem.

Bibliography

"Facing Food Scarcity." Lester R. Brown. *World Watch* 8, no. 6 (November/December, 1995).

"Once and Future Farming." Ronald Bailey. *Garbage* 6, no. 3 (Fall, 1994).

"The World Food Prospect: Entering a New Era." Lester R. Brown. *National Forum* 75, no. 1 (Winter, 1995).

---

the Technical University of Munich. He received his Ph.D. from the university in 1972.

The Study of Photosynthesis

Huber accomplished what many of his fellow scientists believed was impossible: He and his research team crystallized the membrane proteins that take part in the chemical process known as photosynthesis. To grasp the importance of this accomplishment, an understanding of some of the working parts of the cell and of the process of photosynthesis is needed.

The cell is the basic structure of life. Its surrounding membrane controls the passage of materials into and out of the cell. Proteins consist of simple structures known as amino acids. Amino acids perform many functions, one of which is to produce enzymes. Enzymes regulate the chemical reactions that take place in living things.

Photosynthesis is the chemical reaction that takes place when green plants process light energy into chemical energy. Most of the chemical energy in living organisms is the result, directly or indirectly, of photosynthesis. This process helps provide the nutrition for living organisms. Nutrition can be defined as the process of gathering usable material from the environment and utilizing it to carry out the necessary life functions.

Scientists describe photosynthesis as autotrophic nutrition because it forms organic compounds from inorganic structures. The by-product of photosynthesis, glucose, helps provide nutrition for green plants, which gives them the energy that they need to grow and generate the products used by humankind.

In order to study the chemical process of photosynthesis, Huber had to be able to observe proteins more closely because they provide the environment for the production of enzymes, which in turn control the process of photosynthesis. Crystallization allows a more detailed study of a particular object. Huber's success permitted scientists to obtain a deeper understanding of this very important chemical process. He was awarded the 1988 Nobel Prize in Chemistry for his work.

Bibliography
By Huber
"X-Ray Diffraction Analysis of Immunoglobulin Structure," *Hoppe-Seylers Zeitschrift fur*

Physiologische Chemie, 1976

"Crystallographic Structure Studies of an IgG Molecule and Fc Fragment," *Nature*, 1976

"Crystal Structure of the Human Fab Fragment Kol and Its Comparison with the Intact Kol Molecule," *Journal of Molecular Biology*, 1978

"The Refined 2.2-A (0.22-nm) X-Ray Crystal Structure of the Ternary Complex Formed by Bovine Trypsinogen, Valine-Valine, and the Arg15 Analogue of Bovine Pancreatic Trypsin," *European Journal of Biochemistry*, 1984

"Structure of Bovine Pancreatic Trypsin Inhibitor: Results of Joint Neutron and X-Ray Refinement of Crystal Forms II," *Journal of Molecular Biology*, 1984

About Huber

"Huber, Robert." In *The Grolier Library of Science Biographies*. 10 vols. Vol. 5. Danbury, Conn.: Grolier Educational, 1996.

"Robert Huber." In *Larrouse Dictionary of Scientists*, edited by Hazel Muir. New York: Larousse, 1994.

"Robert Huber." In *The Nobel Prize Winners: Chemistry*, edited by Frank N. Magill. Pasadena, Calif.: Salem Press, 1990.

(Richard D. Fitzgerald)

Sir William Huggins

Areas of Achievement: Astronomy and physics

Contribution: By applying the principles of spectrum analysis to stellar light, Huggins determined the chemical constitutions of various stars and nebulas.

Feb. 7, 1824	Born in Stoke Newington, London, England
1854	Joins the Royal Astronomical Society
1856	Builds an observatory attached to his house at Tulse Hill
1862	Begins a collaboration with William Allen Miller and devises a star spectroscope
1863-1864	Publishes work on the spectra of terrestrial elements and stars
1864	Observes the gaseous nature of the nebula Draco
1865	Elected a Fellow of the Royal Society of London
1867	Receives a gold medal, jointly with Miller, from the Royal Astronomical Society
1876	Begins seriously to photograph his observations
1891	Becomes president of the British Association for the Advancement of Science
1897	Knighted at Queen Victoria's diamond jubilee
1900	Becomes president of the Royal Society of London
1902	Receives the Order of Merit
May 12, 1910	Dies at Tulse Hill, London, England

Early Life

William Huggins entered the City of London School in 1837 but left there two years later to continue his education under private tutors. He studied classics, mathematics, and modern languages, but his primary interests lay in science. He had intended to go to Cambridge for university study, but instead he took over the business of his father, a silkmercer and linendraper.

This occupied his time for about twelve years until 1854, when Huggins decided to devote most of his time to the microscope and telescope. In 1856, he built an observatory attached to his house at Tulse Hill, where he conducted all of his astronomical studies.

A New Method

Aside from conventional observations of the sun and planets, Huggins also wanted to examine the peculiar behavior of starlight when refracted by a prism. To accomplish this, he and his neighbor, William Allen Miller, built a device called a spectroscope. They found that a star's spectrum carries a large amount of information about what gaseous chemicals exist in its atmosphere.

Huggins also applied this method of spec-

(Library of Congress)

Spectrum Analysis of Stars

The arrangement of dark lines visible in stellar spectra indicates which gases are present around the star.

By analyzing the spectrum of a star's light, Huggins sought to determine some of the elements existing in its atmosphere. He understood that some elements, when burned, produce bright bands of light in their spectra and that the dark bands of the sun's spectrum are caused by the absorption of light by various elements present in its atmosphere. Huggins perceived that the same is true for stars.

Huggins found that comparing the spectra of stars to those of terrestrial elements indicated what elements existed in those stars. He found that the light of the brightest stars originates from some internal hot source and passes through an atmosphere composed of absorbent gases. He concluded that many of these are ele-

ments often found on Earth, such as hydrogen, sodium, magnesium, and iron.

Huggins applied spectrum analysis to nebulas, which were widely held to be merely groups of stars. He found that some do not emit normal spectra, only the bright bands of light. This indicates that some of these mysterious bodies are indeed giant masses of luminous gas.

Spectrum analysis gave science an effective method for discovering the constitutions of stars and other celestial bodies.

Bibliography

Stars and Their Spectra: An Introduction to the Spectral Sequence. James B. Kaler. Cambridge, England: Cambridge University Press, 1987.

Stellar Spectroscopy, Normal Stars. Margherita Hack. Trieste, Italy: Observatorio Astronomico, 1969.

The Theory of Stellar Spectra. New York: Gordon and Breach, 1970.

trum analysis to other celestial bodies. He observed several nebulas, including the large nebula in the constellation Orion. He also studied comets and novas, using his spectroscope to discover what elements existed in them.

A New Field

Huggins' work helped to unite the two scientific areas of astronomy and physics into a new field of study: astrophysics. Huggins and Miller had published ten papers on their findings by 1866. Their efforts brought them recognition from the Royal Astronomical Society, and in 1865 Huggins was elected a Fellow of the Royal Society of London.

The scientific community understood the importance of Huggins' work in this field. He received honorary degrees from both Cambridge and Oxford, as well as from prestigious universities in Scotland and Ireland. The Royal Society of London lent him several instruments to use at his Tulse Hill observatory, and in 1890 he was granted a civil pension.

Later Career

Huggins' contributions to science continued after his initial research with Miller. He entered into another productive collaboration in 1875, when he married Margaret Lindsay Murray, who was twenty-six years his junior. His wife worked with him over the next thirty-five years, taking part in many astronomical observations.

During this period, Huggins developed methods of photographing stellar spectra, and he also published work on the nature of novas. He held a number of scientific posts and received numerous awards, including knighthood. He continued his observations in his advanced years, but he gave them up in 1908 and returned some of his instruments to the Royal Society of London. He and his wife published a collection of his scientific papers in 1909, and he died the following year after an operation.

Bibliography

By Huggins

On the Results of Spectrum Analysis Applied to the Heavenly Bodies, 1866

The Scientific Papers of Sir William Huggins, 1909

About Huggins

The Analysis of Starlight. J. B. Hearnshaw. Cambridge, England: Cambridge University Press, 1986.

"Huggins, Sir William." In *Dictionary of National Biography: Supplement, 1901-1911*, edited by Sidney Lee. London: Oxford University Press, 1912.

"Huggins, William." Herbert Dingle. In *Dictionary of Scientific Biography*, edited by Charles Coulston Gillispie. New York: Charles Scribner's Sons, 1970.

(Jacob D. Hamblin)

Baron Alexander von Humboldt

Areas of Achievement: Astronomy, botany, earth science, physics, and zoology

Contribution: Humboldt is considered the last of the great naturalists. His explorations of tropical America gave the world new insight not only into the physical environment but also into humanity's relationship to that environment.

Sept. 14, 1769	Born at Schloss Tegel, near Berlin, Prussia (now Germany)
1787-1790	Studies at the universities of Frankfurt-an-der-Oder and Göttingen
1791	Studies at the Frieberg School of Mines
1799-1800	Explores tropical South America, collecting specimens
1800-1801	Studies the plantation economy and labor slavery in Cuba
1802	Climbs Chimborozo volcano to a record elevation of 18,893 feet
1803	Travels to Mexico to study its economic resources and pre-Colombian antiquities
1804	Travels to the United States and visits with President Thomas Jefferson
1804-1808	Lectures in Berlin and Paris
1808	Moves to Paris and continues his scientific research and writings
1829	Conducts a scientific exploration of the Urals and the Altai Mountains of Russia
1845-1862	Writes a five-volume work about science and geography
May 6, 1859	Dies in Berlin, Prussia

Early Life

Friedrich Wilhelm Heinrich Alexander von Humboldt was born in Berlin in 1769. His father served as chamberlain to the king of Prussia, and his mother was a wealthy widow. His brother Wilhelm was the founder of the University of Berlin. When Humboldt was nine years old, his father died. His mother did not show much love to her children, but she saw that they got the best education.

Humboldt and his brother were privately tutored in history, languages, and mathematics at the family estate of Schloss Tegel. Alexander was called "the little apothecary" because of his interest in natural history. He collected things from the natural environment, which he labeled and arranged for display. He read about the explorers of the world and yearned to travel, specifically to the tropics.

At sixteen, Humboldt was introduced to science by a physician who gave lectures in physics and philosophy and conducted experiments at his home. This interested Humboldt, but his mother had plans for him to be trained in economics so he could work for the Prussian government.

Between 1787 and 1788, Humboldt attended the University of Frankfurt-an-der-Oder, and he attended Göttingen University from 1789 to 1790. In 1791, he began his studies in mining and geology at the Freiberg School of Mines. After his graduation in 1792, he worked as an assessor of mines. In 1796, his mother died, and he used his inheritance to begin his studies of science and exploration of the world.

American Exploration

In 1799, Humboldt traveled to South America with the French botanist Aime Bonpland. Arriving in Venezuela, they explored the coastal region and then traveled into the interior to explore the tropics. In his travels along the Orinoco River and the Rio Negro, Humboldt made collections of plants, animals, and geologic specimens. He also made astronomical and magnetic observations.

Humboldt spent three months in 1801 studying the plantation and slavery system of Cuba. He then went to Colombia and to Ecuador, where he climbed the volcano Chimborozo to a height of 18,893 feet (5,759 meters).

He surveyed the headwaters of the Amazon River and traveled through Peru. He studied the current along the west coast of South America. The current and other physical features, as well as political entities, were later named in his honor.

In 1803, Humboldt traveled to Mexico, where he spent a year studying economic resources and pre-Colombian ruins. In May, 1804, he left Mexico for Philadelphia and visited with President Thomas Jefferson, sharing with him information about his travels.

Paris

Upon returning to Europe, Humboldt lived in Paris and Berlin for four years. In 1808, he settled in Paris, where he continued his scientific studies and wrote about his scientific discoveries and travels. His thirty-three-volume publication entitled *Voyage aux régions équinoxiales du Nouveau Continent*, was published between 1805 and 1834. This extensive study of his scientific research and travels caused Humboldt to deplete his financial resources, but it made him famous.

The Decrease of Magnetic Forces from the Poles to the Equator

Humboldt's studies of the geomagnetic field proved that the earth's magnetic field decreases in intensity from the poles to the equator.

Humboldt made observations of the earth's magnetic field in America, Europe, and Asia over a period of thirty-two years. His observations were made from western China to Peru, and covered a distance of 188 degrees in longitude, and ranged from 60 degrees north to 12 degrees south latitude, a distance of 72 degrees.

The intensity of the magnetic field was determined by counting the number of oscillations that the compass needle made from the horizontal position. This is referred to as the inclination of the compass needle and is used to determine the magnetic latitude.

In the American tropics, Humboldt observed that the needle of the same compass that made 245 oscillations in ten minutes in Paris, made 242 in Mexico and 216 at San Carlos del Rio Negro, located at 1 degree 53 minutes north latitude and 80 degrees 40 minutes west longitude.

He discovered the magnetic equator, the line where magnetic inclination is zero, near Cajamarca, Peru. At this point, he noticed that the needle of the compass turned from north to south. For the next fifty years, Humboldt's magnetic intensity measurement at this point served as a reference for all magnetic measurements. The location of this point is at 7 degrees 1 minute south latitude and 80 degrees 40 minutes west longitude, where he measured 219 oscillations.

Humboldt presented his law of the variable intensity of the terrestrial magnetic force at a meeting of the Paris Institut. He attributed the mathematics of his law to Jean-Baptiste Biot and the proof of the theory to the numerical observations that he had made between 1709 and 1803 at 104 localities. His work was published in 1804.

After Humboldt read his paper, Admiral de Rosell related to Biot that he had made six observations of oscillations between 1792 and 1794 in present-day Indonesia. These observations, published in 1808, also proved the law of decreasing magnetic intensity toward the equator.

Earlier observations in the variation of the intensity of the magnetic field were made by Robert de Paul, chevalier de Lamanon on the ill-fated ship *Lapérouse*. The observations were made from Tenerife, in 1785, to the arrival of the ship in Macao, in 1787, and were forwarded to the academy of sciences. In a 1787 letter to the secretary of the academy, Lamanon stated that magnetic intensity increases with latitude.

In *Kosmos* (1845-1862), Humboldt observes that recognition for the law of the decrease of the magnetic forces from the poles to the equator belongs to Lamanon, claiming that his own observations only added credence to the law.

Bibliography

"The Earth's Magnetic Field and Its Variations." Takesi Nagota. In *Rediscovery of the Earth*, edited by L. Motz. New York: Van Nostrand Reinhold, 1979.

"The Earth's Magnetism." S. K. Runcorn. *Scientific American* 193 (1955).

Geomagnetic Instruments Before 1900. Anita McConnell. London: Harriet Wynter, 1980.

Among the many contributions that this publication made, it established that plant distribution is dependent on climate and topography. Humboldt introduced the concept of isotherms, lines of equal temperature that allow the comparison of temperature regimes in different parts of the world. He contributed to the knowledge of the plants of Mexico, Cuba, and South America. From his geomagnetic studies, he concluded that the intensity of the earth's magnetism increases from the equator to the poles.

Berlin
After serving as a diplomat for the king of Prussia, Humboldt moved to Berlin in 1827. During his first year there, he lectured at the University of Berlin and also gave public lectures about geography and the universe.

In 1829, Humboldt made a journey with two scientists, at the request of Czar Nicholas I, to the Urals and the Altai Mountains in Russia. He traveled for six months, collecting information about geography, climate, and the earth's magnetic field.

During his last thirty years of his life, Humboldt wrote *Kosmos*, consisting of five volumes published between 1845 and 1862. In this work, he studied the totality of the universe. It is important in the field of geography because Humboldt demonstrated the relationship between the different components of the physical environment, as well as the relationship between the physical and cultural environments. His studies helped establish geography as a scientific field of study.

Humboldt died in Berlin on May 6, 1859, at the age of eighty-nine.

Bibliography
By Humboldt
Versuche über die gereizte muskel und nervenfaser, 1797 (2 vols.; *Expériences sur le galvanisme et en général sur l'irritation des fibres musculaires et nerveuses*, 1799)
Voyage aux régions équinoxiales du Nouveau Continent, fait en 1799, 1800, 1801, 1802, 1803, et 1804, 1805-1834 (33 vols.; *Personal Narrative of Travels to the Equinoctial Regions of the New Continent During the Years 1799-1804*, 1814-1821, 8 vols.)

(Library of Congress)

Essai politique sur le royaume de la Nouvelle-Espagne, 1808 (2 vols.; *Political Essay on the Kingdom of New Spain*, 1811)
Vue des Cordillères et monuments des peuples indigènes de l'Amérique, 1810 (2 vols.)
Examen critique de l'histoire de la géographie du Nouveau Continent, 1814-1834
Annales des voyages de la géographie, de l'histoire, et de l'archéologie, 1819-1870
Selections from the Works of the Baron de Humboldt, Relating to the Climate, Inhabitants, Productions, and Mines of Mexico, 1824
Essai politique sur l'île de Cuba, 1826 (2 vols.; *The Island of Cuba*, 1855)
The Travels and Researches of Alexander von Humboldt, 1832?
Kosmos: Entwurf einer physischen Weltbeschreibung, 1845-1862 (5 vols.; first 2 vols. trans. as *Kosmos: A General Survey of Physical Phenomena of the Universe*, 1845-1848)
Lettres americaines d'Alexandre de Humboldt (1798-1807), 1905

About Humboldt
Alexander von Humboldt. Lotte Kellner. London: Oxford University Press, 1963.
Humboldt and the Cosmos. Douglas Botting. New York: Harper & Row, 1973.
Humboldt: The Life and Times of Alexander von Humboldt, 1769-1859. Helmut De Terra. Reprint. New York: Octagon Books, 1979.

(*Roberto Garza*)

Christiaan Huygens

Areas of Achievement: Astronomy, invention, mathematics, physics, and technology

Contribution: During Huygens' exceptionally productive career, he discovered the rings of Saturn, invented the pendulum clock, and was instrumental in the development of the wave theory of light.

Apr. 14, 1629	Born in The Hague, the Netherlands
1645	Studies at the University of Leiden
1647	Begins studies at the University of Breda
1654	Publishes his first mathematics paper, on circles
1655	Builds his first telescope with his brother
1655	Discovers Saturn's rings and its moon Titan
1655	Receives an honorary Doctor of Laws degree from the University of Angers
1656	Builds a pendulum clock
1657	Publishes a treatise on probability
1663	Elected a Fellow of the Royal Society of London
1665	Appointed the first foreign resident of the French Académie Royale des Sciences
1666-1681	Lives in Paris and pursues scientific investigations
1678	Writes *Traité de la lumière* (*Treatise on Light*, 1912), which is published in 1690
1682	Returns to The Hague as a result of ill health
July 8, 1695	Dies in The Hague, the Netherlands

Early Life

Christiaan Huygens (pronounced "HOY-gehnz") was born in The Hague in 1629. His father was a very influential and important man who was friends with the philosopher René Descartes. Huygens did not have formal schooling in his early years, but instead studied at home. From the age of fifteen, he read the works of Descartes, which was to have a profound impact on his later views of science.

At the age of sixteen, Huygens was sent to the University of Leiden to study law. In 1647, he transferred to the new University of Breda, which his father directed. Huygens never married, and he devoted his entire life to the advancement of mathematics and the sciences. In 1654, he published a paper on a new way to determine the area of circles accurately.

Astronomy and the Pendulum Clock

In 1655, Huygens worked with his brother to develop a better way of grinding lenses. Together, they built his first telescope, with which he studied Saturn. That same year, Huygens discovered Saturn's largest moon, Titan. He also was able to see that Saturn's strange appearance was attributable to a disk around the planet in the same plane as Titan's orbit.

Huygens published his discovery of Saturn's moon in 1656. For fear of ridicule, however, he did not wish to publish his finding of its rings without further study. In order to prove that he saw the rings first, in case someone else reported them in the meantime, he encoded the discovery in an anagram in his paper about Saturn's moon. In a stroke of genius, he realized that Saturn's rings could not be solid but were likely composed of individual particles.

Huygens was also one of the first persons to measure the rotational period of the planet Mars by timing the passage of surface markings across the face of the planet. He also used a micrometer of his own invention to measure the angular sizes of the planets.

Extending the work of Galileo Galilei, Huygens developed a weight-driven pendulum clock in 1656, the first truly reliable timepiece. The development of a dependable clock began an era of precision measurements of time.

The Principle of Secondary Wave Fronts

Huygens postulated that light propagates as a succession of vibrations in oscillators. Each oscillator in a wave front thus acts as a source for further oscillations.

Waves propagate from a point oscillator as circular wave fronts. This is analogous to the ripples set up on the surface of a still pool of water by a dropped pebble.

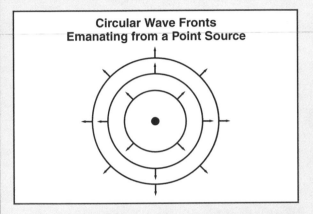

**Circular Wave Fronts
Emanating from a Point Source**

Huygens' idea of nature was essentially mechanistic. He believed that light was produced by oscillations of some sort and that these oscillations would trigger other oscillators. These oscillators would then cause yet more distant oscillators to begin oscillating, thus propagating the light as a wave. Further wave fronts would be formed by the sum of the wave fronts of the many oscillators forming earlier wave fronts. The later wave fronts are called secondary wave fronts. The concept that each part of a wave front

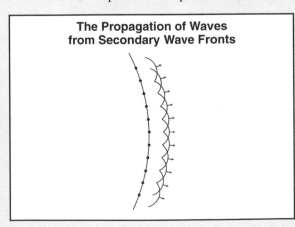

**The Propagation of Waves
from Secondary Wave Fronts**

can be the center of new wave fronts is now called Huygens' principle.

Two major problems arose from Huygens' theory of the wave propagation of light. The first was that his ideas conflicted with Sir Isaac Newton's corpuscular theory of light. As a consequence, Huygens' ideas were for the most part discounted until 1865, when James Clerk Maxwell showed that light does indeed propagate as oscillating electric and magnetic fields.

A second difficulty with Huygens' model arose from his almost wholly mechanistic view of nature. His model supposed that space must be filled with oscillators that can be excited to produce and transmit light. This medium through which light was supposed to travel was called the ether (or aether). It was not until the early twentieth century that the concept of the ether was dismissed.

Light does propagate in waves, but not waves of mechanical oscillations, as supposed by Huygens. Light is instead made of time-varying electric and magnetic fields—concepts not yet realized in Huygens' day.

While Huygens was incorrect regarding a mechanistic method of light propagation through the ether, he was correct in the belief that light propagates as waves. Huygens' principle is still used today to describe the wave properties of light, such as diffraction, interference, and refraction. Many of these topics were unknown to Huygens, although he did study refraction, the bending of light as it passes from one medium to another. While the speed of light in a vacuum is constant, it varies from one medium to another. Huygens showed that as a wave front passes from one medium to another, the waves travel slower through one medium than through another, and so the wave front is bent.

Bibliography

Light, Magnetism, and Electricity. Isaac Asimov. Vol. 2 in *Understanding Physics.* New York: Walker, 1966.

Optics. Eugene Hecht and Alfred Zajac. Reading, Mass.: Addison-Wesley, 1974.

What Is Light? A. C. S. van Heel and C. H. F. Velzel. New York: McGraw-Hill, 1968.

Paris

Having been elected as the first foreign resident and a charter member of France's Académie Royale des Sciences, Huygens moved to Paris to continue his work from 1666 to 1681. During this time, he studied many topics, including a description of the physical pendulum, a topic that was later to lead physicists to the concept of the moment of inertia. Extending his work on the pendulum, Huygens conducted research on rotational motion and centrifugal forces.

Huygens studied collisions, favoring the concept of elastic collisions. He also studied forces, following Descartes' ideas on the topic rather than those of Sir Isaac Newton. Huygens' basic philosophy of nature tended to be mechanistic, again after the ideas of Descartes.

One of the major triumphs of Huygens' time in Paris was his development of a theory of optics. Throughout his stay in France, however, he was ill. In 1682, his poor health finally forced him to return to his homeland.

Light and Optics

One of Huygens' lasting achievements was the development of the wave theory of light. In keeping with his mechanistic view of nature, he supposed that light was created by oscillators of some type and that light propagated itself by triggering other oscillators.

This concept seemed to require a medium through which light must pass. The existence of such a medium, called the ether, was rejected early in the twentieth century. The wave theory of light that Huygens proposed, however, was confirmed by James Clerk Maxwell in the nineteenth century.

Final Days

After returning to The Hague in 1682, Huygens published his treatise on light, written several years earlier in Paris. He also constructed new telescopes and devised a new style of eyepiece that minimized color distortions, now called a Huygian eyepiece.

In his latter days, Huygens studied philosophy and speculated about the cosmos. In a work published in 1698, after his death, he reflected on the other planets of the solar system. With Earth having been shown to be merely one of six known planets, Huygens speculated that the other planets might be worlds similar to Earth, complete with living beings. In 1695, Huygens' poor health finally resulted in his death.

(Library of Congress)

Bibliography

By Huygens

De circuli magnitudine inventa: Accedent ejusdem problematum quorundam illustrium constructiones, 1654

De Saturni luna observatio nova, 1656

De ratiociniis in ludo aleae, 1657 (*Of the Laws of Chance*, 1692)

Horologium, 1658

Horologium oscillatorium sive de mortu pendulorum ad horologia aptato demonstrationes geometricae, 1673 (*Horologium*, 1970)

Traité de la lumière, 1690 (*Treatise on Light*, 1912)

Discours de la cause de la pesanteur, 1690

Cosmotheoros, sive de terris coelestibus, earumque ornatu, conjecturae, 1698 (*The Celestial Worlds Discover'd: Or, Conjectures Concerning the Inhabitants, Plants, and Productions of the Worlds of the Planets*, 1698)

Oeuvres complètes de Christiaan Huygens, 1888-1950 (22 vols.)

About Huygens

Christiaan Huygens and the Development of Science in the Seventeenth Century. Arthur E. Bell. New York: Longmans, Green, 1947.

History of Science: The Beginnings of Modern Science. Rene Taton. New York: Basic Books, 1964.

The World of Physics. Jefferson Hane Weaver. New York: Simon & Schuster, 1987.

(*Raymond D. Benge, Jr.*)

Ida H. Hyde

Areas of Achievement: Medicine, physiology, and zoology

Contribution: Hyde invented the microelectrode and set up scholarships for other female scientists.

Sept. 8, 1857	Born in Davenport, Iowa
1881	Enrolls at the University of Chicago
1891	Earns a B.S. from Cornell University
1893	Attends the University of Strassburg through an Association of Collegiate Alumnae fellowship
1894	Petitions German universities to allow women to graduate
1896	Earns a Ph.D. from the University of Heidelberg
1896	Establishes the Naples Table Association for Promoting Scientific Research by Women
1897	Allowed to conduct research at the Harvard Medical School
1898	Accepts a position as associate professor of physiology at the University of Kansas
1902	Elected a member of the American Physiological Society
1905	Made full professor and head of the physiology department at Kansas
1920	Retires and moves to California
1921	Publishes a paper on her invention of the microelectrode
1927	Establishes the Ida H. Hyde Scholarship
1945	Funds the Ida H. Hyde Woman's International Fellowship
Aug. 22, 1945	Dies in Berkeley, California

The Microelectrode

Hyde's microelectrode delivered electrical charges to individual cells so that cellular reactions could be studied.

After she retired from teaching, Hyde focused on her lifelong studies of the embryological development of circulatory, respiratory, and nervous systems. She investigated the breathing mechanisms of horseshoe crabs and grasshoppers and the respiratory centers of amphibians and mammals.

Hyde was one of the first physiologists to apply "micro" methods to stimulate and study individual cells. She wanted to understand how muscles, nerves, and organ tissues function. Hyde specifically sought explanations of cell reactions to receiving and sending electrochemical signals.

She invented the microelectrode, the first scientific device to deliver electrical and chemical stimuli to cells. She drew a design for her tool and published an explanation of electrophysiology in a 1921 issue of the *Biological Bulletin*.

Hyde revealed that by sending fluid to or removing fluid from a cell, she could record the cell's electrical activity. She also could study the properties of the cell. She primarily applied her investigative procedure to contractile cells.

Although her microelectrode proved significant to neurobiology, Hyde was forgotten as its inventor. Although initially attributed to her, the first microelectrode was not well known. By the 1940's, Ralph Waldo Gerard, a neurophysiologist at the University of Chicago, reinvented the microelectrode and almost received a Nobel Prize for his efforts.

Bibliography

"Developmental Neurobiology." *Science* 274 (November 15, 1996).

"Fabrication and Characterization of Sputtered-Carbon Microelectrode Arrays." G. Sreenivas, Simon S. Ang, and Ingrid Fritsch. *Analytical Chemistry* 68 (June 1, 1996).

"The Measurement of Microelectrode Sensor Characteristics Using Impedance Spectroscopy." A. McNaughtan, R. O. Ansell, and J. R. Pugh. *Measurement Science & Technology* 5 (July, 1994)

Early Life

Ida Henrietta Hyde, the daughter of German immigrants, grew up in Iowa and Illinois. She attended the Chicago Athenaeum while working as a millinery apprentice. When her mother's store was destroyed by the Great Chicago Fire in 1871, however, Ida had to quit school.

Hyde desired an education and, the age of twenty-four, enrolled at the University of Chicago. Lacking tuition money, she taught for several years in Chicago public schools. In 1891, she completed a B.S. in embryology at Cornell University.

At Bryn Mawr College, she was made a Fellow in biology. Hyde excelled, and her embryology experiments attracted international attention. A zoologist at the University of Strassburg, Germany, invited her to work with him.

Advanced Education

Hyde traveled to Europe to conduct zoological research through an Association of Collegiate Alumnae fellowship. She soon encountered discrimination against female scientists. Prevented from graduating at Strassburg, she appealed to the German Ministry of Education and was allowed to transfer to the University of Heidelberg, where she became the first woman to earn a Ph.D. Hyde next worked at a marine biology laboratory in Naples, Italy, and in the physiology department at the University of Bern in Switzerland.

By the autumn of 1896, Hyde returned to the United States as the Irwin Research Fellow at Radcliffe College. She was the first woman permitted to conduct research at the Harvard Medical School laboratories. Inspired by her experiences in Naples, Hyde founded the Naples Table Association for Promoting Scientific Research by Women.

Research and Teaching

In 1898, Hyde accepted employment at the University of Kansas, where she taught zoology and created and chaired the physiology department. During World War I, Hyde organized local women's defense work. Attending Rush Medical College during summers, she also joined the faculty of the University of Kansas School of Medicine.

Hyde wrote two books, *Outlines of Experimental Physiology* (1905) and *Laboratory Outlines of Physiology* (1910). During school breaks, she also conducted research at the University of Liverpool, England, and for the United States Fish Commission at the Marine Biological Laboratory in Woods Hole, Massachusetts.

Retirement

Hyde's diary revealed her frustrations teaching at the University of Kansas. She retired in 1920 and moved to California, where she continued her studies of the embryological development of circulatory, respiratory, and nervous systems. Hyde invented the microelectrode, the first scientific device to stimulate cells electrically. She studied individual cell's reactions (such as muscle contractions) to electrochemical signals. Hyde's invention was crucial for neurobiology, but, because her tool was not publicized, another scientist reinvented it in the 1940's.

Hyde returned to the University of Heidelberg to research how radioactive radium affects living organisms. In 1938, she wrote an amusing account of her trials as a pioneering female scientist. Socially aware, Hyde supported woman suffrage, financed scholarships, and set academic standards.

Hyde was honored for her original and precise research. She wrote numerous reports and was the first woman elected to the American Physiological Society. She died in 1945 at the age of eighty-seven.

Bibliography

By Hyde

"Collateral Circulation in the Cat After Ligation of the Postcava," *Kansas University Quarterly*, 1900

"Differences in Electrical Potential in Developing Eggs," *American Journal of Physiology*, 1904

Outlines of Experimental Physiology, 1905

"A Study of the Respiratory and Cardiac Activities and Blood Pressure in the Skate Following Intravenous Injections of Salt Solutions," *University of Kansas Science Bulletin*, 1909

Laboratory Outlines of Physiology, 1910

"The Influence of Alcohol upon the Reflex Action of Some Cutaneous Sense Organs in the Frog," *University of Kansas Science Bulletin*, 1913 (with Ruth Spray and Irene Howat)

"The Development of a Tunicate Without Nerves," *University of Kansas Science Bulletin*, 1915

"The Influence of Light on Reproduction in Vorticella," *University of Kansas Science Bulletin*, 1915 (with Christine Spreier)

"The Effects of Music upon Electrocardiograms and Blood Pressure" in *The Effects of Music: A Series of Essays*, 1927 (Max Schoen, ed.)

"Before Women Were Human Beings," *Journal of the American Association of University Women*, 1938

About Hyde

"Before Women Were Human Beings: Adventures of an American Fellow in German Universities of the '90's." Leon Stein. *Journal of the American Association of University Women* 31 (1938).

"Reflections on the Life of Ida Henrietta Hyde (1857-1945)." Gail S. Tucker. *The Creative Woman Quarterly* (Spring, 1978).

Women Scientists in America: Struggles and Strategies to 1940. Margaret W. Rossiter. Baltimore: The Johns Hopkins University Press, 1982.

(Elizabeth D. Schafer)

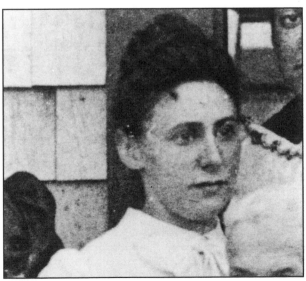

Hyde poses in a group photograph of faculty members and students of the Marine Biological Laboratory at Woods Hole, Massachusetts, where she sometimes conducted research and gave lectures. (Marine Biological Laboratory Archives)

Hypatia

Areas of Achievement: Astronomy and mathematics

Contribution: Hypatia, a respected scholar in ancient Greece, was noted for her lectures on mathematics and was credited with inventing such astronomical instruments as the astrolabe and the planisphere.

c. 370	Born in Alexandria, Greece
c. 415	Dies in Alexandria, Greece

Early Life

Hypatia (pronounced "hi-PAY-shee-uh") was the daughter of Theon, a distinguished professor of mathematics and later director of the University of Alexandria. She grew up immersed in the rarified atmosphere surrounding what was then the greatest seat of learning in the ancient world.

By the fourth century, Greece had been invaded by Roman armies. The Romans did not encourage Greek scholarship, particularly in mathematics. Roman numerals, however, proved clumsy if not impossible to use in mathematical calculations. Greek scholars fought to preserve their tradition of creative inquiry.

Hypatia's father became her teacher, endowing her with his own strong love of the beauty and logic of mathematics, astronomy, and astrology. Astronomy and astrology were considered one science, bonded by mathematics.

She was introduced to all known systems of religion and also studied literature, and philosophy. She received formal training in speech, rhetoric, and the proper use of words in pleasing, gentle tones. Theon set apart a segment of each day for regular physical exercise. She learned to row, swim, ride on horseback, and climb mountains.

Hypatia also traveled extensively abroad, spending some time as a student in Athens at Plutarch the Younger's school. There, she became a gifted, eloquent teacher. In Alexandria, she was invited to succeed Plotinus in his Platonic school.

She taught algebra, geometry, astronomy,

The Muse

Hypatia was a popular and inspirational teacher in her time who was honored for her intellect, eloquence, beauty, and virtue.

Among the many inventions that have been attributed to Hypatia are those used to study astronomy, such as the planisphere (a projection of the stars on a plane with adjustable circles for charting celestial phenomena) and the astrolabe (an instrument for calculating the positions of celestial bodies).

Hypatia's pupil Synesius of Cyrene also credits her with the invention of an apparatus for distilling water, another for measuring the level of water, and a third for determining the specific gravity of liquids. The latter was called an aerometer or hydroscope. Synesius described it as having the form and size of a flute and being graduated so that it could be used to determine the density of liquids.

Socrates, Nicephorus, and Philostorgius—ecclesiastical historians of different persuasions than that of Hypatia—generously praised her character and learning. Historians wrote that Hypatia was thoroughly familiar with the then-known science of natural philosophy. Most of her treatises, such as those on Apollonius' conics or Diophantus' *Arithmetica*, were prepared as textbooks for her students. Little progress was made in mathematical science as taught by Hypatia until the work of René Descartes, Sir Isaac Newton, and Gottfried Wilhelm Leibniz twelve centuries later.

Bibliography

Math Equals: Biographies of Women Mathematicians. Teri Perl. Reading, Mass.: Addison-Wesley, 1978.
Woman in Science. H. J. Mozans. Cambridge, Mass.: MIT Press, 1913.
Women in Mathematics. Lynn M. Osen. Cambridge, Mass.: MIT Press, 1974.

and all fields of philosophy at the university. The historian Socrates wrote that many great scholars challenged her skills at home and in her lecture rooms with unrelenting questions. He believed that she far surpassed all the philosophers of her time.

Adult Life

Students came from the world over to hear Hypatia's lectures on the *Arithmetica* of Diophantus, who was considered the leading algebraist of antiquity. He taught at the University of Alexandria shortly before Hypatia's tenure there. Diophantine equations, which have solutions restricted to integers, are named after him.

Hypatia also became intrigued by the conic work of Apollonius, an Alexandrian who lived five hundred years before her time. Modern science later demonstrated that many natural phenomena can be described by curves that are conic sections. Circles, ellipses, parabolas, and hyperbolas are all figures formed by passing a plane through a single cone. For example, a parabola is the path of all points that are the same distance from a fixed point (the focus) and a fixed line. Parabolic antennae reflect incoming parallel radio or television waves at one point, the focus, at which the receiver is located.

Public Life

Hypatia never married; she considered herself to be "wedded to the truth." Her school of neo-Platonic Greek thought, or scientific rationalism, ran counter to doctrinaire beliefs of dominant Christian thinking. Christians felt threatened by her and considered her teachings heretical.

Hypatia became the victim of the power struggle between Orestes, the Roman prefect of Egypt and her friend and protector, and Cyril, a patriarch of Alexandria and her bitter opponent.

Cyril was committed to obliterating heretical beliefs, and Orestes could not protect Hypatia during one of the resulting outbreaks of hostility. She was brutally murdered by an Alexandrian mob in 415.

Synesius of Cyrene, Hypatia's student, later became a wealthy and influential bishop of Ptolemais. His letters asking for scientific advice are the richest sources of information concerning Hypatia and her works. They also indicate how keenly he valued his intellectual association with her.

Bibliography

By Hypatia
The following titles, tentatively attributed to her, have been lost:
Commentary on the Almagest
Commentary on the Arithmetic of Diophantus
Treatise on Euclid (with Theon)
Treatise on the Astronomical Canon of Ptolemy
Treatise on the Conics of Apollonius

About Hypatia
"Hypatia." John Toland. In *Tetradymus*. London: J. Brotherton and W. Meadows, 1720.
Woman's Record: Or, Sketches of All Distinguished Women from the Creation to A.D. 1854. Sarah Josepha Hale. New York: Harper & Bros., 1860.

(Lillian D. Kozloski)

Alick Isaacs

Areas of Achievement: Biology and virology
Contribution: Isaacs discovered interferon, a protein that explains why only one ribonucleic acid (RNA) virus type can infect the body at a time.

July 17, 1921	Born in Glasgow, Scotland
1944	Graduated from Glasgow University's faculty of medicine
1945	Becomes McCann Research Scholar in Glasgow's bacteriology department
1947	Receives a Medical Research Council Studentship to attend Sheffield University
1948	Wins a Rockefeller Fellowship to study virology in Australia
1949	Marries Susanna Gordon Foss
1950	Becomes director of the World Influenza Centre at the National Institute for Medical Research (NIMR)
1954	Receives an M.D. from Glasgow University
1957	Describes interferon in two articles
1961	Becomes head of the virology division at NIMR
1966	Elected to the Royal Society of London
Jan. 25, 1967	Dies in London, England

(Archive Photos/Express News)

Early Life

Alick Isaacs was born in Glasgow, Scotland, to Louis and Rosine Isaacs. Louis, a merchant-peddler, had four children, of whom Alick was the oldest. Alick attended Glasgow public schools and private Hebrew schools. During his teenage years, he became interested in music and chess; these hobbies continued throughout his life.

In 1944, Isaacs was graduated from Glasgow University with an M.B. and a Ch.B. At the university, he won prizes in dermatology and surgery, but he lacked a calling for clinical medicine. Hence, from 1945 to 1947, he served as a McCann Research Scholar in the bacteriology department at Glasgow.

Because of Isaacs' skill in bacteriology, he won a 1947 Medical Research Council Studentship to Sheffield University. There, while working with eminent microbiologists, his interest in influenza (flu) and flu virus began and would be essential to his later career.

A Visit to Australia

In 1948, Isaacs won a Rockefeller Fellowship to study viruses for a year at the Eliza Hall Institute in Melbourne, Australia. A Medical Research Council award enabled him to stay another year. Throughout this period, Isaacs studied the flu and the viruses that cause it, the body's response to flu virus, and the viral interference phenomenon, which stops more

Interferon

Isaacs helped discover interferon proteins, which fight viral diseases and cancer.

Many communicable diseases are caused by viruses containing ribonucleic acid (RNA) hereditary material, such as colds, influenza (flu), and polio. Unaffected by antibiotics, they are commonly stopped, when the body's immune system cannot fight them off, via preventive vaccines. It has long been known that only one RNA virus disease can be caught at a time, known as the viral interference phenomenon. Isaacs showed that the protein interferon causes this phenomenon. Although he died in 1967 before his work matured, others have shown how interferon action occurs. Viral RNA enters a cell and causes interferon production. Interferon is released from cells killed by the virus. Other cells come into contact with the released interferon and develop resistance to the virus and most other RNA viruses.

Interferons stop several activities: the conversion of cells to virus factories for RNA and proteins that become new viruses (progeny), the assembly of many progeny, the destruction of cells by the progeny and the entry of each new virus into another cell to restart the process, and repeated infections. Interferons cause cells to make oligoadenylate synthetase (OS) and elf-2 kinase (EK). EK prevents progeny protein synthesis by inactivating factor elf-2. OS causes the production of 2, 5-A, which causes the destruction of viral RNA.

Interferon is too expensive for use against common viral diseases, but it is used to cure viral hepatitis, rabies, and cancers caused by viruses. Although much was done after Isaacs' death, he is accredited as the founder of interferon research.

Bibliography

"Interferon." Samuel Baron. In *McGraw-Hill Encyclopedia of Science and Technology*. New York: McGraw-Hill, 1987.

Interferon, the New Hope for Cancer. Mike Edelhart and Jean Lindenmann. Reading, Mass.: Addison-Wesley, 1981.

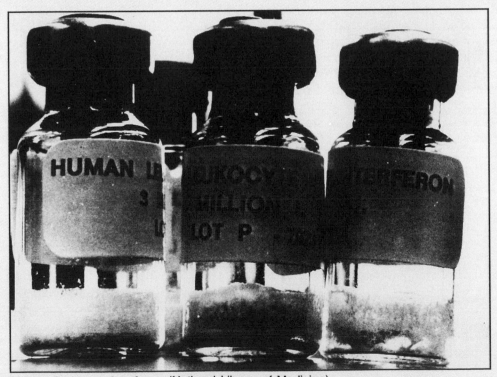

Human leukocyte interferon. (National Library of Medicine)

than one virus from infecting a human or animal at a time.

In 1949, Isaacs married Susanna Gordon Foss. Susanna, a physician, specialized in psychiatry. She and Alick later had twin sons and a daughter. In 1950, they returned to London, where Isaacs directed the World Influenza Centre at the National Institute for Medical Research (NIMR). He guided the identification of flu virus strains and helped pinpoint sites of origin for flu epidemics. He also earned an M.D. from Glasgow University in 1954.

Flu and Interferon

Isaacs' discovery of interferon arose from work on the viral interference phenomenon begun in Australia. He found that interference caused by flu virus was not related to viral penetration of cells during infection. Rather, it appeared to be the result of an event occurring in infected cells.

At NIMR, Isaacs identified the substance interferon in collaborations with visiting Swiss scientist Jean Lindenmann. In 1957, their research culminated in two in vitro observations that were key to the description of interferon: First, the interfering substance was present in the culture fluid that surrounds tissue samples, and, second, infected tissues were stimulated by flu virus to produce the interfering agent, that which Isaacs and Lindenmann named interferon. Next, they showed that interferon either was a protein or required a protein for its biological action.

As Isaacs' work progressed, he received wide recognition from the biomedical community and was asked to head the virology division at NIMR from 1961 to 1965. Throughout his life, his interest in the flu never waned. Isaacs' efforts were lauded as of great importance to the treatment of viral diseases and of potential value to the study of the numerous cancers thought to be caused by viruses.

Premature Death

Isaacs' health failed in 1964, when he had an inoperable subarachnoid hemorrhage. After recovering from the hemorrhage, he gave up his job as an NIMR division head but retained control of the Laboratory for Interferon Research. In 1966, he won more acclaim with his election to the Royal Society of London. He had a fatal recurrence of intracranial hemorrhage, however, and died in London on January 25, 1967, at the age of forty-five.

Bibliography
By Isaacs
"Virus Interference: I. The Interferon," *Proceedings of the Royal Society of London*, 1957 (with Jean Lindenmann)
"Virus Interference: II. Some Properties of the Interferon," *Proceedings of the Royal Society of London*, 1957 (with Lindenmann and R. C. Valentine)

About Isaacs
"Alick Isaacs." C. H. Andrewes. *Biographical Memoirs of the Fellows of the Royal Society* 13 (1967).
Dictionary of National Biography. London: Oxford University Press, 1982.
Obituary. *Nature* 213 (February 11, 1967).

(Sanford S. Singer)

Shirley Ann Jackson

Area of Achievement: Physics

Contribution: Jackson, a theoretical physicist, was the first African American woman to receive a Ph.D. from the Massachusetts Institute of Technology (MIT). In 1995, she achieved a prominent leadership role as chair of the U.S. Nuclear Regulatory Commission.

Aug. 5, 1946	Born in Washington, D.C.
1968	Receives a B.S. degree from MIT
1973	Earns a Ph.D. in theoretical solid-state physics from MIT, the first African American woman to do so in any field
1973-1974	Works as a research associate in theoretical physics at the Fermi National Accelerator Laboratory (Fermilab)
1974-1975	Serves as a visiting scientist at the Conseil Européen pour la Recherche Nucléaire (CERN) in Geneva, Switzerland
1975	Returns as a research associate at Fermilab
1976	Joins the Stanford Linear Accelerator Center and the Aspen Center for Physics
1976-1995	Serves on the technical staff at AT&T Bell Laboratories
1985	Helps found the New Jersey Commission on Science and Technology
1991	Named a professor of physics at Rutgers University
May 2, 1995	Sworn in as a commissioner of the U.S. Nuclear Regulatory Commission (NRC)
July 1, 1995	Assumes the post of chair of the NRC

Early Life

Shirley Ann Jackson was born on August 5, 1946, in Washington, D.C., where she grew up. Her future academic and administrative excellence was foreshadowed when she was graduated from Roosevelt High School as class valedictorian in 1964. She continued her education at the Massachusetts Institute of Technology (MIT), earning a B.S. in physics in 1968.

Jackson achieved the first of her many "firsts" when she chose to stay on at MIT to gain a doctorate in theoretical elementary particle physics. No African American woman had ever been granted a Ph.D. from the university, in any subject.

Academic and Research Pursuits

After receiving her degree in 1973, Jackson embarked on a number of journeys in her pursuit of scientific study: to the Fermi National Accelerator Laboratory (Fermilab), in Batavia, Illinois; to the Conseil Européen pour la Recherche Nucléaire (CERN), also known as the

(United States Nuclear Regulatory Commission)

Peaceful Uses of Nuclear Energy

As chair of the U.S. Nuclear Regulatory Commission (NRC), Jackson was in the position to employ her talents and knowledge as a physicist to monitor the uses of nuclear energy in medicine and technology.

Jackson's background as a research scientist and professor, in addition to her experience as a consultant and corporate director, made her an ideal choice to head the NRC, a post to which she was named in 1995. The NRC was established by Congress in January, 1975, by the Energy Reorganization Act of 1974. This independent agency assumed the duties and responsibilities of the defunct Atomic Energy Commission and was charged with regulating the use of nuclear power and substances in industry, academia, medicine, and commercial products in the United States.

The NRC monitors the public health and safety concerns pertaining to nuclear energy. Within its scope is the management of commercial nuclear power plants, which according to Jackson provided "more than 20 percent of the nation's electricity" in 1996, and the application of nuclear materials to the sterilization of medical instruments and to the diagnosis and treatment of cancer. Such substances are employed increasingly in detection devices, including smoke detectors and gauges used to identify explosives in airport baggage.

Bibliography

Commonsense in Nuclear Energy. Fred Hoyle and Geoffrey Hoyle. New York: W. H. Freeman, 1980.
Concise Encyclopedia of Nuclear Energy. D. E. Barnes et al., eds. New York: Interscience, 1962.
Energy or Extinction?: The Case for Nuclear Energy. Fred Hoyle. 2d ed. London: Heinemann, 1980.

European Organization for Nuclear Research, in Geneva, Switzerland; back to Fermilab; and to the Stanford Linear Accelerator Center in California and the Aspen Center for Physics.

In 1976, she finally settled at the AT&T Bell Laboratories, in Murray Hill, New Jersey, where she would spend the next fifteen years on the technical staff conducting research on theoretical, solid-state, and quantum physics, particularly semiconductors. In 1991, she joined the faculty of Rutgers University as a physics professor in the Department of Physics and Astronomy while continuing her work with Bell Laboratories.

Administrative Leadership

Jackson showed her dedication to the betterment of science and society through service in the public and private sectors. She held numerous memberships in professional organizations, such as the American Academy of Arts and Science and the American Physical Society, and served on an advisory panel for the U.S. Department of Energy and on the research councils of the National Academy of Sciences and the Institute of Nuclear Power Operations (INPO).

She was also a member of the board of directors for such corporations as the Public Service Enterprise Group, CoreStates New Jersey National Bank, and the New Jersey Resources Corporation, and she was granted life member status on the board of trustees at MIT. Jackson helped found the New Jersey Commission on Science and Technology in 1985 and won the Salute to the Policymakers Award from the Executive Women of New Jersey in 1986 and 1988.

Her greatest administrative achievement came in 1995, when Jackson, who had already been sworn in as the first African American commissioner of the Nuclear Regulatory commission (NRC), assumed the post of chair of that influential body—the first African American and the first woman to be so named. The Honorable Shirley Ann Jackson affirmed her commitment to carrying out the primary goal of the NRC: ensuring the protection of public health and safety in the use of nuclear energy.

Jackson married a fellow physicist, Morris A. Washington. Together, they had a son, Alan.

Bibliography

By Jackson
"The Study of a Multiperipheral Model with Continued Cross-Channel Unitarity," 1973 (dissertation)

Educating Young Children Prenatally Exposed to Drugs and at Risk: Report and Resource Compendium, 1993

About Jackson

American Men and Women of Science. 15th ed. Vol. 4. New York: R. R. Bowker, 1982-1983.

Blacks in Science: Astrophysicist to Zoologist. Hattie Carwell. Hicksville, N.Y.: Exposition Press, 1977.

"Jackson, Shirley Ann." In *Notable Twentieth-Century Scientists*, edited by Emily J. McMurray. New York: Gale Research, 1995.

(Tracy Irons-Georges)

François Jacob

Areas of Achievement: Bacteriology, cell biology, genetics, and virology

Contribution: A brilliant theorist, Jacob helped to develop the concepts of messenger RNA and the operon as a model for gene regulation in bacteria.

June 17, 1920	Born in Nancy, France
1947	Receives an M.D. degree
1951	Begins a long collaboration with Elie Wollman, studying the genetic basis of lysogeny
1954	Earn a D.Sc. in science from the Sorbonne in Paris
1956	Named laboratory director at the Institut Pasteur
1960	Becomes chair of the cell genetics department at the Institut Pasteur
1960	With Jacques Monod, proposes the operon as a model for gene regulation in bacteria
1962	With Wollman, devises the technique of interrupted mating in bacteria
1964	Becomes a professor of cell genetics at the Collège de France
1965	Receives the Nobel Prize in Physiology or Medicine
1973	Named a member of the Royal Society of London
1977	Named a member of the Académie des Sciences, in Paris
1987	Publishes his autobiography *La Statue intérieure* (*The Statue Within*, 1988)

Early Life

Born in 1920 in Nancy, France, François Jacob (pronounced "zhah-KOHB") grew up with the

(The Nobel Foundation)

ambition of becoming a surgeon. In 1940, his medical studies at the Faculté de Paris were interrupted by World War II, and he fought with the French Free Forces in northern Africa. Jacob subsequently completed his medical studies, but he was unable to practice surgery because of injuries that he sustained during the war.

Turning to biology, Jacob joined André Lwoff's laboratory at the Institut Pasteur in 1950. Soon thereafter, he began a long and fruitful collaboration with Elie Wollman, initially working on various genetic aspects of bacteriophage (viral) infection of bacteria. Jacob received the D.Sc. degree from the Sorbonne in 1954 and two years later was appointed as a laboratory director at the Institut Pasteur.

Collaboration with Monod
In 1958, Jacob began a second highly successful collaboration, this time with Jacques Lucien Monod and Arthur Pardee, on the control of

bacterial enzyme production. They discovered and described messenger RNA (mRNA), a biological macromolecule that carries genetic information from the deoxyribonucleic acid (DNA) to the ribosomes, where proteins are synthesized. Jacob and Monod were also the first to distinguish structural genes from regulatory genes. Structural genes encode proteins that are important for normal cellular activities, while the products of regulatory genes interact with the structural genes to inhibit or stimulate their expression.

The highlight of the Jacob and Monod collaboration came in 1960 with their proposal of the operon model for the regulation of genes in bacteria. This model made an immediate and profound impact on the science of molecular biology, and they shared the Nobel Prize in Physiology or Medicine for this work a mere five years later, in 1965.

Collaboration with Wollman
Jacob renewed his association with Elie Wollman in 1960, and, the following year, they published what has become a classic text in bacterial genetics: *La Sexualité des bacteries*, 1959 (*Sexuality and the Genetics of Bacteria*, 1961). Their discovery and description of episomes (stable, autonomous, nonchromosomal pieces of DNA) in bacteria had widespread applications. Such elements were later found in corn and fruit flies and have been of critical importance in cancer research.

The single most useful technique for mapping bacterial genes was also devised by Jacob and Wollman. Known as the interrupted mating procedure, it allows for the determination of precise map distances between closely linked genes. This genetic approach established the circularity of the bacterial genome.

Philosophy of Science
Jacob made an abrupt shift in the 1970's to study embryology and development in mice. In particular, he studied teratocarcinoma, a type of germ cell tumor, as a system to investigate early developmental processes in mammals.

In addition, Jacob made excursions into scientific philosophy, resulting in the writing of two well-known books, *La Logique du vivant* (1970; *The Logic of Life*, 1973) and *Le Jeu des*

The *Lac*-Operon

Genes involved with the metabolism of the sugar lactose are actively expressed only in the presence of the inducer, lactose. In the absence of lactose, the lac-repressor binds to the deoxyribonucleic acid (DNA), inhibiting the expression of the genes.

Jacob and Jacques Monod identified three adjacent structural genes involved in lactose utilization, which share a common regulatory control in a scheme that they termed the "*lac*-operon." (In the accompanying figures, *i* is the regulatory gene, *p* is the promoter site, *o* is the operator sequence, *z* is the gene encoding β-galactosidase enzyme, *y* is the gene encoding permease enzyme, *a* is the gene encoding transacetylase enzyme, RP is the repressor protein, rnap is the RNA polymerase, and *L* is lactose.) The operon also includes a short DNA sequence called the operator, located immediately "upstream" from gene *z*.

Outside the operon and even further upstream is found the regulatory gene, *i*. Gene *i* encodes the *lac*-repressor, a protein that has an affinity for the operator. When the *lac*-repressor is bound to the operator, it blocks the movement of the enzyme ribonucleic acid (RNA) polymerase, which at-

taches to the DNA at the upstream promotor. An RNA transcript of the structural genes is thus not made, and the genes are repressed (turned off).

The *lac*-repressor has a much stronger affinity for lactose, however, than it does for the operator. In the presence of lactose, it will leave the operator to bind to lactose, thus allowing RNA polymerase to make messenger RNA (mRNA) copies of the structural genes. All *lac* enzymes will be produced until the lactose is finally exhausted, at which time the *lac*-repressor can again bind to the operator to shut down mRNA synthesis.

Gene regulation is a complex process that can occur at several levels in the cell. The *lac*-operon was the first regulatory mechanism to be described in detail and serves as the model for many subsequent studies.

Bibliography
Genetics. Peter Russell. Boston: Scott, Foresman, 1995.
How Scientists Think. George B. Johnson. Dubuque, Iowa: Wm C. Brown, 1996.
The Lactose Operon. J. R. Beckwith and D. Zipser, eds. Cold Spring Harbor, N.Y.: Cold Spring Harbor Laboratory, 1970.

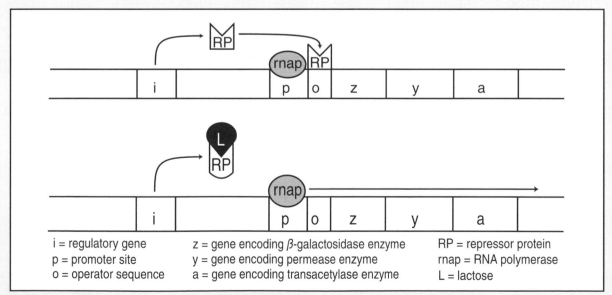

i = regulatory gene
p = promoter site
o = operator sequence
z = gene encoding *β*-galactosidase enzyme
y = gene encoding permease enzyme
a = gene encoding transacetylase enzyme
RP = repressor protein
rnap = RNA polymerase
L = lactose

1. In the absence of lactose, the repressor protein binds to the operator, blocking the movement of RNA polymerase. The genes are turned off.
2. When lactose is present, it preferentially binds the repressor protein, freeing up the operator and allowing RNA polymerase to move through the operon. The genes are turned on.

possibles (1981; *The Possible and the Actual*, 1982). *La Statue intérieure*, published in 1987 and translated as *The Statue Within* (1988), is an autobiographical account that also focuses heavily on Jacob's philosophy of science.

Bibliography
By Jacob
Les Bacteries lysogenes et la notion de provirus, 1954

La Sexualité des bacteries, 1959 (with Elie L. Wollman; *Sexuality and the Genetics of Bacteria*, 1961)

La Logique du vivant: Une Histoire de l'heredité, 1970 (*The Logic of Life: A History of Heredity*, 1973)

Le Jeu des possibles: Essai sur la diversité de vivant, 1981 (*The Possible and the Actual*, 1982)

La Statue intérieure, 1987 (*The Statue Within: An Autobiography*, 1988)

About Jacob
The Eighth Day of Creation: Makers of the Revolution in Biology. Horace F. Judson. New York: Simon & Schuster, 1979.

Great Scientific Experiments: Twenty Experiments That Changed Our View of the World. Ron Harre. New York: Oxford University Press, 1983.

Nobel Lectures in Molecular Biology, 1933-1975. New York: Elsevier, 1977.

(*Jeffrey A. Knight*)

Sir James Jeans

Areas of Achievement: Astronomy and physics

Contribution: Jeans corrected the derivation of Lord Rayleigh's law explaining the distribution of blackbody radiation. Later in life, he popularized science in Great Britain.

Sept. 11, 1877	Born in Ormskirk, Lancashire, England
1903	Earns a master's degree from Trinity College, Cambridge University
1905	Publishes a paper correcting the derivation of Lord Rayleigh's radiation law
1905	Appointed a professor of applied mathematics at Princeton University
1907	Elected to the Royal Society of London
1910	Named Stokes Lecturer in Applied Mathematics at Cambridge
1919	Wins the Adams Prize for his essay *Problems of Cosmogony and Stellar Dynamics*
1919-1929	Elected a secretary of the Royal Society of London
1925-1927	Holds the presidency of the Royal Astronomical Society
1928	Receives a knighthood
1929	Delivers radio lectures that inspire his book *The Universe Around Us*
1938-1940	Elected vice president of the Royal Society of London
1938	Becomes a director of the Royal Academy of Music
Sept. 16, 1946	Dies in Dorking, Surrey, England

Early Life

James Hopwood Jeans was the son of a journalist who wrote about the lives of scientists. James was an aloof, but intellectually curious child who wrote a little book about clocks when he was nine years old.

He entered Trinity College at Cambridge University in 1896; two years later, he took second place in the mathematical tripos examinations for honors in undergraduate mathematics. Despite ill health, Jeans earned the Smith's Prize in 1900. He was elected a Fellow of Trinity College in 1901.

Teaching

Jeans was a professor of applied mathematics at Princeton University from 1905 to 1909. During this tenure, he wrote two textbooks, *Theoretical Mechanics* (1906) and *The Mathematical Theory of Electricity and Magnetism* (1908). He was elected a Fellow of the Royal Society of London in 1907. In that year, he married Charlotte Tiffany Mitchell, a wealthy American.

(Library of Congress)

Jeans was Stokes Lecturer in Applied Mathematics at Cambridge from 1910 until his retirement from teaching in 1912.

Radiation Theory

Jeans is most well known for his correction in a 1905 paper of Lord Rayleigh's law of radiation. That year brought a proposal by Max Planck that difficulties in the proposed laws of radiation could be solved if energy were treated as capable of being emitted only in certain specified units. Jeans resisted this quantum theory until 1914, when he published a report showing that the difficulties could not be avoided by classical methods.

Double Stars and the Solar System

As an undergraduate, Jeans initiated a study of the behavior of compressible and incompressible fluids. He considered two cases: an incompressible liquid mass and a gaseous cloud of negligible mass surrounding a mass concentrated in the center. He maintained that if an incompressible mass were to contract or began to spin more fiercely, the mass would eventually become an unstable, pear-shaped object and would then split into two parts. This mechanism could explain the formation of the many double-star systems in the universe.

In the other case, gas of a negligible mass would become increasingly flat, like a pancake, and finally spin off matter from the edge; this model could explain the formation of spiral nebulas. Jeans concluded that the rotation of a contracting mass could not be the origin of the solar system, in the form of nebular theory proposed by Immanuel Kant and Simon Laplace. Instead, he believed in a tidal theory of origin for the solar system. According to this now-discredited theory, the planets were created when another body passed nearby to the sun and drew out enough mass to form planets.

The Popularization of Science

In 1928, Jeans ceased active work as a researcher and became famous for his work in the popular exposition of science. His last major scientific idea was that matter was coming into being throughout the universe, a predecessor of the steady state theory.

He was awarded the Royal Medal in 1919

Derivation of the Rayleigh-Jeans Radiation Law

According to the Rayleigh-Jeans radiation law, if one knows the temperature of an object, the distribution of energy that it will radiate can be calculated.

A blackbody is an object that completely absorbs all radiation without reflection; there are no perfect blackbodies in nature. In 1896, Wilhelm Wien concluded that the energy that such a body would re-radiate near a given wavelength varied inversely with the fifth power of that wavelength.

It was experimentally demonstrated in 1900 that for a range of smaller frequencies, this Wien-Planck radiation law was incorrect. Lord Rayleigh published a paper in that same year to resolve the discrepancy between the law and the data. Jeans's contribution to the form of the law, in a 1905 paper entitled "The Law of Radiation," was the statement that "it seems to me that Lord Rayleigh has introduced an unnecessary factor 8 by counting negative as well as positive values for his integers." Rayleigh admitted the error.

Their formula indicated that the energy reradi-ated by the blackbody in the neighborhood of a given wavelength varied inversely with the fourth power of that wavelength, a result that was at odds with experiment for the higher frequencies. In addition, the equation did not allow for a maximum frequency beyond which no energy would be radiated. In theory, a cooling body would eventually emit dangerous high-frequency radiation in unlimited amounts, a fact contrary to experience. In 1911, Paul Ehrenfest would call this situation the "ultraviolet catastrophe." Max Planck's new quantum mechanics, introduced in 1905, solved this problem.

Bibliography

Black Body Theory and the Quantum Discontinuity, 1894-1912. Thomas S. Kuhn. Oxford, England: Oxford University Press, 1978.

The Conceptual Development of Quantum Mechanics. Max Jammer. New York: McGraw-Hill, 1966.

The History of Quantum Theory. Friedrich Hund. New York: Barnes & Noble Books, 1967.

and received a knighthood in 1928. After the death of his first wife, he married a concert organist, Suzanne Hock. Jeans died as a result of a heart condition in 1946.

Bibliography

By Jeans
The Dynamical Theory of Gases, 1904
Theoretical Mechanics, 1906
The Mathematical Theory of Electricity and Magnetism, 1908
Report on Radiation and the Quantum Theory, 1914
Problems of Cosmogony and Stellar Dynamics, 1919
The Nebular Hypothesis and Modern Cosmogony, 1923
Atomicity and Quanta, 1926
Eos: Or, The Wider Aspects of Cosmogony, 1928
The Universe Around Us, 1929
The Mysterious Universe, 1930
The Stars in Their Courses, 1931
The New Background of Science, 1933
Through Space and Time, 1934
Science and Music, 1938
Introduction to the Kinetic Theory of Gases, 1940
Physics and Philosophy, 1942
The Growth of Physical Science, 1947

About Jeans
"James Jeans and Radiation Theory." Rob Hudson. *Studies in the History and Philosophy of Science* 20, no. 1 (March, 1989).
"Planck's Principle and Jeans's Conversion." Geoffrey Gorham. *Studies in the History and Philosophy of Science* 22, no. 3 (September, 1991).
Sir James Jeans: A Biography. E. A. Milne. Cambridge, England: Cambridge University Press, 1952.

(Drew L. Arrowood)

Edward Jenner

Areas of Achievement: Immunology and medicine

Contribution: Jenner, a country doctor, invented the method of disease prevention known as vaccination and helped to eradicate smallpox. His work inspired the creation of the branch of science called immunology.

May 17, 1749	Born in Berkeley, Gloucestershire, England
1770	Studies medicine at St. George's Hospital of London
1771	Prepares specimens from Captain Cook's first Pacific voyage
1772	Declines to serve as a naturalist on Cook's second expedition
1788	Becomes a Fellow of the Royal Society of London
1788	Marries Catherine Kingscote
1792	Receives an M.D. from St. Andrew's Hospital
1796	Inoculates a boy with cowpox and confirms his subsequent immunity to smallpox
1798	Publishes his findings regarding inoculation
1802	Awarded thirty thousand pounds by Parliament for his dedication and achievements
1803	Founds the Royal Jennerian Society, which closes in 1806 and is replaced by the National Vaccine Establishment in 1808
1813	Presented with a Doctor in Physic degree by Oxford University 1815
1820	Suffers a stroke
Jan. 26, 1823	Dies in Berkeley, Gloucestershire, England

Early Life

Edward Jenner was born in the village of Berkeley in Gloucestershire, England, on May 17, 1749. His father, Reverend Steven Jenner, the vicar of Berkeley, died when Edward was only five years old. Edward attended local schools administrated by the clergy and developed an affinity for natural history and nature.

Jenner was apprenticed to Daniel Ludlow in Sodbury, located just outside of Bristol. During his apprenticeship, Jenner's interest in smallpox was sparked by a milkmaid's assertion that because she had contracted cowpox, she could not contract smallpox. In 1770, Jenner left Berkeley to study medicine at St. George's Hospital in London, where he lived with and studied under the anatomist John Hunter for two years.

Dr. Jenner Conquers Smallpox

In 1780, Jenner began research and experimentation on smallpox. In 1788, while involved in smallpox research, Jenner married Catherine Kingscote. Together, the couple lived in a house called "The Chantry," which was their

(Library of Congress)

permanent residence for the rest of their lives. The couple produced two sons.

In 1792, Jenner received his doctor of medicine certification and began his medical practice in Gloucestershire. Despite the rigors of rural medical practice, he continued his work with smallpox and, in 1796, successfully inoculated eight-year-old James Phipps using cowpox. He submitted the results and details of his experiment to the Royal Society of London. In response, the society deemed that a single, isolated success was inconclusive.

In 1798, after collecting twenty-three additional case histories to support his original experiment, Jenner published the pamphlet *An Inquiry into the Causes and Effects of the Variolæ-Vaccinæ, a Disease Discovered in Some of the Western Counties of England, Particularly Gloucestershire, and Known by the Name of the Cow Pox.* Interest in Jenner's work was sparked not only within the medical profession but also among laypeople throughout the world.

In 1802, Parliament received a petition to reimburse Jenner for the loss of income caused by his work on the smallpox vaccine. Jenner was against the proposal, but Parliament nevertheless granted him a total of thirty thousand pounds.

Jenner's Work Continues

In 1803, Jenner helped to found the Royal Jennerian Society. The society provided free vaccinations and a facility to collect the lymph fluid necessary to produce the vaccine. After the society was founded, the average number of deaths from smallpox in England dropped from 2,018 to 622 a year. The Royal Jennerian Society closed in 1806 as a result of management problems, but it was replaced by the National Vaccine Establishment in 1808.

Jenner was continually contacted personally by people from around the world wishing to know more about his vaccine and the lymph needed to administer it. The deluge of requests spurred Jenner to call himself the "Vaccine Clerk to the World."

The Development of the Smallpox Vaccine

Jenner discovered that inoculating humans with the milder cowpox or grease strains of the smallpox virus renders them immune to it.

Jenner believed that cowpox (in cows), the grease (in horses), and smallpox (in humans) were caused by the same "distemper," or infectious matter. His evidence was provided by milkmaids, who claimed that they could not contract smallpox. Jenner established the connection between the grease and cowpox by placing matter from the hoof of an infected horse on the udder of a cow, causing it to contract cowpox. Jenner then used pus from sores caused by the diseases to obtain vaccines and tested his method.

Inoculation was more successful than other methods of disease prevention at the time, but Jenner noted a disturbing number of failed vaccinations performed by other physicians. He found that the vaccine was effective only if certain conditions were met: It must be administered through the skin on the eighth day of the disease, and the pustular matter used in the vaccine must be stored properly.

Another cause of ineffective vaccinations was the inoculation of patients with matter from a "spurious cowpox" disease. Cows frequently were stricken with another disease with symptoms similar to those of "true" cowpox. Jenner delineated the difference between the two diseases to help eliminate impotent vaccines.

Jenner's vaccine was key in the eradication of smallpox from human populations. His method of vaccination led to major advances in the control and prevention of other diseases.

Bibliography

Further Observations on the Variolæ-Vaccinæ, or Cow Pox. Edward Jenner. London: Sampson Low, 1799.

An Inquiry into the Causes and Effects of the Variolæ-Vaccinæ. Edward Jenner. London: Sampson Low, 1789.

Magic Shots: A Human and Scientific Account of the Long and Continuing Struggle to Eradicate Infectious Diseases by Vaccination. Allan Chase. New York: William Morrow, 1982.

In 1815, Jenner's wife died, prompting his retirement. He became ill shortly thereafter and died following a stroke (commonly called a "fit of apoplexy") on January 26, 1823. He was buried in the parish church in Berkeley.

Bibliography

By Jenner

An Inquiry into the Causes and Effects of the Variolæ-Vaccinæ, a Disease Discovered in Some of the Western Counties of England, Particularly Gloucestershire, and Known by the Name of the Cow Pox, 1798

Further Observations on the Variolæ-Vaccinæ, or Cow Pox, 1799

About Jenner

The Life of Edward Jenner. John Barron. London: Henry Colburn, 1827.

Pioneers of Public Health: The Story of Some Benefactors of the Human Race. M. E. M. Walker. Edinburgh, Scotland: Oliver & Boyd, 1930.

(Alvin M. Pettus)

J. Hans D. Jensen

Area of Achievement: Physics

Contribution: Jensen was one of the scientists who developed the shell model of the atomic nucleus, explaining the "magic numbers" of neutrons and protons associated with the stability of certain elements and their isotopes.

June 25, 1907	Born in Hamburg, Germany
1927	Enters the University of Freiburg
1932	Receives a doctorate in physics from the University of Hamburg, joining the faculty there
1941	Becomes professor ordinarius at the Institute of Technology at Hannover
1948	Formulates his explanations of shell structure
1949	Joins the faculty of the University of Heidelberg
1955	Publishes *Elementary Theory of Nuclear Shell Structure* in collaboration with Maria Goeppert Mayer
1955	Joins the editorial staff of the journal *Zeitschrift für Physik*
1960	Accepts membership in the prestigious Max Planck Society
1963	Awarded the Nobel Prize in Physics jointly with Eugene Wigner and Mayer
Feb. 11, 1973	Dies in Heidelberg, West Germany

Early Life

Johannes Hans Daniel Jensen (pronounced "YEHN-zuhn") was born the son of gardener Karl Jensen and Helene (Ohm) Jensen in 1907. His talents were recognized by one of his teachers, who helped him acquire a stipend for study at a preparatory school for the natural sciences.

In 1926, Jensen was graduated and attended for a time the University of Freiburg, but he returned to the University of Hamburg to study, where he received his doctorate in 1932. Four years later, he was promoted from assistant lecturer to docent, a position roughly equivalent to assistant professor. His early research was on ionic lattices, networks of fixed points about which ions vibrate in a crystal.

Magic Numbers

Hans E. Suess, a geochemist, and Otto Haxel, an experimental physicist, first directed Jensen's attention to the unexplained nuclear behavior of elements whose protons or neutrons number 50, 82, and 126. Such elements are unusually and highly stable. Other "magic numbers," as the physicist Eugene P. Wigner had called them, were known, including 2, 8, 20, and 28.

Jensen's determination to solve the riddle of magic numbers led to advances in the understanding of atomic structure for which he, along with Wigner and Maria Goeppert Mayer, would receive the Nobel Prize in Physics in 1963.

Shell Theory and Magic Numbers

Jensen helped to explain the structure and behavior of atoms and their constituent particles.

The model of the atom developed largely by the Danish physicist Niels Bohr posited a nucleus something like a liquid drop, which could not be used to explain successfully the subatomic behavior physicists were encountering in their research in the late 1940's. The idea of a shell of orbits within the nucleus had been around since the early 1930's, and, indeed, physicists were aware of the existence of nucleon "spin" and its magnetic effects.

Jensen and Maria Goeppert Mayer independently, and virtually simultaneously, devised a comprehensive shell model in which nucleons have different energies according to the direction of their spin. Spin can be either parallel or antiparallel to the direction of orbit. This coupling of spin and orbit was used to make several predictions contained in *Elementary Theory of Nuclear Shell Structure* (1955) their collaborative book on shell theory; experiments later confirmed the validity of their theory of shell structure, although in a somewhat modified form. Their contribution was to determine the relationship of spin and nuclear stability and to thus solve the mystery of so-called magic numbers, certain numbers of protons or neutrons that make an element highly stable.

In his acceptance speech for the Nobel Prize in Physics, Jensen sketched the history of atomic physics leading up to the problems that had occupied him in his own research. In the early part of the twentieth century, the model for the building blocks of the atom was essentially that of the previous century, with positively and negatively charged particles (protons and electrons) orbiting within the nucleus.

The most important conceptual advancement had come no earlier than the early 1930's, when Sir James Chadwick discovered an uncharged counterpart to the proton in the nucleus. This missing link, the neutron, led to accurate predictions about the structure and behavior of the atom. Eugene P. Wigner and Werner Heisenberg laid much of the groundwork of modern shell theory with their studies of nucleon interactions.

The well-known Italian physicist Enrico Fermi went a step further in describing the neutron and proton as two quantum states of one particle, the nucleon itself. Fermi predicted the existence of neutrinos as the result of transitions between the two states of the nucleon.

In his speech, Jensen pictured the elements of shell theory coming together, as it began to be understood how the spin and orbit of these particles in the nucleus are related, especially once the suspected significance of magic numbers was confirmed and elucidated. Jensen portrayed the contemporary science of physics as a dialogic, collaborative process, and he credited Bohr (whom he often visited in Copenhagen), Hans Suess, Otto Haxel, Mayer, and others with providing insights and observations that advanced his own work.

Bibliography

Theory of the Nuclear Shell Model. R. D. Lawson. Oxford, England: Clarendon Press, 1980.

(The Nobel Foundation)

The War Years

Jensen was not alone among German physicists in leading an ostensibly apolitical life. He pursued science for its own sake during a period of historic upheaval that saw the rise of Nazism, the coming of World War II, and the global polarization of the Cold War, with its constant threat of mutually assured destruction from atomic weapons. Nor were those who conquered Germany interested on the whole in the politics of those physicists active in Germany during the war years.

In Jensen's case, his advancements in shell theory brought him fame beyond a small circle of specialists, and, by the early 1950's, he was a welcome guest at various universities in the United States, with lectureships at the University of Wisconsin, Princeton University, and the University of California, Berkeley.

Later Life

Jensen was not a colorful or flamboyant figure, but a meticulous researcher. This is not to imply, however, that he tended to the extreme of pedantry. Rather, he was a singularly independent-minded physicist whose refusal to adhere to dogmatic schools of thought led to his distinctly original findings and ideas. He was willing to borrow methods and approaches from other disciplines, and he profited from the ease with which he was able to collaborate with colleagues.

Jensen spent most of his career at the University of Heidelberg, where he accepted a position in 1949. He remained professionally active until his death, serving with Otto Haxel as the coeditor of the prestigious German-language physics periodical *Zeitschrift für Physik* from 1955 to 1973.

Bibliography

By Jensen
Elementary Theory of Nuclear Shell Structure, 1955 (with Maria Goeppert Mayer)

About Jensen
"J. Hans D. Jensen." Mark R. McCulloh. In *The Nobel Prize Winners: Physics*, edited by Frank N. Magill. Pasadena, Calif.: Salem Press, 1989.

(Mark R. McCulloh)

Niels K. Jerne

Area of Achievement: Immunology

Contribution: Jerne, considered to be the founder of modern cellular immunology, won the 1984 Nobel Prize in Physiology or Medicine for three major theories explaining the workings of the immune system.

Dec. 23, 1911	Born in London, England
1928	Receives a bachelor's degree in Rotterdam
1943-1955	Conducts research at the Danish State Serum Institute
1951	Receives an M.D. degree
1955	Proposes the natural selection theory of antibody formation
1956-1962	Serves as chief medical officer of the World Health Organization
1960-1966	Teaches at the University of Geneva, the University of Pittsburgh and J. W. Goethe University
1963	Develops the plaque assay
1966-1969	Serves as director of the Paul Ehrlich Institute, Frankfurt
1969-1980	Serves as director of the Basel Institute for Immunology
1971	Presents an explanation of immune system discrimination between "self" and "nonself"
1974	Proposes his immune network theory
1981	Teaches at Institut Pasteur, Paris
1982	Retires to southern France
1984	Wins the Nobel Prize in Physiology or Medicine, jointly with Georges Köhler and César Milstein
Oct. 7, 1994	Dies in Pont du Gard, France

Early Life

Niels Kaj Jerne (pronounced "YEHR-neh") was born on December 23, 1911, in London, England. Shortly after his birth, his family moved to Denmark and later to the Netherlands, where Jerne earned his bachelor's degree at the age of sixteen. He studied physics for two years at the University of Leiden and, twelve years later, entered the University of Copenhagen to study medicine.

While working for his doctorate, Jerne also held a research position at the Danish State Serum Institute. His doctoral research dealt with the strength of interaction between antigens (foreign substances such as viruses, bacteria, and toxins) and antibodies (chemicals produced by immune cells to defend against antigens). He showed that antibody binding strength increases with every exposure to antigen.

Antibody Production and the Plaque Assay

As a research fellow at the California Institute of Technology (Caltech), Jerne published a

(The Nobel Foundation)

The Network Theory

The immune system consists of diverse cells and antibodies that interact in a balanced, self-regulating network. This immune network responds to harmful substances in the body and turns itself on or off as needed.

Lymphocytes are white blood cells that, when activated, defend the body against potentially harm- ful foreign substances (antigens) such as bacteria, viruses, or toxins. Activation occurs when lymphocytes directly interact with antigens in a lock-and-key fashion via special cell surface receptors. Each lymphocyte bears receptors for a different antigen and can be activated only by that antigen.

Two functionally different types of lymphocytes are activated during an immune response. B lymphocytes produce antibodies, chemicals that bind to antigens and promote their neutralization, destruction, or elimination. T lymphocytes help B lymphocytes produce antibodies and also kill infected cells directly.

Antibodies are large proteins consisting of constant and variable regions. The constant regions of most antibodies are chemically identical even if they have different antigen specificities. Variable regions are the relatively small portions of an antibody that physically bind to antigens. These regions determine antigen specificity and are unique to each antibody.

In the early 1960's, several investigators noticed that the injection of antibodies into an animal stimulates the production of new antibodies. Some of the new antibodies are specific for the variable region of the injected antibody and bind to the stimulating antibody in precisely the same place as the antigen. These studies showed that the variable region of an antibody not only binds to antigens but also can itself act as an antigen.

The antigenic component of an antibody is called the idiotype, and the antibody that specifically recognizes the idiotype is the anti-idiotype.

In the network theory, Jerne suggested that, under normal circumstances, idiotype and anti-idiotype antibodies exist in the body as a balanced network, with each idiotype being bound to its respective anti-idiotype. A foreign antigen disrupts the balance by displacing some of the anti-idiotype antibody. The presence of excess anti-idiotype stimulates the immune system to produce more idiotype antibody in an attempt to reestablish equilibrium, thus strengthening the immune response against the invading antigen. When the antigen is eliminated, a balance between idiotype and anti-idiotype is restored, and the immune system is shut down.

The network theory encompasses not only circulating antibodies but also B and T lymphocytes, both of which bear receptors with unique antigen-binding regions that can stimulate the production of anti-idiotype antibody.

One practical outcome of Jerne's theory was the concept that anti-idiotype antibodies could be used to vaccinate against antigens. Since antigens and anti-idiotype antibodies bind to the same idiotype, it follows that they are structurally similar. Therefore, these antibodies would mimic antigens and stimulate an immune response without posing any risk to the individual.

Bibliography
Essential Immunology. Ivan Roitt. London: Blackwell Scientific Publications, 1991.

"Immune System." Niels K. Jerne. *Scientific American* 229 (July, 1973).

Immunology: A Short Course. Eli Benjamini and Sidney Leskowitz. New York: Wiley-Liss, 1991.

landmark paper entitled "The Natural Selection Theory of Antibody Formation," in which he proposed a revolutionary theory explaining an animal's ability to produce antibodies against a virtually limitless array of antigens. This paper provided the basis for the now universally accepted clonal selection theory of Sir Frank Macfarland Burnet.

From 1956 to 1962, Jerne serve as chief medical officer of the World Health Organization (WHO) and then spent four years teaching at the University of Geneva, the University of Pittsburgh, and the J. W. Goethe University. In Pittsburgh, Jerne and Albert Nordin developed the Jerne plaque assay, a now-standard method for counting antibody-producing cells.

The Basel Institute of Immunology

In 1966, Jerne became director of the Paul Ehrlich Institute in Frankfurt, Germany, where he stayed until 1969. He left to become the founding director of a new institute dedicated to basic research in immunology. Jerne recruited a staff of sixty prominent scientists from all over the world, and, on June 16, 1971, the Basel Institute for Immunology was officially opened in Switzerland.

During the 1970's, Jerne presented two more major immunological theories. The first explained how the immune system distinguishes foreign ("nonself") antigens from normal ("self") antigens. Jerne proposed that during a maturation phase in the thymus, immune cells that would react against self components are suppressed, while those that recognize foreign substances are allowed to mature.

The second, known as the network theory, is considered to be his most important. Jerne proposed that all parts of the immune system are linked together in a dynamic, self-regulating network that can turn itself on or off as needed.

The Nobel Prize

Jerne left Basel in 1980, taught for a year at the Institut Pasteur in Paris, and then retired to southern France with his wife, Ursula Alexandra Kohl. In 1984, he was awarded the Nobel Prize in Physiology or Medicine for a lifetime of theoretical contributions to the field of immunology. He died in 1994.

Bibliography

By Jerne

"The Natural Selection Theory of Antibody Formation," *Proceedings of the National Academy of Sciences, U.S.A.*, 1955

"The Somatic Generation of Immune Recognition," *European Journal of Immunology*, 1971

"Immune System," *Scientific American*, 1973

"Plaque-Forming Cells: Method and Theory," *Transplantation Reviews*, 1974

"Idiotype Networks and Other Preconceived Ideas," *Immunological Reviews*, 1984

About Jerne

Milestones in Immunology: A Historical Exploration. Debra J. Bibel. Madison, Wis.: Science Tech, 1988.

The Nobel Prize Winners: Physiology or Medicine. Frank N. Magill, ed. Pasadena, Calif.: Salem Press, 1991.

Notable Twentieth-Century Scientists. Emily J. McMurray, ed. Detroit: Gale Research, 1995.

(Darbie L. Maccubbin)

Wilhelm Ludvig Johannsen

Areas of Achievement: Biology, botany, genetics, and physiology

Contribution: Johannsen helped establish the field of genetics with his experimental support for and invention of the terms "gene," "genotype" and "phenotype."

Feb. 3, 1857	Born in Copenhagen, Denmark
1881	Appointed an assistant chemist at Carlsberg Laboratorium, Copenhagen
1892	Becomes a lecturer at the Royal Veterinary and Agricultural College, Copenhagen
1893	Demonstrates his technique of using ether to break the dormancy of plants
1893-1897	Carries out individual progeny analyses of barley and the Princess bean
1898	Elected to the Royal Danish Academy of Sciences
1902-1909	Conducts pure line studies of the Princess bean
1905	Appointed *professor honoris* in plant physiology at the University of Copenhagen
1909	Coins the terms "gene," "genotype," and "phenotype"
1910	Named *doctor honoris causa* in medicine at the University of Copenhagen
1917	Becomes rector of the University of Copenhagen
1924	Elected president of the International Seed Control Congress
Nov. 11, 1927	Dies in Copenhagen, Denmark

Early Life

Wilhelm Ludvig Johannsen (pronounced "yoh-HAN-suhn") was born in 1857. The son of a Danish army officer, he credited both of his parents for helping him become a scientist. His punctual, orderly father gave him an interest in the material aspects of things, and his mother's love of plants and animals led to his fascination with nature. Wilhelm passed his qualifying examinations for the university at the age of fifteen, but his parents could only afford to send his older brother.

Johannsen was apprenticed to a pharmacist in 1872, passed his examination in 1879 with high honors, and continued his studies in botany and chemistry until he was appointed to the chemical department at Carlsberg Laboratorium in 1881. He gained initial fame and election to the Danish Academy of Sciences with his discovery that ether could be used to "awaken" plants from their winter dormancy. He also traveled to gain additional experience in plant physiology, and, by 1892, he was a lecturer in botany and plant physiology at the Royal Veterinary and Agricultural College in Copenhagen.

The Experimental Years

Johannsen began studying why the characteristics of self-fertilized plants such as barley (*Hordeum vulgare*) and the Princess bean (*Phaseolus vulgaris*) vary. He found that the average weight of seeds from parents and offspring were the same even when he had selected for heavier or lighter seeds. He introduced his concept of "pure lines" in 1903, the same year that he was promoted to professor.

Later that year, Johannsen read about the stability of inherited traits as demonstrated by Gregor Mendel and integrated these ideas into his theory of evolution. His textbook on heredity, *Arvelighedslaerens elementer*, was published in 1905. Johannsen was hired the same year at the University of Copenhagen, a move of which some peers disapproved because he lacked a university education. His increasing fame stifled the criticism.

Writer, Critic, and Historian

Johannsen expanded the above text in German, and it was published in 1909 entitled *Elemente der exakten Erblichkeitslehre*. In it, he introduced statistical methodology and the terms "gene," "genotype," and "phenotype." The book became the most influential genetics text in Europe.

By 1910, Johannsen was named *doctor honoris causa* in medicine. He no longer experimented but instead interpreted and synthesized current thought. He wrote a paper in 1914 entitled *Falske analogier*, in which he criticized the use of speculation and mysticism in biology. He also explored the history of genetics in the popular book named *Arvelighed i historisk og experimentel belysning* (1917).

Resting on His Laurels

Johannsen became rector of the University of Copenhagen in 1917 and received many additional academic honors from outside Denmark. He had originally regretted his lack of university training, but, looking back, he thought that it contributed to his originality. He used his gifts, including a superb memory, fluency, and wit, to make difficult concepts accessible to a broader audience.

Johannsen died in 1927 in Copenhagen at the age of seventy.

Johannsen (left) with William Bateson. (California Institute of Technology)

Bibliography

By Johannsen

Laerebog i plantefisiologi med henblik paa plantedyrkningen, 1892 (textbook on plant physiology with special reference to plant cultivation)

Om arvelighed og variabilitet, 1896 (on heredity and variation)

Das Aether-Verfahren beim Frühtreiben mit besonderer Berücksichtigung der Fliedertreiberei, 1900 (the ether process)

Über Erblichkeit in Populationen und in reinen Linien, Ein Beitrag zur Beleuchtung schwebender Selektionsfragen, 1903 ("Concerning Heredity in Populations and in Pure Lines" in *Selected Readings in Biology for Natural Sciences 3*, 1955)

Arvelighedslaerens elementer: Forelasninger holdte ved Kobenhavns universitet, 1905 (elements of heredity)

Elemente der exakten Erblichkeitslehre, 1909 (elements of an exact science of heredity)

Falske analogier, med henblik paa lighed, slaegtskab, arv, tradition og udvikling, 1914 (false analogies)

Genotype Versus Phenotype

The external appearance of an individual organism (phenotype) is distinguished from the genetic material inherited from its parents (genotype).

Johannsen was the first to divide variation into two components. He studied "pure lines," or all individual plants descended from a single self-fertilized individual, in order to determine whether offspring selected for smaller or larger seed weights would vary significantly from parents. He found no difference between the averages of the parental line and the averages of selected subpopulations of offspring.

Johannsen concluded that change could only result from inherited differences in pure lines. The differences among pure lines, the genotype, included all the genes in the fertilized egg. (He coined the term "gene" but refused to identify it physically.)

He recognized that the genotype interacted with the environment to produce external characteristics, but his first definition of phenotype referred to the population average of the distribution of variation. By the 1926 edition of his book *Elemente der exakten Erblichkeitslehre*, Johannsen had been influenced by Thomas Hunt Morgan's group working on the genetics of the fruit fly (*Drosophila melanogaster*), and he also applied his phenotype concept to the external traits of individual organisms, the contemporary meaning of the term.

The relationship between genotype and phenotype, and how phenotype is expressed and why it varies (phenotypic plasticity), are areas of ongoing research.

Bibliography
Genes V. Benjamin Lewin. Oxford, England: Oxford University Press, 1993.

"Phenotypic Plasticity and the Origins of Diversity." Mary Jane West-Eberhard. *Annual Review of Ecology and Systematics* 20 (1989).

The Selfish Gene. Richard Dawkins. 2d ed. Oxford, England: Oxford University Press, 1989.

Arvelighed i historisk og experimentel belysning, 1917 (heredity in the light of history and experimental study)

About Johannsen
"Johannsen, Wilhelm Ludwig." Leslie Clarence Dunn. In *Dictionary of Scientific Biography*, edited by Charles Coulston Gillispie. Vol. 7. New York: Charles Scribner's Sons, 1970.

The Mendelian Revolution. Peter J. Bowler. Baltimore: The Johns Hopkins University Press, 1989.

The Origins of Theoretical Population Genetics. Peter J. Bowler. Chicago: University of Chicago Press, 1971.

(Joan C. Stevenson)

Frédéric Joliot

Area of Achievement: Physics
Contribution: Joliot and his wife, Irène Joliot-Curie, were among the first to recognize and verify the existence of artificially induced radioactivity in otherwise nonradioactive elements.

Mar. 19, 1900	Born in Paris, France
1920	Enters the École Supérieure de Physique et de Chimie Industrielle to study engineering
1925	Joins the Institut du Radium of the University of Paris
1926	Marries Irène Curie
1930	Receives a doctoral degree from the University of Paris
1932	Conducts experiments leading to the discovery of the neutron
1934	Recognizes artificially induced radioactivity
1935	Receives the Nobel Prize in Chemistry jointly with his wife
1937	Appointed a professor of the Collège de France
1939	Performs experiments on the neutron bombardment of uranium
1942	Joins the Communist Party
1945-1950	Serves as high commissioner of the French atomic energy commission
1950-1958	Directs research at the Centre National de la Recherche Scientifique and at the Collège de France
1951	Awarded the Stalin Peace Prize
1956	Named director of the Institut du Radium's Laboratoire Curie
Aug. 14, 1958	Dies in Paris, France

Early Life

Frédéric Joliot (pronounced "zhoh-LYOH") was born in Paris on March 19, 1900, as the sixth and youngest child of Henri and Émilie (Roederer) Joliot. He was reared an atheist and had no religious involvement throughout his life.

Influenced by one of this teachers at the École Supérieure de Physique et de Chimie Industrielle, where he enrolled in 1920 to study engineering, he accepted a position as assistant to Marie Curie, head of the Institut du Radium, at the University of Paris, in 1925.

Curie's daughter, Irène, was also an assistant at the institute. They were married in October, 1926. In honor of the importance of Marie Curie's work with radioactivity and because Irène had no brothers to carry on the family name, the couple adopted the joint surname of Joliot-Curie. Together, they conducted experiments on radioactivity. Frédéric pursued studies at the University of Paris and received his doctorate in 1930.

Radioactivity and the Nobel Prize

Frédéric and Irène Joliot-Curie investigated the effects of radioactive particles emitted spontaneously from natural sources. At the time that the Joliot-Curies were undertaking their experiments, the entire field of radioactivity was relatively new. Little was known about radioactive emissions, their origin as subatomic particles and rays, and their effects on matter both inanimate and living.

One of their studies dealt with the effects of alpha radiation emitted from polonium as it was directed toward various chemical elements. They, and others, observed that secondary emissions came from the target elements. Although they did not pursue the investigation of these new radioactive emissions, other scientists correctly identified one of these emissions as consisting of a neutral subatomic particle that was soon named the neutron. Another component of these emissions was correctly identified by the Joliot-Curies as having properties analogous to those of the electron but with a positive charge. These particles were later identified by the term "positron."

Among the studies undertaken by the Joliot-Curies was the bombardment of aluminum with alpha radiation. The secondary emissions from the aluminum led them to conclude correctly that some of the aluminum atoms had been transformed into phosphorus atoms and that the heretofore unknown isotope of phosphorus was itself radioactive. They reported their results in January, 1934.

So significant was this discovery—the existence of stable artificially produced radioactive isotopes—that they jointly received the Nobel Prize in Chemistry the following year for the synthesis of radioactive elements.

The War Years
The Joliot-Curies pursued their research following receipt of the Nobel Prize. Now a pro-

Artificial Radioactive Elements

The incorporation of artificial radioactive substances into a variety of chemicals allows researchers to follow the changes that occur during manufacturing processes and in the human body.

Radioactivity is the emission of particles and/or energy rays from the nucleus of an atom. These particles were discovered in 1896 by the French chemist Antoine-Henri Becquerel. The race to isolate natural radioactive elements and studies to identify and characterize their emissions dominated science in the early part of the twentieth century. Irène and Frédéric Joliot-Curie contributed to this knowledge.

Using alpha particles from a natural radioactive source, they studied the effects of alpha bombardment on other substances. They bombarded a thin aluminum film with alpha radiation and observed secondary emission from the aluminum target that persisted even after the primary source of radiation had been removed.

Identifying these secondary rays as neutrons and positrons, they concluded that a transformation had occurred in which the atoms of aluminum had released neutrons from their nuclei, and what remained were atoms of phosphorus. Aluminum, with 13 protons and an atomic mass of 27, when struck by an alpha particle (containing 2 protons and an atomic mass of 4) dislodged a neutron (with a charge of 0 and an atomic mass of 1) and became phosphorus (with 15 protons and an atomic mass of 30).

More significant is that the phosphorus atoms themselves were radioactive, emitting from each of their nuclei a positron (with a charge of +1 and an atomic mass of 0). A relatively stable, artificially produced radioactive form of phosphorus had been made from an element that was not naturally radioactive.

For artificially induced radiations from elements to be achieved, the proper relation must exist between the energy of the incoming primary radiation and the binding energy of the protons and neutrons of the target material. If the protons and neutrons are tightly held in the nucleus of an atom, the penetrating primary radiation must have sufficient energy to dislodge them from one another. Present-day linear accelerators, cyclotrons, and synchrotrons provide energy beams over a wide energy range. With these instruments, it is possible to produce radioactive isotopes of many elements.

Artificial radioactive isotopes, when incorporated along with their nonradioactive forms, serve as tracers, allowing one to follow the path of a substance as it proceeds through various reaction pathways. For example, when radioactive iodine is injected into the human body, it accumulates in the thyroid gland and can be used to monitor the function of a healthy person or, with a larger dose, destroy unhealthy tissue.

Bibliography
Brighter than a Thousand Suns. Robert Jungk. New York: Harcourt Brace Jovanovich, 1958.
Radioisotopes and Radiation. John H. Lawrence, Bernard Manowitz, and Benjamin S. Loeb. New York: Dover, 1969.
"Scientists Honor Centennial of the Discovery of Radioactivity." Stu Borman. *Chemical & Engineering News* 74 (April 29, 1996).
World of Chemistry. Melvin D. Joesten, David O. Johnston, John T. Netterville, and James L. Wood. Philadelphia: Saunders College Publishing, 1991.

(The Nobel Foundation)

fessor at the Collège de France, Frédéric had the necessary laboratory facilities to study the production and effects of radioactive substances more thoroughly.

One of these studies dealt with the effects of neutron bombardment on uranium. It had recently been shown that slow neutrons striking an atom of uranium 237 split the atom into two smaller atoms of approximately equal atomic mass, freed additional neutrons, and released a tremendous amount of energy. In a few years, this discovery, the fission of uranium, would lead to the development of the atomic bomb.

Under the German occupation of France during World War II, the Joliot-Curies continued research not related to the war. Becoming increasingly concerned regarding the politics of war, Frédéric Joliot-Curie joined the Communist Party in 1942. He also became active in the French Resistance.

The Postwar Years

At the end of World War II in 1945, Frédéric Joliot-Curie convinced French president Charles de Gaulle of the importance of nuclear energy. As a result, France established the Commissart à l'Énergie Atomique (atomic energy commission), with Joliot-Curie as its high commissioner. As Cold War tension between the Western allies and the Soviet Union mounted, however, Joliot-Curie's ties with the Communist Party became a growing concern for the French government. Consequently, he was dismissed from his position as high commissioner in 1950, although his scientific research continued.

During this period, he also became active in various movements directed toward achieving world peace. He was instrumental in helping form the United Nations Atomic Energy Commission and the United Nations Educational, Scientific, and Cultural Organization (UNESCO) and was active in other world peace organizations.

Following the death of his wife in 1956, Joliot-Curie assumed her teaching duties at the Sorbonne and as director of the Laboratoire Curie de l'Institut du Radium. He died in Paris at age fifty-eight, from complications brought about by his long exposure to radiation, on August 14, 1958.

Bibliography

By Joliot

"Sur une nouvelle méthode d'étude du dépôt électrolytique des radio-éléments," *Comptes rendus hebdomadaires des séances de l'Académie des Sciences*, 1927

"Sur la nature du rayonnement absorbable qui accompagne les rayons alpha du polonium," *Comptes rendus hebdomadaires des séances de l'Académie des Sciences*, 1929 (with Irène Joliot-Curie)

"Un nouveau type de radioactivité," *Comptes rendus hebdomadaires des séances de l'Académie des Sciences*, 1934 (with Irène Joliot-Curie)

"Sur l'énergie des neutrons libérés lors de la partition nucléaire de l'uranium," *Nature*, 1939 (with L. Dodé, Hans von Halban, and Lew Kowarski)

"Sur la possibilité de produire dans un milieu uranifère des réactions nucléaires en chaîne

illimitée, 30 octobre 1939," *Comptes rendus hebdomadaires des séances de l'Académie des Sciences*, 1949 (with von Halban and Kowarski)
Textes choisis, 1959
Oeuvres scientifiques complètes, 1961 (with Irène Joliot-Curie)

About Joliot
"Frédéric Joliot." In *The Nobel Prize Winners: Chemistry*, edited by Frank N. Magill. Pasadena, Calif.: Salem Press, 1990.
Frédéric Joliot-Curie: A Biography. M. Goldsmith. London: Laurence & Wishart, 1976.
Nobel Laureates in Chemistry, 1901-1992. Laylin K. James, ed. Philadelphia: Chemical Heritage Foundation, 1993.

(Gordon A. Parker)

Irène Joliot-Curie

Areas of Achievement: Chemistry and physics

Contribution: Joliot-Curie and her husband created the world's first artificially produced radioactive elements. Their experiments in radioactivity enabled other scientists to discover the neutron and the positron. Her own experiments led to the discovery of nuclear fission.

Sept. 12, 1897	Born in Paris, France
1907-1909	Attends Marie Curie's private cooperative school
1914	Earns a baccalaureate degree from the Collège Sévigné
1914	Begins studies at the University of Paris
1914	Begins her service as an army nurse during World War I
1918	Becomes an assistant at the Radium Institute
1920	Passes licensing examinations in physics and mathematics
1925	Earns a doctorate from the University of Paris
Oct. 9, 1926	Marries Frédéric Joliot
1935	Shares the Nobel Prize for Chemistry with her husband
1936	Serves as France's Undersecretary of State for Scientific Research
1937	Named a professor at the University of Paris
1946	Named director of the Radium Institute
1946-1950	Serves on the board of directors of France's Atomic Energy Commission
Mar. 17, 1956	Dies in Paris, France

Early Life

Irène Joliot-Curie was born Irène Curie in Paris, France, on September 12, 1897. Her parents, Marie Sklodowska Curie and Pierre Curie, were known for their pioneering studies of radioactivity. Irène received her earliest education at home. In 1907, she began attending a small private cooperative school organized by her mother. In 1909, she began studying at the Collège Sévigné, from which she graduated with a baccalaureate degree in 1914.

Curie began studying at the University of Paris in 1914, but her education was soon interrupted by the outbreak of World War I. While serving as an army nurse, she set up X-ray equipment in military hospitals near the front lines.

When the war ended in 1918, Curie became

The Artificial Production of Radioactive Elements

Exposing nonradioactive elements to various forms of radiation can transform them into radioactive elements.

Radioactivity, or radioactive decay, was discovered near the end of the nineteenth century. It occurs when the nucleus of an atom is in an unstable state that causes it to release particles. The most common forms of radiation are known as alpha, beta, and gamma. Alpha radiation consists of helium nuclei, which contain two neutrons and two protons. Beta radiation consists of electrons or positrons. Gamma radiation consists of photons.

The first two elements studied as sources of natural radioactivity were uranium and thorium. Marie and Pierre Curie discovered the naturally occurring radioactive elements radium and polonium in 1898.

Irène and Frédéric Joliot-Curie created the first artificially produced radioactive elements in 1933. They placed a sample of aluminum next to a sample of polonium. The polonium released alpha particles. The aluminum atoms absorbed these particles and immediately released neutrons. After a few minutes, they released positrons. Chemical tests revealed the exact nature of the transformation taking place.

The nucleus of a normal, nonradioactive aluminum atom consists of thirteen protons and fourteen neutrons. When it absorbs an alpha particle, one of the two new neutrons is ejected immediately. The nucleus then has fifteen protons and fifteen neutrons. The added protons transform the aluminum atom into a phosphorus atom. Unlike an ordinary, nonradioactive phosphorous atom, which contains fifteen protons and sixteen neutrons, this atom is radioactive.

In a few minutes, the unstable nucleus releases a positron, which transforms one of the protons into a neutron. The nucleus then contains fourteen protons and sixteen neutrons. The loss of a proton transforms the radioactive phosphorus atom into a nonradioactive silicon atom. In a similar experiment, the Joliot-Curies transformed nonradioactive boron into radioactive nitrogen, which underwent radioactive decay into nonradioactive carbon.

The half-life of a radioactive element is the amount of time required for half of the atoms in a sample to undergo radioactive decay. Naturally occurring radioactive elements have long half-lives, up to billions of years or more. (If they did not, they would have decayed into nonradioactive elements long ago.) Artificially produced radioactive elements may have very short half-lives. The radioactive phosphorus produced by the Joliot-Curies, for example, had a half-life of about three and one-half minutes.

Certain artificially produced radioactive elements have important applications in medicine. Like ordinary iodine, artificially produced radioactive iodine is absorbed by the thyroid and is used to produce images of this gland. Artificially produced radioactive phosphorus, like ordinary phosphorus, is absorbed by cancer cells to a greater degree than by normal cells. It is used to produce images of cancerous tumors.

Bibliography

Introduction to Nuclear Reactions. G. R. Satchler. New York: John Wiley & Sons, 1980.
The Physics of Nuclear Reactions. W. M. Gibson. Oxford, England: Pergamon Press, 1980.
Transmutation, Natural and Artificial. Thaddeus J. Trenn. London: Heyden, 1981.

an assistant at the Radium Institute, directed by her mother. She passed licensing examinations in physics and mathematics in 1920. In 1921, she began studying the release of alpha radiation from polonium. For this research, she earned a doctorate from the University of Paris in 1925.

The Neutron and the Positron

In 1926, Irène Curie married Frédéric Joliot, who had joined the Radium Institute in 1925; they both changed their surname to "Joliot-Curie." The Joliot-Curies began studying a new kind of radiation produced by exposing light elements such as boron and beryllium to alpha radiation. When paraffin was exposed to this new radiation, protons were ejected at high velocity. The Joliot-Curies thought that the new radiation was a form of gamma radiation. In 1931, the British physicist Sir James Chadwick discovered that it actually consisted of previously unknown particles called neutrons.

Irène and Frédéric Joliot-Curie began using neutron radiation in their studies of cloud chambers. A cloud chamber contains a vapor that condenses into drops of liquid when particles pass through it. They discovered a trail of drops left by a strange new particle. The American physicist Carl David Anderson discovered that this particle was identical to an electron, but with a positive charge rather than a negative charge. The new particle, now known as a positron, was the first known example of an antimatter particle.

Artificial Radioactivity and Nuclear Fission

In 1933, the Joliot-Curies noted that when aluminum was exposed to alpha radiation, it emitted neutrons and positrons. When the source of alpha radiation was removed, the neutron radiation stopped but the positron radiation remained. This indicates that the aluminum had been transformed into a source of positrons. A chemical test proved that the nonradioactive aluminum atoms had been

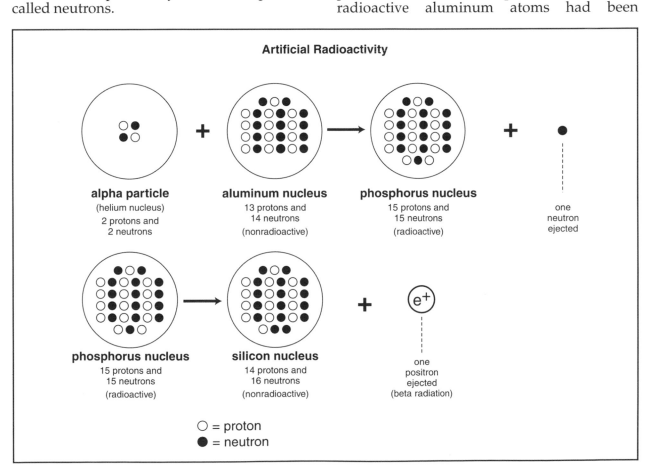

Artificial Radioactivity

alpha particle
(helium nucleus)
2 protons and
2 neutrons

aluminum nucleus
13 protons and
14 neutrons
(nonradioactive)

phosphorus nucleus
15 protons and
15 neutrons
(radioactive)

one
neutron
ejected

phosphorus nucleus
15 protons and
15 neutrons
(radioactive)

silicon nucleus
14 protons and
16 neutrons
(nonradioactive)

one
positron
ejected
(beta radiation)

○ = proton
● = neutron

(The Nobel Foundation)

changed into radioactive phosphorus atoms. For their discovery of artificial radioactivity, the Joliot-Curies shared the Nobel Prize for Chemistry in 1935.

After this triumph, Irène and Frédéric Joliot-Curie began separate careers. Frédéric was appointed a professor at the Collège de France in 1937. Irène was appointed a professor at the University of Paris and continued to work at the Radium Institute.

Irène Joliot-Curie also found time to play an active role in politics. She fought the rise of fascism in Europe by joining the Socialist Party in 1934 and the Vigilance Committee of Anti-Fascist Intellectuals in 1935 and by supporting the Republicans in the Spanish Civil War (1936-1939). From June to September, 1936, she served as Undersecretary of State for Scientific Research in the Popular Front government (a coalition of antifascist political parties) of Léon Blum, the first Socialist premier of France.

In 1938, Joliot-Curie studied the effect of neutron radiation on uranium. She believed that the uranium would absorb neutrons and be transformed into a new, heavier element. Instead, she found evidence that the lighter element lanthanum was present.

The German chemists Otto Hahn and Fritz Strassman repeated her experiments and discovered that the element barium was present also. German physicist Lise Meitner was able to explain these results when she realized that uranium atoms had split apart into lanthanum and barium atoms, a process known as nuclear fission.

World War II and Afterward

During the German occupation of France, from 1940 to 1944, in World War II, the Joliot-Curies remained to continue their research. In 1944, Frédéric went into hiding in Paris, while Irène and their two children escaped to Switzerland. After the war, Frédéric was named high commissioner of France's Atomic Energy Commission.

In 1946, Irène began serving on the board of directors of the commission. The same year, she was named director of the Radium Institute. In 1950, the Joliot-Curies were removed from the commission because of their leftist politics. Irène Joliot-Curie died of leukemia, probably caused by years of exposure to radiation, on March 17, 1956.

Bibliography
By Joliot-Curie
"Sur la vitesse d'émission des rayons alpha du polonium," *Comptes rendus hebdomadaires des séances de l'Académie des Sciences*, 1922

"New Evidence for the Neutron," *Nature*, 1932 (with Frédéric Joliot-Curie)

"Contributions à l'étude des électrons positifs," *Comptes rendus hebdomadaires des séances de l'Académie des Sciences*, 1933 (with Joliot-Curie)

"Production artificielle d'éléments radioactifs," *Journal de physique*, 1934 (with Joliot-Curie)

Les Radioéléments naturels: Propriétés chimiques, préparation, dosage, 1946

Oeuvres de Marie Sklodowska-Curie, 1954 (as editor)

Oeuvres scientifiques complètes, 1961 (with Joliot-Curie)

About Joliot-Curie
Nobel Prize Women in Science. Sharon Bertsch McGrayne. New York: Carol, 1993.
Women in Chemistry and Physics. Louise Grinstein, Rose K. Rose, and Miriam H. Rafailovich, eds. Westport, Conn.: Greenwood Press, 1993.
Women of Science: Righting the Record. G. Kass-Simon and Patricia Farnes, eds. Bloomington: Indiana University Press, 1990.

(Rose Secrest)

Brian D. Josephson

Area of Achievement: Physics

Contribution: While still a graduate student, Josephson described supercurrents in the thin barrier region sandwiched between two superconductors. This theory fostered studies of the complexity of superconducting behavior.

Jan. 4, 1940	Born in Cardiff, Glamorgan, Wales
1962	Becomes a junior research fellow at Trinity College, Cambridge University
1964	Receives a Ph.D. from Cambridge
1965-1966	Serves as research assistant professor at the University of Illinois
1967	Becomes assistant director of research at Cambridge
1973	Wins the Nobel Prize in Physics, jointly with Leo Esaki and Ivar Giaever
1974	Receives full professorship in physics at Cambridge
1980	Serves as one of several editors of *Consciousness and the Physical World*
1981	Publishes "Multistage Acquisition of Intelligent Behaviour"
1987	Publishes "Physics and Spirituality:The Next Grand Unification?"
1994	Coauthors "Music and Mind: A Theory of Aesthetic Dynamics"

Early Life

Brian David Josephson was born in Wales in 1940. Most of his academic career was spent at Cambridge University in England. As an undergraduate, he was noted for his scientific insight, readily pointing out to his superiors oversights in major scientific experiments.

Only twenty-two years old when he made the discoveries that ultimately led to the Nobel Prize in Physics, he was doing graduate work in experimental superconductivity.

One of the youngest Nobel laureates, Josephson shared the prize in 1973 with Leo Esaki and Ivar Giaever. All three had made advances in tunneling phenomena, validating earlier theories of superconductivity. The presenter of the award used the metaphor of a baseball occasionally penetrating a wall rather than bouncing back to explain how electrons tunnel through thin insulating barriers. Thus, because of their work, questions arose about normal perceptions of reality.

By the time he was thirty-three, Josephson was already growing dissatisfied with tradi-

tional physics. He believed that the greatest advance in contemporary physics was John Bell's 1965 theorem arguing on the basis of quantum mechanics that disconnected particles would continue to influence one another, even events in different parts of the universe. A reexamination of appropriate areas of research for the scientist, Josephson suggested, should consider conscious experience.

Expanding the Domain of Science

The restrictiveness of scientific orthodoxy concerned Josephson. In fact, he suggested that scientists were in danger of being too logical, of limiting reality to conventional definitions. He continued to study the relationship between consciousness and intelligence and to call for

Josephson Effect

Josephson predicted the traveling of supercurrents through a thin barrier between two superconductors. This theory led to experiments on superconducting devices, often resulting in technological innovations and new fields of physics.

As a student at Cambridge University, Josephson investigated superconductors, materials that at very low temperatures lose resistance to electric current. He calculated the results of inserting a thin barrier between two superconductors, discovering that the equations predicted a significant current would flow or tunnel through the barrier. Traditional quantum mechanical theory, an explanation of the behavior of subatomic particles, had indicated that no such flow would occur.

Unaccounted for in classical mechanics, the tunneling phenomena is a consequence of modern physics. After learning that supercurrents had been observed flowing through a thin barrier between superconductors, Josephson tried to observe the tunneling supercurrents himself. Discouraged by negative results, he tentatively planned to record them as unsuccessful in a chapter of his thesis. One of his mentors recognized that electrical noise had interfered with the observations, however, and cooperated with a fellow researcher at Bell Laboratories to prove the existence of tunneling supercurrents.

The Josephson effect has two aspects: Supercurrent flows even if no voltage is applied, and current passes through the barrier if constant voltage is applied. This discovery facilitated sensitive measurements of voltages and magnetic fields and made possible complex explorations of superconductors. In particular, Josephson recognized periodically varying supercurrents at a frequency related to the voltage between the two superconducting regions.

His discoveries helped advance technology in the 1980's, offering the possibility of high-speed switching circuits used in instrumentation and computers. In the late 1980's, the Josephson effect was used to build a high-speed oscilloscope several times faster than conventional ones. By recognizing the probability that particles may penetrate barriers previously considered to constrain them, Josephson helped revolutionize semiconductors and superconductors.

Bibliography

High Temperature Superconductivity: An Introduction. Gerald Burns. New York: Harcourt Brace Jovanovich, 1992.

The Path of No Resistance: The Story of the Revolution in Superconductivity. Bruce Schecter. New York: Simon & Schuster, 1989.

Superconductivity: Fundamentals and Applications. Werner Buckel. New York: VCH, 1991.

(The Nobel Foundation)

study of mystical experience and its incorporation into science.

A trip to the United States stimulated his growing interest in psychic phenomena. While in New York in 1971, he learned the transcendental meditation (TM) technique, advancing to a higher version of it in 1979. This philosophy, developed by Maharishi Mahesh Yogi, continued to influence Josephson's scientific research and his accepting the concept of the "Science of Creative Intelligence." Formulated by Maharishi, this view argues that living systems move toward an ideal under favorable conditions. It emphasizes consciousness and movement toward a goal.

As a result of his TM studies, Josephson rejected making decisions based merely on rational arguments. He sought greater spontaneity in human relationships by moving beyond the intellect. This process led him to attempts to substantiate a theory of intelligence, in part by studying children's acquisition of language skills. His psycholinguistic theory assumes that a child tunes into the brain, a channel-receiving programmed system with a pro-grammer known as God or Mind.

After the late 1960's, Josephson's publications explored broadening the scope of science to include inner experience. One of several editors of *Consciousness and the Physical World*, he participated in and commented on the symposium about consciousness and its relationship with intelligence. He concluded the edition by calling for the systematic study of mystical experience and its incorporation into science.

Music

Josephson's interest in unconventional methodology as a means of understanding intelligence led him in the 1990's to study music as a symbol system. In several coauthored publications, he drew parallels between music and deoxyribonucleic acid (DNA) as two informational systems. In comparing these elements, he evoked analogies between aesthetic processes and life processes. Music, a preexisting system according to Josephson, awaits discovery rather than invention.

Areas of Specialty

His early research in superconductivity prompted Josephson to question the dependence of science on empirical studies. Active in the Mind-Matter Unification Project at Cavendish Laboratory, Cambridge, he continued to explore science and mysticism, critical phenomena, and the theory of intelligence.

Bibliography
By Josephson
"Macroscopic Field Equations for Metals in Equilibrium," *Physical Review*, 1966
"Multistage Acquisition of Intelligent Behaviour," *Kybernetes*, 1981
"Physics and Spirituality: The Next Grand Unification?," *Physics Education*, 1987

About Josephson
"Josephson Computer Technology." *Physics Today* (March, 1986).
Nobel Prize Conversations. Norman Cousins, ed. Dallas: Saybrook, 1983.
The Omni Interviews. Pamela Weintraub, ed. New York: Ticknor & Fields, 1984.

(B. Christiana Birchak)

James Prescott Joule

Areas of Achievement: Physics, science (general), and technology

Contribution: Joule was among the last of the self-taught pioneers of science in the first half of the nineteenth century. His elegant experiments led to the confirmation of ideas on the kinetic nature of heat and of the representation of heat as a form of energy.

Dec. 24, 1818	Born in Salford, Lancashire, England
1834-1837	Privately educated at home in science and mathematics
1837	Publishes his first scientific paper, on electric motors
1840	Explores the heating effects of an electric current
1841	Publishes his work on electric batteries and the heating effect in *Philosophical Magazine*
1841	Gives his first public lecture on electric motors
1843	Measures the equivalence of heat and energy
1846	Elected Secretary of the Literary and Philosophical Society in Manchester, England
1847	Lectures to the general public on his views of energy conservation
1850	Elected to the Royal Society of London
1852	Collaborates with William Thomson (later Lord Kelvin) to verify experimentally the Joule-Thomson refrigeration effect
1875	Makes precision measurements of the mechanical equivalent of heat
Oct. 11, 1889	Dies in Sale, Cheshire, England

(Library of Congress)

Early Life

James Prescott Joule (pronounced "jewl") was born into a wealthy family of brewers on Christmas Eve, 1818, near Manchester, England. At that time, the thriving industries in the towns surrounding Manchester were factories, iron foundries, and spinning mills, all of which depended entirely on the steam engine for their source of power. During his boyhood, the rapid growth of railways involving new and more powerful engines, together with his knowledge of the steam engines in the family brewery, helped to promote in Joule a lifelong interest in mechanical energies.

Joule's early education in science and mathematics was undertaken privately by tutors, among whom was the eminent chemist John Dalton, best known for his work on the atomic theory of matter. Dalton's influence would prove to be critical in stimulating the youth's interest in the quantitative formulation of the physical sciences.

During his formative years, Joule was a constant close companion of his older brother, Benjamin. Together, they undertook several in-

The Mechanical Equivalent of Heat

Joule's belief that the caloric theory was incorrect led to a series of carefully planned experiments to show that heat is not a substance but a form of energy. His work would prove that mechanical energies can be converted to precisely equivalent forms of heat.

Until the latter part of the eighteenth century, many scientists ascribed to the caloric theory of heat, which proposed that heat was a fluid that could be transferred but not generated or destroyed. Joule set about to show that the expenditure of physical effort can lead to heat. He suspected that a unique quantitative relationship existed between the physical work done and the quantity of heat that would appear. In a series of careful experiments, he found the rate of exchange between heat and mechanical work, which became known as the mechanical equivalent of heat.

In his best-known experiment, Joule designed an apparatus that would cause a set of slowly falling weights to stir a container of water by means of a system of paddle wheels. The paddle wheels were kept in motion by the repeated raising of a set of weights. In each descent, the rope attached to the weights would slowly rotate the paddles, and so lose the precisely measured amount of gravitational potential energy, in foot-pounds, that had been given them by Joule when he lifted them. After the weights reached the floor, the paddles would be disconnected from the rope system so that stirring did not take place, and they were again lifted. The mechanism was then reattached, the weights would fall, and further stirring took place.

After many such repetitions, a tiny temperature rise in the water of just over 0.5 degree Fahrenheit was observed. The purpose of the baffles within the container was to ensure that the loss of the potential energy by the weights would not simply go toward speeding up the motion of the water, thus increasing its overall kinetic energy. The energy loss of the falling weights was converted directly into equivalent amounts of heat. Joule's accurate thermometers measured the small temperature rise of the water and so allowed the quantity of heat to be precisely determined.

Joule found that 778 foot-pounds of work were equivalent to 1 British thermal unit (Btu) of heat. Several other types of experiments were undertaken, and they too served to confirm the same equivalence. The current scientific name for energy units honors Joule: 1 calorie is equivalent to 4.18 joules of energy. Thus, heat was confirmed to be merely one form that energy can take.

In 1847, Joule made the proposal that within any closed system, the total amount of energy is always conserved. One of the most important and fundamental general principles of the physical sciences, this concept is known as the principle of energy conservation. It would remain unchanged until Albert Einstein's work in 1905 demonstrated that mass itself is yet another form of energy, that it too must be included in the energy balance equation. In the branch of theoretical physics that studies heat, this principle constitutes the first law of thermodynamics.

Bibliography

The Discovery of the Conservation of Energy. Yehuda Elkana. Cambridge, Mass.: Harvard University Press, 1974.

Introduction to Concepts and Theories in Physical Science. Gerald Holton and Stephen Brush. Princeton, N.J.: Princeton University Press, 1985.

Physics. Hans Ohanian. New York: W. W. Norton, 1989.

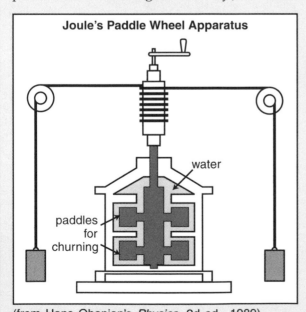

Joule's Paddle Wheel Apparatus

water

paddles for churning

(from Hans Ohanian's *Physics*, 2d ed., 1989)

formal scientific studies of weather, atmospheric electricity, and the power of electric batteries, in one experiment using them to explore the physical tolerance of a family servant to high-voltage electric shock.

Early Experiments
Joule's first experiments were done in the family brewery. Making use of his knowledge of the forces that come into play when electric currents are placed near magnets, Joule proceeded to develop prototypes of what would become the common electric motor. He believed initially that the efficiency of a well-constructed electric motor would far outshine its steam-driven counterpart but that the relative costs of battery components, when compared with the cheap common fuel source of coal, would probably not allow it to replace the steam engine.

In another early series of experiments, Joule explored the forces between conductors carrying electric currents, and he expressed his findings in mathematical forms.

Experiments on Heat
Before any recognition of a general principle of energy conservation for an interacting system of objects is possible, it is clearly important to identify the various forms that energy can assume.

In the nineteenth century, Newtonian mechanics had proven its worth in explaining many facets of the physical universe. One outcome of that successful Newtonian scheme was the notion of the "work" that forces can do on an object, which then may lead to an increase of what Gottfried Wilhelm Leibniz termed its *vis viva* (now called kinetic energy) as it speeds up, or of its potential energy if the force lifts it higher. Both concepts were of great interest to steam engine builders of the period.

Occasions arise, however, when forces are at work and neither kinetic energy nor potential energy appears to increase, such as when hands are rubbed together. Nevertheless, heat appears. Thus, the existence of a crucial ingredient in the operation of the steam engine, termed "caloric" and thought by many scientists to be a kind of weightless fluid, was proposed. It was believed that heat could only be passed on, as from fire to steam, but never created or destroyed.

Joule spent a large part of his scientific career conducting experiments that would prove the inadequacy of the caloric theory. If heat could be shown to be simply another form that energy can take, it might then be possible to conclude that the sum of a system's kinetic, potential, and heat energies will increase when some outside forces are at play but that, in a completely isolated system, the total energy would remain constant.

Joule's most important contributions to the general advance of science, the crucial experiments with which his name is immediately connected, were concerned with demonstrating that heat is a form of energy. This work would ultimately lead to the general idea of energy conservation.

Bibliography
By Joule
The Scientific Papers of James Prescott Joule, 1884-1887 (2 vols.)

About Joule
British Scientists of the Nineteenth Century. J. G. Crowther. London, England: Trubner, 1935.
Great Men of Science: A History of Scientific Progress. P. Lenard. New York: Macmillan, 1938.
James Joule: A Biography. Donald S. Cardwell. Manchester, England: Manchester University Press, 1989.

(David G. Fenton)

Percy Lavon Julian

Areas of Achievement: Chemistry and invention

Contribution: A classical synthetic organic chemist, Julian combined a talent for creating complex molecular structures with a solid sense of how chemical transformations occur.

Apr. 11, 1899	Born in Montgomery, Alabama
1920	Earns a B.S. in chemistry from DePauw University in Indiana
1920-1922	Teaches chemistry at Fisk University in Tennessee
1923	Earns an M.S. in organic chemistry from Harvard University
1923-1929	Teaches at West Virginia State College
1923-1929	Serves as department head at Howard University
1929	Awarded a Rockefeller Foundation General Education Fellowship
1931	Awarded a Ph.D. in chemistry from the University of Vienna
1932-1936	Conducts research at DePauw
1935	Marries Anna Johnson
1936	Joins Glidden as chief chemist and director of research
1950	Elected "Chicagoan of the Year"
1954	Establishes Julian Laboratories
1956	Publishes a paper on the synthesis of cortisone derivatives
1968	Awarded the Chemical Pioneer Award of the American Institute of Chemistry
1973	Elected a member of the National Academy of Sciences
Apr. 19, 1975	Dies in Waukegan, Illinois

Early Life

When Percy Lavon Julian was born in 1899, an intellectual career was virtually impossible for African Americans in Montgomery, Alabama, as there was no secondary school for black children. Julian later told of pressing his nose against the window of the chemistry laboratory of the all-white high school.

Julian's grandparents had been slaves; his grandfather's fingers were cut off as a punishment for learning to write. His grandmother sold produce on the streets so that his father could have more than the usual sixth-grade education. The dream of a college education for her son was realized by her grandson. All six children in the family obtained an education. Julian's brothers became doctors, and his sisters earned master's degrees. Julian always acknowledged his debt to his family.

Limited Opportunity

A private school for African Americans allowed Julian to complete high school in 1916; he was graduated at the head of his class. Julian was admitted to DePauw University in Greencastle, Indiana, where his grandmother had dreamed of sending his father.

His secondary education had been so weak, however, that Julian was admitted on the condition that he complete two years of high school courses along with his college program. This requirement was in addition to his need to earn a portion of his expenses. These additional requirements failed to hold Julian down. He was graduated in 1920 as class valedictorian and Phi Beta Kappa.

Yet, this sterling record was insufficient to allow him to pursue a Ph.D. Several universities tried to soften their rejection, claiming that they were actually trying to help him because neither industry nor academia would hire an African American with a Ph.D. They suggested that he teach at a black school, where he did not need a further degree.

Two years later, Julian earned a fellowship to study chemistry at Harvard University with E. P. Kohler. Even there, discrimination was evident: He was denied an assistantship because he was told that white students would refuse to take instruction from a black man.

(The Associated Publishers, Inc.)

The Synthesis of Large Molecules

Julian spent his career synthesizing organic molecules, such as physostigine or cortisone, to be used as medications.

One of the most exciting competitions of twentieth century organic (or carbon) chemistry was the effort to be the first person to synthesize a molecule of nature. Such a compound might have ten carbons, as in nicotine, or twenty-seven carbons, as in cholesterol. In addition to the degree of intellectual challenge, a molecule is usually selected for synthesis because of its medicinal properties.

Although many types of molecules have been prepared in the laboratory, the alkaloids and steroids generally grab the spotlight. The distinctive features of these compounds include rings of atoms, carbon for the steroids and both carbon and nitrogen for the alkaloids. Thousands of such compounds have been prepared.

The synthetic process begins with a molecule in which the exact sequence of atoms is known. It might be a small molecule consisting of a few atoms, but more often it is the large molecule related to the desired compound. In either case. the product is assembled step by step using chemical reactions that change the starting material in predictable ways.

At each step, it is essential to show that the new intermediate has the structure expected. The conclusion is reached when the synthetic material is shown to be identical to the natural substance in its chemical and physical properties.

Bibliography

Art in Organic Synthesis. Nitya Anand, Jasjit S. Bindra, and Subramania Ranganathan. 2d ed. New York: John Wiley & Sons, 1988.

Organic Chemistry. Marye Anne Fox and James K. Whitesell. 2d ed. Boston: Jones and Bartlett, 1997.

Organic Chemistry. Paula Bruice. Upper Saddle River, N.J.: Prentice Hall, 1995.

Foundation of a Career

In 1929, the Rockefeller Foundation awarded Julian a fellowship that allowed him to attend the University of Vienna. After teaching himself German, he worked with Ernst Späth and earned a doctorate in 1931. He found his lifelong interest in the synthesis of nature's complex molecules.

Julian returned to DePauw, where he made his greatest contribution to pure chemistry. He achieved the synthesis of physostigmine, an important drug for the treatment of the eye disease glaucoma. In 1935, he married Anna Johnson.

In spite of his growing scientific reputation, Julian was denied faculty positions at several colleges. In 1936, he joined the Glidden Company, where he became director of research. From 1954 to 1961, he managed his own firm, Julian Laboratories, exploring the scientific and practical importance of soybeans and discovering an inexpensive synthesis of cortisone. Sadly, even this recognition was accompanied by continued threats and attacks on him and his family.

Julian died in 1975 just after his seventy-sixth birthday. In 1992, he was honored on a U.S. postage stamp.

Bibliography
By Julian

"Studies in the Indole Series: I, The Synthesis of Alpha-Benzylindoles," *Journal of the American Chemical Society*, 1933 (with Josef Pikl)

"Studies in the Indole Series: V, The Complete Synthesis of Physostigmine (Eserine)," *Journal of the American Chemical Society*, 1935 (with Pikl)

"Studies in the Indole Series: XII, Yohimbine (Part 3)—A Novel Synthesis of the Yohimbine Ring Structure," *Journal of the American Chemical Society*, 1949 (with Arthur Magnani)

"The Chemistry of Indoles" (with Edwin W. Meyer and Helen C. Printy) in *Heterocyclic Compounds*, vol. 3., 1952 (Robert C. Elderfield, ed.)

About Julian

"Percy Julian, 1899-1975." James Michael Brodie. In *Created Equal: The Lives and Ideas of Black American Innovators*. New York: William Morrow, 1993.

"Percy Lavon Julian: April 11, 1899-April 19, 1974." Bernard Witkop. In *Biographical Memoirs of the National Academy of Sciences*. Vol. 52. Washington, D.C.: National Academy of Sciences, 1980.

"Percy Lavon Julian, 1899-   )." Louis Haber. In *Black Pioneers of Science and Invention*. New York: Harcourt, Brace & World, 1970.

(K. Thomas Finley)

Ernest Everett Just

Area of Achievement: Biology

Contribution: As a marine biologist, Just conducted pioneering research on invertebrate embryos and the physiology of development.

Aug. 14, 1883	Born in Charleston, South Carolina
1907	Earns a bachelor's degree in biology from Dartmouth College
1909	Joins the faculty of Howard University
1909	Spends the first of twenty summers as a researcher at the Woods Hole Marine Biological Laboratory
1915	Receives the first Spingarn Medal of the National Association for the Advancement of Colored People (NAACP)
1916	Earns a Ph.D. in physiology and zoology from the University of Chicago
1920	Elected a member of the American Association for the Advancement of Science
1920-1931	Named a National Research Council Rosenwald Fellow
1922	Given an honorary doctorate from South Carolina State College
1929	Named a visiting researcher at the Stazione Zoologica in Naples, Italy
1930	Serves as guest professor at the Kaiser Wilhelm Institute in Berlin
1938-1940	Lives in Europe
1939	Publishes *The Biology of the Cell Surface*
Oct. 27, 1941	Dies in Washington, D.C.

Early Life

Ernest Everett Just was born in Charleston, South Carolina, on August 14, 1883. His father died when Just was four years old, and his mother, Mary Cooper Just, reared him and his sister and brother while teaching school.

Determined that her eldest son would also become a teacher, she sent him to a boarding school in South Carolina at the age of thirteen and to the Kimball Union Academy in Meriden, New Hampshire. He excelled at both schools. Just entered Dartmouth College in 1903 as the only African American in the freshman class. He was graduated magna cum laude in biology in 1907.

Howard University and Woods Hole

A young African American scientist with a first-class college degree was a rarity in 1907, and Just was immediately hired by Howard University, an all-black institution in Washington, D.C. Eventually, he rose to full professor of zoology and physiology, becoming one of the university's most distinguished faculty members. In 1912, Just married Ethel Highwarden.

They had two daughters and a son.

In 1909, Frank Rattray Lillie, the director of the Marine Biological Laboratory at Woods Hole, Massachusetts, invited Just to spend the summer conducting research there. Just gladly accepted, not only because such opportunities rarely came to African Americans but also because time-consuming teaching responsibilities at Howard left him little time for his own work.

Just spent the next twenty summers at Woods Hole and earned an international reputation for his studies of marine embryos and his methods of capturing and preparing specimens. In 1916, he earned a doctorate in zoology and physiology from the University of Chicago.

As Just's interest in his research grew, his dissatisfaction with Howard University intensified. He felt overworked there, but no more prestigious university would employ African American professors. Instead, Just had to rely on grants from various foundations to support his work. In 1929, he also received funds for research in Italy. Just felt freer and more appre-

Fertilization and Parthenogenesis

The fertilization of an egg occurs when a sperm cell penetrates it, initiating a new organism, but some eggs can develop on their own, without being fertilized.

Just examined the eggs and embryos of marine organisms in greater detail than any scientist before him. Others had learned that fertilization requires an egg, or ovum, and a male cell, or sperm. When the sperm penetrates the egg wall, its genetic information mingles with that of the egg. The egg then divides, and a new organism begins to develop.

The ova of some plants and animals divide without sperm, a process known as parthenogenesis. This type of development starts with an external chemical or physical stimulus. One of Just's mentors, Jacques Loeb, found that he could artificially start parthenogenesis in sea urchins and frogs. He therefore concluded that the nucleus of the egg determined the organism's development. The presence of sperm, he thought, is

simply a biological trigger and is not even necessary.

Just's research led him to support the theory of his other mentor, Frank Rattray Lillie, who held that during fertilization, chemicals from both the sperm and the egg nucleus participate in launching cell division. Just also showed that different parts of the protoplasm surrounding the egg's nucleus play a part in development, whether begun by fertilization or by parthenogenesis.

Bibliography

Biology of Fertilization. Charles B. Metz and Alberto Monroy, eds. Orlando, Fla.: Academic Press, 1985.

The Expansion of American Biology. Keith R. Benson, Jane Maienschein, and Ronald Rainger, eds. New Brunswick, N.J.: Rutgers University Press, 1991.

Fertilization. Frank J. Longo. New York: Chapman and Hall, 1987.

(The Associated Publishers, Inc.)

ciated in Europe than in the United States. He returned several times during the 1930's.

A Scientific Expatriate

Just had received wide recognition in United States, but, kept from advancing to a higher academic position because of his race, he felt slighted and grew bitter. In 1938, he moved to France, intending to make it his home. He worked intensively there, although he had little money. In 1939, he published *The Biology of the Cell Surface*, the culmination of his life's research. The same year, he remarried. He and his second wife, Hedwig Schnetzler of Germany, had one daughter.

In 1940, Just was arrested and imprisoned by the Nazi occupiers of Paris. Although the U.S. government won his release and returned him to the United States, Just was already ill with cancer and died in 1941.

Bibliography
By Just
"Cortical Reactions and Attendant Physico-Chemical Changes in Ova Following Insemination" in *Colloid Chemistry*, 1928

"Hydration and Dehydration in the Living Cell: I. The Effect of Extreme Hypotony on the Egg of Nereis," *Physiological Zoology*, 1928

"Hydration and Dehydration in the Living Cell: II. Fertilization of Eggs of Arbacia in Dilute Sea Water," *The Biological Bulletin, Marine Biological Laboratory*, 1929

"Hydration and Dehydration in the Living Cell: III. Fertilization Capacity of Nereis Eggs After Exposure to Hypotonic Sea Water," *Protoplasma*, 1930

"Hydration and Dehydration in the Living Cell: IV. Fertilization and Development of Nereis Eggs in Dilute Sea Water," *Protoplasma*, 1930

"A Single Theory for the Physiology of Development and Genetics," *American Naturalist*, 1936

Basic Methods for Experiments on Eggs of Marine Animals, 1939

The Biology of the Cell Surface, 1939

The Cellular and Molecular Biology of Invertebrate Development, 1985 (with Roger H. Sawyer and Richard M. Showman)

About Just
Black Apollo of Science: The Life of Ernest Everett Just. Kenneth R. Manning. New York: Oxford University Press, 1983.

Blacks in Science and Medicine. Vivian Ovelton Sammons. New York: Hemisphere Publishing, 1990.

Distinguished African American Scientists of the Twentieth Century. James H. Kessler, J. S. Kidd, Renée A. Kidd, and Katherine A. Morin. Phoenix: Oryx Press, 1996.

(Roger Smith)

Heike Kamerlingh Onnes

Areas of Achievement: Invention, physics, and technology

Contribution: Kamerlingh Onnes was a pioneer in the field of low-temperature physics, being the first to liquify helium and the first to recognize superconductivity.

Sept. 21, 1853	Born in Groningen, the Netherlands
1870	Admitted to the University of Groningen
1872	Spends three semesters at the University of Heidelberg
1878	Appointed an assistant to the director of the Polytechnic School
1879	Awarded a Ph.D. from Groningen
1882	Appointed a professor and the director of the physics laboratories at the University of Leiden
1892	Builds a cascade-type gas liquefaction refrigeration device
1901	Founds the Society for the Promotion of the Training of Instrument Makers
1906	Creates liquid hydrogen
1908	Creates liquid helium
1911	Discovers superconductivity
1913	Receives the Nobel Prize in Physics for his work in low-temperature physics
1924	Demonstrates the unusual behavior of helium near 2.2 degrees Kelvin
Feb. 21, 1926	Dies in Leiden, the Netherlands

Early Life

Heike Kamerlingh Onnes (pronounced "KA-mehr-ling OHN-ehs") was born in the Nether-lands, in the city of Groningen, on September 21, 1853, as the son of the owner of a tile factory. His parents were fairly strict and taught him the values of diligence and patience.

In 1870, Kamerlingh Onnes began studies in physics and mathematics at the University of Groningen. After winning academic awards during his first two years, he studied for three years at the University of Heidelberg under Robert Bunsen and Gustav Kirchhoff. He then returned to Groningen and was awarded a Ph.D. magna cum laude in 1879.

Just before finishing his graduate studies, Kamerlingh Onnes was appointed assistant to the director of the Polytechnic School. He held this position for several years and became acquainted with the work of Johannes van der Waals. The molecular theory of matter that van der Waals had developed was to play a major part in Kamerlingh Onnes' research.

A Crossroads in Science

In 1882, at the age of only twenty-nine, Kamerlingh Onnes was appointed a professor and the director of the physics laboratories at the University of Leiden. As director of the physics laboratories, he stressed the importance of meticulous measurements. He ordered that the motto Door Meten tot Weten (through measurement to knowledge) be placed over every laboratory door. Kamerlingh Onnes helped to usher in the new era of science in which detailed quantitative measurements replaced qualitative studies.

Under his direction, the Leiden laboratories became a model for science laboratories of the twentieth century. He recognized that no longer would major scientific advancements be made chiefly in the laboratory of a single scientist working alone. Instead, scientific investigations were becoming complicated enough that many investigations would require teams of researchers and support staff working together. He encouraged an open door policy at his laboratories, inviting scientists from around the world to come and work with his researchers.

To assist the scientists under his direction, Kamerlingh Onnes worked to establish the Society for the Promotion of the Training of Instrument Makers in 1901. The society was charged with providing glass blowers and other instrument makers with the basic knowledge and skills to help construct the specialized instruments used by scientists in the laboratories. Instrument makers trained at Leiden soon became highly valued all over Europe.

The Liquefaction of Gases

In 1892, Kamerlingh Onnes constructed a cascade-type gas liquefaction device to supply liquid nitrogen and oxygen to his laboratories. This refrigeration unit used the principle of cooling in a series of stages, with the early stages cooling the gases that would be used in the next stages. This device would remain in operation for several decades.

By 1906, Kamerlingh Onnes had liquefied hydrogen, although he was not the first to do so. Helium, therefore, remained as the only known gas not to have been liquefied. Kamerlingh Onnes applied his understanding of van der Waals' work to estimate the temperature needed to liquefy helium. By 1908, Kamerlingh Onnes was the first to liquefy this gas, at a temperature of only a few degrees above absolute zero.

Superconductivity and the Nobel Prize

By 1911, Kamerlingh Onnes had shifted his research interests away from helium to the properties of other substances at low temperatures. In 1911, he discovered that the electrical resistance of mercury suddenly dropped below his ability to measure it at a temperature of 4.2 degrees Kelvin. In 1913, he announced that not only mercury but also tin and lead showed a sudden vanishing of resistance at low temperatures, and he coined the term "superconductivity" to describe this sudden drop of resistance.

In 1913, Kamerlingh Onnes was awarded the Nobel Prize in Physics for his work in low-temperature physics, including the liquefaction

Three tiny household magnets, joined by toothpicks, float over a dish filled with metal pellets cooled by liquid nitrogen. This effect has become the basic test for true superconductivity. (Lawrence Berkeley National Laboratory)

Superconductivity

Superconductivity is a state of matter existing primarily at very low temperatures in which electrical resistance vanishes.

Kamerlingh Onnes' interest in the electrical properties of matter at low temperatures came from suggestions from physicists Sir James Dewar and Lord Kelvin that electrical resistance decreases as temperature decreases. Kamerlingh Onnes found that at very low temperatures, however, the resistance stopped falling. He correctly interpreted this result as attributable to impurities in his samples. In 1911, he decided to study samples of mercury, a substance that he obtain in an extremely pure form.

As expected, the resistance of the mercury samples dropped with temperature, according to Dewar's predictions. Surprisingly, however, Kamerlingh Onnes found that at 4.2 degrees Kelvin, the resistance suddenly vanished below his ability to measure it. Later, he found other substances that suddenly lost resistance at a very low temperature that depended on the particular substance. This point is called the critical temperature. Kamerlingh Onnes, realizing that he had found a new state of matter, coined the term "superconductivity" to describe the sudden loss of resistance at low temperatures.

Initially, Kamerlingh Onnes hoped that superconductors could be used to create powerful electromagnets and to carry large electrical currents without resistive loss. Unfortunately, he found that superconductors reverted to ordinary conductors in the presence of even small magnetic fields or modest currents. The largest magnetic field in which a superconductor can exist is called the critical field, and the largest electrical current that a superconductor can carry is called the critical current. It was several years after Kamerlingh Onnes' death that a new type of superconductor was found that was able to handle larger currents and magnetic fields.

Although superconductivity was discovered in 1911, no one really understood the mechanism whereby superconductors achieved their remarkable properties until 1957, when John Bardeen, Leon N Cooper, and John Schrieffer proposed a theory, often called the BCS theory, that explains superconductivity. These scientists eventually received the 1972 Nobel Prize in Physics for their work on superconductivity.

The BCS theory states that electrons in the superconductor interact with each other, forming what are known as Cooper pairs. These pairs are temporary interactions between electrons that move through the superconductor in such a way that the total momentum of electrons in the material remains constant. Thus, no electrical energy is lost in electron collisions.

The biggest problem to be overcome in using superconductors was that they had to be kept near the temperature of liquid helium, which was difficult and expensive. In 1986, J. Georg Bednorz and Karl Alexander Müller announced that they had produced a ceramic material that had a superconducting critical temperature near 30 degrees Kelvin, far higher than any other superconductor, and suggested that even higher critical temperatures were possible. In 1987, Paul Chu fabricated a superconductor that had a critical temperature above that of liquid nitrogen. Bednorz and Müller received the 1987 Nobel Prize in Physics for their work.

Bibliography

Introduction to Superconductivity. A. C. Rose-Innes and E. H. Rhoderick. 2d ed. New York: Pergamon Press, 1978.

Matter at Low Temperatures. P. V. E. McClintock, D. J. Meredith, and J. K. Wigmore. Glasgow, Scotland: Blackie, 1984.

States of Matter. David L. Goodstein. New York: Dover, 1985.

of helium and the discovery of superconductivity. During his Nobel lecture, Kamerlingh Onnes correctly suggested that superconductivity may be related to the newly discovered quantization of energy.

Later Work

Kamerlingh Onnes never retired; he worked until his death in 1926. Shortly after 1920, he returned to his studies of helium and showed that the density of this gas peaked at 2.2 de-

Kamerlingh Onnes (left) with Johannes Diderik van der Waals. (California Institute of Technology)

grees Kelvin. He noticed other peculiar properties of helium at this temperature, but he died before he could complete his studies and announce the discovery of a phenomenon that would later be called superfluidity.

Bibliography
By Kamerlingh Onnes
"Algemeene theorie der vloeistoffen," *Verhandelingen der K. Akdemie van Wetenschappen*, 1881

"On the Cryogenic Laboratory at Leiden and the Production of Very Low Temperatures," *Communications from the Physical Laboratory at the University of Leiden*, 1894

"The Importance of Accurate Measurements at Very Low Temperatures," *Communications from the Physical Laboratory at the University of Leiden*, 1904

"Die Zustandsgleichung," *Communications from the Physical Laboratory at the University of Leiden*, 1912

"Untersuchungen über die Eigenschaften der Körper bei niedrigen Temperaturen, welche Untersuchungen unter anderen auch zur Herstellung von flüssigem Helium geführt haben," *Communications from the Physical Laboratory at the University of Leiden*, 1913

"On the Lowest Temperature Yet Obtained," *Communications from the Physical Laboratory at the University of Leiden*, 1922

Through Measurement to Knowledge: The Selected Papers of Heike Kamerlingh Onnes, 1853-1926, 1991 (Kostas Gavroglu and Yorgos Goudaroulis, eds.)

About Kamerlingh Onnes
The Path of No Resistance: The Story of the Revolution in Superconductivity. Bruce Schechter. New York: Simon & Schuster, 1989.

Pioneers of Science: Nobel Prize Winners in Physics. Robert L. Weder. London: Institute of Physics, 1980.

The Quest of Absolute Zero. Kurt Mendelssohn. 2d ed. New York: Halsted Press, 1977.

(Raymond D. Benge, Jr.)

Pyotr Leonidovich Kapitsa

Areas of Achievement: Chemistry, invention, physics, and technology
Contribution: Kapitsa discovered the superfluidity of helium and invented apparatuses for the liquefaction of helium and air. These achievements were of great significance both for industry and for theoretical physics.

July 9, 1894	Born in Kronshtadt, Russia
1918	Graduated from the Petrograd Polytechnic Institute
1921	Leaves for Cambridge, England
1923	Completes a doctorate under Ernest Rutherford
1924	Becomes assistant director of magnetic research at the Cavendish Laboratory
1925	Becomes a Fellow of Trinity College, Cambridge University
1929	Becomes a Fellow of the Royal Society of London and Corresponding Member of the Soviet Academy of Sciences
1930	Becomes the director of the Royal Society Mond Laboratory
1934	Detained in the Soviet Union
1935	Named director of the Institute for Physical Problems, Moscow
1938	Discovers the superfluidity of helium
1948	Dismissed from his position and placed under house arrest
1955	Reinstated as director
1978	Awarded the Nobel Prize in Physics
Apr. 8, 1984	Dies in Moscow, Soviet Union

Early Life

Nobel laureates ordinarily are known solely for their work. A few are known as much for the circumstances of their lives. Pyotr Leonidovich Kapitsa (pronounced "KA-pyiht-suh") is one of these individuals.

He was born in 1894, in Kronshtadt, Russia, to a general in the czarist army engineering corps and the daughter of a general. After secondary school in Kronshtadt, he received electrical engineering training at the Petrograd Polytechnical Institute. Upon his graduation in 1918, he stayed on as a lecturer.

In 1921, after his wife and two small children perished in the great influenza epidemic, Kapitsa left for Cambridge, England, and its Cavendish Laboratory, which was then headed by noted physicist Ernest Rutherford.

In Cambridge, England

Kapitsa and Rutherford developed a close relationship. After Kapitsa earned his Ph.D., Rutherford asked him to stay on at the Cavendish Laboratory.

Kapitsa began in nuclear physics at Cambridge, but soon his inclination toward engineering asserted itself. He set to work creating very strong magnetic fields, in order to investigate atomic properties, by sending much greater currents through the coil of his electromagnet than the coil could sustain—but for less time than it would take the coil to burn out.

His experiments with strong magnetic fields led to work at low temperatures, at which these strong fields could be achieved. The Royal Society of London provided funds to build a new laboratory, to be directed by Kapitsa, who was at the same time appointed a Royal Society professor.

Although a loyal Soviet citizen, Kapitsa put down roots in Cambridge. He married Anna Krylova, the daughter of a prominent Soviet mathematician, whom he met while on vacation in Paris. They had two sons.

In the summer of 1934, the Kapitsas went to the Soviet Union, as they had a number of previous summers. This time, however, they were not permitted to leave.

In the Soviet Union

Kapitsa refused at first to do any work in the Soviet Union. The government built him a laboratory and purchased his Cambridge ap-

Discoveries at Low Temperatures

Kapitsa's work was a combination of fundamental physics and the invention of devices.

Kapitsa's investigations with strong magnetic fields led to work in low temperatures because of the cooling necessary to produce the strong fields. He invented a method for liquefying helium in which gaseous helium expanded and moved a piston, dropping in temperature as a result. This method had not been employed for liquefying helium previously because lubricants would not function at the very low temperatures required. Kapitsa overcame this difficulty by allowing gaseous helium to leak into the piston housing and thereby act as the lubricant. The technique became the basis for the commercial Collins liquefier.

At low temperatures, he conducted studies of helium itself. He discovered the phenomenon of superfluidity, which is the loss of viscosity, or resistance to flow. It is analogous to superconductivity, which is the loss of resistance to the flow of electricity. At temperatures below 2.2 Kelvins, helium becomes a superfluid: It creeps out of its container by literally climbing the walls, a phenomenon unknown for ordinary fluids.

During World War II, Kapitsa contributed to the Soviet war effort by designing an apparatus to liquefy air in quantity. As the temperature is lowered, oxygen is the first constituent of air to liquefy. This apparatus then led to a method for obtaining pure oxygen, which is widely used in industry.

Bibliography

Landmark Experiments in Twentieth Century Physics. George L. Trigg. New York: Crane, Russak, 1975.

"Superfluidity." Eugene M. Lifshitz. *Scientific American* 198 (June, 1958).

(AP/Wide World Photos)

"premeditated sabotage of national defense." Only after Joseph Stalin's death in 1953 was he reinstated in his former position.

Throughout the rest of his life, Kapitsa was an outspoken critic of the Soviet government; he was one of its most prominent dissidents. In his seventies, he was finally allowed to travel outside the Soviet Union.

He was awarded the 1978 Nobel Prize in Physics for both his inventions and his discoveries in fundamental physics. Kapitsa died in April, 1984, a symbol of integrity.

Bibliography

By Kapitsa

Elektronika Bol'shikh Moshchnostei, 1962 (*High-power Microwave Electronics*, 1964)

Collected Papers of P. L. Kapitsa, 1964-1967

Peter Kapitsa on Life and Science, 1968

Fizicheskie zadachi, 1972

Eksperiment, Teoriia, Praktika, 1974 (*Experiment, Theory, Practice*, 1980)

About Kapitsa

Kapitza in Cambridge and Moscow: Life and Letters of a Russian Physicist. J. W. Boag, P. E. Rubinin, and D. Shoenberg, eds. New York: North-Holland, 1990.

Kapitza, Rutherford, and the Kremlin. Lawrence Badash. New Haven, Conn.: Yale University Press, 1985.

"Pyotr Kapitza, Octogenarian Dissident." Grace Marmor Spruch. *Physics Today* 32 (September, 1979).

(*Grace Marmor Spruch*)

paratus. When it became quite clear that he would not be released, Kapitsa commenced work in his custom-built Institute for Physical Problems.

In 1948, he was abruptly dismissed from his position and compelled to live under house arrest. Kapitsa had refused to cooperate on the Soviet atomic bomb project and was accused of

Jacobus Cornelius Kapteyn

Area of Achievement: Astronomy

Contribution: Kapteyn helped organize the systematic collection and cataloging of basic stellar data, and investigated the distribution and motions of stars in the system today called the Milky Way.

Jan. 19, 1851	Born in Barneveld, the Netherlands
1868	Enters the University of Utrecht
1875	Accepts a position at Leiden Observatory
1878	Appointed a professor of astronomy at the University of Groningen
1896-1900	Publishes *Cape Photographic Durchmusterung*
1904	Announces his discovery of "star streaming" at the International Congress of Science in St. Louis
1905	Takes a trip to South Africa with the Astronomical Society of the Atlantic
1906	Publishes *Plan of Selected Areas*
1919	Named a Fellow of the Royal Society of London
1921	Retires from Groningen
1922	Publishes "Theory of the Arrangement and Motion of the Sidereal System"
June 18, 1922	Dies in Amsterdam, the Netherlands

Early Life

Jacobus Cornelius Kapteyn (pronounced "kahp-TINE") was born into a large family in 1851 in Barneveld, the Netherlands, where his parents ran a boarding school. Young Kapteyn showed considerable intellectual promise,

passed the entrance examination for the University of Utrecht at the age of sixteen, studied physics and mathematics, and obtained his doctorate with a thesis on vibrating membranes.

In 1875, Kapteyn obtained a position at Leiden Observatory, and three years later he was appointed to a professorship in astronomy and theoretical mechanics at the University of Groningen. He married Elise Kalshoven in 1879; they had a son and two daughters, one of whom married the famous Danish astronomer Ejnar Hertzsprung.

Cataloging Stars

Kapteyn's primary contributions were in stellar astronomy. He was a meticulous and critical researcher who excelled in the careful analysis of data and strongly encouraged international scientific cooperation. Among his first major

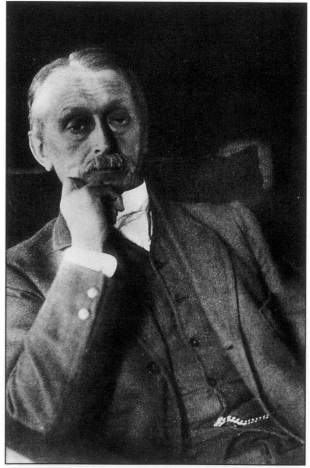

(Yerkes Observatory, University of Chicago)

The Rotation of Galaxies

The Galaxy is a somewhat flattened, rotating system of stars. Stars closer to the galactic center than the sun have higher orbital velocities, while stars further from the galactic center have lower orbital velocities.

A star's radial velocity, together with its proper motion and parallax, enables the star's space motion (with respect to the solar system) to be determined. Kapteyn carried out detailed statistical analyses of space velocities of stars in different directions. Such studies enabled him to determine that stellar motions are not random, but rather fall into groups, which he called streams.

It is now known that stars are in orbit about the center of the Milky Way. Stars generally in the direction of the galactic center (toward the constellation Sagittarius) have mean velocities somewhat different from those of stars generally in the opposite direction (toward the constellation Perseus). More recent studies have indicated that the differential rotation of the galactic disk is actually quite complicated. Nevertheless, stars in the galactic disk tend to move in more or less circular orbits about the galactic center as the galaxy rotates.

The situation is somewhat different for stars well above or below the galactic plane. These stars tend to move in much more eccentric orbits and at higher velocities.

Bibliography

Exploration of the Universe. George O. Abell, David Morrison, and Sidney C. Wolff. 6th ed. Philadelphia: W. B. Saunders, 1991.

Galactic Astronomy. Dimitri Mihalas and James Binney. 2d ed. San Francisco: W. H. Freeman, 1981.

Introductory Astronomy and Astrophysics. Michael Zeilik, Stephen A. Gregory, and Elske v. P. Smith. 3d ed. Philadelphia: W. B. Saunders, 1992.

accomplishments was the compilation, in collaboration with David Gill, director of the Royal Observatory in Cape Town, South Africa, of the *Cape Photographic Durchmusterung* (1896-1900). This was a catalog of photographic magnitudes and positions of more than 450,000 stars, down to the tenth magnitude, in the southern hemisphere, an extremely valuable (and accurate) reference work; it complemented the earlier *Bonner Durchmusterung* for northern hemisphere stars.

At the time when this catalog was being compiled, Kapteyn recognized the need for vastly increasing the quantity of other stellar data, such as radial velocities, proper motions, and parallaxes. In order to promote an organized, systematic approach, in 1906 he proposed to the international astronomical community a plan to concentrate work on 206 specific selected areas. This plan was largely accepted by the world's observatories, and soon considerable quantities of data were being collected for these selected areas.

The Stellar System: Structure and Dynamics

Another major effort of Kapteyn was the attempt to ascertain, from statistical analyses, the space density of stars (the number of stars per unit volume of space) and their luminosity function (the distribution of absolute magnitudes). This problem is complicated by the fact that observable quantities such as apparent magnitude and proper motion (angular motion against the background sky) are functions of distance. The conclusion of Kapteyn and his coworkers was that the local stellar system was a somewhat flattened spheroidal system (lens-shaped) more or less centered on the sun—the so-called Kapteyn Universe). It is now known that interstellar absorption by dust grains, especially near the galactic plane, seriously affects apparent magnitudes; the solar system is far from the center of the Galaxy.)

Continuing his statistical analyses of the motions of stars, Kapteyn found that the stellar motions are not random but rather form two different groups that he called star streams. It was later pointed out by his student Jan Oort that Kapteyn had, in fact, discovered galactic rotation. Kapteyn continued his studies of stellar dynamics and discovered the star with the second largest proper motion, now called Kapteyn's star, with an annual motion of 8.73 seconds of arc. He died in 1922.

Bibliography
By Kapteyn
Cape Photographic Durchmusterung, 1896-1900 (with David Gill)
Plan of Selected Areas, 1906
Contributions from the Mount Wilson Solar Observatory, 1920 (with P. J. van Rhijn)
"First Attempt at a Theory of the Arrangement and Motion of the Sidereal System," *Astrophysical Journal*, 1922
Mount Wilson Catalogue of Photographic Magnitudes in Selected Areas 1-139, 1930 (with F. H. Seares and van Rhijn)

About Kapteyn
"Jacobus Cornelius Kapteyn." Arthur S. Eddington. *Observatory* 45 (1922).
Kosmos. Willem de Sitter. Cambridge, Mass.: Harvard University Press, 1932.

(George W. Rainey)

Lord Kelvin (Sir William Thomson)

Areas of Achievement: Earth science, invention, physics, and technology
Contribution: Kelvin formulated the second law of thermodynamics. He contributed to most areas of physics and produced numerous inventions.

June 26, 1824	Born in Belfast, Ireland
1834	Begins study at University of Glasgow
1841	Enrolls at Peterhouse (St. Peter's College), Cambridge University
1841	Publishes his first scientific paper
1845	Graduated from Cambridge
1845	Takes a position at Henri-Victor Regnault's laboratory
1846	Becomes a chairperson at the University of Glasgow
1848	Recommends the adoption of an absolute temperature scale
1851	Presents the second law of thermodynamics
1854	Starts work on a telegraph
1865	Successful transatlantic submarine telegraph cabling is developed using his model
1866	Knighted
1890	Elected president of the Royal Society of London
1892	Created Baron Kelvin of Largs
Dec. 17, 1907	Dies at Netherhall near Largs, Ayrshire, Scotland

Early Life
William Thomson, later known as Lord Kelvin, was the son of James Thomson, a professor of

engineering, who taught William at home during his childhood in Belfast, Ireland. James Thomson accepted a professorship at the University of Glasgow in 1832, and William was enrolled at that university when he was only eleven. At sixteen, he won a medal for an undergraduate essay on the figure of the earth that applied principles of physics and mathematics, not geology. This foundational, analytic approach characterized his work thenceforth.

Under Professor William Meickleham and others, Thomson read and developed an appreciation for brilliant continental analysts such as Joseph-Louis Lagrange. At fifteen, he understood Joseph Fourier's theory of heat, the celestial mechanics of Pierre-Simon Laplace, and Lagrange's analytical mechanics. He mapped an attraction in an electric fluid problem into a heat flow problem, finding the behavior of these systems equivalent, which resulted in his first scientific paper.

At Cambridge University, he curtailed these deeper insights for a more rigid and rigorous pursuit of grades. Nevertheless, he kept abreast of continental analysis. Peterhouse was less rigid than other parts of Cambridge and accepted Thomson without a formal degree from Glasgow.

His tutor, William Hopkins, was the best mathematics coach at Cambridge, genuinely interesting to students, and understanding of Thomson's unique ability. Hopkins recognized that while Thomson was not the best at examinations, he had a broader, more analytic mind, capable of original thought. Thomson also met Sir George Gabriel Stokes, beginning a lifetime of numerous correspondences, with Thomson synthesizing and Stokes critically refining.

Paris: Experiments and Meetings
In 1845, Thomson was graduated from Cambridge. Seeing dismal job prospects, he went south, to Paris. In addition to a job, Henri-Victor Regnault's laboratory offered Thomson opportunities to experiment and learn of recent continental progress. Baron Augustin Louis Cauchy, Charles-François Sturm, and others were great sources of ideas, and meeting them proved enlightening to Thomson. He developed strong ties with the French mathematician Joseph Liouville.

In the discussions between Thomson and Liouville, the disparity between the models for electricity of Michael Faraday and of Siméon-Denis Poisson (and Charles-Augustin Coulomb) became a major point of interest. The result was a dissociation of the physical and mathematical aspects of these theories and their eventual unification. Thomson published these results in the 1840's, and they later influenced Scottish physicist James Clerk Maxwell.

Glasgow: Thermodynamics and Electricity
In 1846, Meickleham died, and Thomson returned to the University of Glasgow to accept his position in natural philosophy. Thomson's inaugural speech was on the age of the earth, a recurrent theme in his career. He soon applied his experiences in France to developing Great Britain's first academic laboratory. With university support, he continued his experiments and introduced students to laboratory meth-

(Library of Congress)

The Second Law of Thermodynamics

One modern formulation of the second law of thermodynamics states that, given any system, a function of the state of that system exists, termed entropy, that increases for irreversible systems and stays constant for reversible systems.

Lord Kelvin's original formulation of the second law of thermodynamics was needed to reconcile Sadi Carnot's models with those of James P. Joule and several contemporaries. Carnot's theory assumed, as an apparent requirement, that heat is a substance that can be neither created nor converted. Joule viewed heat as a mechanical effect or motion.

Carnot's principle on the motive power of heat basically describes the relationship between work produced and the measure of heat transferred from a subsystem of one temperature to another. One standard "heat engine" cited by Carnot involves a piston. A fixed amount of heat transfer produces a fixed amount of work. A substance transfer occurs, from a place of high heat density to a place of low heat density. Carnot's principle formally requires several conditions, such as returning to initial states and, for optimality, no heat "leaks."

Kelvin expressed the importance of Carnot's work but progressively refined it. He doubted the concept of heat as a substance; Joseph Fourier's work did not require it, and Kelvin disliked unnecessary axiomatic baggage. On the other hand, Joule assumed that the heat engine concept was simply an issue of matter, with forces operating and motion produced. To him, heat could be completely created or destroyed by mechanical systems, without dependence on heat flow from high to low density.

Kelvin started with Carnot's assumptions but scrutinized them. If a heat engine is to return to an initial state, the motion created must originate from the flow of heat. The flow producing the effect is still from high to low temperature. Kelvin then derived the equation for computing the maximum effect from this flow, which could be achieved only by a perfect engine. From his observations, heat (and thus perfection) would be lost, a fraction dissipating into the system and environment. Later, he modeled a second type of perpetual motion machine and demonstrated this principle by its impossibility. The state of entropy was produced, in which the unavailable energy in a closed thermodynamic system varies directly with a change in heat and inversely with a change in absolute temperature. In its production, the difference between cause and effect in irreversible reactions of the heat engine was absorbed.

The entropy principle, when coupled with the conservation principle (the first law of thermodynamics), sets the framework for much research in physics and engineering. The wonder of air-conditioning is only one area that benefited from this analysis.

Bibliography
Thermodynamics for Chemists. Samuel Glasstone. Huntington, N.Y.: Krieger, 1972.
Thermodynamics for Chemists and Biologists. Terrell L. Hill. Reading, Mass.: Addison-Wesley, 1968.
Thermodynamics I: An Introduction to Energy. John R. Dixon. Englewood Cliffs, N.J.: Prentice Hall, 1975.
Thermodynamics: Principles and Applications. Frank C. Andrews. New York: Wiley-Interscience, 1971.

ods. In 1848, he recommended the adoption of an absolute temperature scale for scientific work, which is called the Kelvin scale.

James P. Joule's work in thermodynamics interested Thomson. While on the continent and studying Regnault's work on steam, he was exposed to Sadi Carnot's work on heat. Carnot had died in 1832 with a small part of his life's work published as a short document. Thomson learned of Carnot's research from intermediate sources and, in applying it in the late 1840's, introduced its true importance to the world.

Twenty years later, Carnot's brother published a second edition of Carnot's monograph that includes many of the previously excluded notes and examples. In 1851, Thomson formulated the second law of thermodynamics as part of a paper on heat production and the conservation of energy. Thomson again unified two approaches, those of Carnot and Joule.

Telegraphy and Marine Instruments

From his work at Regnault's laboratory, one of Thomson's lifelong goals was the continual development of precise instruments of measurement. In numerous papers starting in 1854, he presented principles and refinements for making the transatlantic telegraph possible. Public fame followed, yet he remained industrious and humble. His paper on signal delay predicted problems in early disastrous attempts at telegraph cabling.

Thomson also invented the mariner's compass, mirror galvanometers, siphon recorders, cable stranding, high-quality transmission cable, and many other electronic devices for detecting and measuring. Among other marine tools, he constructed sonic depth, tidal, and marine positional apparatuses and methodologies. He was both theoretician and experimentalist.

Later Years

Sir William Thomson, having been knighted in 1866, received the title of Baron Kelvin of Largs in 1892, in honor of his service as the most productive scientist and inventor of the British Empire. He remained active throughout his life, publishing several papers in his final year, and some of his research was published posthumously.

After a lifetime of more than three hundred papers and many more correspondences, Lord Kelvin died in 1907 and joined Sir Isaac Newton, Sir John Herschel, and the other great physicists who are buried in Westminster Abbey.

Bibliography

By Kelvin

Reprint of Papers on Electrostatics amd Magnetism, 1872

Mathematical and Physical Papers, 1882-1911 (6 vols.)

Popular Lectures and Addresses, 1889-1894 (3 vols.)

About Kelvin

Energy and Empire. Crosbie Smith and Norton Wise. Cambridge, England: Cambridge University Press, 1989.

Lord Kelvin. Andrew Gray. New York: Chelsea House, 1973.

Lord Kelvin and the Age of the Earth. Joe D. Burchfield. New York: Science History Publications, 1975.

Lord Kelvin: The Dynamic Victorian. Harold Sharlin. University Park: Pennsylvania State University Press, 1979.

(John Panos Najarian)

Edward Calvin Kendall

Areas of Achievement: Chemistry and physiology

Contribution: Kendall discovered the thyroid hormone thyroxine and the adrenal steroid cortisone.

Mar. 8, 1886	Born in South Norwalk, Connecticut
1908	Earns a B.S. in chemistry from Columbia University, New York
1909	Earns an M.S.
1909-1910	Named a Goldschmidt Fellow at Columbia
1910	Receives a Ph.D.
1910-1911	Works as a research chemist at Parke, Davis, in Detroit
1911-1914	Works in the chemical pathology laboratory at St. Luke's Hospital, New York
1914	Becomes head of biochemistry at the Mayo Clinic, in Rochester, Minnesota
1914	Isolates thyroxine from animal thyroid tissue
1915	Marries Rebecca Kennedy
1921-1951	Teaches physiological chemistry at the Mayo Foundation and the University of Minnesota
1949	Discovers the clinical value of cortisone
1950	Awarded the Nobel Prize in Physiology or Medicine
1951	Named professor emeritus at Mayo, research professor at Princeton University, and visiting researcher at Merck and Co.
1951	Receives an honorary Sc.D. from Columbia
May 4, 1972	Dies in Princeton, New Jersey

Early Life

Edward Calvin Kendall's family was professional: His father was a dentist, and his uncles were a physician and a clergyman. He was directed away from his first interest, physics, and into chemistry by his high school chemistry teacher in Stamford, Connecticut. At Columbia University, Kendall demonstrated the wisdom of this choice.

After the statutory year of commercial research at Parke, Davis, and Co. in Detroit, Kendall moved to a clinical position at St. Luke's Hospital in New York City. After three years, however, he decided that he preferred the laboratory setting of the Mayo Clinic in Rochester, Minnesota.

Research Years

His choice proved out quickly. Within his first year at the Mayo Clinic, working with abundant thyroid tissue from midwestern slaughterhouses, he isolated crystalline thyroxine, the iodine-rich hormone necessary for oxidation of the energy-producing small mole-

Kendall and his wife return to the United States in 1951 following his lecture tour in Great Britain. (AP/Wide World Photos)

The Discovery of Thyroxine and Cortisone

The metabolic hormone thyroxine and the clinical agent cortisone were discovered and isolated by essentially the same laboratory methods. Although thyroxine is a valuable drug in hypothyroidism, cortisone commanded the attention of the Nobel Prize committee because of its dazzling array of therapeutic applications.

Natural product compounds, plant or animal, are isolated and purified according to procedures that vary in detail but are alike in broad outline. The source is ground up and extracted with water, water solutions, or solvents. The resulting solutions are separated into fractions by methods including chromatography or fractional distillation.

When a fraction is shown to contain a single component, that substance is induced to crystallize as a means of final purification. The crystalline product is examined both physically and chemically and is sometimes evaluated clinically, after which the long, arduous process of determining its structure is undertaken.

Up to this point, the isolation of thyroxine and cortisone is highly similar except for the starting materials—thyroid and adrenal tissue, respectively. The difference lies in the applications that Kendall, working at the Mayo Clinic, was so well equipped to explore in depth. Thyroxine is a metabolism booster; it counteracts the effects of hypothyroidism, such as lethargy, obesity, and mental slowness. This is its only medical use; as such, it must be taken on a lifelong basis.

The steroid cortisone, on the other hand, is a short-term therapeutic, used to treat a range of conditions. When symptoms are alleviated, treatment is discontinued because, among other reasons, overtreatment can result in psychic disturbances, irreversible eye disorders, and other undesirable side effects. What distinguishes cortisone is its broad range of applications and its mode of action: It does not merely maintain metabolic functions; it actively attacks dysfunctions. This is the property that was recognized by the Nobel Prize committee and that captured the popular imagination, making cortisone appear to be an instant panacea.

Bibliography
"Edward Calvin Kendall." Dwight Ingle. *Biographical Memoirs of the National Academy of Sciences* 47 (1975).
"Edward Calvin Kendall, Philip Showalter Hench, Tadeus Reichstein." Theodore L. Sourkes. In *Nobel Prize Winners in Medicine and Physiology, 1901-1965*. London: Abelard-Schuman, 1966.

cules produced by digestion in the mammalian body. For a decade or more, he tried to determine the chemical structure of thyroxine, but he was "scooped" in 1926 by C. R. Harington in England.

After a few years spent isolating and determining the structure of the tripeptide yeast enzyme glutathione, Kendall turned to extracts of the adrenal cortex, a gland associated with the kidneys whose secretions were known to be related to animal metabolism. During the 1930's and 1940's, Kendall (as well as Tadeus Reichstein in Switzerland) isolated and demonstrated the structures of six hormones that Kendall called "Compound A" through "Compound F." These were of little clinical interest until Philip Showalter Hench tried Compound E in the treatment of rheumatoid arthritis.

The effects were dramatic, and Compound E, renamed cortisone, quickly found applications in the treatment of rheumatic fever, allergies, skin and eye inflammations, various blood diseases, ulcerative colitis, Addison's disease, and hypopituitarism. This finding led to the 1950 Nobel Prize in Physiology or Medicine for Kendall, Hench, and Reichstein.

Later Life
After Kendall retired from the Mayo Clinic in 1951, he continued his research activities at Princeton University and at the academically minded Merck and Co. in nearby Rahway, New Jersey. He received an enormous number of medals and awards over his professional lifetime, including seven honorary doctorates in addition to one from Columbia. Kendall died in 1972 at the age of eighty-six.

Bibliography

By Kendall

Influence of the Thyroid Gland on Oxidation in the Animal Organism, 1925
Oxidative Catalysis, 1927
Thyroxine, 1929
Cortisone: Memoirs of a Hormone Hunter, 1971

About Kendall

"Edward Calvin Kendall." Robert M. Hawthorne, Jr. In *American Chemists and Chemical Engineers*, edited by Wyndham D. Miles and Robert F. Gould. Guilford, Conn.: Gould Books, 1994.
"Edward Calvin Kendall, Ph.D., Sc.D., 1886-   ." Leonard G. Rowntree. In *Amid Masters of Twentieth Century Medicine*. Springfield, Ill.: Charles C Thomas, 1958.
"Kendall, Edward Calvin." In *Dictionary of Scientific Biography*, edited by Charles Coulston Gillispie. Vol. 15. New York: Charles Scribner's Sons, 1970.

(Robert M. Hawthorne, Jr.)

John Cowdery Kendrew

Areas of Achievement: Biology and chemistry

Contribution: Kendrew determined the three-dimensional structure of the protein myoglobin, which earned for him the Nobel Prize in Chemistry.

Mar. 24, 1917	Born in Oxford, England
1939	Earns a B.A. from Trinity College, Cambridge University
1939-1945	During World War II, develops radar for the British Ministry of Aircraft Production and serves as scientific adviser for the air commander in chief for Southeast Asia
1943	Receives an M.A. from Cambridge
1949	Receives a Ph.D. under J. H. Taylor at the Cavendish Laboratory
1949-1957	Investigates the structure of myoglobin using X-ray diffraction
1954-1968	Serves as Reader at the Davy-Faraday Laboratory, Royal Institution, London
1958	Publishes a paper on myoglobin structure in *Nature*
1959-1987	Founds and acts as editor in chief of *Journal of Molecular Biology*
1962	Receives the Nobel Prize in Chemistry with Max Perutz
1962-1975	Serves as deputy chair of the Laboratory for Molecular Biology
1975-1982	Founds and acts as director general of the European Molecular Biology Laboratory in Heidelberg, Germany
1981-1987	Serves as president of St. John's College, Oxford

Early Life

John Cowdery Kendrew was the only child of a climatologist and an art historian at Oxford University; his childhood was spent in an academic atmosphere. He attended English public (that is, preparatory) schools, and he chose Cambridge University for the study of chemistry, with time out for service in World War II, before he did his final graduate work.

His thesis work compared the structures of fetal and adult hemoglobin, which gave him experience with X-ray crystallography but no major structural conclusions. Kendrew chose myoglobin for a serious study of structure because it is about one-quarter the size of hemoglobin, which Max Ferdinand Perutz had already begun to study, and because it was relatively plentiful, being an oxygen-retention molecule found in the blood and muscles of whales.

Myoglobin Research

Little was known about the detailed structure of proteins when Kendrew and Perutz began their separate work. It was clear that the protein molecule, of whatever type or source, was made up of small molecules called amino acids, twenty different ones, and that these were hooked together head-to-tail in a single unbranched chain, containing from eight or ten to many thousands of amino acids. (Myoglobin contains about four hundred.) It was also known that the chains assumed secondary structures, possibly helices (pleated sheets) and what appeared to be amorphous masses.

Kendrew and his coworkers tackled the structure problem using X-ray diffraction. This technique can be compared to beaming a strong light through a lattice of regularly spaced, shiny Christmas-tree balls (representing atoms); photographing the spots of light reflected off balls in the lattice; and calculating where the balls had to be, based on the pictures thus obtained.

This process took about nine years, and the results were so important that the Nobel Prize in Chemistry went to Kendrew and Perutz in 1962—the same year that the prize for determining the double-helix structure of deoxyri-

---

Determining Myoglobin Structure Through X-Ray Crystallography

Myoglobin was found to consist of a large, flat, nitrogen-containing heme molecule that holds oxygen, attached to protein chains that limit heme access to oxygen.

The first problem for Kendrew in determining the structure of myoglobin was obtaining the perfect crystals necessary for clean X-ray diffraction pictures. Finding the right crystallization conditions for myoglobin took many months.

The next problem was taking X-ray images that made sense. The first runs, on the myoglobin molecule itself, produced diffraction patterns in which the three-dimensional positions of the atoms could not be ascertained. Only when a heavy-metal atom was complexed to the heme—requiring more than ten thousand trials to achieve success—was a useful depth marker put into place.

Finally came the interpretation of the pictures. High-powered computers were available to calculate electron densities at points in the crystal, but no software was available to say what these densities meant. Kendrew and his coworkers had to plot lines of equal electron density—rather like altitude lines on a topographical map—by hand, for slices angstroms apart through the entire crystal, and to visualize the arrangement of atoms in space from these lines. Later, they recalculated the lines at 2 angstroms for more detail.

In the end, they determined the structure of myoglobin, but only through years of grueling work, seasoned with more than a little luck.

Bibliography

"The 'Mad Pursuit': X-Ray Crystallographers' Search for the Structure of Hemoglobin." R. C. Olby. *History and Philosophy of the Life Sciences* 7 (1985).

"Myoglobin and the Structure of Proteins." J. C. Kendrew. *Science* 139 (1963).

"The Three-Dimensional Structure of a Protein Molecule." J. C. Kendrew. *Scientific American* 205 (1961).

(The Nobel Foundation)

bonucleic acid (DNA) went to Francis Crick, James D. Watson, and Maurice H. F. Wilkins.

Later Career
Kendrew did little important research after about 1960. Instead, he was increasingly drawn into the administration of research facilities in molecular biology. Various honors were given to him, such as fellowship in the Royal Society of London, St. John's and Oxford Universities, and Peterhouse College, Cambridge, as well as honorary membership in American scientific associations. He was knighted in 1963 and given the Order of the British Empire.

Bibliography
By Kendrew
The Thread of Life: An Introduction to Molecular Biology, 1966

"Books: How Molecular Biology Got Started," *Scientific American*, 1967 (book review of *Phage and the Origins of Molecular Biology*, John Cairns, ed.)

"Some Remarks on the History of Molecular Biology," *Biochemical Society Symposia*, 1970

About Kendrew
"The Development of Specialties in Science: The Case of X-Ray Protein Crystallography." J. Law. *Science Studies* 3 (1973).

"John Kendrew, 1917-   ." Robert M. Hawthorne, Jr. In *Notable Twentieth-Century Scientists*, edited by Emily J. McMurray. Detroit: Gale Research, 1995.

Nobel Laureates in Chemistry, 1901-1992. Laylin K. James, ed. Washington, D.C.: American Chemical Society, 1993.

The Nobel Prize Winners: Chemistry. Frank N. Magill, ed. Pasadena, Calif.: Salem Press, 1990.

(Robert M. Hawthorne, Jr.)

Johannes Kepler

Areas of Achievement: Astronomy, mathematics, and physics

Contribution: Kepler founded modern astronomy, supported and expanded the Copernican system, discovered the laws of elliptical orbits, and set the stage for Newtonian physics.

Dec. 27, 1571	Born in Weil, Swabia (now Weil der Stadt, Württemberg, Germany)
1584-1586	Attends the Lutheran seminary at Adelberg
1588	Graduated from the college at Maulbronn
1588-1594	Attends the University of Tübingen and learns Copernican astronomy
1594	Teaches at the Lutheran school of Graz in Styria
1596	Publishes a paper that results in correspondence with Tycho Brahe and Galileo
1598	Flees Graz when Lutherans are banned
1600	Accepts a position under Brahe at the observatory near Prague
1601	Appointed by Emperor Rudolph II to succeed Brahe
1609	Publishes a paper stating two laws of planetary motion
1612	Moves to Linz, becoming the mathematician to Upper Austria
1619	Publishes *Harmonices mundi*, containing a third law of motion
1618-1621	Publishes *Epitome astronomiae Copernicanae* (*Epitome of Copernican Astronomy*, 1939)
Nov. 15, 1630	Dies in Ratisbon, Bavaria (now Regensburg, Bavaria, Germany)

Early Life

Johannes Kepler was born to Lutheran parents in 1571 in Weil, near present-day Stuttgart, Germany. His home life was unstable, fraught with financial problems. Nevertheless, his parents showed him the awesome comet of 1577 and took him out to see an eclipse of the moon. Johannes did well in his studies at one of the Latin elementary schools established in Lutheran communities to educate promising boys. He was frail, sensitive, devoutly religious, and fascinated by nature. His parents and teachers agreed that he should study for the ministry.

An outstanding examination for his bachelor's degree at Maulbronn earned for Kepler acceptance as a student at the University of Tübingen, which stood alongside Wittenberg as an outstanding center of German learning. There, Michael Mästlin taught Kepler the controversial theory of Nicolaus Copernicus, which held that Earth moved and circled the sun.

Completing his master's degree in divinity, Kepler was surprised to be recommended for a position teaching mathematics and astronomy at the Lutheran school at Graz. He had hoped to continue in theology. Apparently, the faculty had no reservations about Kepler's orthodoxy for the pulpit, but they saw him as clearly standing out among his classmates in mathematics. Financially, Kepler was obligated to accept.

Philosophy of Science

Kepler did not attract students at Graz, but, in a short time, he published his work. He was taken with finding God's underlying design for the solar system. There were six known planets at the time. Kepler asked "Why six?" and "Why are they not equally spaced?" Believing that geometry preceded creation in the mind of God, Kepler was struck with the idea that God had used the five perfect Pythagorean solids, one inside the other, to locate the planets in their orbits around the sun. In 1596, he published *Mysteriium cosmographicum*, which contained these ideas, and at the same time openly supported the Copernican system. While his interesting design theory has been discarded, at the time Kepler gained fame and correspondence with noted astronomers Gali-

Kepler's Three Laws of Planetary Motion

Kepler showed that each planet follows an oval-shaped path, called an ellipse, around the sun and that the planets do not travel at uniform speeds in circular orbits or combinations of circles.

What is now called Kepler's second law was discovered first. His analysis of the elliptical motion of Mars revealed that it moved faster when it was closer to the sun and slower when it was farther away. This led to his statement that when a line is connected from a planet to the sun, the line will sweep over an equal area in an equal amount of time, no matter where the planet happens to be in its orbit (see figure).

It then followed that every planet must travel in an ellipse around the sun. An ellipse is a closed curve defined by a fixed total distance from two points called foci (singular: focus). The sun is located at one of the foci. This is the first law of planetary motion.

The third law is that the cubes of the average distance of any planets from the sun are proportional to the squares of their periods (the time that it takes a planet to revolve around the sun). In other words, if Earth is by definition 1.000 astronomical units (AU) from the sun and its period is one Earth year, then Mars is 1.524 AU from the sun and its period is 1.881 Earth years. If the distance from the sun is cubed and the period is squared, they should be equal. For Mars, $(1.524)^3$ should equal $(1.881)^2$. The results are 3.540 and 3.538, which is close enough in celestial physics and allows for the smaller effects of one planet's gravitational effect on another, which becomes more evident with the outer planets.

Kepler might have applied his discoveries to comets, but he did not believe that comets were in orbit around the sun. He thought that the tail of a comet indicated that the sun was driving it away, never to return.

Kepler's discoveries were impressive for two reasons. First, he dispensed with Earth-centered hypotheses and successfully applied the Copernican theory. Second, in the process he overthrew the ancient assumption that heavenly bodies travel in circles or in complicated circles within circles called epicycles. Circles were thought to represent a type of perfection in design. To break with this old idea was no easy matter. In *Astronomia nova, seu physicsa coelestis, tradita commentariis de motibus stellae Martis* (1609), he stated his first two laws of elliptical orbits. These two laws, and later a third, showed that the nature of a satellite's path is mechanistic and set the stage for Sir Isaac Newton to formulate his laws of universal gravitation and motion to explain the forces that control movement.

It is interesting to note that Kepler may not have seen his laws of motion as the most important discoveries in his career. Arthur Koestler, one of his biographers, maintains that Kepler thought that these laws were mere details in his quest for God's grand design.

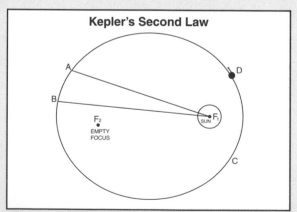

Kepler's Second Law

Kepler concluded that planets traveling in an ellipse move faster when they are closer to the sun. In this exaggerated drawing of an elliptical orbit, assume that the time for the planet to travel from A to B is equal to the time for its travel from C to D. If so, Kepler's second law states that the areas of ABF$_1$ and CDF$_1$ will also be equal. This relationship requires the planet to vary its speed depending on its distance from the sun.

Bibliography

"The Solar System." In *The Cambridge Encyclopaedia of Astronomy*, edited by Simon Mitton. New York: Crown, 1977.

"Space Orbits and Trajectories." Samuel Glasstone. In *Sourcebook on the Space Sciences*. Princeton, N.J.: Princeton University Press, 1965.

"The Theory of Gravitation." Richard P. Feynman. In *Six Easy Pieces: Essentials of Physics Explained by Its Most Brilliant Teacher*. Reading, Mass.: Addison-Wesley, 1995.

leo Galilei and Tycho Brahe. The friendly contact with Brahe was critical to Kepler's future.

Flight to Brahe's Observatory

In 1598, all Lutheran teachers and preachers were banned from Graz by the Catholic archduke. Kepler was given some latitude by friendly Jesuits and could have stayed by converting to Catholicism, but he refused. By 1600, he welcomed Brahe's offer to work in his observatory near Prague. Brahe put Kepler to work on a major problem: the seemingly erratic orbit of Mars.

In a year, Brahe died, and Kepler was appointed head of the observatory and inherited all of Brahe's data on the movements of the planets. Kepler was in an ideal position to contribute to a greater understanding of the solar system.

The Discovery of Elliptical Orbits

In 1604, still working on the problem of the orbit of Mars using Brahe's records, Kepler reached his basic and paradigm-shattering conclusion: The data fit better if the speed of Mars varied and its path was an ellipse. The discovery was impressive. In the process, Kepler applied Copernican theory and also overthrew the two-thousand-year-old belief that heavenly bodies traveled in circles. In *Astronomia nova, seu physicsa coelestis, tradita commentariis de motibus stellae Martis* (1609), he stated his first two laws of elliptical orbits.

Later Life

In 1611, Kepler's wife died of fever, and his three children were lost to smallpox. Emperor Rudolph II died, and Prague became a battlefield. In 1612, Kepler, still retaining his position, moved to Linz to become the mathematician to Upper Austria. There, he remarried and resumed his studies.

Still driven to seek out God's underlying designs, Kepler published *Harmonices mundi* in 1619, which described the spheres of the planets as producing musical tones. The pitch of each sphere varied with the speed of the planet. Mercury had the highest average pitch, and Saturn was given the lowest. These ideas sound strange today, but Kepler found a mystical beauty and truth in this type of thinking.

(Library of Congress)

This book also contains his third law of elliptical motion.

Next, he produced a popular work in parts from 1618 to 1621 called *Epitome astronomiae Copernicanae*, which clearly generalized his laws of motion to all planets. In 1627, Kepler completed *Tabulae Rudolphinae*, based on the ideas of Copernicus, which predicted planetary motion more accurately than any previous tables. In 1630, Kepler died while on a trip to Ratisbon, Bavaria, to plead for his overdue wages.

Bibliography

By Kepler

Mysteriium cosmographicum, 1596 (partial trans. in *The Physicist's Conception of Nature*, 1958)

Astronomiae pars optica, 1604 (also known as *Ad Vitellionem Paralipomena*)

De stella nova in pede Serpentarii, 1606

Astronomia nova, seu physicsa coelestis, tradita commentariis de motibus stellae Martis, 1609

Epitome astronomiae Copernicanae, 1618-1621 (3

parts; *Epitome of Copernican Astronomy*, 1939)

Harmonices mundi, 1619 (partial trans. as *Harmonies of the World* in *Great Books of the Western World*, 1952)

De cometis libelli tres, 1619-1620

Chilias logarithmorum, 1624

Tabulae Rudolphinae, 1627

Somnium, seu opus posthumum de astronomia lunari, 1634 (*Kepler's Dream*, 1965; also as *Kepler's Somnium: The Dream, or Posthumous Work on Lunar Astronomy*, 1967)

About Kepler

Johannes Kepler and Planetary Motion. David C. Knight. New York: Franklin Watts, 1962.

Johannes Kepler: Life and Letters. Carola Baumgardt. New York: Philosophical Library, 1951.

John Kepler. Angus Armitage. New York: Roy, 1966.

The Watershed: A Biography of Johannes Kepler. Arthur Koestler. Garden City, N.Y.: Doubleday, 1960.

(Paul R. Boehlke)

Helen Dean King

Areas of Achievement: Cell biology and genetics

Contribution: King produced standard strains of laboratory rats used worldwide for experimental studies.

Sept. 27, 1869	Born in Owego, New York
1892	Earns an A.B. from Vassar College
1899	Earns an A.M. and a Ph.D. from Bryn Mawr College
1899-1904	Hired as a biology assistant at Bryn Mawr
1899-1907	Teaches science at Miss Florence Baldwin's School in Bryn Mawr, Pennsylvania
1906	Designated among the top one thousand U.S. scientists in the first edition of *American Men of Science*
1906-1908	Named a biology research fellow at the University of Pennsylvania
1908-1913	Serves as an anatomy assistant at the Wistar Institute of Anatomy and Biology
1913-1927	Named assistant anatomy professor at the Wistar Institute
1919	Publishes *Studies on Inbreeding*
1924-1927	Edits *Journal of Morphology and Physiology*
1927-1949	Named an embryology professor at the Wistar Institute
1932	Shares the Ellen Richards Prize
1939	Publishes *Life Processes in Gray Norway Rats During Fourteen Years in Captivity*
Mar. 7, 1955	Dies in Philadelphia, Pennsylvania

Early Life

Helen Dean King, the daughter of George Alonzo and Leonora Louise Dean King, grew up in a prosperous family. After being graduated from the Owego Free Academy, King enrolled at Vassar College in 1888. Vassar supported scientific study for women, purchasing new equipment and hiring talented professors who were familiar with current theories and techniques.

King completed her degree in 1892 and worked in the biology laboratory. By 1895, she began a doctorate at Bryn Mawr College. She focused on morphology, studying with noted geneticist Thomas Hunt Morgan, who encouraged women to pursue independent research projects.

King worked as Morgan's assistant for five years after her graduation in 1899. She published her doctoral dissertation about embryonic development of toads in 1901. During this time, she also taught science in a local school.

Research with Inbreeding

By 1906, King was employed as a biological research fellow at the University of Pennsylvania. Interested in fertilization, she examined factors such as environmental, genetic, and chemical influences on gender determination.

In 1908, she was named an assistant at the Wistar Institute of Anatomy and Biology, where King's most significant work occurred. She began her albino rat-breeding experiments in 1909. She bred two males and two females from the same litter. King then carefully selected their offspring, ultimately producing twenty-five succeeding generations.

The King colony established a uniform stock

Animal Research

King developed standard strains of rats used in research laboratories. The use of animals in experimentation, however, has been a controversial topic.

Animal research is the use of animals in experiments to test surgical techniques, drug effects, and disease treatments. Scientists and animal rights activists have debated the use of animals in scientific and medical investigations.

Throughout history, humans have utilized animals for scientific pursuits. Early scientists dissected animals to understand anatomy. Since the nineteenth century, animals have been used to produce vaccines against diseases. Louis Pasteur developed protective animal cultures to combat cholera and anthrax.

Animal research advocates stress biomedical gains, including the vaccine to fight Hemophilus influenza type B (Hib), which causes meningitis. Laboratory animals have enabled researchers to extract insulin, produce antibiotics and antibacterial agents, perfect organ transplants, and practice heart surgery.

The animal rights movement emerged in the 1970's, demanding humane treatment of laboratory animals. Its leaders argue that animal research cannot consistently be applied to humans and that laboratory results are often misleading.

These critics claim that specimens, under stress in laboratory conditions, produce antibodies and hormones that skew tests. They argue that drugs deemed nontoxic in animals have caused severe reactions, even fatalities, in humans.

Urging scientists to embrace alternatives, animal rights activists suggest that researchers observe humans and consider factors such as genetic, environmental, and biochemical causes of diseases. The ethical and moral aspects of animal research present a complex issue that is not readily resolved.

Bibliography

The Animal Research Controversy: Protest, Process, and Public Policy. Andrew N. Rowan, Franklin M. Loew, and Joan C. Weer. Medford, Mass.: Center for Animals and Public Policy, Tufts University School of Veterinary Medicine, 1995.

"Forum: The Benefits and Ethics of Animal Research." Andrew N. Rowan. *Scientific American* 276, no. 2 (February, 1997).

In the Name of Science: Issues in Responsible Animal Experimentation. F. Barbara Orlans. New York: Oxford University Press, 1993.

The Monkey Wars. Deborah Blum. New York: Oxford University Press, 1994.

of white rats that were used in laboratories worldwide. The rats were large, fertile, and long-lived. King admitted that she could not solely credit inbreeding with these improved traits but emphasized that inbreeding had not caused the damage that Charles Darwin had hypothesized.

Negative Publicity and Further Studies

Many American newspapers portrayed King as an immoral woman for her genetic research. Reporters questioned her femininity because she handled rats and hinted that she believed human inbreeding would strengthen society. Outraged readers sent her angry letters, including death threats. King ignored public opinion, however, and continued to teach and to conduct research. She served on the Wistar Institute's advisory board and was editor of its bibliographic service.

In 1919, King pursued new inbreeding studies with rats. She domesticated the wild Norway rats that roamed Philadelphia's streets. She successfully bred six pairs of the Norway rats through twenty-eight generations.

King noticed slight mutations in the animals. Some were hairless, while others had wavy hair. New fur colors were seen, and a "waltzing rat" ran around in circles. She concluded that captivity encouraged diversity, not similarity. These new types of rats proved useful in laboratory research. King bred rats for scientists wishing to examine specific characteristics or problems.

Honors

King's rat-breeding experiments earned scientific accolades. She was elected vice president of the American Society of Zoologists in 1937 and was named a Fellow of the New York Academy of Science. Her entry was starred in the first edition of *American Men of Science* (and following editions), indicating her status as being among the top one thousand U.S. scientists and attesting her peers' respect for her research.

King was honored with the Ellen Richards Prize for outstanding experimental work conducted by a female scientist. King's successes inspired breeders of racehorses and sporting animals to improve their livestock through in-

breeding. Her rats enabled valuable scientific investigations and medical advances that have benefitted humanity. King died in 1955 at the age of eighty-five.

Bibliography

By King

"The Maturation and Fertilization of the Egg of *Bufo Lentiginosus*," *Journal of Morphology*, 1901

"The Growth and Variability in the Body Weight of the Albino Rat," *Anatomical Record*, 1915

"The Relation of Age to Fertility in the Rat," *Anatomical Record*, 1916

"Ruby-Eyed Dilute Gray, a Third Allelomorph in the Albino Series of the Rat," *Journal of Experimental Zoology*, 1918 (with P. W. Whiting)

"Studies on Inbreeding: I. The Effects of Inbreeding on the Growth and Variability in the Body Weight of the Albino Rat," *Journal of Experimental Zoology*, 1918

"Studies on Inbreeding: II. The Effects of Inbreeding on the Fertility and on the Constitutional Vigor of the Albino Rat," *Journal of Experimental Zoology*, 1918

"Studies on Inbreeding: III. The Effects of Inbreeding, with Selection, on the Sex Ratio of the Albino Rat," *Journal of Experimental Zoology*, 1918

"Studies on Inbreeding: IV. A Further Study of the Effects of Inbreeding on the Growth and Variability in the Body Weight of the Albino Rat," *Journal of Experimental Zoology*, 1919

Studies on Inbreeding, 1919

Life Processes in Gray Norway Rats During Fourteen Years in Captivity, 1939

About King

"Dr. Helen King, 85, Noted Zoologist." *New York Times* 104 (March 10, 1955).

"Helen Dean King." Ann Lindell. In *Notable Women in the Life Sciences*, edited by Benjamin F. and Barbara Smith Shearer. Westport, Conn.: Greenwood Press, 1996.

"Helen Dean King." Mary Bogin. In *Dictionary of Scientific Biography*. Vol. 17, suppl. 2. New York: Charles Scribner's Sons, 1990.

(*Elizabeth D. Schafer*)

Gustav Robert Kirchhoff

Areas of Achievement: Astronomy, chemistry, and physics

Contribution: Kirchhoff, one of the greatest physicists of the nineteenth century, helped established the science of spectrum analysis. He discovered the laws of absorption and emission of radiation by material objects and the principles governing the flow of electricity in circuits.

Mar. 12, 1824	Born in Königsberg, Prussia (now Kaliningrad, Russia)
1847	Receives a Ph.D. in physics from Königsberg University
1847	Marries Clara Richelot
1850-1854	Teaches physics at the University of Breslau
1854-1874	Teaches physics at the University of Heidelberg
1857	Offers a general theory of the motion of electricity in conductors
1859-1860	Conducts joint research in spectroscopy with Robert Bunsen
1859	Announces the law of absorption and emission of radiation by material bodies
1860	Discovers the elements cesium and rubidium
1862	Introduces the concept of blackbody radiation
1875	Named a Fellow of the Royal Society of London
1875	Appointed a professor of physics at the University of Berlin
Oct. 17, 1887	Dies in Berlin, Germany

(Popperfoto)

Early Life

Gustav Robert Kirchhoff (pronounced "KIHRK-huhf") was born in Königsberg, Prussia, in 1824. At the time, the country was still under a feudal form of government and was in a period of economic growth resulting from its late entrance into the Industrial Revolution. Improvements in technology depended on scientific methods, and the period was favorable to developments in both chemistry and physics.

Kirchhoff studied at the University of Königsberg and obtained his doctorate in 1847 at the age of twenty-three. He married Clara Richelot, the daughter of one of his professors, the same year. He began his academic career in 1848 as a lecturer in Berlin.

While at Königsberg, Kirchhoff came under the influence of Franz Neumann, who introduced into Germany the methods of the important French schools of mathematical physics. His lessons were evidently well learned, since Kirchhoff strove throughout his life for rigorous clarity in the mathematical expression of his experimental results.

The Absorption and Emission of Radiation

Kirchhoff studied the laws of absorption and emission of radiation by material objects and the spectral lines that result.

The solar spectrum is that band of colors that is obtained when sunlight is passed through a glass prism. The light is dispersed by the prism because the various wavelengths that make up white light have different indices of refraction, so each bends slightly differently resulting in the spreading out of the various colors into the familiar rainbow pattern. Seen at this low resolution, the solar spectrum appears to be a band spectrum in which each color blends gradually into the next. Heated solids produce similar band spectra.

Incandescent gases, however, behave differently. When a gas is heated to incandescence, it gives off a series of discrete spectral lines that are exactly reproducible and characteristic of the specific gas being studied. A sufficiently hot flame can convert any element to the gaseous state so that its spectrum may be analyzed.

The specific lines in the spectra of the various elements result from electrons changing from one energy level to another as they absorb or emit energy. Atomic spectroscopy involves heating a material until it is vaporized and the atoms are excited so that the electrons jump to higher energy levels. As these electrons return to their original level, the excess energy is emitted in the form of electromagnetic radiation. This radiation is passed through a prism or some other dispersing element and examined for its wavelength content. This process is known as atomic emission spectroscopy.

High-resolution study of the spectrum of the outer layer of gases in the sun shows many narrow lines of varying degree of darkness. The spectral locations of these lines are found to correspond exactly to those of certain elements whose emission spectra have already been cataloged. For example, the brightly colored lines in the emission spectrum of hydrogen are missing in the spectrum of the solar gases, which indicates the presence of hydrogen gas in the sun's outer atmosphere. The complete composition of the sun's atmosphere has been identified using this version of spectroscopy, called atomic absorption spectroscopy.

Lines found in emission spectra have been identified with the transition of electrons from higher to lower energy levels, losing energy as they drop. Lines in absorption spectra result when electrons make upward transitions between the same sets of energy levels. It is clear then that materials absorb and emit the same set of spectral lines. This discovery has made possible the determination of the composition of the stars, the sun, and the identification of unknown materials on Earth.

Historically, visible spectroscopy was developed first, but similar patterns of spectral lines are found in the infrared and ultraviolet regions of the electromagnetic spectrum as well. These patterns make spectroscopy a gold mine of information about the elements and the energy levels of their electrons.

Bibliography

"New Applications of Light: Spectrum Analysis." A. R. Wallace. In *The Wonderful Century: Its Successes and Its Failures*. London: Swan Sonnenschein, 1898.

Spectroscopy and Molecular Structure. Gerald W. King. New York: Holt, Rinehart and Winston, 1964.

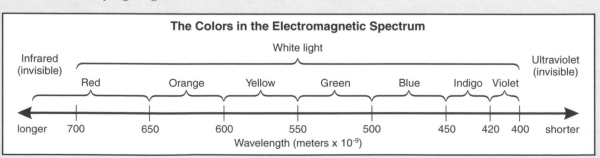

Kirchhoff's first important contribution to physics was made while he was still a student studying under the direction of Neumann in the new field of electromagnetism. During 1845 and 1846, he studied networks of conducting circuits and derived the equations known as Kirchhoff's laws. These laws allow the current in any branch of a complex circuit to be determined if the resistances and sources of potential difference are known.

In 1850, Kirchhoff was appointed to the post of Extraordinary Professor of Physics at the University of Breslau. The following year, Robert Bunsen came to Breslau, and the two scientists began a fruitful collaboration. Bunsen moved to the University of Heidelberg in 1852, and Kirchhoff followed him in 1854, being appointed Ordinary Professor of Physics.

The Heidelberg Years

Bunsen had developed his famous gas furnace, which gave an almost colorless flame, in the 1850's. He and Kirchhoff used it to study the colors given off by heated metals and their salts. Kirchhoff suggested that a prism should be used to disperse the light emitted. Together, they developed the spectroscope, with which they discovered that each element gives off a characteristic set of spectral lines. They used the spectroscope to classify systematically the elements by their fingerprint-like spectra.

Bunsen and Kirchhoff noticed that ordinary salt (NaCl), when heated in the burner flame, produces a yellow line that falls in the exact position as a dark line in the sun's spectrum, the D line. Kirchhoff tried to observe the dark D line and the sodium line simultaneously by shining sunlight and the sodium light into the spectroscope. The amazing result was that the D line became darker, not lighter.

Kirchhoff used the analogy of resonance vibrations to explain this phenomenon. The white light from the sun, upon passing through the sodium flame, lost those vibrations that correspond to the yellow line. Kirchhoff identified other elements in the solar spectrum in a similar way, discovered the elements cesium and rubidium, and simultaneously developed the theoretical aspects of this work. From these experiments, he concluded that when light passes through a gas, those wavelengths of light are absorbed that would be emitted if the gas were incandescent.

Importance to Physics

Kirchhoff's contributions to physics had important practical and theoretical consequences. While studying electric circuits, he showed theoretically that an alternating current would propagate at the speed of light in a conductor of zero resistance. This was important in the eventual development of the electromagnetic theory of light by James Clerk Maxwell in the 1860's.

The development of spectroscopy led directly to the discovery of several new elements and provided an important analytical tool for determining the composition of the stars and of unknown materials on Earth. The study of atomic spectra in the late nineteenth and early twentieth centuries led to the model of the atom of Niels Bohr and the eventual description of the quantum atom.

Kirchhoff's theories concerning the absorption and emission of the same spectral lines by matter led to the concept of a "blackbody," an object that absorbs and emits all wavelengths equally. While no true blackbody exists in nature, Kirchhoff showed how one can be constructed. The study of blackbody radiation by Max Planck led to the first suggestion of the quantized nature of radiation and represented the first step in the development of quantum mechanics.

Kirchhoff spent the remainder of his career as a professor of physics at the University of Berlin. He died in 1887 at the age of sixty-three.

Bibliography

By Kirchhoff

Untersuchungen über des Sonnenspectrum und die Spectrum der chemischen Elemente, 1861 (*Researches on teh Solar Spectrum and the Spectra of the Chemical Elements*, 1862-1863)

Vorlesungen über mathematische Physik (in 4 parts: *Mechanik*, 1876; *Mathematische Optik*, 1891; *Electricität und Magnetismus*, 1891; *Theorie der Wärme*, 1894)

Gesammelte Abhandlungen, 1882

Nachtrag, 1891

Chemische Analyse durch Spectralbeobachtungen, 1895 (with Robert Bunsen)

About Kirchhoff

The Life and Experiences of Sir Henry Enfield Roscoe Written by Himself. H. Roscoe. London: Macmillan, 1906.

"The Velocity of Light and the Evolution of Electrodynamics." L. Rosenfeld. *Nuovo cimento* 4, suppl. 5 (1956).

(Grace A. Banks)

Shibasaburo Kitasato

Areas of Achievement: Bacteriology and immunology

Contribution: A pioneering bacteriologist, Kitasato conducted investigations into tetanus and diphtheria that opened the new discipline of serology, which became immunology.

Dec. 20, 1852	Born in Oguni, Kumamoto, Japan
1872	Enrolls at the Kumamoto Medical Academy and comes under the influence of Dutch physician C. G. van Mansveldt
1883	Graduated from Tokyo University with a medical degree and joins the Public Health Bureau of Japan
1886	Travels to Germany for advanced training with Robert Koch in Berlin
1889	Succeeds in producing the first pure culture of *Clostridium tetani*
1890	With Emil Adolf von Behring, publishes a paper on immunity to diphtheria and tetanus
1892	Returns to Japan and helps establish the Institute for Infectious Diseases, in Tokyo
1894	Studies the outbreak of bubonic plague in Hong Kong
1899-1914	Serves as director of the Institute of Infectious Diseases
1914	Establishes the Kitasato Institute for microbiological research
1917	Becomes the first dean of the school of medicine at Keio University, Tokyo
1925	Elected the first president of the Japanese Medical Association
June 13, 1931	Dies in Nakanojo, Gumma, Japan

Early Life

Shibasaburo Kitasato (pronounced "kee-tah-Zah-toh") was the eldest son of Korenobu Kitasato, the mayor of the Oguni village in Kumamoto prefecture, located in the southern island of Kyushu in Japan. The location of his birthplace influenced his future career as a medical microbiologist. In the mid-nineteenth century, before the Meji Restoration, native Japanese people had limited access to foreign educational influence except in Nagasaki, a city also located on Kyushu, where Dutch intellectuals were allowed to teach and practice medicine.

In his early years, Kitasato was not much interested in book learning, and his parents thought that he would become a farmer. According to Kitasato scholar James R. Bartholomew, however, three physicians influenced him: "his great-uncle, Hashimoto Ryu'un, a teacher named Tanaka Shiba, and a Dutch navy doctor C. G. van Mansveldt." At the age of nineteen, Kitasato entered Kumamoto Medical Academy and came under the strong influence of Mansveldt for three years.

From Mansveldt, the young Kitasato learned about medicine, the German language, and Western culture and was introduced to bacteria through microscopy. His mentor advised Kitasato to continue his studies at Tokyo University and then proceed to Germany. He was graduated from Tokyo in 1883 with a medical degree and then joined the newly established Public Health Bureau of Japan as a government medical officer. In the following year, Kitasato married Torako Matsuo.

Koch's Protégé

In 1886, Kitasato, sponsored by the Public Health Bureau, traveled to Berlin, Germany, to train with Robert Koch, the most renowned bacteriologist of his era. Before he returned to Japan in 1892, Kitasato had established a reputation as an eminent researcher in bacteriology by publishing papers that later came to be acknowledged as classics. The year 1889 turned out to be a peak in Kitasato's productivity. He published a total of fifteen papers, among which two were of significance. In one paper, he established that a bacillus bacterium, *Clostridium tetani*, causes tetanus. In another paper,

he described a method of culturing anaerobic *C. chauvoei*, the causative agent of black leg in cattle.

In 1889, Emil Adolf von Behring, an army physician, joined Koch's research team. Kitasato collaborated with Behring to develop a strategy for protection against diphtheria (one of the lethal diseases to which children often succumbed) and tetanus. A year later, they coauthored a paper entitled "Über das Zustandekommen der Diphtherie-Immunität und der Tetanus-Immunität bei Thieren" (the mechanism of immunity in animals to diphtheria and tetanus), which appeared in *Deutsche Medizinische Wochenschrift*. This paper is now acknowledged as one of the foundation stones of the discipline of immunology.

A Dispute About Bubonic Plague

Kitasato returned to Japan in 1892, and, when an outbreak of bubonic plague occurred in Hong Kong two years later, he was sent there by the Japanese government. He accepted the

(National Archives)

The Demonstration of Passive Immunity

Immunity acquired by an individual from a passive transfer—such as the immunity of newborns resulting from the transfer of antibodies in the ingestion of colostrum in mother's milk or the immunity that results from the administration of antitoxins or antivenoms—is known as passive immunity.

The phenomenon of passive immunity was described by Emil Adolf von Behring and Kitasato in their classic 1890 paper. They immunized rabbits against a culture containing virulent tetanus bacilli. Then, they collected blood from the carotid artery of the rabbits and injected 0.2 to 0.5 milliliter of serum (blood fluid before coagulation) into the abdominal cavity of mice. They inoculated the mice with virulent tetanus bacilli and observed the effect of immunity after twenty-four hours.

Behring and Kitasato made the following inferences from their observations. First, the blood of rabbits immune to tetanus had the ability to neutralize or destroy the tetanus toxin. Second, this property existed also in extravascular blood and in cell-free serum. Third, this property is so stable that it remained effective even in the body of other animals. Thus, through blood or serum transformations, one can achieve outstanding therapeutic effects.

The paper by Behring and Kitasato presented the first evidence that some substances produced in the serum in response to infection are able to neutralize foreign materials. The term "antitoxin" was first introduced in this paper, in its German variant as "antitoxisch."

This discovery opened the possibility of specific therapy for diseases through the injection of immune serum. Kitasato is recognized for his experimental rigor and exploratory skills in demonstrating the immunological phenomenon of passive immunity.

Bibliography

"Behring Discovers the Diphtheria Antitoxin." In *Great Events from History II: Science and Technology Series*, edited by Frank N. Magill. Pasadena, Calif.: Salem Press, 1991.

"A Centennial Review: The 1890 Tetanus Antitoxin Paper of von Behring and Kitasato and the Related Developments." Sachi Sri Kantha. *Keio Journal of Medicine (Japan)* 40 (1991).

challenge of identifying the causative pathogen of the plague. Alexandre Yersin, a Swiss-born medical doctor, also arrived in Hong Kong from the then-French colony of Indochina (now Vietnam).

In the ensuing competition between these scientists, Kitasato described his pathogen as a gram-positive bacillus, *Pasteurella pestis*, while Yersin found the bacillus to be gram-negative (according to a test called Gram staining). Later investigations showed that Yersin had described the true causative organism of the plague and that Kitasato might have mistaken a contaminant as the causative pathogen.

An Institution Builder

Apart from being a reputed scientist of his era, Kitasato also invested much of his time to building scientific institutions in the then-developing Japan. He played a role in establishing the Institute of Infectious Diseases in Tokyo and served as its director from 1899 to 1914. His notable protégés included Kiyoshi Shiga, who identified the pathogen of dysentery, and Sahachiro Hata, who gained recognition as bacteriologist Paul Ehrlich's associate in the discovery of the antisyphilitic drug Salvarsan.

In 1914, Kitasato set up his private Kitasato Institute for research in microbiology. In 1923, he was elected as the first president of the Japanese Medical Association. After a productive five-decade career in research and science administration, Kitasato died of a stroke at the age of seventy-nine.

Medical historians now believe that Kitasato was unfortunate in not being named a joint winner of the first Nobel Prize in Physiology or Medicine, in 1901, which was awarded solely to Behring for the discovery of natural immunity. Kitasato made substantial contributions to the research described in the 1890 paper on natural immunity that he coauthored with Behring.

Bibliography
By Kitasato
"Über den Tetanuserreger," *Deutsche Medizinische Wochenschrift*, 1889
"Über den Rauschbrandbacillus und sein Culturfahren," *Zeitschrift für Hygiene und Infektionskrankheiten*, 1889
"Über das Zustandekommen der Diphtherie-Immunität und der Tetanus-Immunität bei Thieren," *Deutsche Medizinische Wochenschrift*, 1890 (with Emil Adolf von Behring)
"Heilversuchean tetanuskranken Thieren," *Zeitschrift für Hygiene und Infektionskrankheiten*, 1892
Baikingaku Kenkyu, 1893
"The Bacillus of Bubonic Plague," *Lancet*, 1894

About Kitasato
"Baron Shibasaburo Kitasato." H. Fox. *Annals of Medical History*, n.s. 6 (1934).
Biographical Dictionary of Medicine. Jessica Bendiner and Elmer Bendiner. New York: Facts on File, 1990.
Dictionary of Scientific Biography. Charles Coulston Gillispie, ed. Vol. 7. New York: Charles Scribner's Sons, 1973.
"Diagnosis of Plague: An Analysis of the Yersin-Kitasato Controversy." David J. Bibel and T. H. Chen. *Bacteriological Reviews* 40 (September, 1976).
The Formation of Science in Japan: Building a Research Tradition. James R. Bartholomew. New Haven, Conn.: Yale University Press, 1989.

(Sachi Sri Kantha)

Robert Koch

Areas of Achievement: Bacteriology and medicine

Contribution: Koch, considered by many to be the greatest pure bacteriologist, isolated the etiological agents for a variety of infectious diseases, including anthrax, tuberculosis, and cholera.

Dec. 11, 1843	Born in Clausthal, Prussia (now Germany)
1866	Earns a medical degree at the University of Göttingen
1866	Works as a medical assistant at Hamburg General Hospital
1870-1871	Serves as a physician with the German army during the Franco-Prussian War
1873-1876	Conducts research on anthrax, resulting in the isolation of the etiological agent
1880	Becomes a staff member of the Imperial Health Office in Berlin
1881-1882	Studies tuberculosis, isolating the causative bacillus
1883	Formulates what has become known as Koch's postulates
1883-1884	Conducts research on cholera, culminating in the isolation of the etiological agent
1885	Appointed Professor of Hygiene at the University of Berlin
1890	Announces a tuberculosis cure that is later proved incorrect
1900	The Robert Koch Institute for Infectious Diseases opens in Berlin
1905	Awarded the Nobel Prize in Physiology or Medicine
May 27, 1910	Dies in Baden-Baden, Germany

Early Life

Heinrich Herrman Robert Koch (pronounced "kawk") was born in 1843 in the small mining town of Clausthal, Prussia, as the third of thirteen children. The strongest influence in his life, relevant to his later pursuits, was his uncle, Eduard Biewend, who strongly encouraged Koch's interests in both nature and photography. Koch entered the Gymnasium in 1851, at the age of eight, and demonstrated a strong aptitude for both mathematics and the sciences.

Koch's interest in a university education, particularly one in science, resulted in his enrollment in the University of Göttingen in 1862. While there, he won a prize of thirty ducats for his anatomical study of the nerve distribution in uterine ganglia. Koch used his prize money to attend a professional meeting in Hanover, where he had the opportunity to meet some of the most renowned scientists in Germany. This study, which resulted in his first professional publication, also became the basis for his doctoral dissertation. At the age of twenty-three, Koch was graduated with a doctoral degree from the university.

(Library of Congress)

Interests in Research

Following his graduation, and engaged to marry, Koch accepted a position at the Hamburg General Hospital. It was there that he developed his first interests in research. Unable to support a family on his salary at the hospital, however, Koch resigned in favor of a position in Langenhagen, in an institution for the care and education of retarded children. Koch remained there two years.

Koch spent several years in medical practice in a variety of towns. Eventually, he settled in Rakwitz, where his medical skills became well known. In 1870, the Franco-Prussian War intervened. Koch spent two years serving as a physician with the German forces. Following his discharge, he was accepted for the position of *Kreisphysikus*, or district medical officer, in the city of Wollstein.

In Wollstein, Koch began his study of anthrax. Although bacilli had already been observed in the blood of sick animals, their role in the disease remained uncertain. In 1873, Koch began his research on the illness by repeating the microscopic observations of others.

While studying bacterial cultures isolated from the blood of animals sick with anthrax, Koch made the observation that these bacteria form spores, a dormant stage that allows them to survive. He also demonstrated that pure cultures of these bacteria can be used to infect test animals, causing development of the disease. This work later formed the basis for what became known as Koch's postulates, a means of associating disease with specific bacterial agents.

Isolation of the Tuberculosis Bacillus

In 1880, Koch moved to Berlin as a staff member of the Imperial Health Office. There, he applied his earlier research on microscopy and microbial isolation to the problem of tuberculosis.

Koch began his work on the isolation of the tuberculosis bacillus in August, 1881. Using a variety of staining techniques, he was able to demonstrate the presence of the bacterium within infected lung tissue. He was also able to culture the organism in the laboratory and to demonstrate that pure cultures of the bacilli could cause the same disease in guinea pigs.

Isolation of the Tuberculosis Bacillus

During the nineteenth century, tuberculosis was the deadliest respiratory disease in the world; one-seventh of all deaths were caused by this disease. Koch's isolation of the etiological (causative) agent established the infectious nature of the disease.

In his earlier research, Koch had developed principles of photomicroscopy and bacterial culture in the study of microorganisms. He was able to apply these principles to the isolation of the tuberculosis bacillus and the demonstration of its role in the disease.

Koch began his first experiment on the problem on August 18, 1881. Other scientists had attempted to isolate the organism; indeed, as a specific disease, tuberculosis had been known for thousands of years. Such attempts were never successful, however, and the causative agent had never even been observed in tissue.

In this respect, Koch brought a unique quality to the research: patience. Many scientists had been at work on the problem, but repeated negative results had frustrated them. Koch was convinced that the organism was there. What was required was the discovery of appropriate techniques for their study.

His initial experiments dealt with developing a method to observe the organism. Through intense work, he found that a procedure using an alkaline dye was successful in staining the microbe; he was thus able to observe rod-shaped organisms in the lung tissue from patients with tuberculosis. This work proved to be the most important step in establishing the cause of the disease.

The application of what have become known as Koch's postulates confirmed the role of these microbes as the cause of tuberculosis. Koch was able to observe large numbers of these organisms in all infected tissue; if the nature of the disease improved and the patient recovered, fewer organisms were observed.

To establish firmly the role played by these bacteria, however, it would be necessary to culture (grow) them in the laboratory and to demonstrate that pure cultures could be used to transmit the disease. (Again, an aspect of the postulates.) Koch found that the organism has very strict nutritional requirements and will only grow in a special medium containing coagulated blood. Nevertheless, he was able to grow the organism; guinea pigs inoculated with the cultures became ill.

Koch announced the results of the study at a lecture to the Berlin Physiological Society on March 24, 1882. Not only did he report the work, he also brought an extensive array of material to demonstrate his methodology: test tubes with cultures, a microscope, chemicals for staining, and photographs. When Koch published the results of his work some weeks later in the journal *Berliner klinischen Wochenschrift*, it created intense excitement throughout both the general population and the scientific world.

Bibliography

The Forgotten Plague. Frank Ryan. Boston: Little, Brown, 1994.

A History of Bacteriology. William Bulloch. London: Oxford University Press, 1938.

The White Plague. Rene Dubos and Jean Dubos. Boston: Little, Brown, 1956.

Koch reported his results to the Berlin Physiological Society in March, 1882, only seven months after beginning his work.

Isolation of the Cholera Bacillus

In 1883, Koch was appointed head of the German Cholera Commission, which was sent to Egypt to investigate the outbreak of an epidemic of cholera. By the time that the commission reached Egypt, the epidemic had already begun to wane. Consequently, Koch followed the outbreak to India, where, as before, he was able to isolate and grow the agent that causes the disease.

Koch returned to Germany in 1884. He was greeted as a hero and eventually became the head of his own institute.

The Final Years

Koch again turned his research to the problem of tuberculosis. He became obsessed with the idea that inactivation of the causative bacillus could be used as the basis for a tuberculosis vaccine (tuberculin). Unfortunately, the idea proved invalid and discredited some of his work.

Despite some failures, Koch was recognized in his later years as perhaps the greatest pure bacteriologist in the world. In addition to his isolation of the bacilli that cause several of the most important infectious diseases, Koch's culture methods and development of photomicroscopy revolutionized science.

In 1905, Koch was awarded the Nobel Prize in Physiology or Medicine for his work, ostensibly for isolation of the tuberculosis bacillus but in reality to honor a man who had done so much. In 1910, Koch died from a sudden heart attack.

Bibliography

By Koch
"Über das Vorkommen von Ganglienzellen an den Nerven des Uterus," 1865

"Die Ätiologie der Milzbrand-Krankheit, begründet auf die Entwicklungsgeschichte des Bacillus Anthracis," *Beitrage zur Biologie der Pflanzen*, 1876 ("The Etiology of Anthrax Based on the Life History of *Bacillus anthracis*" in *Milestones in Microbiology*, 1961)

"Verfahren zur Untersuchung, zum Konservieren und Photographiren der Bakterien," *Beiträge zur Biologie der Pflanzen*, 1877

Untersuchungen über die Ätiologie der Wundinfectionskrankheiten, 1878 (*Investigations into the Etiology of Traumatic Infective Diseases*, 1880)

"Zur Untersuchung von pathogenen Organismen," *Mittheilungen aus dem kaiserlichen Gesundheitsamte*, 1881 ("Methods for the Study of Pathogenic Organisms" in *Milestones in Microbiology*, 1961)

"Die Ätiologie der Tuberkulose," *Berliner klinischen Wochenschrift*, 1882 ("The Etiology of Tuberculosis [Koch's Postulates]" in *Milestones in Microbiology*, 1961)

"Über die Cholerabakterien," *Deutsche medizinische Wochenschrift*, 1884

"Fortsetzung der Mittheilungen über ein Heilmittel gegen Tuberkulose," *Deutsche medizinische Wochenschrift*, 1891

"Erste Bericht uber die Thätigkeit der Malariaexpedition," *Deutsche medizinische Wochenschrift*, 1899

About Koch
The Battle Against Bacteria, Peter Baldry. Cambridge, England: Cambridge University Press, 1976.

Microbe Hunters. Paul De Kruif. New York: Harcourt, Brace & World, 1953.

"Robert Koch." Linda Fisher. In *The Nobel Prize Winners: Physiology or Medicine*, edited by Frank N. Magill. Pasadena, Calif.: Salem Press, 1991.

Robert Koch: A Life in Medicine and Bacteriology. Thomas D. Brock. New York: Springer-Verlag, 1988.

(Richard Adler)

Arthur Kornberg

Areas of Achievement: Biology, genetics, and medicine

Contribution: Kornberg was awarded the 1959 Nobel Prize in Physiology or Medicine for his isolation of deoxyribonucleic acid (DNA) polymerase, the enzyme in bacteria that catalyzes the replication of genetic material. He later used the enzyme to synthesize biologically active DNA in a test tube.

Mar. 3, 1918	Born in Brooklyn, New York
1937	Receives a B.S. from the City College of New York
1941	Graduated with an M.D. from University of Rochester School of Medicine
1942	Enlists in the U.S. Coast Guard
1942-1945	Transferred to the nutrition section of the National Institute (later "Institutes") of Health (NIH)
1946	Studies enzymatic techniques at New York University
1947	Trains with Carl and Gerty Cori at the Washington University School of Medicine in St. Louis
1947-1952	Returns to NIH as chief of the enzyme and metabolism section
1953-1959	Serves as professor and chair of the microbiology department at the Washington University School of Medicine
1959-1969	Serves as professor and chair of the biochemistry department at the Stanford University School of Medicine
1959	Awarded the Nobel Prize in Physiology or Medicine
1967	Publishes work on the enzymatic synthesis of DNA
1970	Elected a member of the Royal Society of London

Early Life

Arthur Kornberg was born in 1918 as the son of a sewing machine operator in the sweatshops of the Lower East Side of New York City. A brilliant student who skipped several grades, Arthur was graduated from Abraham Lincoln High School at the age of fifteen and enrolled in a premedical program at the City College of New York.

Receiving his B.S. degree in 1937, Kornberg entered the medical school at the University of Rochester. While a student, Kornberg became aware of a mild jaundice (yellowing) in his eyes. He observed a similar condition among other students and patients at the hospital and published these findings, his first professional paper, in the *Journal of Clinical Investigation*.

Following his graduation in 1941, Kornberg enlisted in the U.S. Coast Guard, being assigned duty as a medical officer in the Caribbean. Officials at the National Institute of Health, aware of his brief excursion into the subject of jaundice, arranged for Kornberg's

(The Nobel Foundation)

transfer to the institute. He spent the remainder of World War II years carrying out research in the nutrition laboratory there.

In 1943, Kornberg married Sylvy Levy. In addition to being the mother of three children, Sylvy was a researcher herself. Her suggestions and advice would play major roles in Kornberg's research.

Enzyme Research

Bored with nutrition studies, Kornberg decided on a leave of absence to study enzyme function. He spent a year with Severo Ochoa at the New York University School of Medicine and a year with Carl and Gerty Cori at the Washington University School of Medicine.

During the summer of 1953, Kornberg enrolled in a microbiology course offered by Cornelius van Niel in Pacific Grove, California. Kornberg had recently accepted a position as chair of the department of biochemistry at the Washington University School of Medicine in St. Louis, and he felt the need for more formal instruction in the subject.

In addition to receiving a historical overview of the subject, Kornberg became intrigued with bacteria as a source of enzymes for his research. In particular, he became interested in biosynthetic pathways for the building blocks of deoxyribonucleic acid (DNA). Once he was able to work out their synthesis, it was a logical step to search for the enzyme that assembled them into DNA itself.

By 1957, Kornberg was able to report the isolation of the DNA-synthesizing enzyme, which he called DNA polymerase. In recognition of his work, Kornberg was awarded the 1959 Nobel Prize in Physiology or Medicine. In 1967, Mehran Goulian and Kornberg reported that their enzyme was able to synthesize biologically active DNA in a test tube.

Recognition

The Nobel Prize was one of many awards for Kornberg. Among other aspects of national and international recognition were the Paul-Lewis Award from the American Chemical Society in 1951, the Scientific Achievement Award from the American Medical Association in 1968, and the National Medal of Science in 1980. In addition, Kornberg was elected as a foreign member of the Royal Society of London.

The Isolation of DNA Polymerase

Using extracts from the bacterium Escherichia coli, *Kornberg and his coworkers were able to purify the enzyme that replicates deoxyribonucleic acid (DNA), called DNA polymerase.*

Kornberg did not initially set out with the intention of isolating the replicative enzyme for DNA. His work at the Washington University School of Medicine during this period dealt with the question of the pathway for synthesis of nucleotide bases found in ribonucleic acid (RNA) and DNA. Much of the research during 1953 and 1954 dealt with purification of the enzymes that synthesize the precursors of DNA. By 1954, Kornberg's team had firmly established how the nucleotides are synthesized. The next logical step was to study how they are assembled into DNA or RNA.

Initial experiments with extracts from animal cells were unsuccessful, and Kornberg turned to extracts from the bacterium *Escherichia coli* (*E.*

coli). In November, 1955, Kornberg and coworkers Robert Lehman and Maurice Bessman began the purification of the DNA replicative enzyme.

Kornberg determined that preformed DNA had to be present in the assay mixture. By June, 1956, he was able to report they had isolated a fraction from *E. coli* that could synthesize DNA.

The next months consisted of further isolations. By the summer of 1957, Kornberg had completed the purification, demonstrating that the enzyme was capable of synthesizing DNA. Ironically, the papers that were submitted with reports of the findings were initially rejected.

Bibliography

DNA Replication. Arthur Kornberg and Tania Baker. 2d ed. New York: W. H. Freeman, 1992.

Molecular Cell Biology. James Darnell et al. New York: W. H. Freeman, 1990.

Molecules to Living Cells. San Francisco: W. H. Freeman, 1980.

Bibliography

By Kornberg

"Latent Liver Disease in Persons Recovered from Catarrhal Jaundice and in Otherwise Normal Medical Students as Revealed by Bilirubin Excretion Test," *Journal of Clinical Investigation*, 1942

"Mechanism of Production of Vitamin K Deficiency in Rats by Sulfonamides," *Journal of Biological Chemistry*, 1944

"Enzymatic Synthesis of Deoxyribonucleic Acid: I. Preparation of Substrates and Partial Purification of an Enzyme from *Escherichia coli*," *Journal of Biological Chemistry*, 1958

"Biologic Synthesis of Deoxyribonucleic Acid," *Science*, 1960

Enzymatic Synthesis of DNA, 1961

"Enzymatic Synthesis of DNA: XXIII. Synthesis of Circular Replicative Form of Phage φX174 DNA," *Proceedings of the National Academy of Sciences*, 1967 (with Mehran Goulian)

"Enzymatic Synthesis of DNA: XXIV. Synthesis of Infectious Phage φX174 DNA," *Proceedings of the National Academy of Sciences*, 1967 (with Goulian and R. Sinsheimer)

DNA Synthesis, 1974

DNA Replication, 1980 (2d ed., 1992, with Tania Baker)

"Initiation of Enzymatic Replication at the Origin of the *Escherichia coli* Chromosome," *Proceedings of the National Academy of Sciences*, 1985 (with T. Ogawa, T. Baker, and A. van der Ende)

"DNA Replication," *Journal of Biological Chemistry*, 1988

For the Love of Enzymes: The Odyssey of a Biochemist, 1989

The Golden Helix: Inside Biotech Ventures, 1995

About Kornberg

"Arthur Kornberg." In *The Nobel Prize Winners: Physiology or Medicine*, edited by Frank N. Magill. Pasadena, Calif.: Salem Press, 1991.

Nobel Prize Winners. Tyler Wasson, ed. Bronx, N.Y.: H. W. Wilson, 1987.

Notable Twentieth-Century Scientists. Emily J. McMurray, ed. Detroit: Gale Research, 1995.

(Richard Adler)

Albrecht Kossel

Areas of Achievement: Chemistry and physiology
Contribution: A pioneer in the chemistry of nucleic acids, Kossel isolated and established the composition of these cell constituents.

Sept. 16, 1853	Born in Rostock, Mecklenburg (now Germany)
1878	Earns an M.D. from the University of Strasbourg
1883	Named chemical director of the Institute of Physiology in Berlin
1884	Identifies histone proteins in the nucleus
1885	Discovers adenine and guanine in nucleic acids
1891	Identifies the presence of a carbohydrate in nucleic acids
1894	Discovers cytosine and thymine in nucleic acids
1895	Becomes a professor of physiology at Marburg University
1895	Named editor of the *Zeitschrift für physiologische Chemie*
1896	Discovers the amino acid histidine
1901	Becomes director of the Institute of Physiology at the University of Heidelberg
1910	Awarded the Nobel Prize in Physiology or Medicine
1912	Proposes that nuclear proteins are the chemical basis for biological specificity
July 5, 1927	Dies in Heidelberg, Germany

Early Life

Karl Martin Leonhard Albrecht Kossel (pronounced "KOHS-uhl") developed an interest in botany as a teenager, becoming an expert on the flora of the Rostock region of Germany. His father, a merchant, discouraged him in this interest, seeing no future economic value in it. In 1872, Kossel entered the University of Strasbourg as a medical student. He received an M.D. in 1878 but never practiced medicine. He remained at Strasbourg until 1883 as a research scientist in the new field of biochemistry.

From 1883 to 1895, he was the chemical director of the Institute of Physiology in Berlin. In 1886, he married Luise Holtzmann; their son, Walther, became an eminent theoretical physicist.

Research in Strasbourg and Berlin

Kossel's first publications appeared in 1878. In 1879, he began to study substances of unknown nature in the cell nucleus. He made these his life's work.

Kossel developed the first reliable methods to isolate and analyze nuclear substances. He

(The Nobel Foundation)

separated them into protein, nonprotein, and phosphoric acid components. In 1885, he discovered that the nonprotein part contained adenine and guanine. These were purines, nitrogen-containing heterocyclic organic bases. By 1894, he found two additional bases, cytosine and thymine. These were pyrimidines, another group of heterocyclic substances.

By 1894, Kossel had discovered yet another component of nucleic acids. There was a carbohydrate entity present, but he was never able to determine its nature.

The Marburg Years

Kossel's position at the Institute of Physiology was financially unattractive, and his heavy administrative duties limited his research activity. In 1895, he became a professor of physiology at the University of Marburg. He was now able to develop his research plans and attract an international group of graduate and postdoctoral students.

At Marburg, he became increasingly interested in the proteins of the cell nucleus. He recognized that the nucleic acids are always associated with them and named this new class of conjugated proteins "nucleoproteins."

Many nuclear proteins had a basic and relatively simple nature, and these he named "histones." Their hydrolysis yielded several basic amino acids, including a hitherto unknown one, histidine, in 1896. He believed histones to be the core building blocks of the complex proteins of the body.

From 1895, Kossel was editor of the *Zeitschrift für physiologische Chemie*, the first journal devoted exclusively to the subject later named biochemistry.

Heidelberg and World War I

From 1901 to his retirement in 1924, Kossel was director of the physiological institute at Heidelberg University. In 1910, he received the Nobel Prize in Physiology or Medicine for his studies on the chemistry of cell constituents.

His fortunes faded from 1914. He was ostracized by his fellow German academics because he opposed World War I and refused to sign the 1914 pronouncement of German professors justifying the war. Kossel never regained the influence that he once had. He died in 1927.

The Role of Nucleic Acids in the Cell

Kossel's findings on nucleic acids were the foundation for the discovery of their biological function.

Kossel obtained all the chemical components of nucleic acids, but much remained unclear. No one knew how the organic bases, carbohydrate, and phosphoric acid were linked in nucleic acids or what was the nature of the carbohydrate. His successors solved these problems by the 1940's, disclosing that nucleic acids had one of two carbohydrates. Some had D-ribose; some had deoxy-D-ribose. This discovery became the basis for classifying nucleic acids into ribonucleic acid (RNA) and deoxyribonucleic acid (DNA) types.

Kossel speculated about the biological role of nucleic acids. He proposed that they were essential for the growth of tissues. He knew that nucleoproteins are found in the chromosomes of germ cells and thus are transmitted to new cells. He believed, however, that nucleic acids were too simple and that only the proteins had sufficient diversity to function in the transmission of hereditary characteristics.

Kossel's findings took on new meaning as scientists in the 1950's discovered that DNA produces genetic effects and that RNA conveys genetic information to cells. These discoveries put Kossel's work into the context of a new molecular genetics. DNA became the storage molecule of genetic information, RNA the molecule of gene expression, and Kossel's histone the molecule of gene suppression.

Bibliography
"Chromosomal Proteins and Gene Regulation." Gary Stein, Janet Stein, and Lewis Kleinsmith. *Scientific American* 232 (February, 1975).
Nucleic Acids. P. A. Levene and Lawrence Bass. New York: Chemical Catalog Company, 1931.
The Path to the Double Helix. Robert Olby. Seattle: University of Washington Press, 1974.

Bibliography
By Kossel
Untersuchungen über die Nukleine und ihre Spaltungsprodukte, 1881 (investigations into the nucleins and their cleavage products)
Zur Chemie die Zellkernig, 1882 (chemistry of the cell nucleus)
Leitfaden für medizinisch-chemische Kurse, 1888 (textbook for medical-chemical courses)
Die Gewebe des menschlichen Körpers und ihre mikroskopische Untersuchung, 1889-1891 (with Paul Schiefferdecker and Wilhelm Julius Behrens; the tissues in the human body and their microscopic invsestigation)
Die Probleme der Biochemie, 1908
"Beziehungen der Chemie zur Physiologie" (the relationship between chemistry and physiology) in *Die Kultur der Gegenwart ihre Entwicklung und ihre Ziele: Chemie*, 1913 (E. von Meyer, ed.)
The Protamines and Histones, 1928
The Chemical Composition of the Cell, 1911-1912

About Kossel
"Albrecht Kossel." In *Great Chemists*, edited by Eduard Farber. New York: Interscience, 1961.
Molecules and Life. Joseph S. Fruton. New York: Interscience, 1972.
"Some Recollections of Albrecht Kossel." Ernest Kennaway. *Annals of Science* 8 (1952).

(Albert B. Costa)

Sir Hans Adolf Krebs

Areas of Achievement: Cell biology, chemistry, and physiology
Contribution: One of the founders of biochemistry, Krebs correctly postulated, with limited evidence, the existence of the citric acid cycle, an important metabolic pathway.

Aug. 25, 1900	Born in Hildesheim, Germany
1918-1925	Studies medicine at various German universities
1923	Publishes his first original research
1930-1932	Discovers the ornithine-urea cycle
1932-1937	Conducts research on the tricarboxylic acid cycle
1932	Publishes "The Ornithine Cycle of Urea Synthesis"
1933	Removed by the Nazis from his position at the University of Freiburg and escapes to England
1935	Begins teaching at Sheffield University
1937	Publishes "The Role of Citric Acid in Intermediary Metabolism in Animal Tissues"
1953	Awarded the Nobel Prize in Physiology or Medicine, jointly with Fritz Lipmann, for his work on metabolism
1954	Moves to Oxford University
1958	Knighted by Queen Elizabeth II
Nov. 22, 1981	Dies in Oxford, England

Early Life

Hans Adolf Krebs was born in 1900 in the small German town of Hildesheim. His father, a surgeon, encouraged Hans to have high standards both personally and professionally, a practice that Krebs continued all of his life.

After his graduation from the gymnasium and a brief military service, Krebs entered the University of Göttingen in 1918, frequented other universities, as was common in Europe, and was graduated from the University of Hamburg in 1925.

Professional Development

While at the University of Freiburg, Hans was attracted by the research philosophy of Hans Knoop, who was studying the chemical conversion of fatty acids to simpler molecules. Under Knoop's inspiration, Krebs began his first original work and later expressed his gratitude to his first mentor.

Krebs passed his medical examinations following studies at both Munich and Berlin. He then decided to combine clinical work with chemical research. He was particularly interested in applying basic science to medical problems. He accepted a position at the Kaiser Wilhelm Institut für Biologie in Berlin.

It was a thrilling time for Krebs because of the opportunity to work with Otto Heinrich Warburg, a world-renowned scholar. A laboratory where large numbers of brilliant scientists came to conduct research was stimulating and rewarding. Warburg was the 1931 winner of the Nobel Prize in Physiology or Medicine, and Krebs admired his intellectual prowess and practicality. In 1979, he honored his mentor with a biography, one of the few written by one world-class scientist about another.

Escape to England

The spring of 1933 marked the rise of Adolf Hitler and the Nazi Party in Germany, and Krebs met with the same persecution as many of his fellow Jews. He was denied his position at Freiburg, where he had returned in 1931, but his career was saved because other scientists had already noticed his creativity. Albert Szent-Györgyi, a 1937 Nobel Prize winner in physiology or medicine, helped bring Krebs to Cambridge University in England.

Once more, the young scientist was in the midst of a galaxy of his intellectual peers. At Cambridge, Krebs continued the work that would bring him the Nobel Prize and finished at Sheffield University, where in 1935 he was offered the opportunity to develop his own re-

The Krebs Cycle

The extraction of energy from complex molecules such as carbohydrates and fats during their conversion to carbon dioxide and water occurs in discrete chemical reactions. Krebs argued that the nature of this important pathway demands the use of a product of the final step as a starting material for the first reaction of the subsequent cycle.

The key element in the metabolism of food in most organisms is the funneling of a molecule derived from various sources into a chemical reaction that begins a cyclic process. In the Krebs cycle, acetyl coenzyme A is this common molecule, and it reacts with oxaloacetate to form citrate. The last in a series of about ten separate chemical reactions results in the formation of a new oxaloacetate molecule and the beginning of a new cycle. At two of these intermediate steps, molecules of carbon dioxide are released, accounting for the overall oxidative chemistry of the carbon-rich foodstuffs.

The actual introduction of molecular oxygen from respiration occurs in a later process, and the detailed chemical mechanism must explain how oxidation occurs in the absence of oxygen. This requirement demands a broader definition of oxidation. During the electronic shifts associated with changing bonds in chemical transformations, the loss of electrons by a chemical is called oxidation, and the gain of those electrons by another chemical is called reduction. The reduced materials in many biochemical reactions are known as coenzymes; they are later reoxidized by oxygen itself.

The individual steps of the Krebs cycle involve the specific compounds known to be present in cells; these compounds must occur rapidly enough to maintain their observed concentrations. Since these exacting demands have been met in a large number of experiments, the validity of Krebs's hypothesis is universally accepted. Furthermore, it is known that the same process that occurs in the animal world occurs in the plant and microbial worlds as well. It is estimated that two-thirds of all cellular oxidation takes place through the Krebs cycle.

When Krebs first outlined his hypothesis, the entire picture of oxidation was far from being

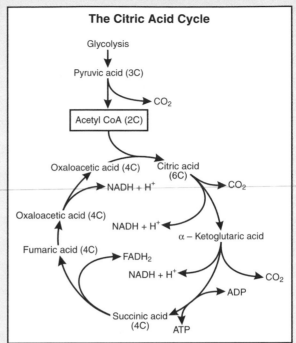

The Citric Acid Cycle

In this diagram of the citric acid (or Krebs) cycle, C is carbon, CO_2 is carbon dioxide, acetyl CoA is acetyl coenzyme A, NADH is a reduced form of nicotinamide adenine dinucleotide (NAD), H is hydrogen, ADP is adenosine diphosphate, ATP is adenosine triphosphate, and $FADH_2$ is a form of flavin adenine dinucleotide (FAD).

solved. The research that his work stimulated added immensely to the theoretical and practical tools available to future biochemists.

Bibliography

Biochemistry. Lubert Stryer. 4th ed. New York: W. H. Freeman, 1995.

The Chemistry of Living Systems. Robert F. Steiner and Seymour Pomerantz. New York: D. Van Nostrand, 1981.

Essentials of Human Metabolism. W. C. McMurray. New York: Harper & Row, 1977.

"How Living Things Obtain Energy: A Simpler Explanation." Donald E. Igelsrud. *The American Biology Teacher* 51 (February, 1989).

"Krebs Describes the Citric Acid Cycle." K. T. Finley and P. J. Siegel. In *Great Events from History II: Science and Technology*, edited by Frank N. Magill. Pasadena, Calif.: Salem Press, 1991.

search group. Krebs always recognized those to whom he owed gratitude, and to Szent-Györgyi he made a personal tribute during a symposium honoring his friend, found in *Search and Discovery: A Tribute to Albert Szent-Györgyi* (1977).

The Ornithine-Urea Cycle

Krebs had published a groundbreaking study of how the liver disposes of the toxic ammonia generated when nitrogen-containing molecules are oxidized. He was the first to show the involvement of a cyclic process. The amino acid ornithine changes ammonia into the amino acid citrulline and then into a third amino acid, called arginine. Later, arginine breaks down into nontoxic urea and ornithine. The excretion of urea in urine had long been known; the ornithine begins another cycle.

Krebs's scientific strategy often involved the application of new technical methods to problems considered unsolvable. Such a new device was invented by Warburg for measuring

(The Nobel Foundation)

rates of chemical reactions by gas pressure changes. In just a year, and with the help of one medical student, Kurt Henseleit, Krebs determined the rate at which urea is formed from many nitrogen sources.

The Citric Acid Cycle

In the early 1930's, the way in which cells convert carbohydrates into carbon dioxide was partially known, but no one had suggested a complete picture. Well prepared from previous work, Krebs was able to propose the outline of his second cyclic pathway in just two years, again with the help of only a single research student, William A. Johnson. This pathway was named the citric acid cycle, the tricarboxylic acid cycle, or simply the Krebs cycle.

When Krebs won the 1953 Nobel Prize in Physiology or Medicine, this feat was called, "the greatest imaginative and experimental accomplishment of biochemistry."

Success Has Reasons

Krebs wrote that his choice of urea synthesis was lucky, because other attractive possibilities proved to be more difficult. Luck, along with skill and diligence, played a role, but it still failed to explain his outstanding success. Colleagues remarked that Krebs had a talent for selecting the most significant work from other laboratories and seeing its relationship to his studies.

The critical difference was Krebs's courage in making speculative hypotheses. With the ornithine-urea cycle, it was fourteen years before methods were perfected allowing the determination of the exact routes by which enzyme catalysts cause the chemical transformations to occur. Although decades of study have added to the understanding of this process, the Krebs cycle has remained intact.

Krebs was knighted by Queen Elizabeth II in 1958. He died in 1981 in Oxford, England, at the age of eighty-one.

Bibliography

By Krebs
"The Role of Citric Acid in Intermediary Metabolism in Animal Tissues," *Enzymologia*, 1937 (with William A. Johnson)

"Cyclic Processes in Living Matter," *Enzymologia*, 1947

"The Citric Acid Cycle" in *Les Prix Nobel en 1953*, 1954

Energy Transformations in Living Matter, 1957 (with Hans L. Kornberg)

"The History of the Tricarboxylic Acid Cycle," *Perspectives in Biology and Medicine*, 1970

"The Disovery of the Ornithine Cycle" in *The Urea Cycle*, 1976 (Santiago Grisolia, R. Baguena, and F. Mayor, eds.)

Otto Warburg: Zellphysiologe, Biochemiker, Mediziner, 1883-1970, 1979 (with Roswitha Schmid)

Reminiscences and Reflections, 1981 (with Anne Martin)

About Krebs

"H. A. Krebs: A Pathway in Metabolism." Hans L. Kornberg. In *The Metabolic Roles of Citrate*. New York: Academic Press, 1968.

"Sir Hans Adolf Krebs." Sanford S. Singer. In *The Nobel Prize Winners: Physiology or Medicine*, edited by Frank N. Magill. Pasadena, Calif.: Salem Press, 1991.

(*K. Thomas Finley*)

August Krogh

Areas of Achievement: Physiology and zoology

Contribution: Krogh demonstrated that oxygen and carbon dioxide exchanges between air and blood in the lungs occurs by passive diffusion and not by secretion. He determined the functions of capillaries in water and ion transport in various organs.

Nov. 15, 1874	Born in Grenå, Jutland, Denmark
1893	Graduated from Århus cathedral school
1899	Earns an M.S. from the University of Copenhagen and becomes an assistant to Christian Bohr
1904	Relates carbon dioxide pressure and the binding of oxygen by blood
1908	Becomes a lecturer in physiology at Copenhagen
1912	Measures the blood flow through the lungs
1916	Publishes a monograph on respiratory exchanges in mammals
1919	Demonstrates the increase in capillary surface in muscle during exercise
1920	Awarded the Nobel Prize in Physiology or Medicine
1922	Publishes a monograph on the anatomy and physiology of capillaries
1939	Investigates the exchanges of water and ions across cell surfaces and membranes
1940	Escapes to Sweden following the Nazi occupation of Denmark
1944	Retires
Sept. 13, 1949	Dies in Copenhagen, Denmark

Early Life

Schack August Steenberg Krogh (pronounced "krawg"), the son of a brewer in Grenå, Denmark, was educated by his mother in his early years. Later, in school, he became interested and experimented in the biological sciences.

At the University of Copenhagen, Krogh initially studied medicine but then switched to zoology, receiving his master of science degree in that field in 1899. It was then that he became associated with physiologist Christian Bohr, the father of physicist Niels Bohr, and began to focus his attention on blood and gas exchanges in the lungs and tissues.

From Frogs to Mammals

Christian Bohr had tentatively proposed that oxygen was transported by secretion, an energy-requiring process. Krogh showed over the period from 1900 to 1910 that oxygen moves by passive diffusion. This work was carried out initially in frogs and then in mammals.

Krogh had married a medical student, Marie Jørgensen, in 1905. She continued her studies and received her medical degree but also collaborated in many of Krogh's studies. In 1910, he was given the Laboratory of Animal Physiology but changed its name to the Laboratory of Zoophysiology in order to avoid attacks by antivivisectionists. He stayed in this laboratory until 1928, when a new, more modern laboratory was made available through funds provided by the Rockefeller Foundation.

Recognition

Krogh achieved international recognition early in his career and received many visiting investigators and students in his laboratory, many of them Americans. His observations and research on the capillaries were the basis for his award of the Nobel Prize in Physiology or Medicine in 1920. This gave him even greater standing in the scientific community.

He published extensively but listed himself

Oxygen, Blood Flow, and the Capillaries

Krogh studied oxygen and carbon dioxide transport across the lungs, blood flow through the lungs, and the capillary system.

Christian Bohr had proposed that oxygen (and carbon dioxide) might be secreted by an energy-requiring process between the gas phase of the lungs and the blood in the capillaries. Krogh greatly refined the measurements of oxygen and carbon dioxide concentrations in the blood and gas phase.

Krogh demonstrated that the oxygen tension in blood was less than in the gas phase, while the tensions of carbon dioxide were almost equal. He concluded that the absorption of oxygen and the elimination of carbon dioxide in the lungs takes place by diffusion. He had answered a critical physiological question.

By the end of the nineteenth century, it was known in a general way that blood flow through the lungs increases with exercise, permitting a greater uptake of oxygen and excretion of carbon dioxide in response to increased needs. Quantification, however, was difficult.

Krogh and J. Lindhard developed a procedure that gave accurate measures of blood flow through the lungs. The amount of blood pumped by the heart per unit time (the cardiac output) ranged from 3 to 8 liters per minute at rest to about 22 liters per minute during exercise. These studies quantified the remarkable ability of the heart to respond to demand.

Krogh also correlated the structure and function of the capillaries, the small channels facilitating the exchange of nutrients and waste products between blood and tissues. He demonstrated that more capillaries are open in muscles during exercise than at rest. His studies extended to a variety of species, and he was able to determine the response of these vessels and their tributaries (arterioles and venules) to various stimuli. These studies brought him the Nobel Prize in Physiology or Medicine.

Bibliography

The Anatomy and Physiology of the Capillaries. August Krogh. Rev. ed. New Haven, Conn.: Yale University Press, 1929.

Textbook of Physiology. A. C. Guyton. 8th ed. Philadelphia: W. B. Saunders, 1988.

(The Nobel Foundation)

rejection because of the repression and brutality by the Nazis. Although unable to join the resistance in active revolt, he still became a target for "liquidation." He managed to escape to Sweden, where he stayed until the end of the war.

On his return, Krogh resumed some research activities in insect and plant physiology. He received many honorary degrees, gave numerous important lectures, and continued to have a remarkable influence on many developments in physiology and clinical medicine. He died on September 13, 1949, in Copenhagen.

Bibliography

By Krogh
"Über einen in biologischer Beziehung wichtigen Einfluss, den die Kohlensäurespannung des Blutes auf dessen Sauerstoffbindung übt," *Skandinavische Archiv für Physiologie*, 1904 (with C. Bohr and K. Hasselbalch; "A Biologically Important Influence of the Carbon Dioxide Tension of the Blood on Its Oxygen Binding Capacity" in *Pulmonary and Respiratory Physiology*, 1976)

"On the Tension of Gases in the Arterial Blood," *Skandinavische Archiv für Physiologie*, 1910 (with Marie Krogh)

"On the Mechanism of Gas-Exchange in the Lungs of the Tortoise," *Skandinavische Archiv für Physiologie*, 1910

"Measurements of the Blood Flow Through the Lungs of Man," *Skandinavische Archiv für Physiologie*, 1912 (with J. Lindhard)

The Anatomy and Physiology of the Capillaries, 1922; rev. ed., 1929

About Krogh
August and Marie Krogh. Bodil Schmidt-Nielsen. New York: Oxford University Press, 1995.

"August Krogh, 1874-1949." Cecil K. Drinker. *Science* 112 (1950).

"Obituary Notice: August Krogh, 1874-1949." G. Liljestrand. *Acta Physiologica Scandinavica* 20 (1950).

(Francis P. Chinard)

as an author only if he had actively participated in the work itself. Thus, he provided leadership in research, more as a collaborator than as a director or administrator. He saw himself as a catalyst.

Krogh was a frequent visitor to the United States, where he had many friends and greatly enjoyed the science and the culture. He was described as modest and informal, direct in expressing himself but kindly and with a sense of humor.

The Later Years

In 1940, the German army invaded Denmark and Norway and oppressively occupied those countries until 1945. Before World War II, Krogh had respected and even admired German science and welcomed many German students to his laboratory. These feelings turned to

Gerard Peter Kuiper

Area of Achievement: Astronomy
Contribution: Kuiper contributed to the theoretical understanding of the solar system. He discovered moons of Uranus and Neptune, proposed a model of how the solar system formed, and predicted a disk of comets, called the Kuiper belt, outside Neptune's orbit.

Dec. 7, 1905	Born in Harenkarspel, the Netherlands
1927	Earns a B.S. degree from the University of Leiden
1933	Awarded a Ph.D. in astronomy from Leiden
1933	Named a Fellow at the Lick Observatory, the University of California
1936	Appointed a lecturer in astronomy at Harvard University
1937	Becomes an assistant professor of astronomy at the Yerkes Observatory, the University of Chicago
1947-1949	Serves as director of the Yerkes Observatory
1948	Discovers Miranda, a moon of Uranus
1949	Discovers Nereid, a moon of Neptune
1951	Proposes that comets originate in a disk outside the orbit of Neptune
1960-1973	Serves as director of the Lunar and Planetary Laboratory at the University of Arizona
1964	Persuades the University of Hawaii to build an observatory on the summit of Mauna Kea
Dec. 23, 1973	Dies in Mexico City, Mexico

(AP/Wide World Photos)

Early Life

Gerard Peter Kuiper (pronounced "KOY-pur") was born on December 7, 1905, to Gerard and Anna Kuiper in Harenkarspel, the Netherlands.

Kuiper enrolled at the University of Leiden, where he studied physics and astronomy and received a bachelor of science degree in 1927. He then began a research project on binary stars, a pair of stars that orbit around each other. Kuiper received a Ph.D. in astronomy at Leiden in 1933 and moved to the United States, where he became a Fellow at the Lick Observatory of the University of California.

In 1936, Kuiper was appointed a lecturer in astronomy at Harvard University. The next year, he accepted a position as an assistant professor of astronomy at the Yerkes Observatory of the University of Chicago. There, he continued his research on binary stars, studying systems in which the two stars are so close to each other that they complete an orbit in only a few hours.

Research in Planetary Science

Kuiper's interest shifted from the study of the stars to the study of the planets and moons of Earth's solar system. In 1944, he obtained the first evidence for an atmosphere surrounding a moon, detecting methane surrounding Titan, the largest moon of Saturn. In 1948, he discovered Miranda, a moon of Uranus, and, in 1949, he discovered Nereid, a moon of Neptune.

Kuiper and several colleagues proposed that the solar system formed from a rotating disk of gas and dust, much greater in mass than the current mass of the planets. In 1951, he suggested that remnants of the disk of matter from which the planets formed might still exist be-

The Origin of the Solar System

Kuiper offered a model of the development of the solar system from a disk of matter.

At the end of World War II, the models for the origin of stars suggested that stars formed by condensation of interstellar gas clouds. A contradiction arose, however, because the known rocky planets—Earth, Mars, Venus, and Mercury—are larger than the lower size limit for the products of such condensation implied by these models.

Kuiper became interested in the origin of the planets. In October, 1949, he proposed a different scenario for how the solar system formed. In his model, the mass of the gas and dust was much greater, about seventy times greater, than the current mass of the planets. Under these conditions, smaller "protoplanets," moon-sized objects out of which planets could grow, were capable of forming.

An outgrowth of this model was Kuiper's suggestion that in the outer region of the solar system, beyond the orbit of Neptune, many of these protoplanets, never having grown to the size of planets, might remain intact. He suggested that, occasionally, one of these objects would be disturbed from its nearly circular orbit and thrown into the inner solar system as a comet. The first of these objects was discovered in 1992, and this remnant of the original solar disk is now called the Kuiper belt.

Bibliography

Evolution of the Solar System. Hannes Alfvén and Gustaf Arrhenius. Washington, D.C.: NASA U.S. Government Printing Office, 1976.

"On the Origin of the Solar System." Gerard P. Kuiper. In *Astrophysics,* edited by J. A. Hynek. New York: McGraw-Hill, 1951.

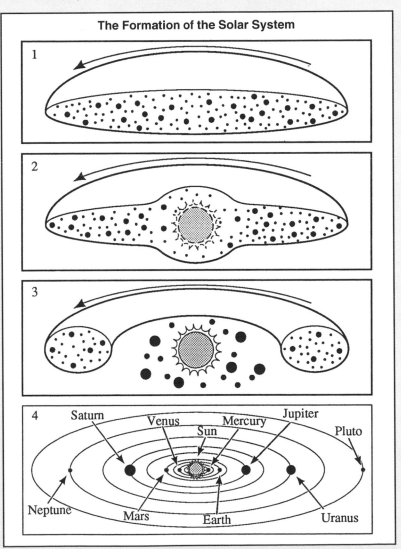

The Formation of the Solar System

Kuiper was one of several scientists who proposed that the solar system had formed from a rotating cloud of gas and dust.

yond the orbit of Neptune. The first object in this disk, now called the Kuiper belt, was discovered in 1992.

Astronomical Observatories
In 1960, Kuiper was named director of the Lunar and Planetary Laboratory at the University of Arizona, where he worked to develop better astronomical observatories. In 1964, he persuaded the governor of Hawaii to build a road to the summit of Mauna Kea and the University of Hawaii to construct an observatory on that site.

Kuiper was among the first astronomers to recognize that jet aircraft could carry telescopes high enough to minimize interference from the atmosphere. He made infrared observations of Venus, which detected water vapor in its atmosphere, from a jet. In January, 1974, in recognition of Kuiper's influence, the National Aeronautics and Space Administration (NASA) named its C-141 aircraft, which carries a 90-centimeter telescope, the Kuiper Airborne Observatory.

Kuiper died on December 23, 1973, while in Mexico on a trip to examine sites for a new observatory.

Bibliography
By Kuiper
The Atmospheres of the Earth and Planets: Papers Presented at the Fiftieth Anniversary Symposium of the Yerkes Observatory, September, 1947, 1949
"On the Origin of the Solar System" in *Astrophysics*, 1951 (J. A. Hynek, ed.)
The Solar System, 1953 (vol. 1, *The Sun*, 1953, as editor; vol. 2, *The Earth as a Planet*, 1954, as editor; vol. 3, *Planets and Satellites*, 1961, as editor, with Barbara M. Middlehurst; vol. 4, *The Moon, Meteorites, and Comets*, 1963, as editor, with Middlehurst)

About Kuiper
Gerard Peter Kuiper. Dale P. Cruikshank. Washington, D.C.: National Academy Press, 1993.
Orbiting the Sun. Fred Whipple. Cambridge, Mass.: Harvard University Press, 1981.
Watchers of the Skies. Willy Ley. New York: Viking Press, 1963.

(George J. Flynn)

Louis O. Kunkel

Areas of Achievement: Botany and virology
Contribution: Kunkel solved major questions about the transmission and treatment of viral diseases of plants. As a skillful administrator, he helped build institutions of research and brought together many of the early leaders in plant virology.

May 7, 1884	Born in Mexico, Missouri
1914	Earns a Ph.D. in botany from Columbia University
1914-1920	Works as a plant pathologist at the Bureau of Plant Industry, United States Department of Agriculture
1915-1916	Receives a fellowship to study in Germany and Sweden
1920-1923	Serves as an associate pathologist with the Hawaiian Sugar Planters' Association
1920	Demonstrates aphid transmission of sugar cane mosaic virus
1924-1931	Works as a pathologist and Administrator at the Boyce Thompson Institute for Plant Research
1931-1949	Serves as director of the division of plant pathology at the Rockefeller Institute for Medical Research
1932	Elected a member of the National Academy of Sciences
1949-1955	Named an emeritus member of the Rockefeller Institute
1956	Given the Botanical Society of America's Certificate of Merit
1959	Receives the New York Botanical Garden's Distinguished Service Award
Mar. 20, 1960	Dies in Newtown, Pennsylvania

Early Life

Louis Otto Kunkel, the son of a farmer, grew up near Mexico, Missouri. At the age of sixteen, he left school to work in agriculture. He returned to high school in 1903 and entered the University of Missouri at Columbia in 1906, receiving a B.S. in 1909, an A.B. in 1910, and an M.A. in 1911.

Following his graduation, Kunkel studied for a year at the Henry Shaw School of Botany in St. Louis before transferring to Columbia University in New York City. At Columbia, he became fascinated with microscopic fungi, receiving a Ph.D. in botany in 1914 for his dissertation on the fungus *Neurospora sitophila*.

A Research Plant Pathologist

In 1914, Kunkel became a plant pathologist with the United States Department of Agriculture (USDA), where he studied diseases of potato and cabbage caused by pathogenic fungi. During a fellowship in Germany and Sweden from 1915 to 1916, his interests in viral diseases developed.

An opportunity to work on viruses led Kunkel to accept a position in 1920 as associate pathologist with the Hawaiian Sugar Planters' Association. Within four months, he had discovered how insects transmit the virus that causes sugar cane mosaic, a disease that had long puzzled scientists.

The Boyce Thompson Institute

In 1923, Kunkel took a position as pathologist at the new Boyce Thompson Institute for Plant Research in Yonkers, New York. He studied the nature of plant viruses, with a particular emphasis on those that caused yellows diseases, attempting to resolve whether they were microorganisms or nonliving chemicals and probing the relationship between viruses, host plants, and insect vectors. As director of research in plant pathology, Kunkel gathered a splendid group of scientists, including Wendell Meredith Stanley, who would win the 1946 Nobel Prize in Chemistry.

Rockefeller Institute

When the Rockefeller Institute for Medical Research at Princeton University began a pro-

Aster Yellows Disease

Aster yellows is caused by an insect-transmitted virus displaying the properties of heat sensitivity and crossprotection.

Kunkel demonstrated that the aster yellows pathogen is transmitted to plants by a leafhopper insect known as *Macrosteles fascifrons*. He collected insects that feed on asters and tested them on healthy seedlings in a greenhouse in order to find the insect vector. He also showed that the causal agent is a virus (now known to be a phytoplasma) that attacks more than forty different plant families and reproduces in both the plant and the leafhopper.

Kunkel proved for the first time that heat therapy could be used to treat yellows-type diseases. This discovery led to commercial treatments that employ enough heat to kill a virus but that will not injure the host plant.

Kunkel significantly advanced the understanding of the phenomenon of crossprotection, in which infection of a plant by one strain of a virus protects against another, even more virulent strain. He also demonstrated similar crossprotection in the insect vectors of aster yellows.

Aster yellows disease affects many vegetables, ornamental plants, and weeds in North America, Europe, and Japan. Understanding its nature has led to control strategies and to the growth of knowledge about similar destructive plant diseases.

Bibliography
Introduction to Plant Diseases: Identification and Management. George B. Lucas, C. Lee Campbell, and Leon T. Lucas. 2d ed. New York: Van Nostrand Reinhold, 1992.
An Introduction to the History of Virology. A. P. Waterson and Lise Wilkinson. Cambridge, England: Cambridge University Press, 1978.
The Virus: A History of the Concept. Sally Smith Hughes. New York: Science History, 1977.

(National Archives)

gram of comparative pathology in 1932, Kunkel was recruited to head its new division of plant pathology. He was already widely recognized as a leader in his field both as a scientist and as an administrator.

Kunkel studied the use of heat treatments against certain viruses. This research produced a major breakthrough in disease control and proved very beneficial to commercial plant growers.

When the Princeton branch of the institute merged with its parent institution in New York City in 1949, Kunkel supervised the construction of new laboratory and greenhouse facilities, furnishing them with the most modern equipment. In July, 1949, he became an emeritus member of the Rockefeller Institute, although he remained as head of the division of plant pathology until his retirement in 1955. For the remainder of his life, he concentrated on research, continuing to produce groundbreaking studies of plant viruses. Kunkel died in 1960.

Bibliography
By Kunkel
"Studies on Aster Yellows," *American Journal of Botany*, 1926
"Filterable Viruses" in *Lectures on Plant Pathology and Physiology in Relation to Man*, 1928
"Virus Diseases of Plants" in *Filterable Viruses*, 1928 (Thomas M. Rivers, ed.)
"Insect Transmission of Peach Yellows," *Contributions from the Boyce Thompson Institute for Plant Research*, 1933
"New Views in Virus Disease Research" in *Science in Progress*, 1939 (George A. Baitsell, ed.)
"Heat Cure of Aster Yellows in Periwinkles," *American Journal of Botany*, 1941

About Kunkel
"Louis Otto Kunkel." Wendell M. Stanley. *National Academy of Sciences Biographical Memoirs 38*. New York: Columbia University Press, 1965.
"Louis Otto Kunkel, 1884-1960." F. O. Holmes. *Phytopathology* 50 (November, 1960).

(Paul D. Peterson, Jr.)

Jean-Baptiste Lamarck

Areas of Achievement: Biology, botany, and zoology

Contribution: Lamarck proposed that evolutionary change takes place by the use and disuse of organs and helped popularize the idea that acquired traits are inherited. He also developed a system for the classification of invertebrates based on anatomy and made major contributions to the classification of plants.

Aug. 1, 1744	Born in Bazentin-le-Petit, Picardy, France
1755-1759	Attends the Jesuit College of Amiens
1761-1768	Performs military service in the infantry
1770-1778	Studies medicine and botany in Paris
1779	Elected to the Académie des Sciences
1783	Promoted to associate botanist
1793	Helps found the Musée d'Histoire Naturelle and is placed in charge of invertebrates
1801	Publishes a revised classification of invertebrates based on anatomical research
1802	Publishes *Hydrogéologie* (*Hydrogeology*, 1964) offering a history of the earth as a series of floods and the building up of deposits to form continents
1809	Proposes laws governing the ascent of life to higher stages and the inheritance of acquired characteristics
1815-1822	Publishes a seven-volume text summarizing his work on the classification of invertebrates
Dec. 28, 1829	Dies in Paris, France

Early Life

Jean-Baptiste-Pierre-Antoine de Monet, chevalier (knight) de Lamarck (pronounced "luh-MAHRK"), the youngest of eleven children, was born in Bazentin-le-Petit, France, in 1744 to a minor noble family. His father, a lieutenant in the infantry, decided that Jean-Baptiste should study for the priesthood. At the age of eleven, he entered the college of the Jesuits at Amiens, but, after his father died in 1759, he left school and joined the French army, fighting valiantly in the Seven Years' War.

When Lamarck was quartered at various posts along the Mediterranean, he observed the unusual vegetation there, stimulating his interest in French plants. When he left the military service because of ill health in 1768, he supplemented his army pension by working at a Paris bank. He studied medicine for four years and attended a botanical course at the Jardin du Roi (royal gardens).

Botany, Invertebrate Zoology, Meteorology

Lamarck abandoned medicine to study botany. After ten years, he published his three-volume *Flore françoise* in 1778, which brought him acclaim because it was useful for the identification of French plants and was written in French instead of Latin. This success and support from the Comte de Buffon (Georges Louis Leclerc) led to Lamarck's appointment to the Académie des Sciences. In 1781-1782, he traveled extensively as Royal Botanist, visiting botanical gardens in Central Europe.

When Lamarck returned, he was appointed curator of the royal herbarium, with a salary barely sufficient to support his wife and growing family. After the French Revolution in 1789, he reorganized the royal collection in natural history. Lamarck published *Introduction à la botanique* (1803), which indicated that species could change.

Lamarck became interested in other scientific fields and published *Recherches sur les causes des principaux faits physiques* (1794) and *Réfutation de la théorie pneumatique* (1796), supporting the Aristotelian doctrine of four elements instead of Antoine-Laurent Lavoisier's new theories. Lamarck's findings in meteorology did not produce new ideas, but they helped him understand the effects of climate on living things.

Lamarck's work in invertebrate zoology and paleontology was the product of his research at the newly founded Musée d'Histoire Naturelle. He was placed in charge of the invertebrate collection and observed how fossils compare to living forms. In *Système des animaux sans vertèbres* (1801), he revised

the classification of invertebrates by utilizing the anatomical studies of Baron Georges Cuvier.

His invertebrate classification served as a useful guide for naturalists throughout the nineteenth century and is the reason why he is considered the founder of the field of invertebrate zoology. His refusal to accept the idea

Lamarck's Theory of Evolution and Philosophical Outlook

Lamarck's evolutionary theory was philosophical, rather than empirical, because it did not rest on numerous observations as did Darwinian evolution.

Lamarck's theory was also vitalistic and environmental, proposing that minerals, plants, and animals spontaneously developed from gelatinous and mucilaginous particles, animals forming from the gelatinous particles and plants from the mucilaginous ones. Animal and plant wastes were then turned into minerals by the action of heat and electricity.

Lamarck suggested that an inner force within all creatures was striving to improve the organism and the species. If this force was not impeded, a continuously ascending chain of organisms—from the simplest creatures all the way up to human beings—would be the result. Since Lamarck did not believe in extinction, he thought that all forms of life were perfect because their imperfections had been corrected.

Lamarck's theory explained organic change as the result of motion: External motion caused body fluids to move to their surrounding solid parts, directing the organs to form better-adapted structures. Changes in external conditions stimulated the organism to produce better-adapted forms through the use or disuse of organs and through an unconscious effort or inner feeling directing modification.

Lamarck postulated that this inner feeling directed the agitation of the nervous fluid to form habits necessary for the organism's survival. The more advanced an animal was—and, consequently, the better developed its nervous system—the more efficiently this force would operate in developing a particular structure or function to fulfill a specific need, such as the search for food in order to relieve hunger. Thus,

animals were modified by habit and lifestyle.

Lamarck's work was an important forerunner to the contributions of Charles Darwin, particularly his recognition that environment is a factor in evolution. From his lengthy studies of plants and animals, Lamarck intuitively developed the idea that living things were capable of change and that previous systems of classification were inadequate.

The opposition of George Cuvier and other influential biologists, however, caused Lamarck's work to be ridiculed or neglected, even though pre-Darwinian evolutionists invoked some of his ideas, such as the inheritance of acquired characteristics. Darwin's grandfather, Erasmus Darwin, was an early evolutionist who adapted some elements of Lamarckism, and Charles Darwin himself utilized the inheritance of acquired characters as a means of explaining how traits were passed on because he had no knowledge of Mendelian genetics. Later, after Darwin's death, the essential parts of Lamarck's theory competed with Darwinian evolution until the 1930's. Then, a synthesis between genetics and evolution took place, thereby establishing modern biology, which basically upheld the Darwinian model of evolution by means of natural selection.

Bibliography
The Death of Adam: Evolution and Its Impact on Western Thought. John C. Greene. Ames: Iowa State University Press, 1959.

Forerunners of Darwin, 1745-1859. H. Bentley Glass, O. Temkin, and W. L. Strauss, eds. Baltimore: The Johns Hopkins University Press, 1959.

The Growth of Biological Thought: Diversity, Evolution, and Inheritance. Ernst Mayr. Cambridge, Mass.: The Belknap Press of Harvard University Press, 1987.

(Library of Congress)

that the fossil forms became extinct, however, led him to advance the notion that they evolved into new species.

Geology and the Theory of Evolution

Lamarck's work in geology and understanding of the vastness of geologic time helped him develop his theory of evolution. In *Hydrogéologie* (1802; *Hydrogeology*, 1964), he suggested that water was the primary force producing geologic change and that the arrangement of fossils in sediment illustrated the conditions existing when the deposits were formed. His understanding that a gradually changing environment influenced organisms to change led him to advance the idea that living things underwent slow modification with the passage of geologic time.

Lamarck's *Recherches sur l'organisation des corps vivans* (1802) discussed how organisms achieve greater complexity, and *Philosophie zoologique* (1809; *Zoological Philosophy*, 1963) explained that traits develop in an organism because of a need created by its environment. These changes are then inherited by its offspring. The organs formed in this process are further perfected by repeated use, and the less useful ones likewise are weakened by infrequent use. The best-known example is the giraffe. Lamarck claimed that it stretched to reach leaves and thus passed on a longer neck to its offspring.

Later Years

Lamarck's theory was very controversial and was opposed by the influential Cuvier. Without support and going blind, Lamarck worked his remaining years on his seven-volume *Histoire naturelle des animaux sans vertèbres* (1815-1822), a summary of his evolutionary ideas and his invertebrate classification.

Much of the time, Lamarck and his family lived in poverty, heightened by the death of his first three wives. He died penniless in 1829, a scientific outcast, unable to leave anything to his children.

Bibliography
By Lamarck
Flore françoise, 1778 (3 vols.)
Recherches sur les causes des principaux faits physiques, 1794 (2 vols.)
Réfutation de la théorie pneumatique: Ou, De la nouvelle doctrine des chimistes modernes, 1796
Système des animaux sans vertèbres: Ou, Tableau générale des classes, des ordres, et des genres de ces animaux, 1801
Hydrogéologie, 1802 (Hydrogeology, 1964)
Recherches sur l'organisation des corps vivans, 1802
Introduction à la botanique, 1803 (2 vols.)
Philosophie zoologique: Ou, Exposition des considérations relative à l'histoire naturelle des animaux, 1809 (2 vols.; *Zoological Philosophy: An Exposition with Regard to the Natural History of Animals*, 1963)
Histoire naturelle des animaux sans vertèbres, 1815-1822 (7 vols.)

About Lamarck
The Age of Lamarck: Evolutionary Theories in France, 1790-1830. Pietro Corsi. Translated by Jonathan Mandelbaum. Berkeley: University of California Press, 1988.
Lamarck. L. J. Jordanova. New York: Oxford University Press, 1984.
Lamarck, the Founder of Evolution: His Life and Work. Alpheus S. Packard. New York: Longmans, Green, 1901.
The Spirit of System: Lamarck and Evolutionary Biology. Richard W. Burkhardt. Cambridge, Mass.: Harvard University Press, 1977.

(Joel S. Schwartz)

Edwin Herbert Land

Areas of Achievement: Chemistry, invention, and physics

Contributions: Land, the founder of the Polaroid Corporation, was a pioneer in the development of polarizing filters, instant photography, and theories of color perception.

May 7, 1909	Born in Bridgeport, Connecticut
1926	Enters Harvard University
1927	Takes a leave of absence to develop a polarizing filter
1929	Marries Helen Maislen and returns to Harvard
1932	Leaves to form Land-Wheelwright Laboratories
1934	Obtains his first patent for polarizing filters
1937	Forms the Polaroid Corporation
1947	Introduces instant black-and-white photography
1951-1953	Named president of the American Academy of Arts and Sciences
1957	Awarded an honorary doctorate in science by Harvard
1959	Demonstrates the Land effect in color vision
1960	Founds the Rowland Foundation to support scientific research
1963	Develops instant color photography
1966-1967, 1974	Conducts lectures in psychology and physics at Harvard
1977	Introduces an instant film and camera for motion pictures
1980	Retires from Polaroid
Mar. 1, 1991	Dies in Cambridge, Massachusetts

Early Life

Edwin Herbert Land, the inventor of Polaroid filters and instant photography, grew up in Bridgeport and Norwich, Connecticut, as the son of a businessman. His interest in photography began as a teenager, when he built a laboratory to develop his own photographs. His interest in optics, the physics of light, began while he was attending Norwich Academy, where he excelled both academically and at debating and sports.

In 1926, while in his first year at Harvard, Land conceived of a way of cheaply producing light-polarizing filters, which organize light waves along the plane of a single axis. The filters reduce the brightness or glare of reflected light. It took six years of intensive experimentation, however, to turn Land's insight into a usable product, and he ultimately left Harvard without obtaining a degree.

The Polaroid Corporation

In 1932, in partnership with Harvard physicist George Wheelwright III, Land created the Land-Wheelwright Laboratories in order to commercialize his invention, which he called the Polaroid filter. Although profit was definitely in his mind, Land saw his filters as primarily a means of enhancing creativity, comfort, and safety through such products as antiglare headlights, sunglasses, and camera filters. Companies such as Eastman Kodak and the American Optical Company were licensed to manufacture these products.

The laboratory remained a research organization, with headquarters in Cambridge, Massachusetts. In 1937, it was reorganized as the Polaroid Corporation. To finance his new enterprise, the twenty-eight-year-old inventor asked for and received the backing of such prominent New York financiers as Averell Harriman, James P. Warburg, and Leo Strauss—unusual validation of the young scientist's capabilities by generally cautious investors.

Instant Photography

In 1943, while on a family vacation in New Mexico, Land's young daughter asked why she could not see immediately the photographs taken during the trip. Six years of research inspired by this question resulted in the Polaroid

Land Camera and a film that would develop a black-and-white photograph within a minute.

The film that Land created, which combined both light-sensitive and developing chemicals, was a marvel of research and insight. The camera was an immediate commercial success but was clumsy to operate, and Land regarded his invention as incomplete. In 1973, he introduced the SX-70 camera. Small and compact, it could fit in a jacket pocket and produced a color photograph within seconds, automatically.

Philosophy

Land was an unusual individual. He became wealthy as the head of a large corporation. He was granted more than 525 patents for his inventions in optics and photography. He received fourteen honorary degrees from colleges and universities, and more than forty U.S. and foreign scientific organizations and institutions presented him with awards or medals.

Yet, Land saw himself primarily as a scientist, and profits or awards were never the primary goals of his research. He regarded his sophisticated scientific insights, and the inventions that followed, primarily as a means to allow ordinary individuals to extend their creative abilities. For Land, the goal of his work was not a larger corporation but the creation of a more satisfying, life-enriching human experience. He died in 1991 at the age of eighty-one.

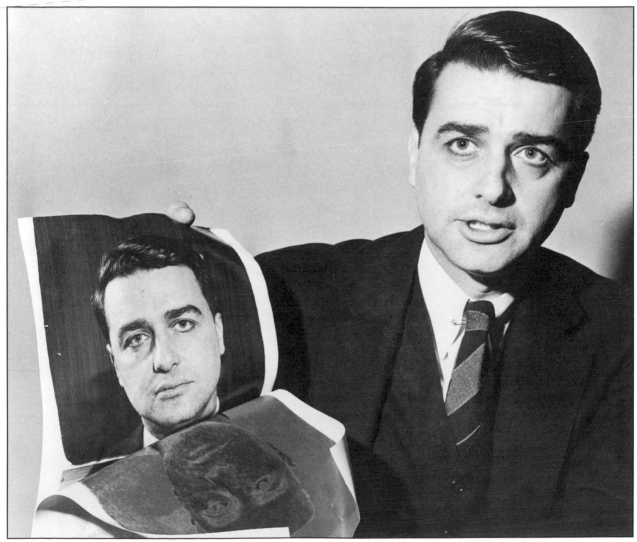

Land demonstrates his Polaroid process. (Library of Congress)

The Retinex Theory

Land's work in optics, as well as photography, resulted in a new explanation of how humans perceive and interpret color.

Light can be described as a wave. The length of a wave determines its frequency, or the rate at which it is vibrating. Different colors have different frequencies. For example, red has a high frequency, green has a middle-range frequency, and blue has a low frequency. Traditional theory held that the receptor rods and cones in the retina of the eye were selectively sensitive to the frequencies of the primary colors of blue, green, and red light, which then were combined to create the full range of colors of the natural world.

Land discovered that projecting on a screen two overlapped photograph negatives of a multicolored object, each taken with filters sensitive to a particular color frequency, would reproduce the full range of color in the image. From this result, Land concluded that color vision is based on the relationship of the ratio of long-to-short light frequencies received by the eye. If sufficient variation exists between any two frequencies, the brain will adjust to reproduce the true range of color.

Land proposed that the brain, not the eye, determines color perception and that somewhere in the cortex of the brain is a center for extrapolating, or filling in, the missing information. His retinex theory, while not fully accepted by all scientists, has stimulated a rethinking of the process by which humans perceive the world in color.

Bibliography
Human Color Perception: A Critical Study of the Experimental Foundation. Joseph Sheppard. New York: American Elsevier, 1968.
"The Retinex Theory of Color Vision." Edwin Land. *Scientific American* (December, 1977).

Bibliography
By Land
"A New One-Step Photographic Process," *Journal of the Optical Society of America*, 1947
"Some Aspects of the Development of Sheet Polarizers," *Journal of the Optical Society of America*, 1951
"The Retinex Theory of Color Vision," *Scientific American*, 1977

About Land
Fire of Genius. Ernest Heyn. Garden City, N.Y.: Anchor Press/Doubleday, 1976.
The Instant Image: Edwin Land and the Polaroid Experience. Mark Olshaker. New York: Stein & Day, 1978.

(Robert R. Gradie III)

Lev Davidovich Landau

Area of Achievement: Physics
Contribution: An outstanding theoretical physicist, Landau helped explain superfluids, superconductors, the composition of stars, nuclear processes, and the properties of quanta.

Jan. 22, 1908	Born in Baku, Azerbaijan, Russian Empire
1924	Graduated from the University of Baku at the age of sixteen
1924-1927	Attends Leningrad University
1927	Becomes a graduate student at the Leningrad Institute of Physics and Technology
1929-1931	Studies with Niels Bohr in Copenhagen, Denmark
1932	Serves as director of theoretical physics at the Physics-Technical Institute of the Ukrainian Academy of Sciences
1932	Named a professor at the Kharkov Institute of Mechanical Engineering
1934	Awarded doctorates in physics and mathematics
1935	Becomes a professor at Kharkov University
1937	Directs the theoretical section at the Institute for Physical Problems, Soviet Academy of Sciences in Moscow
1938-1939	Jailed on charges of espionage
1945	Elected as a full member of the Soviet Academy of Sciences
1962	Awarded the Nobel Prize in Physics
1962	Nearly killed in a car accident, left partially paralyzed
Apr. 1, 1968	Dies in Moscow, Soviet Union

Early Life

Lev Davidovich Landau was born in Baku on the Caspian Sea in 1908 to a science-minded family. His father worked as a petroleum engineer in nearby oil fields, and his mother was a physiologist and physician. His older sister Sofia later became a chemical engineer.

Landau showed remarkable talent for mathematics in primary school and raced through the curricula of the public schools, graduating at the age of thirteen. Obeying his father's wish, he then accompanied his sister to the Economic Technical School to study finance, but, after a year, he transferred to Baku University to pursue his real interests, physics and mathematics. In 1924, he transferred again, this time to Leningrad University; he was graduated in 1927, having already published his first professional article the previous year when he was nineteen years old.

Bohr and Quantum Physics

After his graduation, Landau immediately began graduate studies at the Leningrad Institute of Physics and Technology, where he concentrated on quantum mechanics. He investigated quantum electrodynamics and introduced the density matrix for energy, a widely used concept thereafter.

At the time, the mecca for quantum physics was Niels Bohr's institute in Copenhagen, Denmark. Accordingly, Landau went there in 1929 to work with Bohr. Although much different in temperament, the two great physicists became fast friends; Landau considered Bohr his mentor and spiritual guide.

Landau also worked with many other founders of modern physics during his eighteen months away from the Soviet Union, including Wolfgang Pauli, Paul Ehrenfest, Ernest Rutherford, Werner Heisenberg, and Rudolf Peierls. He advanced the understanding of relativistic quantum mechanics and diamagnetism, astonishing his colleagues with the quickness of his mind and his sweeping grasp of mathematics.

The Theoretical Minimum

In 1931, Landau resumed graduate studies in Leningrad, pursuing a variety of theoretical problems. He moved to the Ukraine in 1932,

Superfluids

Superfluidity occurs in some forms of matter when they are cooled to just above absolute zero (0 degrees Kelvin or −459.67 degrees Fahrenheit). They acquire special properties, such as the loss of resistance.

Landau studied the changes of state that matter undergoes at varying critical temperatures. These phase changes, he argued, are of two kinds. A first-order phase change involves obvious alterations in the appearance of a material, as when water changes from a liquid to a solid during freezing or from a gas to a liquid during precipitation. A second-order phase change is more subtle: The appearance of the material stays the same, but some of its physical properties transform.

A superfluid is one product of a second-order phase change. Pyotr Kapitsa, a senior colleague of Landau, first observed superfluidity in helium 4 in 1938. Scientists achieved superfluidity in a second isotope, helium 3, in the 1960's. Helium never freezes solid: At 4.2 degrees Kelvin, it becomes a liquid, and, at 2.19 degrees Kelvin, it suddenly loses all its resistance to motion, or viscosity, and conducts heat with enormous efficiency. Superfluids can flow through the pores in most solids and therefore are difficult to keep in containers.

Landau realized that superchilled helium 4 obeys the rules of quantum mechanics because all of its atoms assume a common state of minimum energy. The atoms then behave as if they were a single large atom, moving together. On the basis of this insight, Landau was able to compose a mathematical theory of superfluids. He predicted that a superfluid conducts both pressure waves (sound waves), as does ordinary matter, and heat waves ("second-sound" waves), each of which moves at a different speed. Other scientists soon verified this prediction through experiments.

Landau also realized that superfluidity is similar to superconductivity, another form of second-order phase change in which electrons move without resistance through metals cooled below a critical temperature. His theory of superconductivity, which was influential but later superseded, pointed out that when pairs of electrons move through a conductor, they essentially behave like a superfluid. Landau's theories laid the foundation for the burst of technology dependent on superconductors, including high-power magnets, supercomputer circuits, and medical imaging equipment.

Almost no applications for superfluids exist, although an experimental gyroscope using superfluid helium has been built. Nevertheless, superfluids help physicists understand the nature of matter and provide clues to such large-scale phenomena as the origin of galaxies and the existence of cosmic strings, bizarre loops of rolled-up space-time that are supposed to have formed in the early universe.

Bibliography

A History and Philosophy of Fluid Mechanics. G. A. Tokaty. New York: Dover, 1994.
The New Physics. Paul Davies, ed. New York: Cambridge University Press, 1986.
The Quantum Universe. Tony Hey and Patrick Walters. Cambridge, England: Cambridge University Press, 1987.

successively holding positions at the Ukrainian Institute of Physics and Technology and at the Institute of Mechanical Engineering in Kharkov; in 1935, he became a professor at Kharkov University. He married Concordia (Cora) Drobantseva in 1937. Their son, Igor, became an experimental physicist.

Widely recognized as having one of the most talented minds in physics, Landau soon was called to the center of Soviet science. In 1937, Pyotr Kapitsa appointed him director of the theoretical section of the Soviet Academy of Sciences' Institute of Physical Problems.

Landau had already shown skill as a teacher, as well as a theoretician, and he developed a famous sequence of nine demanding examinations, called the theoretical minimum, designed to identify the most talented students. In 1938, he also published *Statisticheskaya fizica* (*Statistical Physics*, 1938), the first volume of his course of theoretical physics, a detailed survey of all physics disciplines.

Landau's outspoken nature and brilliance attracted students who became leaders of Soviet physics and space science. Landau's sharp criticisms, however, also attracted suspicion from Soviet leader Joseph Stalin. In 1938, the secret police whisked him away to the Butyrskaya state prison, accused him of spying for Nazi Germany, and gave him a ten-year sentence, although, as a Jew, Landau was a very unlikely Nazi sympathizer. A year later, Kapitsa managed to free Landau.

Phase Changes

For the rest his life, Landau trained theoreticians and published widely influential articles on an exceptionally diverse variety of topics—such as low-temperature physics, different types of magnetism, particle behavior in a plasma, shock waves, turbulence, the detonation of explosives, the analysis of spectral lines, and quantum field theory. He is best known, however, for his theories explaining the superconductivity and superfluidity of materials chilled to temperatures just above absolute zero.

Both his native country and other nations showered him with honors, among them the Lenin Prize, the Hero of the Soviet Labor, the Order of Lenin, the Fritz London Prize, and the Max Planck Medal and memberships in the Danish, Dutch, American, and Soviet academies of sciences and the Royal Society of London.

In 1962, Landau received the Nobel Prize in Physics for his work in low-temperature physics, the superfluidity of helium in particular. He could not attend the awards ceremony, however, because he was in a Moscow hospital recovering from a near-fatal automobile accident. Although Landau was able to resume some of his duties, the accident ended his career, for he never recovered fully. He died six years later, at only sixty years of age.

(The Nobel Foundation)

Bibliography

By Landau

Statisticheskaya fizica, 1938 (with Evgenii Mikhailovich Lifshitz; *Statistical Physics*, 1938)

Teoria polya, 1941 (with Lifshitz; *The Classical Theory of Fields*, 1951)

Mekhanika sploshnykh sred, 1944 (with Lifshitz; *Fluid Mechanics*, 1959)

Kvantovaya mekhanika, 1948 (with Lifshitz; *Quantum Mechanics: Non-Relativistic Theory*, 1958)

Lekstskii po teori atomnogo yadra, 1955 (with Yakov Smorodinsky; *Lectures on Nuclear Theory*, 1958)

Elektrodynamika sploshnykh sred, 1957 (with Lifshitz; *Electrodynamics of Continuous Media*, 1960)

Mekhanika, 1958 (with Lifshitz; *Mechanics*, 1960)

Chto takoe teoriia otnositel' nosti, 1959 (with G. B. Rumer; *What Is Relativity?*, 1960)

Collected Papers of L. D. Landau, 1965

Kratkii kurs teoreticheskoi fiziki, 1969-1972 (with Lifshitz; *A Shorter Course on Theoretical Physics*, 1972)

About Landau

Landau, a Great Physicist and Teacher. Anna Livanova. New York: Pergamon, 1980.

"Lev Davidovich Landau." In *The Nobel Prize Winners: Physics*, edited by Frank N. Magill. Pasadena, Calif.: Salem Press, 1989.

The Man They Wouldn't Let Die. Alexander Dorozynski. New York: Macmillan, 1965.

Thirty Years That Shook Physics: The Story of Quantum Physics. George Gamow. Garden City, N.Y.: Doubleday, 1966.

(Roger Smith)

Karl Landsteiner

Areas of Achievement: Biology, genetics, immunology, and medicine

Contribution: A pioneer in the development of immunology, Landsteiner received the Nobel Prize in Physiology or Medicine for his discovery of human blood groups.

June 14, 1868	Born in Vienna, Austria
1891	Graduated in medicine, from the University of Vienna
1891-1896	Receives training at the laboratories of Arthur Hantzsch, Emil Fischer, and E. Bamberger
1896	Serves as an assistant to Max von Gruber at the Hygiene Institute
1898	Becomes an assistant in pathological anatomy at Vienna
1900-1901	Demonstrates the existence of different types of human blood (A, B, and O groups)
1908	Appointed as a dissector at the Wilhelminaspital and an adjunct professor of pathological anatomy at Vienna
1919	Moves to the Netherlands and takes a position as a dissector at a small Catholic hospital
1922	Joins the Rockefeller Institute for Medical Research in New York City as a researcher
1927-1928	With Philip Levine, reports the discovery of additional blood groups (M, N, and MN) in humans
1930	Awarded the Nobel Prize in Physiology or Medicine for his discovery of blood groups
1940	With Alexander S. Wiener, reports the existence of Rh blood groups
June 26, 1943	Dies in New York, New York

(Library of Congress)

Early Life

Karl Landsteiner's father, Leopold, was a prominent Viennese journalist who died when his son was only six years old. Thus, Karl was brought up by his widowed mother, Fanny Hess Landsteiner.

After his graduation from the University of Vienna with a medical degree in 1891, Landsteiner received sound training in organic chemistry from Arthur Hantzsch at the University of Zurich, in Switzerland, as well as from Emil Fischer at the University of Würzburg, and E. Bamberger at the University of Munich, both in Germany.

The Discovery of Blood Groups

While employed as an assistant at the department of pathological anatomy at the University of Vienna, Landsteiner wrote a footnote in his only paper published in 1900 which dealt with natural antibodies. The footnote contained a significant observation: "The serum of healthy human beings not only agglutinates animal red cells, but also often those of human origin, from other individuals."

Landsteiner used his own blood in the agglutination experiments and, in 1901, published a short, definitive paper entitled "Über Agglutinationscheinungen normalen menschlichen Blutes" (on the agglutination of normal human blood), describing his classic effort on the identification of three blood groups: A, B, and O.

Focus on Microbiology

For almost two decades, from 1903 to 1922, Landsteiner shifted gears and focused his attention on microbiology. Although he was able to work in Vienna during World War I, wartime deprivations in Austria, marriage to Helene Wlasto in 1916, and the birth of a son, Ernst, in 1917 made him find a position as a chief dissector in a small Catholic hospital in The Hague, the Netherlands, in 1918. In addition to the routine demands of conducting autopsies and analyzing urine and blood samples, he continued his research.

Landsteiner contributed to the development of microbiology and immunology by elucidating the pathogenesis of paroxysmal hemoglobinuria, introducing dark-field microscopy for the diagnosis of syphilis, developing a complement fixation test for syphilis, identifying the viral origin of poliomyelitis, cultivating *Rickettsia* in tissue cultures, studying the pathogenesis of contact dermatitis, introducing the concept of haptens (parts of antigens that react with antibodies), and clarifying the specificity of plant agglutinins.

After emigrating to the United States in April, 1922, and accepting a research position at the Rockefeller Institute for Medical Research, Landsteiner again returned to study the blood groups. At last, he also had a laboratory of his own.

The Nobel Prize

Three decades after his publication of the existence of different blood groups in humans, Landsteiner was honored with the Nobel Prize in Physiology or Medicine in 1930. In his Nobel lecture, delivered on December 11, 1930, he highlighted the multiple applications of his discovery. These included the ability to trace the origin of and relationships among human races, a higher rate of success in blood transfusion practices, and forensic investigations to verify paternity claims and help in "inducing some fathers to recognise their illegitimate child."

Later Years

After his Nobel Prize, Landsteiner did not rest on his laurels. He wrote a definitive work, *Die Spezifität der serologischen Reaktionen*, which was published in 1933. Its English translation,

Differences in Human Blood

The four major different types of human blood—A, B, O, and AB—are the result of substances known as isoagglutinogens with two different structures, of which both or one may be present or both absent in an individual's red blood cells.

Landsteiner was the first to report the existence of three blood types after a classic experiment. He collected blood from five of his associates and some of his own blood, mixed equal amounts of serum and 5 percent red blood cell suspension in 0.6 percent saline, and observed what happened. He noticed that some of the cell suspensions were clumped by the serums of certain individuals but not of others.

Landsteiner tabulated the findings as follows, under the caption, "Concerning the Blood of Six Apparently Healthy Men," with the + sign indicating agglutination (clumping).

Sera						
Dr. St	−	+	+	+	+	−
Dr. Plecn	−	−	+	+	−	−
Dr. Sturl	−	+	−	−	+	−
Dr. Erdh	−	+	−	−	+	−
Zar	−	−	+	+	−	−
Landst	−	+	+	+	+	−
Red blood cells of	Dr. St	Dr. Plecn	Dr. Sturl	Dr. Erdh	Zar	Landst

Landsteiner inferred that there are active substances known as isoagglutinins in the serum (liquid portion of the blood) and that they are present in a specific distribution. Every serum contains those agglutinins that react with the agglutinogens not present in the red blood cells. Thus, in his Nobel lecture, he presented the following relationship, with the + sign indicating agglutination.

Serum of group	Agglutinins in serum*	Red blood cells of group			
		O	A	B	AB
O	αβ	−	+	+	+
A	β	−	−	+	+
B	α	−	+	−	+
AB	−	−	−	−	−

* α, anti-A; β, anti-B

The discovery of blood groups by Landsteiner and the later findings that the blood group characteristics are inherited in accordance with Gregor Mendel's laws of genetics made possible the safe transfusion of blood from one person to another and paternity screening in legal cases.

Bibliography

"Is Karl Landsteiner the Einstein of the Biomedical Sciences?" Sachi Sri Kantha. *Medical Hypotheses* 44 (1995).

"Karl Landsteiner, M.D.: History of Rh-Hr Blood Group System." Alexander S. Wiener. *New York State Journal of Medicine* 69 (November 15, 1969).

"The Purpose of Immunity: Landsteiner's Interpretation of the Human Isoantibodies." Pauline M. H. Mazumdar. *Journal of the History of Biology* 8 (Spring, 1975).

"A Review of Landsteiner's Contributions to Human Blood Groups." Philip Levine. *Transfusion* 1 (1961).

The Specificity of Serological Reactions, first appeared in 1936.

Then, in 1940, at the age of seventy-two, Landsteiner and his junior colleague Alexander S. Wiener reported another landmark discovery, an agglutinable factor in human blood recognized by its immune serum for the blood from a Rhesus monkey, now known as Rh factor. Until his death in June, 1943, when Landsteiner suffered a heart attack while working in his laboratory, he continued to publish papers on the Rh factor.

Landsteiner's discoveries influenced many biomedical disciplines, such as immunochemistry, medical anthropology, forensic medicine, genetics, and pathology.

Bibliography
By Landsteiner

"Zur Kenntnis der antifermentativentytischen und agglutinierenden Wirkungen des Blutserum und der Lymph," *Centralblatt für Bakteriologie Parasitenkunde und Infektionskrankheiten*, 1900

"Über Agglutinationscheinungen normalen menschlichen Blutes," *Wien Klin Wochenschr*, 1901

"Über die verwertbarkeit individueller Blut differenzen für die forensische Praxis," *Zeitschr Medizin*, 1903 (with M. Richter)

"Demonstriert mikroskopische praparate von einem menschlichen und zwei affenrucken-marken," *Wien Klin Wochenschr*, 1908 (with H. Raubitschek)

"A New Agglutinable Factor Differentiating Individual Human Bloods," *Proceedings of the Society for Experimental Biology and Medicine*, 1926-1927 (with Philip Levine)

"Further Observations on Individual Differences of Human Blood," *Proceedings of the Society for Experimental Biology and Medicine*, 1926-1927 (with Levine)

"Über Individuelle unterschiede des menschlichen Blutes" in *Les Prix Nobel en 1930*, 1931 ("Individual Differences in Human Blood," *Science*, 1931)

Die Spezifität de serologischen Reaktionen, 1933 (*The Specificity of Serological Reactions*, 1936)

"An Agglutinable Factor in Human Blood Recognized by Immune Sera for Rhesus Blood," *Proceedings of the Society for Experimental Biology and Medicine*, 1940 (with Alexander S. Wiener)

About Landsteiner

"Karl Landsteiner." In *The Nobel Prize Winners: Physiology or Medicine*, edited by Frank N. Magill. Pasadena, Calif.: Salem Press, 1991.

"Karl Landsteiner: Dissector of the Blood." Elmer Bendiner. *Hospital Practice* 26, 3A (March 30, 1991).

"Karl Landsteiner: Founder of Immunohematology." Jain I. Lin. *Laboratory Medicine* 15 (February, 1984).

Species and Specificity: An Interpretation of the History of Immunology. Pauline Mazumdar. New York: Cambridge University Press, 1995.

(Sachi Sri Kantha)

Samuel Pierpont Langley

Areas of Achievement: Astronomy, invention, mathematics, physics, and technology
Contribution: Langley, a pioneer in solar astrophysics, also made contributions to the development of heavier-than-air flight.

Aug. 22, 1834	Born in Roxbury, Massachusetts
1851-1864	Works as an architectural draftsman
1865	Works as an assistant at the Harvard Observatory
1866	Appointed assistant professor of mathematics and director of the observatory at the U.S. Naval Academy
1867-1887	Teaches physics and astronomy and directs the Allegheny Observatory at the Western University of Pennsylvania
1879-1881	Invents the bolometer, which can measure minute changes in solar energy accurately
1881	Organizes an expedition to climb Mount Whitney in order to gather data to calculate the solar constant
1887-1906	Serves as secretary of the Smithsonian Institution
1887	Helps create the National Zoological Park, Washington, D.C.
1890	Opens the Smithsonian Astrophysical Observatory
1896	Makes the first successful flight of an unpiloted, powered, heavier-than-air flying machine
1903	Makes two unsuccessful attempts to fly a piloted, full-scale version of his aircraft
Feb. 22, 1906	Dies in Aiken, South Carolina

Early Life

Samuel Pierpont Langley, son of a wealthy Boston merchant, was descended from a long line of distinguished New England business and political leaders, skilled craftsmen, and military leaders. He was distantly related to presidents John Adams and John Quincy Adams.

As a boy, Langley showed an aptitude for mechanics and mathematics, as well as skill at drawing. He hoped to combine these talents with his first love, astronomy. With few employment prospects in this field, however, he instead decided to pursue a career as an architectural draftsman. In 1864, after twelve years working mostly in the Midwest, Langley finally returned to Boston to pursue astronomy.

In 1865, he secured a job as an assistant to Joseph Winlock at the Harvard Observatory. With this experience, Langley finally realized his ambition of a fully professional position in astronomy when he was appointed assistant professor of mathematics and director of the observatory at the U.S. Naval Academy in 1866.

The Allegheny Observatory

After only a year at the Naval Academy, Langley accepted the post of professor of physics and astronomy, as well as director of the Al-leghany Observatory, at the Western University of Pennsylvania (now the University of Pittsburgh), a position that he would hold for twenty years. Upon his arrival, Langley was shocked to find the observatory at Allegheny to be in deplorable condition. When he was finally able to begin his astronomical work in earnest, he focused on the sun. His principal interest was infrared astronomy, the area of the spectrum beyond visible wavelengths. Between 1879 and 1881, he developed an instrument that he called the bolometer to measure heat energy in the infrared range of the spectrum.

Langley used his bolometer to pursue one of his central astronomical quests—an accurate measurement of the solar constant, the value of the sun's heat energy before it is absorbed by the earth's atmosphere. In 1881, he organized a large expedition to Mount Whitney, in California, to measure solar energy at higher elevations, where the atmosphere is thinner, in order to calculate the solar constant.

In addition to his academic research, Langley was a great believer in popular science education. He published extensively in newspapers and magazines, and he frequently delivered public lectures. By the 1880's he was

Expanding the Infrared Spectrum

Langley's precise measurement of the infrared portion of the spectrum demonstrated significant radiation beyond the wavelength of two microns, which had been thought to be the limit of solar radiation.

At the turn of the nineteenth century, Sir William Herschel discovered that a temperature increase occurs when one moves from shorter to longer wavelengths of the visible spectrum. He further noticed that this temperature increase continued beyond the visible range into what is now called the infrared portion of the spectrum. Langley was interested in not only detecting this solar energy but also measuring it accurately.

Between 1879 and 1881, Langley developed an instrument called the bolometer that could identify and precisely measure these minute changes in temperature. The device was at least two orders of magnitude more sensitive than anything else then in use. During his expedition up Mount Whitney, in California, Langley detected significant radiation well beyond a wavelength of 2 microns. Previously, a level of 2 microns was considered the limit of solar radiation. Langley's discovery of an expanded range of the infrared, what he termed "The New Spectrum," opened new avenues in the study of the sun.

Bibliography

Exploration of the Universe. George O. Abell, David Morrison, and Sidney C. Wolff. Philadelphia: Saunders College Publishing, 1991.
Infrared: The New Astronomy. David Allen. New York: John Wiley & Sons, 1975.
McGraw-Hill Encyclopedia of Astronomy. S. P. Parker and J. M. Pasachoff, eds. New York: McGraw-Hill, 1993.

(North Wind Picture Archives)

ing arm device to investigate the effects of air flow over different shapes. At the Smithsonian, he turned to building actual flying machines with a series of steam-powered and gasoline-powered unpiloted model craft that he called aerodromes. Modest success with these small aircraft led to the construction of a full-scale, piloted version in 1903. Two humiliating public failures with the so-called Great Aerodrome, however, severely compromised Langley's reputation. (That same year, the Wright Brothers successfully flew the first airplane.) Langley died a despondent man in 1906.

Bibliography

By Langley
"Researches on Solar Heat and Its Absorption by the Earth's Atmosphere: A Report of the Mount Whitney Expedition," *Professional Papers of the Signal Service*, 1884

The New Astronomy, 1887

Experiments in Aerodynamics, 1891

The New Spectrum, 1901

"Langley Memoir on Mechanical Flight" in *Smithsonian Contributions to Knowledge*, 1911

About Langley
A Dream of Wings: Americans and the Airplane, 1875-1905. Tom D. Crouch. New York: W. W. Norton, 1981.

"Founding the Astrophysical Observatory: The Langley Years." John A. Eddy. *Journal for the History of Astronomy* 21 (1990).

Langley: Man of Science and Flight. J. Gordon Vaeth. New York: Ronald Press, 1966.

Sons of Science: The Story of the Smithsonian Institution and Its Leaders. Paul H. Oehser. New York: Greenwood Press, 1968.

(Peter L. Jakab)

popularly regarded as one of America's leading scientists.

The Smithsonian and Aeronautics
Langley was appointed secretary of the Smithsonian Institution in 1887, a post that he held for the remainder of his life. He continued his interest and work in astronomy, opening the Smithsonian Astrophysical Observatory in 1890. His central research focus, however, shifted to aeronautics during the Smithsonian years.

He began experiments in aerodynamics while still at Allegheny using a 70-foot whirl-

Irving Langmuir

Areas of Achievement: Chemistry, physics, and technology

Contribution: Langmuir, an industrial physical chemist, did pioneering work in electrical technology, surface chemistry, the structure of matter, electrical discharge, thermionic emission, plasma physics, and weather modification.

Jan. 31, 1881	Born in Brooklyn, New York
1906	Earns a Ph.D. from the University of Göttingen
1906-1909	Works as an instructor at the Stevens Institute of Technology
1909	Joins the General Electric Research Laboratory
1918	Elected to the National Academy of Sciences
1929	Named president of the American Chemical Society
1932	Wins the Nobel Prize in Chemistry
1932-1950	Made associate director of the General Electric Research Laboratory
1938	Serves as Pilgrim Trust Lecturer for the Royal Society of London
1941	Elected president of the American Association for the Advancement of Science
1943	Awarded the Faraday Medal
1946	Named Hitchcock Foundation Lecturer at the University of California
1948-1950	Serves on the Board of Trustees for the State University of New York
1950	Retires from General Electric
Aug. 16, 1957	Dies in Falmouth, Massachusetts

Early Life

Irving Langmuir was the third of four sons born to Charles and Sadie (Comings) Langmuir. He attended public school in Brooklyn until 1892, Parisian boarding schools from 1892 to 1895 (starting when his father became director of European agencies for the New York Life Insurance Company), and the Chestnut Hill Academy in Philadelphia from 1895 to 1896.

Langmuir was graduated from the Pratt Institute's Manual Training High School of Brooklyn in 1899, obtained a metallurgical engineering baccalaureate in 1903 from the Columbia School of Mines, and traveled to Germany to earn a Ph.D. in 1906 at the University of Göttingen under the physical chemist Walther Nernst. Langmuir then taught chemistry for three years at the Stevens Institute of Technology in Hoboken, New Jersey, but he found little opportunity for research there.

Joining General Electric

In 1909, Langmuir took a summer job under Willis Whitney at the Research Laboratory of

(Library of Congress)

Surface Chemistry

The surface of solids and liquids can be covered with a single layer of adsorbed molecules called a monolayer, whose presence influences interfacial phenomena and whose orderly structure is related to molecular properties.

Chemists of the early twentieth century lacked a comprehensive theory for the phenomenon of adsorption. Langmuir proposed that adsorption involves the formation of a single layer of molecules arranged evenly on a surface. The famous Langmuir isotherm expression was derived to measure the extent of surface coverage by this monolayer and confirmed its existence.

Langmuir's new concept of adsorption was applied to films of organic molecules spread onto the surface of water. The Langmuir film balance, developed at the General Electric Research Laboratory, was used to measure the size, shape, surface orientation, packing, and intermolecular forces of molecules in organic monolayers ranging from simple fatty acids to proteins.

Monolayers provide models for biological membranes and are employed in the fabrication of sophisticated optical and electronic devices. The principles of surface chemistry summarized so clearly by Langmuir are applied in heterogeneous catalysis, lubrication, colloidal dispersion, and other interfacial phenomena.

Bibliography

Introduction to Surface Chemistry and Catalysis. Gabor A. Somorjai. New York: Wiley-Interscience, 1994.
Langmuir-Blodgett Films: An Introduction. Michael C. Petty. Cambridge, England: Cambridge University Press, 1996.
Lipid and Biopolymer Monolayers at Liquid Interfaces. K. S. Birdi. New York: Plenum Press, 1989.
Physical Chemistry of Surfaces. Arthur W. Adamson. 5th ed. New York: Wiley-Interscience, 1990.
Surfactant Aggregation. John H. Clint. New York: Chapman & Hall, 1992.

the General Electric Company in Schenectady, New York, which became his lifelong employer. He established the international reputation of a celebrity who ultimately received fifteen honorary degrees and twenty-three scientific medals and prizes, including the Nobel Prize in Chemistry, awarded in 1932 for his surface chemistry work.

Industrial scientists at the General Electric Research Laboratory were free to pursue projects based on personal interest and scientific merit. Enormous long-term profits from practical applications of Langmuir's discoveries encouraged other corporations and governmental agencies to fund pure research, which continued as a national trend until the mid-1980's.

A Prolific Scientist

Langmuir published more than two hundred scientific papers, often arranged into the following interrelated categories: chemical reactions at high temperatures and low pressures (1906-1921); thermal effects in gases (1911-1936); atomic structure (1919-1921); thermionic

emission and surfaces in vacuums (1913-1937); chemical forces in solids, liquids, and surface films (1916-1943); electrical discharges in gases (1923-1932); and atmospheric science (1938-1955).

The "octet rule" for "covalent" and "electrovalent" (ionic) chemical bonding were terms proposed by Langmuir to clarify the initial ideas of Gilbert Lewis. Langmuir also coined the word "plasma" and developed the field of magnetohydrodynamics to describe ionized gas as a fourth state of matter. This work provided fundamental concepts for understanding electrical discharges, thermonuclear fusion, and astrophysics. He offered a pioneering theory for thermionic emission from hot metals and the Child-Langmuir space-charge equation for the current between electrodes.

Langmuir's innovations, involving more than sixty patents, include the gas-filled incandescent lamp, atomic hydrogen welding, and the mercury-condensation pump used to produce high-vacuum power tubes for radio broadcasting. He worked on submarine detection during World War I and studied protective

788   Lankester, Sir Edwin Ray

smoke screens and aircraft icing during World War II. He continued military research as the head of Project Cirrus, which led to the first artificial rain and snow produced by cloud seeding.

Langmuir died in 1957 at the age of seventy-six.

Bibliography
By Langmuir
"Atomic Hydrogen as an Aid to Industrial Research," *Science*, 1928
"Surface Chemistry," *Chemical Reviews*, 1933
"Molecular Films in Chemistry and Biology" in *Molecular Films, the Cyclotron, and the New Biology*, 1942 (Hugh Scott Taylor, ed.)
"Science, Common Sense, and Decency," *Science*, 1943
Phenomena, Atoms, and Molecules: An Attempt to Interpret Phenomena in Terms of Mechanisms or Atomic and Molecular Interactions, 1950
"Control of Precipitation from Cumulus Clouds by Various Seeding Techniques," *Science*, 1950
The Collected Works of Irving Langmuir, 1960-1962 (12 vols.; C. Guy Suits, ed.)

About Langmuir
"Classics and Classicists of Colloid and Interface Science: 9. Irving Langmuir." Milton Kerker. *Journal of Colloid and Interface Science* 133 (1989).
"Irving Langmuir." C. Guy Suits and Miles J. Martin. *Biographical Memoirs of the National Academy of Sciences* 45 (1974).
"Irving Langmuir and the 'Octet' Theory of Valence." Robert E. Kohler. *Historical Studies in the Physical Sciences* 4 (1974).
"Irving Langmuir and the Pursuit of Science and Technology in the Corporate Environment." Leonard S. Reich. *Technology and Culture* 24 (1983).
The Quintessence of Irving Langmuir. Albert Rosenfeld. Oxford, England: Pergamon Press, 1966.

(Martin V. Stewart)

Sir Edwin Ray Lankester

Area of Achievement: Zoology
Contribution: Lankester was a zoologist whose research interests included all major groups of both fossil and living animals. He also helped reform science education in English universities.

May 15, 1847	Born in London, England
1868	Earns a bachelor's degree in zoology and geology from Cambridge University
1870-1872	Studies at universities in Austria, Germany, and Italy
1873	Named a Full Fellow at Exeter College, Oxford University
1875	Elected a Fellow of the Royal Society of London
1875-1890	Appointed a professor at University College, London
1878	Named sole editor of the *Quarterly Journal of Microscopical Science*
1884	Founds the Marine Biological Association
1888-1929	Elected president of the Marine Biological Association
1898-1907	Directs the British Museum of Natural History
1907	Knighted
1907-1914	Writes a popular science column for *The Daily Telegraph*, collected in *From an Easy Chair* (1909) and *Science from an Easy Chair* (1910)
1908	Receives the Darwin-Wallace Medal from the Linnaean Society
1913	Wins the Copley Medal of the Royal Society of London
Aug. 15, 1929	Dies in London, England

Early Life

Edwin Ray Lankester, the son of a respected microscopist who cofounded the *Quarterly Journal of Microscopical Science*, met many scientists as a child. As a schoolboy, he attended popular lectures given by Thomas Henry Huxley, who became his mentor, and, in 1861, he published his first paper, a letter to *The Geologist* on a fossil animal.

In the mid-1860's, Lankester published several papers on earthworms, attracting the attention of Charles Darwin. After receiving a Radcliffe Traveling Fellowship, Lankester made microscopical studies of marine species in Naples, Italy, and learned German laboratory techniques and methods of teaching. In 1872, he earned his master's degree.

Emphasis on the Laboratory

At this time, science education was very weak at both Oxford and Cambridge Universities. Lankester became convinced that science education in England had to be reformed on the German model.

At Oxford, he petitioned to teach in the museum but was refused. At University College, London, however, he taught in the zoological laboratory in the museum, where he emphasized practical laboratory work. His equipment included aquariums for saltwater and freshwater species. Lankester's efforts at University College turned it into a major center for teaching and research into evolutionary relationships.

His studies in Naples instilled in Lankester the desire to establish a laboratory to study marine species in England. Lankester's public addresses played an important role in generating popular and official interest, leading to the founding of the Marine Biological Association in 1884. In 1888, its laboratory at Plymouth opened and was the only English facility able to participate in an international study of the North Sea from 1899 to 1901.

The Lister Institute

In 1882, Lankester discovered a blood parasite in frogs that scientists later recognized as a relative of the parasite that causes malaria. He also rediscovered in frogs a parasite related to those causing sleeping sicknesses. These discoveries led him to realize that microbiology held implications for medicine. During the 1890's, he thus became involved in the estab-

Working Out Evolutionary Relationships

Comparisons of invertebrate embryology (development) and morphology (structure and form) can help establish evolutionary relationships.

After the acceptance of evolution in the 1860's, biologists began to search for common ancestors. One of Lankester's most important studies was on the horseshoe crab, thought to be related to crabs or lobsters. Lankester compared the horseshoe crab with the scorpion, organ for organ, and concluded that the horseshoe crab, like the scorpion, was an arachnid, a group also including spiders. The common ancestor of the horseshoe crab and scorpion is an extinct sea scorpion.

On the other hand, Lankester was aware that similarities in structures could mislead a morphologist into concluding that two animals had an evolutionary link. Studying embryos, he showed that the appearance of similarity in some adult structures did not exist in their embryo-

logical structures. Adaptation to similar environments produced such similarities in adults, a phenomenon that he called homoplasy.

Lankester helped systematize the field of embryology, coining the terms "stomadaeum" (the part of the embryo's ectoderm that forms the mouth and oral cavity), "blastophore" (the opening to the digestive cavity), and "invagination" (the process in which the embryological layers turn inward).

Bibliography

Archetypes and Ancestors: Paleontology in Victorian London, 1850-1875. Adrian Desmond. Chicago: University of Chicago Press, 1982.

Essays in the History of Embryology and Biology. Jane M. Oppenheimer. Cambridge, Mass.: MIT Press, 1967.

Ontogeny and Phylogeny. Stephen J. Gould. Cambridge, Mass.: Harvard University Press, 1977.

(Library of Congress)

lishment of what became the Lister Institute of Preventative Medicine.

A Full Life
Lankester's contemporaries regarded him as one of the most prominent scientists of his time. He received several awards from both the Royal Society of London and the Linnaean Society. Among his friends were political philosopher Karl Marx and novelist Thomas Hardy.

Lankester became the sole editor of the *Quarterly Journal of Microscopical Science* in 1878 and remained until 1920. During his later years, he also wrote popular science articles and books on a wide variety of subjects. He died in 1929 at the age of eighty-two.

Bibliography
By Lankester
Comparative Longevity in Man and the Lower Animals, 1870
Degeneration: A Chapter in Darwinism and Parthenogenesis, 1880
Zoological Articles Contributed to the "Encyclopaedia Britannica," 1891
A Treatise on Zoology, 1900-1909
The Kingdom of Man, 1907
From an Easy Chair, 1909
Extinct Animals, 1909
Science from an Easy Chair, 1910
Diversions of a Naturalist, 1915
Secrets of Earth and Sea, 1920
Great and Small Things, 1923

About Lankester
"Charles Darwin and Associates, Ghostbusters." Richard Milner. *Scientific American* 275 (October, 1996).
E. Ray Lankester and the Making of Modern British Biology. Joseph Lester. Edited by Peter J. Bowler. London: British Society for the History of Science, 1995.
"The Friendship of Edwin Ray Lankester and Karl Marx: The Last Episode in Marx's Intellectual Evolution." Lewis S. Feuer. *Journal of the History of Ideas* 40 (1979).

(Kristen L. Zacharias)

Max von Laue

Areas of Achievement: Earth science and physics

Contribution: Laue won the Nobel Prize in Physics for his discovery of X-ray diffraction, which proved that X rays are electromagnetic waves and enabled scientists to measure the position of atoms in crystals

Oct. 9, 1879	Born in Pfaffendorf, near Kolenz, Germany
1898	Enters the University of Strasbourg
1903	Earns a Ph.D. in physics from the University of Berlin, studying under Max Planck
1905	Assists Planck at the Institute for Theoretical Physics
1909-1911	Teaches at the University of Munich and publishes one of the first books on Albert Einstein's relativity theory
1912	Works out mathematical equations for determining the structure of crystals and the wavelength of X rays
1912	Joins the faculty at the University of Zurich
1914	Awarded the Nobel Prize in Physics
1914	Made full professor of physics at the University of Frankfurt
1919	Returns to the University of Berlin as professor of physics
1932	Awarded the Max Planck Medal by the German Physical Society
1933	Opposes Einstein's dismissal from the Kaiser Wilhelm Institute for Physics
1950	Directs the Fritz Haber Institute of Physical Chemistry
Apr. 23, 1960	Dies in Berlin, West Germany

Early Life

Max Theodor Felix von Laue (pronounced "LOW-uh") was born in Pfaffendorf, in western Germany, on October 9, 1879. His father, Julius, was a civilian employed in the Prussian court system. By his early teenage years, Laue had a marked interest in physics. He began to attend regular meetings of a scientific society when the family lived in Berlin.

Laue entered the University of Strasbourg to study physics in 1898. One year later, he transferred to the University of Göttingen in northern Germany and then, within the same year, was accepted as a student of world-famous physicist Max Planck at the University of Berlin. Laue earned his Ph.D. in physics in July, 1903. He focused his doctoral research on mathematically explaining how light waves are affected when they intersect one another.

Teaching and Research

In 1905, Laue was invited to become Planck's chief assistant at the Institute for Theoretical

(The Nobel Foundation)

Physics in Berlin. In 1909, he moved to the University of Munich to join the faculty and continue his research, returning to his earlier interests in light and optics.

By 1907, he realized that his work in optics could be applied to Albert Einstein's theory of relativity. He became one of the first German professors to endorse Einstein's theory, providing critical experimental and theoretical support.

X-Ray Diffraction

In 1912, Laue began working on an article to explain wave optics, including how light waves are diffracted (bent) when passing through various substances. He also began to consider the perplexing question as to whether X rays are actually short, electromagnetic waves. While discussing the problem with a colleague who was studying another question of the day—the internal physical structure of crystals—it occurred to Laue that exposure of X rays to a crystal could measure their wavelength.

Two assistants conducted the experiment on April 21, 1912, and obtained a pattern of dark points on a photographic plate placed behind the crystal. Laue realized that he could relate the positions of the points on the plate both to the position of the atoms in the crystal and to the length of the X rays themselves.

Laue's discovery, hailed by Einstein as one of the greatest discoveries in physics, resulted in the 1914 Nobel Prize in Physics. He had simultaneously provided a means of determining the position of atoms within crystals and other substances and of measuring exactly the length of X rays. Scientists would use these insights to study a wide range of physical structures and substances.

Later Life

In 1932, Laue was awarded the Max Planck Medal, Germany's highest scientific honor at the time. The next year, however, he placed himself at risk by opposing Adolf Hitler's dismissal of Einstein from the Kaiser Wilhelm Institute for Physics and by corresponding with Einstein in the United States.

Laue remained in Germany during World War II and was arrested at the war's end, along with other scientists, and taken to Great Britain for questioning. He returned to Germany, however, and helped to rebuild its scientific com-

X-Ray Diffraction

When an X-ray beam strikes matter, the atoms scatter the X radiation in various directions and at varying intensities. The interference patterns produced from the scattered radiation produce patterns of maximum and minimum intensity. This process is known as X-ray diffraction.

Scientists can study the light and dark patterns—termed "Laue patterns" in honor of Max von Laue's original discovery—that are produced by X-ray diffraction in order to determine both the atomic arrangement of the material that was exposed to the X rays and the wavelength of the X rays themselves.

X-ray diffraction functions in this way because of the relationship between the wavelength of X rays and the distances between planes within crystals. X rays range in wavelength from about 100 nanometers down to 0.1 nanometer (smaller than a single atom). In crystals, the planes of atoms are spaced at roughly 10 nanometers. X rays that are also roughly this wavelength will be scattered by the atomic planes within the crystal.

Scientists, following Laue's pioneering work, have applied X-ray diffraction methods to a wide variety of materials to determine crystal structures, differentiate between crystalline and amorphous materials, determine electron distribution within atoms, determine textures of polygrained materials, measure strain within a material, measure grain-sized matter, and study aspects of the structure of gases and liquids as well as of many solids.

Bibliography

Light. Michael I. Sobel. Chicago: University of Chicago Press, 1989.

X-Rays. Rob Morrison. New York: SRA School Group, Macmillan/McGraw-Hill, 1994.

munity. In 1950, he was appointed director of the Fritz Haber Institute of Physical Chemistry in Berlin-Dahlem. He died in 1960 at the age of eighty from injuries suffered in a traffic accident.

Bibliography
By Laue
Vorlesungen über Elektrodynamik und Theorie des Magnetismus, 1907 (as editor)
Das Relativitätsprinzip, 1911
Über einen Versuch zur Optik der bewegten Körper, 1911
Die Relativitätstheorie, 1921
Geschichte der Physik, 1946 (*History of Physics*, 1950)
Theorie der Supraleitung, 1947 (*Theory of Superconductivity*, 1952)
Vorlesungen über Thermodynamik, 1954 (as editor)
Gesammelte Schriften und Vorträge, 1961 (3 vols.)
"My Development as a Physicist: An Autobiography" in *Fifty Years of X-Ray Diffraction*, 1962 (Peter Paul Ewald, ed.)

About Laue
From X-Rays to Quarks: Modern Physicists and Their Discoveries. Emilio Segrè. San Francisco: W. H. Freeman, 1980.
Nobel Prize Winners: An H. W. Wilson Biographical Dictionary. Tyler Wasson, ed. New York: H. W. Wilson, 1987.
Reality and Scientific Truth: Discussions with Einstein, von Laue, and Planck. Ilse Rosenthal-Schneider. Detroit: Wayne State University Press, 1980.

(*Dennis W. Cheek*)

Alphonse Laveran

Areas of Achievement: Medicine, pharmacology, and zoology

Contribution: Laveran was the first to demonstrate that protozoa can cause disease. His work with malaria won for him the Nobel Prize in Physiology or Medicine in 1907.

June 18, 1845	Born in Paris, France
1867	Graduated from the École du Service de Santé Militaire in Strasbourg
1878-1883	Serves in Algeria and begins his studies into the cause of malaria
1879	Publishes a two-volume work on pathology and clinical medicine
Nov. 6, 1880	Makes a critical observation of a malaria parasite
1884	Publishes a treatise on palustrial fevers
1889	Receives the Bréant Prize from the Académie des Sciences
1896	Joins the Institut Pasteur
1901	Elected a member of the Académie des Sciences
1904	Publishes *Trypanosomes et trypanosomiases* (*Trypanosomes and Trypanosomiases*, 1907)
1907	Receives the Nobel Prize in Physiology or Medicine
1912	Made a commander in the Legion of Honor
May 18, 1922	Dies in Paris, France

Early Life
Charles Louis Alphonse Laveran (pronounced "la-VRAHN") was born in Paris in 1845. Several members of his family were physicians or

military officers, a heritage that he continued in his career.

When Laveran was only five, his family moved to Algeria, where he was taught mostly by his father. After returning to Paris, he completed his secondary education at the Lycée Louis-le-Grand and studied medicine in Strasbourg. In 1874, by taking a competitive examination, he earned the chair formerly held by his father at the Val-de-Grace military academy in Paris.

Army Life and Opportunity

The French army never noticed Laveran's talent for research, and he was frequently sent to posts with extensive administrative duties and no research opportunities. It is a tribute to his character that he would not allow these circumstances to nullify his gifts. During a potentially wasted assignment in Algeria, he carried out his most important work, the identification of the cause of malaria.

The comparison of fresh blood from both healthy and afflicted soldiers led to his hypothesis that a protozoan offered the best explanation of the various known facts about the disease. The accepted idea that bacteria were the cause of malaria, however, led most medical workers to insist that water, air, or soil must contain a causative bacterium. Laveran's work was disregarded for four years.

Ultimately, the weight of evidence became overpowering, and his research gained nearly universal acceptance. During this period, he had continued active research on the subject but had been unable to work out the full development of the parasite's life cycle. The problem was complicated: In Algeria, there are three separate, and common, forms of malaria. Laveran published his opinion that the mosquito is responsible for the life of the parasite outside the human body.

Working in India, Sir Ronald Ross later proved that the *Anopheles* mosquito is the required host for malaria. When he won the 1902 Nobel Prize in Physiology or Medicine, Ross gave Laveran credit for putting him on the right track.

(The Nobel Foundation)

Enough of the Army—Not of the Protozoa

Even with the general acceptance of his work, the army refused to provide for the development of Laveran's skills. Reluctantly, despite the pleas of several fellow officers, he resigned his commission in 1896 and joined the Institut Pasteur in Paris. There, in the company of able colleagues, he found an environment in which he could grow; he intensified and expanded his studies of protozoa and disease.

Over the next twenty years, Laveran continued to make important studies of these tiny creatures. He made contributions to the eventual identification of the parasite that causes sleeping sickness. In other studies of tropical fevers, he greatly advanced the techniques required for the laboratory study of protozoa.

It is a curious fact that the Nobel Prize must be given for "recent work." Thus, Laveran technically received this belated recognition for his work "on the role played by protozoa in causing disease," not for his discovery concerning malaria.

Laveran was made a commander in the Legion of Honor in 1912. He died in 1922 at the age of seventy-six.

Protozoa as Medical Parasites

It was common knowledge at the end of the nineteenth century that disease was caused by bacteria, but Laveran's discovery of a protozoan in the blood as the cause of malaria came as a great surprise to the medical world.

After Louis Pasteur proved his germ theory of disease, people believed that bacteria were the ultimate disease-causing organisms. Two Italian scientists published research claiming that a specific bacterium, *Bacillus malariae*, found in the soil and water of fever-infested areas caused malaria.

Blood from the corpse of a fever victim shows a black pigment, or melanemia. When blood is taken from the liver capillaries of a living malaria patient, the red blood cells have pigmented bodies with distinctive shapes and color. The patient's white blood cells also contain the black pigment, and outside the blood cells are crescent and spherical bodies with black fragments.

A critical observation of the malaria protozoa can be made when a blood sample is taken from a patient during a fever attack. In addition to the crescent-shaped bodies, those cells having a spherical shape show a series of fine, transparent filaments. These flagella, which are characteristic of the one-celled animals called protozoa, move actively among the red blood cells. Some of the flagella separate and disappear; these represent the male component in the sexual reproduction of protozoa.

Bibliography
Foundations of Parasitology. Gerald D. Schmidt and Donald A. Klein. 2d ed. St. Louis: C. V. Mosby, 1981.

The Marvelous Animals: An Introduction to the Protozoa. Helena Curtis. New York: Natural History Press, 1968.

Microbiology. Lansing M. Prescott, John P. Harley, and Donald A. Klein. Dubuque, Iowa: Wm. C. Brown, 1990.

Bibliography
By Laveran
Nouveaux éléments de pathologie et de clinique medicales, 1879 (2 vols.; with J. Teissier)

"Un Nouveau Parasite trouvé dans le sang des maladies atteints de fièvre palustre" in *Bulletin de Mémoriale Société de Médicale Hôpital de Paris,* 1880 (a new parasite found in the blood of sick with palustrial fever)

Traité des fièvres palustres: Avec la déscription des microbes du paludisme, 1884 (*Traits of Palustrial Fever with a Description of the Palustrial Microbes,* 1884)

Trypanosomes et trypanosomiases, 1904 (with F. Mesnil; *Trypanosomes and Trypanosomiases,* 1907)

About Laveran
"Alphonse Laveran." Lisa A. Lambert. In *The Nobel Prize Winners: Physiology or Medicine,* edited by Frank N. Magill. Pasadena, Calif.: Salem Press, 1991.

"Laveran, Charles Louis Alphonse." Marc Klein. In *Dictionary of Scientific Biography.* New York: Charles Scribner's Sons, 1973.

(K. Thomas Finley)

Antoine-Laurent Lavoisier

Area of Achievement: Chemistry
Contribution: Lavoisier's discoveries of oxygen and hydrogen established chemistry as a separate science. His laboratory methods and system for naming chemical elements and compounds became standards in the field.

Aug. 26, 1743	Born in Paris, France
1754	Begins his formal education at Collège Mazarin
1763	Earns a law degree and enters the Order of Advocates
1764	Publishes a scientific paper on the properties of gypsum
1765	Awarded for his proposal for lighting the streets of Paris
1768	Becomes a member of the Académie Royale des Sciences
1771	Marries Marie-Anne Paulze
1772	Shows that phosphorus absorbs air while burning
1775	As Superintendent of the Arsenal, improves France's supply of gunpowder
1782-1783	Creates a calorimeter to measure the heat produced in chemical reactions
1783	As part of his research on heat, proves that water is composed of two gases
1787	Suggests a new method of naming chemical elements and compounds
1791	Proposes a tax reform plan to the revolutionary government
May 8, 1794	Dies in Paris, France

(Library of Congress)

Early Life

Antoine-Laurent Lavoisier (pronounced "lah-vwah-ZYAY") was born in Paris, France, on August 26, 1743, to a comfortably middle-class family. He attended the Collège Mazarin, one of the best secondary schools, in order to prepare for a career in law, which was the profession of his father and his grandfather. Lavoisier studied humanities for six years and won prizes in French, Latin, and Greek at the end of the sixth year. He then began a three-year program in mathematics and philosophy. After studying mathematics for a year, he left to study law.

Lavoisier earned his law degree in 1763 and was admitted to practice law at the *parlement*, the court of twelve judges in Paris, but he was more interested in scientific research. He attended public lectures at the Jardin du Roi, the royal museum of natural history, botany, and zoology. The king's garden was the best institution of its kind in Europe. There, Lavoisier heard lectures by prominent scientists and mathematicians.

Lavoisier's maternal grandmother died in 1768, leaving him a large amount of money, which he used to buy a government position as a tax collector. This position did not require all his time and energy, so Lavoisier left the legal profession and began a new career in science.

Marriage and Early Success

The terms of his contract with the French government required Lavoisier to inspect the work of many tax collectors. He was away from Paris, traveling in the countryside, during 1769 and 1770. Lavoisier reported to Jacques Paulze, his future father-in-law.

Paulze's wife had died after giving birth to three sons and a daughter, Marie-Anne. The girl was reared in a convent, according to the custom of the time, and Paulze introduced his daughter to Lavoisier. An older man, politically powerful but not wealthy, had asked to marry Marie-Anne, who had inherited a fortune from her mother and her mother's family. Instead, Lavoisier and Marie-Anne were married on December 16, 1771. The bride was not yet fourteen, and the groom was twenty-eight.

Before 1750, chemistry was the business of

The Chemical Revolution

Lavoisier brought great changes to chemistry by proving experimentally that elements can exist as gases, liquids, and solids and that air and water are chemical compounds.

Combustion was the central problem in chemistry when Lavoisier began his experiments with phosphorus in 1772. Georg Ernst Stahl, a German chemist, had developed the generally accepted theory that combustion, or burning, involved the release of "phlogiston," leaving less material than existed before combustion. No chemist, however, had isolated phlogiston from other elements.

Stahl's theory of combustion explained many experiments, until Lavoisier noticed that iron weighs more after being burned than it does before. Lavoisier reasoned that if phlogiston were released during combustion, then iron should weigh less after combustion, not more. He also conducted experiments with phosphorus which convinced him that air combines with phosphorus during combustion. Lavoisier learned that the weight of the air lost during combustion equaled the weight gained by the phosphorus.

During these experiments, Lavoisier developed a new method of chemistry. With the most precise scales that could be made, he weighed all the instruments and all the materials before and after the experiments. He stored the materials carefully so that they would not be contaminated. He cleaned the instruments so that no foreign material would affect the experiment. He timed the experiments. His wife, Marie-Anne, kept precise records of everything that happened. He gave the name "oxygen" (meaning "acid-maker") to the air that had combined with the phosphorus. Thus, he began to write a new language for chemistry.

Lavoisier knew that the English chemists Joseph Black and Joseph Priestley had discovered several kinds of air because Marie-Anne had translated their reports into French. When he learned that dew appeared inside the glass vessel when Henry Cavendish, another English chemist, burned air, he knew that water was a chemical compound and air was part of it. Lavoisier replicated this experiment and was the first to understand what the result meant. Lavoisier named the new air, or gas, "hydrogen" (meaning "water-maker").

In a decade, Lavoisier brought about a revolution in chemistry. He proved that elements can exist as gases, as liquids, and in solid states. He proved that air and water are not elements, as had been believed for thousands of years, but chemical compounds made of the same gases combined in different weights.

Bibliography

Antoine-Laurent Lavoisier: Chemist and Revolutionary. Henry Guerlac. New York: Charles Scribner's Sons, 1975.

Historical Studies in the Language of Chemistry. Maurice Crosland. Cambridge, Mass.: Harvard University Press, 1962.

Lavoisier and the Chemistry of Life. Frederic Lawrence Holmes. Madison: University of Wisconsin Press, 1985.

Lavoisier, Antoine-Laurent

doctors and pharmacists. From the beginning, Lavoisier hoped that his experiments would be revolutionary: He wanted to make chemistry a separate science like physics or astronomy. Lavoisier began his experiments on combustion in 1772. At that time, all scientists accepted the theory of Aristotle, the ancient Greek philosopher, that there were four elements—earth, air, fire, and water.

Lavoisier accomplished his revolution within ten years. He proved that air and water are chemical compounds. He also proved that many elements can exist in several states—as gases, as liquids, or as solids. Marie-Anne recorded all of his experiments, noting the time required and drawing illustrations of the arrangements of the laboratory equipment that Lavoisier used.

The French Revolution

Lavoisier continued to work on important government projects while conducting the research that made him the founder of modern chemistry. For years, he advocated the reform of the tax system. He kept his government position after the French Revolution began in 1789.

A new government, however, was formed in 1791. The leaders were suspicious of Lavoisier because of his success and fame as a scientist

and as a public administrator under the old royal governments. When they ordered the imprisonment of tax collectors, Lavoisier and his father-in-law were among those arrested for conspiring against the people.

Although no evidence existed that he had broken any laws or deceived the public, Lavoisier was condemned to death. On May 8, 1794, he went to the guillotine. His widow, Marie-Anne, devoted the rest of her life to restoring his reputation.

Traité élémentaire de chimie, 1789 (*Elements of Chemistry in a New Systematic Order, Containing All the Modern Discoveries*, 1790)

Oeuvres de Lavoisier, 1862-1893 (6 vols.)

Oeuvres de Lavoisier: Correspondance, 1955-1986 (René Fric, ed.)

About Lavoisier

Antoine Lavoisier: Science, Administration, and Revolution. Arthur Donovan. Oxford, England: Blackwell, 1993.

Lavoisier: The Crucial Year. Henry Guerlac. Ithaca, N.Y.: Cornell University Press, 1961.

(Hugh L. Guilderson)

Ernest Orlando Lawrence

Area of Achievement: Physics

Contribution: Lawrence invented the cyclotron, a device for studying high-energy collisions of subatomic particles. Using this invention, he made key discoveries in nuclear reaction physics and identified several new isotopes of chemical elements.

Aug. 8, 1901	Born in Canton, South Dakota
1922	Earns a B.S. from the University of South Dakota
1923	Awarded an M.A. in physics from the University of Minnesota
1925	Earns a Ph.D. from Yale University
1928	Hired as an associate professor of physics at the University of California, Berkeley (UCB)
1930	Builds the first cyclotron
1932	Marries Mary Kimberly Blumer
1934	Elected to the National Academy of Sciences
1936	Appointed director of UCB's Radiation Laboratory
1937	Given the Comstock Prize by the National Academy of Sciences
1939	Awarded the Nobel Prize in Physics
1940	Helps found the Massachusetts Institute of Technology's Radiation Laboratory for research in radar detection systems
1942-1945	Studies the electromagnetic separation of uranium isotopes as part of the Manhattan Project
1952	Awarded the Faraday Medal
Aug. 27, 1958	Dies in Palo Alto, California

(Library of Congress)

Early Life

Ernest Orlando Lawrence was born in Canton, South Dakota, in 1901. Both of his parents were teachers, and Lawrence learned the importance of education at an early age. After finishing high school, he enrolled at St. Olaf College in Minnesota in 1917 and shortly thereafter transferred to the University of South Dakota.

After receiving his undergraduate degree in 1922, Lawrence moved to the University of Minnesota, where he received a master's degree in 1923 under the supervision of W. F. G. Swann, a physicist. Lawrence followed Swann to the University of Chicago and then to Yale.

Lawrence's early research focused on the photoelectric effect, a method by which free electrons are produced through shining light on a metal. After earning his Ph.D. in 1925, Lawrence was hired as a research fellow at Yale. He rapidly established a reputation as an outstanding experimental physicist and soon received several offers for permanent faculty positions. In 1928, he became a physics professor at the University of California, Berkeley (UCB).

The Cyclotron

A cyclotron is a device that can accelerate charged particles to high energies. Cyclotrons and related particle accelerators are used to study fundamental processes in particle physics.

A cyclotron is a circular particle accelerator. Ions are injected into the center of the cyclotron, where they are accelerated by a high-voltage alternating electric field. A uniform magnetic field of fixed strength is used to force the particles to travel in a circular path. Unlike with a linear accelerator, particles in a cyclotron make several passes through the accelerating field. Therefore, a relatively small cyclotron can be used to achieve particle beams of high energy.

For a cyclotron operating at a fixed frequency for the alternating electric field, the maximum energy at which protons can be accelerated is approximately 15 million electronvolts. At this point, the protons are traveling close to the speed of light, and relativistic effects prevent further increases in energy. This problem is solved in a device called a synchrocyclotron, in which a variable-frequency alternating electric field is used for particle acceleration. Proton energies as high as 800 million electronvolts have been generated in such devices. If the magnetic field used to cause the charged particles to travel in a circular path is also varied, even greater particle energies can be achieved. These devices, called synchrotrons, have been used in the discovery of quarks, the building blocks of the family of particles called baryons.

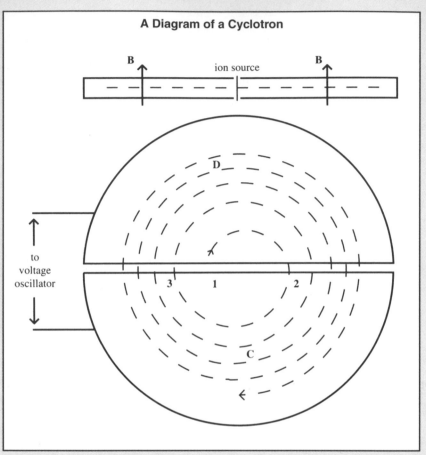

A Diagram of a Cyclotron

Ions are injected into the cyclotron at position 1. Upon entering semicircle D, which is free from electric fields, the ions are pulled to the semicircle C, which is charged to the opposite potential by the voltage oscillator. The polarity then reverses, forcing the ions back across the gap. The strong magnetic field at B keeps the ions confined to a semicircle. Eventually, they reach a circumference represented by positions 1, 2, and 3.

Bibliography

"The Next Generation of Particle Accelerators." R. R. Wilson. *Scientific American* (January, 1980).

Particle Accelerators and Their Uses. Waldemar Scharf. New York: Harwood Academic Publishers, 1986.

Principles of Charged Particle Acceleration. Stanley Humphries. New York: John Wiley & Sons, 1986.

The Invention of the Cyclotron

Shortly after arriving in California, Lawrence began investigating methods for producing high-energy subatomic particles. He realized that a combination of a high-frequency alternating electrical voltage combined with a large permanent magnet could be used to accelerate particles along a circular pathway. In this manner, a relatively small device could be used to produce particles of high energy.

Lawrence built the first cyclotron in 1930. A modified version of this instrument, built later in the year, was able to accelerate protons to an energy of 80,000 electronvolts. Successive improvements over the next few years led to instruments producing particles with energies of millions of electronvolts.

Lawrence used his cyclotrons to study elementary nuclear processes. In 1932, he confirmed earlier experiments showing that helium nuclei could be produced from the disintegration of lithium. In subsequent experiments, Lawrence discovered a large number of radioactive isotopes, including carbon 14, iodine 131, and uranium 233. In 1939, he was awarded in Nobel Prize in Physics for his invention of the cyclotron.

Later Accomplishments

In 1936, Lawrence was appointed the first director of the Radiation Laboratory at UCB, which was established to carry out research in high-energy physics. Shortly after the start of World War II, Lawrence helped found a second radiation laboratory at the Massachusetts Institute of Technology (MIT) for the development of radar detection systems. From 1942 to 1945, he worked on the electromagnetic separation of uranium isotopes as part of the Manhattan Project to develop the atomic bomb.

After the war, Lawrence became less active in research and more involved in the debate concerning the development of more powerful nuclear weapons. Lawrence died in 1958 following an exhausting trip to Switzerland to attend a meeting on the detection of violations to test bans on atomic weapons.

Bibliography

By Lawrence
"On the Production of High Speed Protons," *Science*, 1930 (with N. E. Edlefsen)
"Disintegration of Lithium by Swiftly Moving Protons," *Physical Review*, 1932 (with M. Stanley Livingston and Milton G. White)
"The Production of High Speed Light Ions Without the Use of High Voltages," *Physical Review*, 1932 (with Livingston)

The first successful cyclotron, built by Lawrence and graduate student M. Stanley Livingston in 1930. (Lawrence Berkeley National Laboratory)

"An Improved Cyclotron," *Science*, 1937 (with Donald Cooksey)

"Nuclear Physics and Biology" in *Molecular Films, the Cyclotron, and the New Biology: Essays*, 1942 (Hugh Scott Taylor, ed.)

"High Energy Physics," *American Scientist*, 1948

"High Current Accelerators," *Science*, 1955

About Lawrence

An American Genius: The Life of Ernest Orlando Lawrence. Herbert Childs. New York: E. P. Dutton, 1968.

Atomic Scientists: A Biographical History. Henry A. Boorse, Lloyd Motz, and Jefferson Hane Weaver. New York: John Wiley & Sons, 1989.

Lawrence and His Laboratory: Nuclear Science at Berkeley, 1931-1961. J. L. Heilbron, R. W. Seidel, and B. R. Wheaton. Berkeley: University of California Press, 1981.

Lawrence and Oppenheimer. Nuel Pharr Davis. New York: Simon & Schuster, 1968.

(*Jeffrey A. Joens*)

Henrietta Swan Leavitt

Area of Achievement: Astronomy

Contribution: A pioneer in the photographic measurements of the brightness of stars, Leavitt discovered 2,400 variable stars and established the period-luminosity law for measuring the distances to galaxies.

July 4, 1868	Born in Lancaster, Massachusetts
1885-1888	Studies at the Oberlin College Conservatory of Music
1892	Earns an A.B. at the Society for the Collegiate Instruction of Women (now Radcliffe College)
1895	Volunteers as a research assistant at the Harvard College Observatory
1902	Appointed to the staff of the Harvard College Observatory
1904	Begins observing the galaxies called the Magellanic Clouds
1907	Begins a survey of stars as chief of the photographic photometry department
1908	Publishes her study of 1,777 variables in the Magellanic Clouds
1912	Proposes the period-luminosity law for Cepheid variable stars
1917	Publishes "The North Polar Sequence," offering a brightness standard for stars in the Milky Way
1920	Provides the basis for Harlow Shapley's determination of the size of the universe
Dec. 12, 1921	Dies in Cambridge, Massachusetts

Early Life

Henrietta Swan Leavitt, one of seven children, was the daughter of a prominent Congregationalist minister with a parish in Cambridge, Massachusetts. Both parents were of colonial

The Period-Luminosity Law for Cepheid Variable Stars

The average luminosity of Cepheid variable stars increases with the period (time) of their pulsations.

Using photographic photometry, Leavitt discovered 2,400 variable stars, about half of those known at the time. In her 1908 paper "1,777 Variables in the Magellanic Clouds," she derived periods (varying from 1.25 days to 127 days) for seventeen variables and noted that the brighter variables have longer periods. Such variable stars had been observed earlier in the constellation Cepheus and were called Cepheid variables.

Extending her analysis in 1912 to twenty-five stars in the Small Magellanic Cloud, Leavitt took advantage of the fact that they were all at nearly the same distance from Earth. Thus, she could move beyond the apparent magnitude (brightness) of stars to their absolute magnitude (luminosity), since any apparent differences could be attributed not to relative distances but rather to their actual emission of light as determined by their size and surface brightness. In this way, she showed that the intrinsic luminosity of Cepheid variables increases in a simple way with their period.

Once the luminosity of a star is known, its measured brightness can be used to estimate its distance from Earth. By 1920, Harlow Shapley had calibrated the luminosities of the Cepheid variables and used the period-luminosity law to

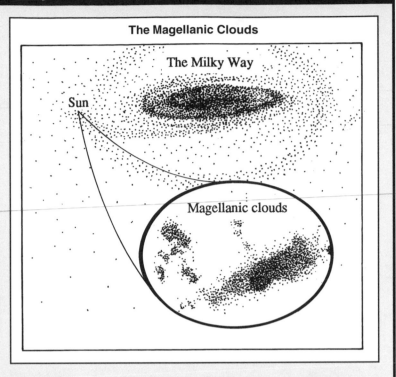

The Magellanic Clouds

The Milky Way

Sun

Magellanic clouds

ascertain the size of the Milky Way. In 1924, Edwin Hubble used the law to find the distance to other galaxies.

Bibliography

"Pulsating Stars." John R. Percy. *Scientific American* 232 (June, 1975).

Source Book in Astronomy. Harlow Shapley, ed. Cambridge, Mass.: Harvard University Press, 1960.

"Women and the Stars." Joseph L. Spradley. *The Physics Teacher* (September, 1990).

stock and instilled stern Puritan virtues in their daughter. She attended public schools in Cambridge but entered Oberlin College in 1885 after her family moved to Cleveland, Ohio. She enrolled in the Conservatory of Music there, even though her hearing was seriously impaired.

In 1892, Leavitt completed her undergraduate education at the Society for the Collegiate Instruction of Women, nicknamed the "Harvard Annex" and now known as Radcliffe College. Her interest in astronomy began with a

course during her senior year; following her graduation, she took an advanced astronomy course. After a period of traveling and further graduate work, she became a volunteer research assistant at the Harvard College Observatory. In 1902, she received a permanent position there, measuring the brightness of variable stars on photographic plates.

The Harvard College Observatory

The director of the Harvard College Observatory at the end of the nineteenth century, Ed-

(Science Photo Library)

ward C. Pickering, was a pioneer in the hiring of women, asking them to analyze the increasing volume of telescopic data collected on photographic plates. Leavitt advanced rapidly to become chief of the photographic photometry department with several young women working for her, some with only minimal training in astronomy. She devoted the rest of her life to the accurate measurements of the brightness of stars.

In 1907, Leavitt began a survey of stars near the north celestial pole to establish a standard photographic sequence, comparing 299 plates from thirteen telescopes. In 1913, Leavitt's "north polar sequence" became the standard for brightness measurements of stars in the Milky Way and was adopted in 1913 by the International Committee on Photographic Magnitudes for its projected astrographic map of the sky. It was eventually published in the *Annals of the Harvard College Observatory* in 1917.

Magellanic Cloud Studies

In 1890, the Harvard College Observatory set up a 24-inch telescope above the city of Are-

quipa, Peru. Two particular areas of study were the Great and Small Magellanic Clouds, which are the faint patches of light first observed by explorer Ferdinand Magellan's crew in 1521. A series of sixteen long-exposure photographic plates, sent from Arequipa to Cambridge, revealed very faint stars within the Magellanic Clouds, now known as small satellite galaxies of the Milky Way.

Leavitt's first conclusion from her analysis of the Magellanic Cloud photographs was that a large number of its stars had a variable brightness. In 1908, she published her discovery of 1,777 variables in the Magellanic Clouds in the *Annals of the Harvard College Observatory*. By 1912, she had established the period-luminosity law for a special category of these variables.

Unfortunately, Leavitt's career was cut short. She died of cancer in Cambridge, Massachusetts, on December 12, 1921, at the age of only fifty-three.

Bibliography
By Leavitt
"1,777 Variables in the Magellanic Clouds," *Annals of the Harvard College Observatory*, 1908

"Ten Variable Stars of the Algol Type," *Annals of the Harvard College Observatory*, 1908

"Periods of Twenty-Five Variable Stars in the Small Magellanic Cloud," *Harvard College Observatory Circular*, 1912

"The North Polar Sequence," *Annals of the Harvard College Observatory*, 1917

About Leavitt
"Henrietta Swan Leavitt." Dorrit Hoffleit. In *Notable American Women*, edited by Edward T. James. Cambridge, Mass.: The Belknap Press of Harvard University Press, 1971.

"Henrietta Swan Leavitt and Cepheid Variables." Helen Buss Mitchell. *The Physics Teacher* (March, 1976).

History and Work of the Harvard College Observatory. Solon I. Bailey. New York: McGraw-Hill, 1931.

(*Joseph L. Spradley*)

Joshua Lederberg

Areas of Achievement: Bacteriology, genetics, and medicine

Contribution: Lederberg's extensive work in bacterial genetics established the presence of sexual reproduction among bacteria. He also demonstrated the possibility of genetic manipulation of bacterial genetic material.

May 23, 1925	Born in Montclair, New Jersey
1941	Graduated from Stuyvesant High School in New York City
1942	Enlists in the U.S. Navy, entering a premedical program
1944	Graduated with honors from Columbia University
1944-1946	Attends the College of Physicians and Surgeons at Columbia
1946	Works as a research assistant at Yale University
1947-1958	Serves as assistant professor and professor of genetics at the University of Wisconsin
1948	Receives a Ph.D. from Yale
1958	Awarded the Nobel Prize in Physiology or Medicine
1958-1959	Serves as chair of the genetics department at Wisconsin
1959-1978	Appointed professor of genetics and chair of the genetics department at Stanford
1962	Named director of the Kennedy Laboratories for Molecular Medicine at Stanford
1978-1990	Serves as president of Rockefeller University
1993-1994	Elected president of the New York Academy of Sciences

Early Life

Joshua Lederberg was born in 1925 in Montclair, New Jersey. His parents, Zvi and Esther Lederberg, had recently emigrated from Palestine; his father was a rabbi. Lederberg considered himself a precocious youth with an inquiring mind. He received an excellent education in the New York City schools, including the opportunity to conduct independent research in a laboratory after school.

From 1941 to 1944, Lederberg attended Columbia University on a tuition scholarship from the Hayden Trust, being graduated with honors in zoology. He conducted research and developed an interest in the genetic analysis of plants. He also had the opportunity to discuss genetics with Francis Ryan and to observe his research using the mold *Neurospora*.

In 1942, Lederberg enlisted in the U.S. Navy, where he entered a premedical/medical program designed to train physicians. He was assigned to duty at the St. Albans Naval Hospital on Long Island. In 1944, Lederberg entered the medical school at Columbia University.

(The Nobel Foundation)

Studies in Genetics

Lederberg's desire for a career in research interrupted his medical studies. His interest in genetics led Ryan to suggest that Lederberg contact Edward Lawrie Tatum at Yale University. Tatum and his colleague, George Wells Beadle, were in the process of completing their work on the association of genes with proteins in *Neurospora*. In 1946, Lederberg joined Tatum as a research assistant. That year, he also married Tatum's assistant, Esther Zimmer.

Lederberg's success at Yale brought him an offer from the University of Wisconsin. Despite pejorative references to Lederberg's religion, he accepted a position there as assistant professor of genetics.

Lederberg's successful work on genetic recombination and his demonstration of conjugation, the genetic transfer of deoxyribonucleic acid (DNA), between bacteria, placed him at the forefront of bacterial genetics. By 1954, he had been promoted to full professor. In recognition of his important work, Lederberg, along with Beadle and Tatum, was awarded the 1958 Nobel Prize in Physiology or Medicine.

In 1959, Lederberg accepted an offer to become chair of the new department of genetics at Stanford University. In 1962, he was appointed director of the Kennedy Laboratories for Molecular Medicine at Stanford. He remained in California until 1978, when he was appointed president of Rockefeller University.

Awards and Recognition

Lederberg received numerous awards and honorary degrees. Among his most prized were honorary medical degrees from Tufts University and the University of Turin; ironically, Lederberg never completed his medical studies.

He received the Eli Lilly Award, presented to outstanding young scientists, and the Alexander Hamilton Medal from Columbia University. He also received the National Medal of Science in 1989. He was elected a member of the National Academy of Sciences and the Royal Society of London and served as president of the New York Academy of Sciences in 1993-1994. He also served as an adviser to the World Health Organization and the National Space Agency.

Sexual Reproduction in Bacteria

The demonstration of sexual processes in bacteria was instrumental in the development of the field of bacterial genetics.

The role of deoxyribonucleic acid (DNA) as genetic material was first reported in 1944. It was clear that genes must themselves be DNA. Eukaryotic organisms such as molds had been demonstrated to carry out sexual reproduction through the exchange of DNA; it was not clear that bacteria could do the same.

Lederberg and Edward Lawrie Tatum initially carried out a number of genetic crosses between different bacterial strains. In doing so, they were able to obtain a new strain that carried genes from each parent. They concluded that bacteria could carry out a form of sexual reproduction called conjugation, the one-way transfer of DNA between bacteria.

Lederberg and Tatum observed that the genetic markers they followed behaved like linked genes; the characteristics mapped in linear order, as would be true if they were aligned along the same chromosome. Lederberg later demonstrated a second means by which genes could transfer between bacteria: transduction. In this process, a virus serves as a vector (carrier) for genetic exchange.

Lederberg's work demonstrated that several methods exist by which bacteria may exchange genetic material. The process of conjugation in particular was later shown to be of particular importance, as genes encoding resistance to antibiotics may also be exchanged among bacteria.

Bibliography

The Eighth Day of Creation. Horace Judson. Cold Spring Harbor, N.Y.: Cold Spring Harbor Press, 1996.

The Genetics of Bacteria and Their Viruses. William Hayes. New York: John Wiley & Sons, 1964.

Molecular Biology of Bacterial Viruses. Gunther Stent. San Francisco: W. H. Freeman, 1963.

Bibliography
By Lederberg
"Detection of Biochemical Mutants of Microorganisms," *Journal of Biological Chemistry*, 1946 (with Edward L. Tatum)
"Gene Recombination in *Escherichia coli*," *Nature*, 1946 (with Tatum)
"Gene Recombination in the Bacterium *Escherichia coli*," *Journal of Bacteriology*, 1947 (with Tatum)
"Gene Recombination and Linked Segregations in *Escherichia coli*," *Genetics*, 1947
Papers in Microbial Genetics: Bacteria and Bacterial Viruses, 1951
"Replica Plating and Indirect Selection of Bacterial Mutants," *Journal of Bacteriology*, 1952 (with E. M. Lederberg)
"Genetic Exchange in *Salmonella*," *Journal of Bacteriology*, 1952
"Sex in Bacteria: Genetic Studies, 1945-1952," *Science*, 1954
"Viruses, Genes, and Cells," *Bacteriological Reviews*, 1957
"Biological Future of Man" in *Man and His Future*, 1963 (Gordon Wolstenholme, ed.)
"Edward Lawrie Tatum," *Annual Review of Genetics*, 1979
"Forty Years of Genetic Recombination in Bacteria," *Nature*, 1986
The Excitement and Fascination of Science: Reflections by Eminent Scientists, vol. 3, 1990 (with others)
Emerging Infections: Microbial Threats to Health in the United States, 1992 (as editor, with Robert E. Shope and Stanley C. Oaks, Jr.)
Encyclopedia of Microbiology, 1992 (as editor)

About Lederberg
"Joshua Lederberg." In *The Nobel Prize Winners: Physiology or Medicine*, edited by Frank N. Magill. Pasadena, Calif.: Salem Press, 1991.
Nobel Prize Winners. Tyler Wasson, ed. Bronx, N. Y.: H. W. Wilson, 1987.
Notable Twentieth-Century Scientists. Emily J. McMurray, ed. Detroit: Gale Research, 1995.

(Richard Adler)

Leon M. Lederman

Area of Achievement: Physics
Contribution: Lederman, one of the foremost high-energy physicists of the latter part of the twentieth century, conducted an experiment revealing the existence of the muon neutrino, which led to the postulation of the standard model of physics and earned for Lederman the 1988 Nobel Prize in Physics.

July 15, 1922	Born in the Bronx, New York
1951	Earns a Ph.D. at Columbia University and joins the faculty
1956	Discovers the neutral K-meson at the Brookhaven National Laboratory
1960	Becomes the director of the Nevis Laboratories at Columbia
1960-1962	Conducts experiments that produce the world's first beam of neutrinos
1965	Receives the National Medal of Science
1966-1970	Serves on a panel of the Atomic Energy Commission
1973	Named the Eugene Higgens Professor of Physics at Columbia
1977	Discovers the upsilon particle
1979	Becomes the director of the Fermi National Accelerator Laboratory in Batavia, Illinois
1988	Shares the Nobel Prize in Physics
1989	Serves as a professor of physics at the University of Chicago
1992	Becomes a professor of science at the Illinois Institute of Technology

(AP/Wide World Photos)

Early Life
Leon Max Lederman was born in New York City on July 15, 1922, the son of Russian immigrants Morris and Minna Lederman. The elder Ledermans owned a laundry in the Bronx and sent their children to New York public schools.

Leon attended New York's City College, receiving a bachelor's degree in chemistry in 1943. He then joined the U.S. Army Signal Corps and served for the remainder of World War II as a second lieutenant. Lederman returned to New York after the war, changed his major to physics, and earned a master's degree and a Ph.D. in physics from Columbia University.

A Researcher in New York
After completing his doctorate, Lederman was invited to remain at Columbia, where he taught and conducted research at Columbia's Nevis Laboratories, using its powerful particle accelerator that could boost atoms or subatomic particles to energies of several hundred million electronvolts (eV). Lederman was also a guest scientist at the Brookhaven National Laboratory on Long Island. In 1956, his work at Brookhaven resulted in the discovery of a new subatomic particle, the neutral K-meson. In 1960 he was named director of the Nevis Laboratories.

His work at Brookhaven climaxed in 1960-1962 experiments that produced the world's first beam of neutrinos. Lederman, with fellow physicists Melvin Schwartz and Jack Steinberger, used the new 33 billion electronvolt Alternating-Gradient Synchrotron (AGS) at Brookhaven to propel protons into a beryllium target.

As expected, the beryllium atoms disintegrated into loose protons, neutrons, and other subatomic particles, including unstable pions that disintegrated into muons and neutrinos. The now-famous experiment revealed the existence of the muon neutrino and later led to the postulation of the standard model of physics. This experiment earned for Lederman, Schwartz, and Steinberger the 1988 Nobel Prize in Physics.

Lederman's work at the Nevis and Brookhaven laboratories spanned twenty-seven years and resulted in many significant discoveries. In addition to those described above, Lederman created the antimatter version of deuteron (heavy hydrogen). Shifting his research to the Fermi National Accelerator Laboratory (Fermilab) in Batavia, Illinois, he discovered the upsilon particle in 1977. The appearance of this new particle, with an extraordinarily high mass of 10 giga electronvolts (ten times heavier than the proton) and a surprisingly long lifetime, resulted in a dramatic new interpretation of subatomic particles. It was believed that the upsilon particle could not be made from the four known types of quarks (subatomic particles). Thus the prediction was made that upsilon was made of a yet-unknown type of quark, a fifth, or the "bottom" quark.

The Director of Fermilab
In 1979, Lederman was named director of Fermilab. While he was there, the laboratory's 2 trillion electronvolt Tevatron accelerator was completed.

At Fermilab, Lederman found himself more an administrator and less an experimenter. He created a new computing center, established an astrophysics group, encouraged the formation of an industrial affiliates organization, promoted a neutron therapy facility for cancer patients, and initiated fifteen education programs, including a Saturday morning class for high school physics teachers and students that he taught himself. Concerned about the level of scientific literacy in high school graduates, he helped found the Illinois Science and Mathematics Academy in Aurora, Illinois.

In 1989, a year after being awarded the No-

A Major Step Toward the Standard Model of Atomic Structure

Experiments conducted by Lederman, Melvin Schwartz, and Jack Steinberger revealing the existence of the muon neutrino led to the postulation of the Standard Model of physics.

The scientific search for fundamental particles has been going on for 2,500 years. Leucippus, a fifth century B.C.E. Greek philosopher, postulated a theory called "atomism" (from the Greek word *atoma*, meaning "uncuttable"). He believed that atoms were fundamental, that is indivisible, and that there was nothing else in the universe but the void of empty space.

In 1897, Sir J. J. Thomson discovered the first subatomic particle, the electron. Because atoms are electrically neutral and the electron is negatively charged, he assumed that the rest of the atom must balance the electron and is therefore positively charged. Thus, the atom, despite its name, is not "uncuttable." For his work, Thomson was awarded the 1906 Nobel Prize in Physics, and the race to find other such particles intensified.

By the middle of the twentieth century, more than two hundred subatomic particles, including the muon and the neutrino, had been identified. Neutrinos are subatomic particles that have no detectable mass or electrical charge and that can pass through almost anything without impact. Two vexing questions of the 1950's were "Was the neutrino that was present in electron experiments identical to the one that appeared in muon interactions?" and "Could there possibly be two hundred different fundamental particles?"

A particle accelerator is an instrument that can produce a stream of very-fast-moving atomic or subatomic particles. Lederman, Schwartz, and Steinberger used the powerful AGS particle accelerator at the Brookhaven National Laboratory in Upton, New York, to create a beam of neutrinos by propelling protons at a beryllium target. The impact separated beryllium nuclei into pro-

tons and neutrons and created, out of pure energy, other subatomic particles, including the pion. Pions are extremely unstable, and each disintegrated into a muon and a high-energy neutrino.

After the collisions, a steel barrier, 40 feet thick, stopped all the moving particles except for the neutrinos. Therefore, the only particles emerging from the back side of the barrier were the neutrinos. Behind the steel barrier was a 10-ton aluminum detection spark chamber, which the laboratory had built to detect any neutrino collisions.

The work at Brookhaven climaxed in the 1960-1962 experiments that produced the world's first beam of neutrinos. In all, about 100 trillion neutrinos were produced during the eight months of experimentation, and about 50 neutrino collisions were detected. By detecting the previously unknown muon neutrino, the experiment showed that there is, indeed, more than one type of neutrino.

Their results have been used to study the properties of other subatomic particles and led to the formulation of the Standard Model theory of atomic structure. This theory proposes that instead of some two hundred fundamental particles, a small number of quarks and leptons are the fundamental building blocks of other subatomic particles.

Bibliography
Neutrino Physics. Klaus Winter. New York: Cambridge University Press, 1991.
Nuclear and Particle Physics. W. Burchham and Melvyn Jobes. New York: John Wiley & Sons, 1995.
The Particle Garden: Our Universe as Understood by Particle Physicists. Gordon Kane. Reading, Mass.: Addison-Wesley, 1995.
The Particle Hunters. Yuval Ne'eman and Yoram Kirsh. New York: Cambridge University Press, 1996.

bel Prize, Lederman declined an offer to begin a third term as director of Fermilab. He decided instead to return to teaching at the University of Chicago. In his years in Chicago, first at the university and later at the Illinois Institute of Technology, Lederman became a strong advocate for primary school science education, including science teacher preparation. He was instrumental in establishing Chicago's Academy for Mathematics and Science Teachers.

Philosophy of Science Teaching

Lederman proposed "turning the high school science curriculum up-side-down." Physics, he said, is fundamental to chemistry, which is fundamental to the life sciences. Physics, therefore, should be taught to freshmen, at a far more empirical and less abstract level than it is currently taught to upperclassmen. Chemistry can then expand on the study of matter and energy into a study of molecules and chemical change, which would then lead smoothly into the study of organic molecules in living things.

Lederman became a tireless advocate of pure scientific research and the perfection of equipment with which to do that research. He believed that science and scientific research should be in every citizen's domain.

Bibliography
By Lederman
Neutrino Physics, 1963
From Quarks to the Cosmos: Tools of Discovery, 1989 (with David Schramm)
Science: The End of the Frontier?, 1991
The God Particle: If the Universe Is the Answer, What Is the Question?, 1993 (with Dick Teresi)

About Lederman
"Lederman, Leon." In *Current Biography Yearbook*. New York: H. W. Wilson, 1989.
"Lederman, Leon Max." In *Larousse Dictionary of Scientists*, edited by Hazel Muir. New York: Larousse, 1994.
"Leon M. Lederman." In *The Nobel Prize Winners: Physics*, edited by Frank N. Magill. Pasadena, Calif.: Salem Press, 1989.

(Kenneth J. Schoon)

Tsung-Dao Lee

Areas of Achievement: Astronomy, mathematics, and physics
Contribution: Lee did important work in statistical mechanics and particle physics. Lee and Chen Ning Yang suggested experiments in which parity was not conserved, leading to greater theoretical understanding and experimental discoveries in the physics of elementary particles.

Nov. 25, 1926	Born in Shanghai, China
1943	Enters National Chekiang University
1945	Evacuated to National Southwest Associated University
1946	Departs for the United States
1950	Completes his Ph.D. under Enrico Fermi and becomes a research associate at Yerkes Observatory
1950-1951	Becomes a research associate and lecturer at the University of California, Berkeley
1951-1953	Joins the Institute for Advanced Study at Princeton University
1953-1956	Serves as assistant, associate, and then full professor at Columbia University
1957	Named Loeb Lecturer at Harvard University
1957	Receives the Albert Einstein Science Award from Yeshiva University and the Nobel Prize in Physics
1964	Becomes Enrico Fermi Professor of Physics at Columbia
1980	Inaugurates the CUSPEA program for Chinese students

Early Life

Tsung-Dao Lee, the third of six children, was born the son of a businessman. After middle school, he entered the National Chekiang University in 1943, but the invasion of Japanese troops necessitated evacuation to Kunming, where he attended the National Southwest Associated University. There, he studied with Ta-You Wu, who procured a Chinese government fellowship for Lee and took him to the United States in 1946.

Lee had difficulty entering a graduate program, having completed only his sophomore year. The University of Chicago, however, accepted students without formal degrees if they were familiar with certain "great books." Lee was able to convince the admissions officer that he was knowledgeable in the Chinese equivalent of these Western classics, and he was accepted. Chicago probably had the best science department at that time, with a distinguished faculty and equally talented students. One of these was Chen Ning (Frank) Yang,

(The Nobel Foundation)

whom Lee had met in Kunming. The two became close friends.

In 1948, Lee began his doctoral thesis, on white dwarf stars, under the great physicist Enrico Fermi. In 1950, he completed his Ph.D. and married Hui Chung (Jeannette) Chin; they would have two sons.

Research

After working with astrophysicist Subrahmanyan Chandrasekhar at the Yerkes Observatory for eight months, followed by one year at the University of California, Berkeley, Lee spent two years at the Institute for Advanced Study at Princeton University, where Yang had a position. Lee and Yang published two important papers in statistical mechanics.

Lee became an assistant professor at Columbia University in New York in 1953 and was promoted to full professor in 1956, the youngest on the Columbia faculty. Lee was associated with Columbia University for almost his entire scientific career.

At Columbia, Lee first worked in field theory, on what is now called the Lee model, a mathematically solvable model against which new computational techniques or theorems can be checked. He then turned to particle physics, in particular to the major problem of the mid-1950's, the theta-tau puzzle. This led to work with Yang on the nonconservation of parity, for which they shared the Nobel Prize in Physics in 1957, within weeks of Lee's thirty-first birthday.

Through the next decades, Lee, with different collaborators, worked in a variety of fields and produced some two hundred papers. The subjects included statistical mechanics, the properties of particles known as intermediate vector bosons, mathematical problems associated with particles without mass, and general relativity.

The Return of a Favor

In 1980, Lee established the China-United States Physics Examination and Application (CUSPEA) Program, which enables qualified Chinese physics students to study for a doctoral degree at American universities. Lee stated that among the relevant factors for creativity, luck is perhaps the most important and the least understood. Appreciation of the opportunity that

The Theta-Tau Puzzle and Nonconservation of Parity

The puzzle involved a particle, a K-meson, that seemed to have two forms. The theta form decayed into two particles, and the tau form decayed into three; otherwise, they were the same. Scientists were reluctant to identify them as the same particle because doing so meant that the concept of parity would be violated.

Parity is related to right- and left-handedness—that is, to an object and its mirror image. A person raising the right hand in front of a mirror will see the image raising its left hand. The laws of physics had been assumed to be the same whether described by a right-handed system of coordinates or by a left-handed system, the mirror image of a right-handed system. In other words, nature was assumed to be symmetric with respect to right and left; object could not be distinguished from image.

An analogy used by Lee describes two cars that are alike except that one is the mirror image of the other. Car A has the driver's seat on the left, with the gas pedal near the driver's right foot; car B has the driver's seat on the right, with the gas pedal near the left foot. A's driver starts the car by turning the ignition key clockwise; B is started by turning the key counterclockwise. If gas and pressure on the pedal are the same for both, the two cars should move at the same speed. Then, what is called "right" or "left" is entirely relative. This is the right-left symmetry principle, which was accepted until 1956.

In trying to solve the theta-tau paradox, Lee and Yang examined experiments that had already been performed. They found that the symmetry, or parity, law held in two of the three types of interactions examined—the strong and the electromagnetic interactions—but that the experiments did not test the law for the so-called weak interactions because the results would have been the same whether parity was conserved or not. They then suggested experiments that would test the law.

In one experiment, nuclei of cobalt 60 were aligned by a magnetic field at low temperatures. If nuclei are envisioned as small spheres, each spinning on its axis as Earth turns about its axis, then alignment means spinning, for example, clockwise with respect to the direction of the magnetic field. Nuclei emit electrons in the weak interaction process called beta decay. If symmetry held, as many electrons would be emitted in the hemisphere moving in the direction of the field as in the opposite hemisphere. In fact, however, the emission of the electrons was asymmetric; there was a preferred direction. In terms of Lee's car analogy, the two cars, one the mirror image of the other, moved at different speeds.

A law of physics was overturned: Parity was not conserved in the weak interactions. Such laws are not overturned with any frequency. Usually, they are not overturned at all; hence, the designation "law." When they are overturned, there are important consequences. The effects of parity nonconservation provided a major source of information about weak interactions.

Bibliography
The Ambidextrous Universe. Martin Gardner. New York: Basic Books, 1964.

he had in 1946 to study in the United States led him to organize this program so that similar good fortune might come to others.

Bibliography
By Lee
Particle Physics and Introduction to Field Theory, 1981
T. D. Lee: Selected Papers, 1986 (Gerald Feinberg, ed.)
Symmetries, Asymmetries, and the World of Particles, 1988
"Happiness Is When Old Friends Come from Far Away" and "Reminiscences" in *Thirty Years Since Parity Nonconservation: A Symposium for T. D. Lee,* 1988 (Robert Novick, ed.)

About Lee
Thirty Years Since Parity Nonconservation: A Symposium for T. D. Lee. Robert Novick, ed. Boston: Birkhäuser, 1988.
"Tsung-Dao Lee." In *The Nobel Prize Winners: Physics,* edited by Frank N. Magill. Pasadena, Calif.: Salem Press, 1989.

(Grace Marmor Spruch)

Antoni van Leeuwenhoek

Areas of Achievement: Bacteriology, biology, cell biology, and medicine

Contribution: As the first microscopist to create powerful lenses, Leeuwenhoek made many discoveries concerning the description and reproduction of bacteria, protozoa, plants, and animals.

Oct. 24, 1632	Born in Delft, the Netherlands
1650	Becomes a shopkeeper
1654	Marries Barbara de Mey, with whom he has five children
1660	Becomes a civil servant
1665	Constructs his first microscopes
1668	Develops the theory of blood circulation through capillaries
1671	Marries Cornelia Swalmius following the death of his first wife in 1666
1674	Describes red blood corpuscles
1675	Describes microorganisms, including bacteria and protozoa, which he termed "animalicules"
1677	Describes animal sperm and eggs and provides evidence against the theory of spontaneous generation
1680	Elected as a Fellow of the Royal Society of London
1685	Investigates plant reproduction
1699	Appointed as a correspondent of the Académie des Sciences in Paris
1716	Awarded a silver medal by the Louvain College of Professors
Aug. 26, 1723	Dies in Delft, the Netherlands

Early Life

Antoni van Leeuwenhoek (pronounced "LAY-vehn-hewk"), the son of a middle-class basket maker who died when Antoni was six years old, attended grammar school in a village near Leiden, the Netherlands. He never received a university education and instead went to Amsterdam to apprentice himself to a cloth merchant. After setting up a shop in Delft and marrying his first wife, he accepted a civil post in Delft, serving the city in various capacities. After the death of his first wife, he remarried, but the death of his second wife preceded his own by almost thirty years.

Leeuwenhoek's scientific career began as a hobby. He gained mathematical skills, which were necessary for his duties as a civil servant, and he taught himself to make tiny magnifying lenses, initially for the purpose of inspecting the quality of cloth. He ground these lenses by hand from glass globules. He had excellent vision, mathematical exactitude, tremendous manual dexterity, and patience—all of which contributed to his success.

The Microscope

With these lenses, Leeuwenhoek constructed microscopes with magnifying powers of up to 500 times normal viewing power. These devices allowed him to visualize objects with a diameter of about 1 micron. His art, however, died with him. Microscopes equivalent to those that he made did not become available until the advent of the compound microscope in the nineteenth century.

Leeuwenhoek's scientific activities first began when he was almost forty years old. Because of his meager education, he knew only one language, Dutch, and could not communicate with foreign scientists. He worked in near isolation, seldom leaving the Netherlands. He wrote nearly two hundred letters to the Royal Society of London, his primary scientific contact, but these had to be translated.

Initially, Leeuwenhoek's observations were questioned, and scientists traveled great distances to Delft to confirm his reports. His reports caused quite a furor in the Royal Society of London. He was the first to describe eukaryotic microorganisms, as well as the three principal shapes of bacteria (spherical, rod-shaped, and spiral-shaped). He erroneously thought of microorganisms as little animals and called them "animalicules." He observed sperm and egg cells from many different species, argued against the then-prevalent theory of spontaneous generation, and set the groundwork for the present understanding of fertilization. He also devoted much time to the characterization of blood circulation and muscle structure, thereby providing a basis for an understanding of animal physiology.

Leeuwenhoek's devotion to his studies led to worldwide recognition. His discoveries at the frontier of microscopy were followed with interest throughout England and Europe. He became so famous that many dignitaries, including kings and princes, visited him. Among these were Queen Anne of England, Peter the

The First Microscopist

Leeuwenhoek can be considered the world's first microscopist. Although he also examined inanimate objects, almost all of his valued discoveries resulted from the description of living things, such as bacteria, yeast, ciliates, and many higher organisms, including humans.

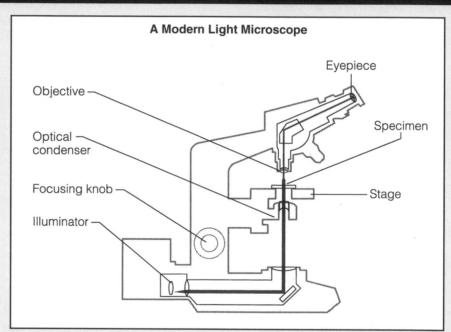

A Modern Light Microscope

(Hans & Cassady, Inc.)

Many of Leeuwenhoek's important discoveries opposed the then-prevalent theory of spontaneous generation. He showed that weevils and other insects did not derive from decaying organic matter. Instead, they arose from sperm and eggs, as do mammals. His studies set the stage for the modern view of fertilization as the unified basis for reproduction in all higher organisms.

In addition to his important advances in the study of animals and microbes, Leeuwenhoek described many important aspects of plants. He drew elaborate diagrams that led to an understanding of their physiological functions. He usually interpreted the structures that he observed correctly, in spite of (or maybe because of) his lack of familiarity with the scientific thought of his time.

Despite his numerous observational advances and his amazing interpretive insight, Leeuwenhoek missed some important concepts. For example, he never came to appreciate the cellular basis of life. Furthermore, in his description of microorganisms such as protozoa and bacteria, he always viewed them as miniature animals rather than as distinct life-forms. These deficiencies and misconceptions presumably reflected the time in which he lived. Modern thought has evolved gradually, as a result of continual change from established dogma.

Bibliography
Measuring the Invisible World: The Life and Works of Antoni van Leeuwenhoek. Abraham Schierbeek. London: Abelard-Schuman, 1959.

The Microbe Hunters. Paul De Kruif. San Diego: Harcourt, Brace, 1926.

(Library of Congress)

Great of Russia, and Frederick the Great of Germany. Leeuwenhoek continued his work for nearly half a century until his death at the age of ninety.

Bibliography
By Leeuwenhoek
His collected Dutch edition, the *Brieven*, consists of four volumes.

Vol. 1: *Brieven, Geschreven aan de Wyt-vermaarde Koninglijke Wetenschapzoekende Societeit, tot Londen in Engeland,* 1684-1694 (10 parts; with a *Register*, 1695)

Vol. 2: *Vervolg Der Brieven, Geschreven aan de Wytvermaarde Koninglijke Societeit in Londen,* 1688; *Tweede Vervolg Der Brieven,* 1689; *Derde Vervolg Der Brieven,* 1693; and *Vierde Vervolg Der Brieven,* 1694

Vol. 3: *Vijfde Vervolg Der Brieven, Geschreven aan verscheide Hoge Standspersonen En Geleerde Luijden,* 1696; *Sesde Vervolg Der Brieven,* 1697; and *Sevende Vervolg Der Brieven,* 1702

Vol. 4: *Send-Brieven,* 1718

The Select Works of Antony van Leeuwenhoek, 1798-1807 (2 vols.; Samuel Hoole, ed.)

The Collected Letters of Antoni van Leeuwenhoek, 1939-1967 (8 vols.)

About Leeuwenhoek
Antony van Leeuwenhoek and His "Little Animals." C. Dobell. 2d ed. New York: 1958.

Measuring the Invisible World: The Life and Works of Antoni van Leeuwenhoek. Abraham Schierbeek. London: Abelard-Schuman, 1959.

(Milton H. Saier, Jr.)

Jean-Marie Lehn

Areas of Achievement: Chemistry, science (general), and technology

Contribution: Lehn was instrumental in the development of supramolecular chemistry. His work has improved the understanding of how molecules "recognize" one another, opening the door for the synthesis of artificial enzymes, cells, and molecular devices.

Sept. 30, 1939	Born in Rosheim, France
1960	Earns a B.S. in chemistry from the University of Strasbourg
1963	Earns a Ph.D. in organic chemistry at Strasbourg
1963	Awarded a Bronze Medal from the Centre National de la Recherche Scientifique
1964	Named a postdoctoral research associate at Harvard University
1965	Returns to Strasbourg as a lecturer
1966	Appointed an assistant professor of chemistry at Strasbourg
1970	Promoted to full professor at Strasbourg
1972	Awarded a Silver Medal from the Centre National de la Recherche Scientifique
1976	Named to the French National Order of Merit
1980	Elected to a chair at the Collège de France in Paris
1981	Awarded a Gold Medal from the Centre National de la Recherche Scientifique
1983	Named to the French Legion of Honor
1987	Awarded the Nobel Prize in Chemistry

(The Nobel Foundation)

Early Life

Jean-Marie Lehn (pronounced "layn") was born in 1939, the first of Pierre and Marie Lehn's four sons. Entering high school in 1950, he studied classics, with an emphasis on philosophy, but developed an interest in science as well. In 1957, he received his *baccalauréat* in both philosophy and experimental sciences.

In the fall of 1957, Lehn entered the University of Strasbourg, where he intended to study philosophy, but he soon reconsidered. He was quite taken with the experimental power of organic chemistry, which was able to interconvert complicated substances following well-defined rules and routes.

After receiving his bachelor of science degree in chemistry in 1960, Lehn remained at Strasbourg to begin his graduate studies with Guy Ourisson. He received his Ph.D. in only three years, after which he spent a year at Harvard University as a postdoctoral research associate, working with Robert Burns Woodward on the total synthesis of vitamin B_{12}.

Supramolecular Chemistry

Certain large molecules can recognize and bind other molecules having a complementary shape. Such binding significantly alters the chemical and physical properties of the pair.

The term "supramolecular chemistry" refers to interactions in which host molecules with cavities of precisely defined sizes and shapes recognize and bind to smaller guest molecules of a complementary size and shape, much in the same way that a key fits into a lock. The host-guest interaction is very specific; only guests of the appropriate structure can be accommodated by a particular host.

This sort of molecular recognition is vital to all life processes. For example, enzymes, substances which catalyze specific biochemical reactions, must be able to recognize and act on only the appropriate substrate molecules. A given enzyme might be able to break down the proteins in food, but it must not also break down the proteins in the body's own cells.

Lehn has described three functions as being characteristic of supramolecular species: recognition, transformation, and translocation. The earliest cryptands performed only the first of these three functions. To be truly useful, however, complexation must be followed either by a chemical reaction that would not occur otherwise or by the transport of the guest molecule across some barrier that it would not cross on its own.

Lehn and other researchers in this rapidly growing field soon succeeded in producing supramolecular compounds that could do so as artificial enzymes (transformation), and some others that could selectively transport drugs or other chemicals to and from specific tissues within the body (translocation). Still other applications of supramolecular chemistry are under development, such as artificial cells and molecular-level circuit components. The principles of supramolecular chemistry guide the research efforts of many scientists.

Bibliography

"Cages, Cavities, and Clefts." Ivars Peterson. *Science News* 132 (August 8, 1987).

Comprehensive Supramolecular Chemistry. Jean-Marie Lehn et al., eds. Tarrytown, N.Y.: Pergamon Press, 1996.

Supramolecular Chemistry: An Introduction. Fritz Vogtle. New York: John Wiley & Sons, 1993.

The Function of Enzymes

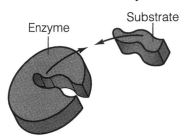

An enzyme combines with a substrate that has molecules of a complementary shape.

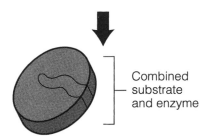

Combined substrate and enzyme

The interaction between the enzyme and substrate causes a chemical change in the substrate, splitting it in two.

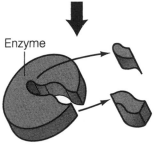

The enzyme is unchanged and can repeat the process with another substrate molecule.

(Hans & Cassady, Inc.)

Early Academic Career

Lehn returned to Strasbourg in 1965 and was appointed assistant professor of chemistry in 1966. Initially, he worked in the area of physical organic chemistry: the relationship between the structure and shape of an organic (carbon-containing) molecule and its physical properties.

Lehn's interest in the physical and chemical processes occurring within the nervous system made him wonder if a chemist could contribute to their study. Nerve cells communicate, in part, by enforcing an imbalance in the concentration of certain positively charged atoms called cations—most notably sodium and potassium—inside and outside the cell. Noting that certain natural antibiotics were able to make cell membranes permeable to cations, Lehn reasoned that it should be possible to devise and synthesize chemical substances that could accomplish the same feat.

A New Direction

Lehn also took note of the recently discovered crown ethers, doughnut-shaped molecules having remarkable abilities to bind cations tightly, yet reversibly, to form what was called a supramolecular complex. Crown ethers are essentially planar molecules. Shape determines function, Lehn reasoned, and if a two-dimensional crown ether can form a strong complex with specific cations, then a three-dimensional analogue should do the job even better. This hypothesis turned out to be true.

Lehn chose the term "cryptand" to describe his new class of molecules, because their interior cavities resembled crypts in which some other molecule could be "entombed." Work on the synthesis of the first cryptand began in October, 1967, and was completed the following September. This molecule forms a complex with the potassium cation that is ten thousand times stronger than the strongest one formed between potassium and any crown ether.

Amazingly, by altering the structure of the simplest cryptand only slightly, Lehn and his coworkers succeeded in synthesizing molecules that could act as artificial enzymes. Similarly, they synthesized molecules that can selectively separate toxic from nontoxic metal cations.

In recognition of his pioneering efforts in the field of supramolecular chemistry, Lehn was awarded the 1987 Nobel Prize in Chemistry, jointly with Donald J. Cram and Charles J. Pedersen.

Bibliography

By Lehn

"Design of Organic Complexing Agents: Strategies Toward Properties," *Structure and Bonding*, 1973

"Cryptates: The Chemistry of Macropolycyclic Inclusion Complexes," *Accounts of Chemical Research*, 1978

"Cryptates: Inclusion Complexes of Macropolycyclic Receptor Molecules," *Pure and Applied Chemistry*, 1978

"Macrocyclic Receptor Molecules—Aspects of Chemical Reactivity: Investigations into Molecular Catalysis and Transport Processes," *Pure and Applied Chemistry*, 1979

"Physicochemical Studies of Crown and Cryptate Complexes" (with A. I. Popov) in *Coordination Chemistry of Macrocyclic Compounds*, 1979 (G. A. Melson, ed.)

"Cryptate Inclusion Complexes. Effects on Solute-Solute and Solute-Solvent Interactions and on Ionic Reactivity," *Pure and Applied Chemistry*, 1980

"Supramolecular Chemistry: Receptors, Catalysts, and Carriers," *Science*, 1985

"Photophysical and Photochemical Aspects of Supramolecular Chemistry" in *Supramolecular Photochemistry*, 1987 (V. Balzani, ed.)

"Supramolecular Chemistry—Scope and Perspectives," *Angewandte Chemie, International Edition in English*, 1988

Comprehensive Supramolecular Chemistry, 1996 (as editor, with others)

About Lehn

"Jean-Marie Lehn." In *The Nobel Prize Winners: Chemistry*, edited by Frank N. Magill. Pasadena, Calif.: Salem Press, 1990.

Nobel Laureates in Chemistry, 1901-1992. Laylin K. James, ed. Washington, D.C.: American Chemical Society, 1993.

(Thomas H. Eberlein)

Luis F. Leloir

Areas of Achievement: Biology and chemistry

Contribution: Leloir discovered angiotensin and did Nobel Prize-winning work on the biochemistry of carbohydrates, particularly sugar nucleotides and glycogen.

Sept. 6, 1908	Born in Paris, France
1932	Receives an M.D. from the University of Buenos Aires
1934	Begins work in research science with Bernardo Houssay
1936	Studies at Cambridge University's Biochemistry Laboratory
1943	Marries Amelie Zuherbuhler
1943	Moves to the United States to conduct research at both Washington and Columbia Universities
1945	Returns to Argentina to work with Houssay
1947	Named the director of the Buenos Aires Institute for Biochemical Investigations
1962	The institute becomes part of the University of Buenos Aires
1970	Wins the Nobel Prize in Chemistry for his work on sugar nucleotides and their role in carbohydrate biochemistry
Dec. 2, 1987	Dies in Buenos Aires, Argentina

Early Life

Luis Federico Leloir (pronounced "lay-LWAHR") was born in Paris on a visit of his parents, Federico and Hortensia Aguirre Leloir, to France. Later, they returned home to Buenos Aires, Argentina, where Luis attended elementary and secondary school. He then attended the University of Buenos Aires and re-

ceived a medical degree in 1932. Leloir practiced medicine at the university hospital, but he was soon disenchanted with Argentinean medicine.

This led him into research at the university's Institute of Physiology with Bernardo Alberto Houssay, a 1947 Nobel Prize winner. There, Leloir studied adrenal glands and carbohydrates, earning a Ph.D. In 1936 he did postdoctoral study at Cambridge University's Biochemistry Laboratory in England. He worked for Sir Frederick Gowland Hopkins, a giant in endocrinology (the study of hormones). At Cambridge, Leloir studied enzymes, biological catalysts that build and break down essential body components.

A Prelude to Great Things

Leloir returned to Buenos Aires to explore the kidney's role in regulating blood pressure. He participated, with Houssay, in the discovery of kidney angiotensin, the hormone involved in the control of blood pressure. Leloir's life did

(The Nobel Foundation)

not run smoothly, however, and 1943 was a crucial year, both good and bad. On the good side, he married Amelie Zuherbuhler, with whom he had a daughter. On the bad side, Juan Perón rose to power in Argentina and soon removed Houssay from the Institute of Physiology.

The latter event led to the disbanding of Houssay's research group and a move to the United States for the Leloirs. Leloir worked, for a while, at Washington University in St. Louis, Missouri, with Carl Cori. He then moved to Columbia University in New York City to work with David Green. These experiences broadened Leloir's expertise in endocrinology and carbohydrate metabolism. In 1945, he returned to Argentina to work again with Houssay, who was back in favor and the director of research at the Buenos Aires Institute of Biology and Experimental Medicine.

The Study of Milk Sugar

In 1947, Leloir, with financial aid from textile tycoon Jaime Campomar, became director of the Institute for Biochemical Investigations. Its first goal was understanding the biochemistry of lactose (milk sugar). Leloir researched how the body makes lactose, which led him to identify two substances essential to the process: glucose-1, 6-diphosphate and a sugar nucleotide named uridine diphosphate glucose (UDPG).

Leloir believed that UDPG was essential to many other aspects of carbohydrate biosynthesis and proved it. He also discovered glycogen, the main storehouse of carbohydrate energy and found that it arises from UDPG. In addition, Leloir and his coworkers explained the biosynthesis of other carbohydrates, such as sucrose (table sugar), from UDPG.

In 1955, Perón was overthrown and Leloir's institute grew. In 1962, it joined the University of Buenos Aires. Leloir also became chair of the department of biochemistry there. In 1970, he won the Nobel Prize in Chemistry for his discovery of sugar nucleotides and their role in carbohydrate biosynthesis; he became a hero to Argentineans. Leloir also made important discoveries in lipid biochemistry.

Leloir also helped found the Society for Biochemical Research and the Panamerican Association of Biochemical Societies. His rewards

Sugar Nucleotides and Carbohydrates

Leloir studied how sugars and polysaccharides are made and interconverted via sugar nucleotides.

Carbohydrates are sugars and sugar chains called oligosaccharides or polysaccharides, depending on chain length. They constitute more than 50 percent of all calories eaten. The oligosaccharides (for example, sucrose) and polysaccharides (for example, starch) arise from sugar nucleotides, which are uridine diphosphate-sugars and adenosine diphosphate-sugars (UDP-sugars and ADP-sugars).

In Leloir's day, little was known about carbohydrate production or bioconversion. Leloir discovered UDP-sugars and glycogen, a polysaccharide, and also explored carbohydrate enzymology.

Leloir's background was important to his success. First, he obtained a Ph.D. with Argentine Nobel Prize winner Bernardo Alberto Houssay. Then, postdoctoral study at Cambridge University taught him about enzymes. He also worked with Carl Cori and David Green, two knowledgeable American biochemists.

It was amazing that Leloir developed his ability in scientifically weak Argentina. There, he was aided by a benefactor, Jaime Campomar, and the National Institutes of Health (NIH) in the United States. Most important, however, were his hard work and skill conducting excellent scientific experiments using limited resources.

Bibliography
"Carbohydrate Metabolism." L. F. Leloir and C. E. Cardini. *Annual Review of Biochemistry* 22 (1953).
"Far Away and Long Ago." L. F. Leloir. *Annual Review of Bio-Chemistry* 52 (1983).
"Nucleotide and Saccharide Synthesis." L. F. Leloir. *Conference on Polysaccharides in Biological Transactions* (1958).
"Research on Sugar Nucleotides Brings Honor to Argentinean Biochemist." Enrico Cabin. *Science* 170 (1970).

were prizes and memberships in premier scientific societies such as the National Academy of Science, the Royal Society of London, and the French Académie des Sciences. He died in Buenos Aires on December 2, 1987.

Bibliography
By Leloir
"Fatty Acid Oxidation in the Liver," *Biochemistry Journal*, 1939 (with J. M. Muñoz)

Renal Hypertension, 1946, (with Eduardo Braun-Menéndez, Juan Carlos Fasciolo, et al.)

"Carbohydrate Metabolism," *Annual Review of Biochemistry*, 1953 (with C. E. Cardini)

"Nucleotide and Saccharide Synthesis," *Conference on Polysaccharides in Biological Transactions*, 1958

"Far Away and Long Ago," *Annual Review of Biochemistry*, 1983

About Leloir
"Luis F. Leloir." In *The Nobel Prize Winners: Chemistry*, edited by Frank N. Magill. Pasadena, Calif.: Salem Press, 1990.

McGraw-Hill Modern Scientists and Engineers. McGraw-Hill, 1980.

"Research on Sugar Nucleotides Brings Honor to Argentinean Biochemist." Enrico Cabib. *Science* (1970).

(Sanford S. Singer)

Georges Lemaître

Areas of Achievement: Cosmology and mathematics

Contribution: Lemaître proposed the "primeval atom" theory of the origin of the universe, which later came to be known as the "big bang."

July 17, 1894	Born in Charleroi, Belgium
1914	Joins the Fifth Corps of Volunteers during World War I
1920	Completes a dissertation on the approximation of real functions in several variables at the University of Louvain
1920	Enters the Maison Saint Rombaut to study for the priesthood
1923	Ordained to the priesthood
1923-1924	Studies at Cambridge University
1924-1925	Studies at the Massachusetts Institute of Technology (MIT)
1927	Becomes professor of astrophysics at Louvain
1933	Publishes *Discussion sur l'évolution de l'Univers*
Oct. 28, 1936	Becomes a member of the Pontifical Academy of Science
1946	Publishes *L'Hypothèse de l'atome primitif* (*The Primeval Atom*, 1950)
1950	Publishes *L'Univers*
1960	Becomes president of the Pontifical Academy of Science
June 20, 1966	Dies in Louvain, Belgium

Early Life
Georges Henri Lemaître (pronounced "luh-MEHTR"), the son of a Belgian lawyer, attended a parish grade school and a Jesuit high school. His father moved the family to Brussels

The Primeval Atom

The "primeval atom" is Lemaître's term for the superdense state of matter at the beginning of the universe.

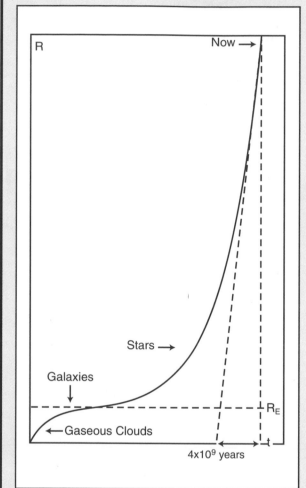

The history of the universe as Lemaître envisioned it, from the superdense primeval atom at the far left of the curve to the present at the far right. R is the size of the universe, t is the age, and the upward slope of the curve represents the expansion of the universe. (from *Cosmology of Lemaître*, by O. Godart and M. Heller, 1985).

Lemaître combined the work of Alexander Friedmann, a Russian mathematician who developed a mathematical model for an expanding universe, with the work of Edwin Hubble, the American astronomer who discovered the expansion of the universe.

Before Lemaître, Friedmann's work was considered to be a form of theoretical physics that was merely a mathematical exercise. Lemaître developed the theory into an account for the physical origin of the universe. He claimed that the universe was once a "primeval atom," an atom that contained all the matter of the universe. Just as the elements of atomic number 92 (uranium) and higher are radioactive, he proposed that this primeval atom, with an atomic number equal to the number of all the protons and neutrons in the universe, would be "super-radioactive."

The fission of this cosmic egg into smaller and smaller parts and the force of the decay would result in the outward expansion of the universe that Hubble observed. Later, Lemaître claimed, some of this matter would condense to form stars and galaxies.

His was the first modern cosmology to combine relativistic mathematics and observational evidence from astronomy to describe the creation of the universe. Later theories that built on Lemaître's theory were first dubbed "big bang" theories by Sir Fred Hoyle in a British radio broadcast in 1950.

Bibliography

Astronomy and Cosmology. John North. New York: W. W. Norton, 1995.

The Big Bang. Joseph Silk. 2d ed. New York: W. H. Freeman, 1989.

In Search of the Big Bang. John Gribbin. New York: Bantam Books, 1986.

in 1910, where Georges attended a Jesuit school, studying mathematics in preparation for a career as a research scientist. He was graduated from the College of Engineering in 1913 and took a job as a mining engineer.

Just days after Germany invaded Belgium, Lemaître joined the Fifth Corps of Volunteers.

Early in the war, he dug trenches in preparation for battle. He was later transferred to an artillery unit, where he fought in the trenches. He reached the rank of master sergeant and was cited for bravery.

After the war, Lemaître devoted himself to finishing an advanced degree in the sciences and to studying for the priesthood. He took a degree in mathematics in 1920 and was ordained in 1923.

Cosmological Theory

Lemaître studied for a year in Cambridge, England, under Sir Arthur Stanley Eddington and for a year at the Massachusetts Institute of Technology (MIT), where he worked closely with Harlow Shapley of Harvard University. His career was marked by an ability to apply higher mathematics to problems in astrophysics and celestial mechanics.

His work under Eddington and Shapley drew Lemaître to problems in astrophysics. After working on the problem of the motion of galaxies, he turned to the work for which he is most famous. Lemaître proposed the first theory that brought together relativity theory and observational astronomy into a model for the origin of the universe. This model, which he called the "primeval atom," is the basis for modern big bang cosmology.

Science and Religion

Lemaître's priesthood was a source of some interest for many of his colleagues in the sciences—he was often referred to by his Catholic title, "The Abbé Lemaître," to reinforce his connection with the Catholic Church.

Lemaître was reticent, however, to bring the world of science and the world of religion together. He admonished Pope Pius XII not to associate his primeval atom with the Creation account in Genesis, and he often spoke of the different ways of thinking that for him divided questions of science and questions of religion.

Numerical Calculations

Lemaître continued his work in pure mathematics throughout his career, and he is known for having brought the first computer to Belgium. He was an active participant in all facets of the computer's operation—its programming, application to mathematical problems, and administration.

He removed himself from cosmological work as the steady state model of Fred Hoyle, Herman Bondi, and Thomas Gold gained popularity, but he lived long enough to see his concept of the primeval atom, by then called

Lemaître (second from right, in clerical garb) visits Mount Wilson Observatory in 1932. Next to him is Edwin Powell Hubble (second from left). (AP/Wide World Photos)

the big bang theory, vindicated by the observation of cosmic background radiation in 1965. He died in Louvain on June 20, 1966.

Bibliography
By Lemaître
"Un Univers homogene de masse constante et de rayon croissant rendant compte de la vitesse radiale des nebuleuses extragalactiques," *Annales de la Société Scientifique de Bruxelles*, 1927 ("A Homogeneous Universe of Constant Mass and Increasing Radius Accounting for the Radial Velocity of Extra-Galactic Nebulae," *Monthly Notices of the Royal Astronomical Society*, 1931)

"The Expanding Universe," *Monthly Notices of the Royal Astronomical Society*, 1931

Discussion sur l'évolution de l'Univers, 1933

L'Hypothèse de l'atome primitif: Essai de cosmogonie, 1946 (*The Primeval Atom: An Essay on Cosmogony*, 1950)

L'Univers, 1950

The Expanding Universe: Lemaître's Unknown Manuscript, 1985 (M. Heller and O. Godart, eds.)

About Lemaître
The Big Bang and Georges Lemaître. A. Berger, ed. Boston: D. Reidel, 1984.

Cosmology of Lemaître. O. Godart and M. Heller. Tucson, Ariz.: Pachart, 1985.

The Red Limit. Timothy Ferris. New York: William Morrow, 1977.

(Craig Sean McConnell)

Rita Levi-Montalcini

Areas of Achievement: Cell biology and physiology

Contribution: Levi-Montalcini discovered a substance known as nerve growth factor, which is critical to the development of the nervous system.

Apr. 22, 1909	Born in Turin, Italy
1936	Earns an M.D. from the University of Turin
1936-1938	Works as a research assistant to Giuseppe Levi
1939	Works at the Neurological Institute in Brussels, Belgium
1940-1943	Conducts research at her home
1943-1944	Lives in hiding in Florence, Italy
1945-1946	Resumes work with Levi
1946-1952	Conducts research at Washington University in St. Louis
1952-1953	Works at the Institute of Biophysics in Rio de Janeiro, Brazil
1953-1959	Conducts research with Stanley Cohen at Washington
1961-1969	Works at the Higher Institute of Health in Rome, Italy
1968	Elected to the National Academy of Sciences
1969	Promoted to full professor at Washington
1969-1979	Directs the Laboratory of Cell Biology in Rome
1977	Named professor emeritus at Washington
1986	Shares the Nobel Prize in Physiology or Medicine with Cohen
1987	Awarded the National Medal of Science

Early Life

Rita Levi-Montalcini (pronounced "LAY-vee MOHN-tahl-CHEE-nee") was born Rita Levi in Turin, Italy, on April 22, 1909. Her father, Adamo Levi, was an engineer, and her mother, Adele Montalcini Levi, was a painter. As an adult, Levi-Montalcini added her mother's maiden name to her own last name in order to distinguish herself from the many other Levis in Turin.

Levi-Montalcini entered medical school at the University of Turin in 1930, despite the protests of her father, and earned an M.D. in 1936. She continued to work with Giuseppe Levi, one of her professors at the university, for two more years, studying the development of nerve cells.

In 1938, Benito Mussolini, the leader of Italy's Fascist government, issued a decree banning Jews from all professional careers. As a Jew, Levi-Montalcini was forbidden from practicing medicine or from working at a university. After briefly working illegally as a physician, she found employment at the Neurological Institute in Brussels, Belgium, in early 1939. Later that year, the impending invasion of Belgium by the Nazi government of Germany forced her to return to Turin.

The Secret Laboratory

From 1940 to 1943, Levi-Montalcini set up a small research laboratory in her home in Turin. She worked in secret by purchasing fertile eggs from farmers and studying the development of nerves in chicken embryos. She was inspired in her work by reading about similar work done by American embryologist Viktor Hamburger.

In 1943, the Fascist government of Italy fell, and the Nazis invaded the country. Levi-Montalcini and her family left Turin and fled south to Florence. They remained in hiding until the Germany was defeated in southern Italy

(The Nobel Foundation)

in 1944. Levi-Montalcini worked as a physician treating war refugees until the Germans were defeated in northern Italy in 1945. She returned to Turin to continue her work with Giuseppe Levi, who had often worked with her during these years in hiding.

Research in the United States and Brazil

In 1946, Hamburger invited Levi-Montalcini to come to the United States to work with him. She accepted and began her long association with Washington University in St. Louis, Missouri. Together, Hamburger and Levi-Montalcini continued to study the growth of nerve cells in chicken embryos. They discovered that certain mouse tumors, when attached to chicken embryos, seemed to promote nerve growth.

In 1952, Levi-Montalcini traveled to Rio de Janeiro, Brazil, to work with Hertha Meyer at the Institute of Biophysics. Meyer was an expert in the newly developed technique of

Nerve Growth Factor

Levi-Montalcini discovered a substance called nerve growth factor, which directs the development of nerve cells.

The nervous system consists of two parts. The central nervous system is made up of the brain and spinal cord. The peripheral nervous system is made up of nerve cells called neurons, which connect the central nervous system with the rest of the body. These neurons contain long extensions called axons that allow the neurons to communicate with other cells.

Neuroembryologists (scientists who study the development of nerves in organisms at an early stage of life) discovered that neurons grow toward body tissues in ways which suggest that the tissue has some control over the process. For example, when a limb is surgically removed from a young amphibian, neurons stop growing in that direction. When a new limb is attached, even one from another species, neurons begin growing toward it again. Later experiments showed that certain kinds of tissues cause accelerated neuron growth when placed near nerve tissue. This finding showed that these tissues produce a substance that induces nerve growth in their direction. The effect was seen not only in living organisms but also in nerve tissue grown in glass dishes.

When this substance, now known as nerve growth factor (NGF), was isolated, it was discovered to be a protein consisting of two identical chains of 118 amino acids. NGF appears to have two functions in the developing organism.

First, it seems to be necessary to the survival of immature neurons, as indicated by an experi-ment in which newborn mice were injected with antibodies to nerve growth factor. These antibodies destroyed the normal NGF in the bodies of the mice, and the mice failed to develop normal neurons.

Second, nerve growth factor seems to direct growing neurons toward body tissues. This phenomenon, known as neurotropism, was indicated in an experiment in which isolated neurons were placed between two chambers, one with NGF and one without. The neurons grew only in the direction of the chamber containing NGF.

In the developing organism, nerve growth factor is believed to be released by the cells of body tissues. It travels through the fluid in the spaces between cells until it reaches an immature neuron. When it binds to the neuron, the neuron begins to form an axon. As this axon grows, it encounters more NGF from the tissue cells, which guides it in the direction of these cells. When the axon reaches the tissue, the neuron is able to perform its function of communicating with it.

The discovery of nerve growth factor added greatly to the understanding of the development of the nervous system and was the first of many growth factors to be discovered.

Bibliography

Growth and Trophic Factors. José Regino Perez-Polo, Jean De Vellis, and Bernard Haber. New York: A. R. Liss, 1983.

Nerve Growth Factors. Robert A. Rush. New York: John Wiley & Sons, 1989.

Neuronal Growth Factors. M. Bothwell. New York: Springer-Verlag, 1991.

working with tissues grown in glass dishes. This method allowed results to be obtained much more quickly than did working with live animals.

When Levi-Montalcini placed a piece of mouse tumor near a piece of chicken nerve tissue, within hours the nerve tissue was surrounded by a halo of new nerve fibers. This experiment proved that the tumor was producing a substance that caused nerve growth.

Levi-Montalcini returned to Washington University in 1953 and began working with biochemist Stanley Cohen. They discovered that the substance in the mouse tumors, now called nerve growth factor (NGF), could also be found in snake venom, rodent salivary glands, and many other tissues. In 1959, they made antibodies to NGF by injecting it into rabbits and then withdrawing serum from the rabbits. These antibodies, manufactured by the rabbits' immune system, acted to destroy NGF. When injected into newborn mice, they blocked the growth of nerves almost completely.

Return to Italy
Cohen left Washington University in 1959. In 1961, Levi-Montalcini began spending only six months a year at Washington and the other six months in Italy working at the Higher Institute of Health in Rome. In 1968, she was elected to the U.S. National Academy of Sciences, and, in 1969, she was promoted to full professor at Washington. That same year, she began spending her time in Italy directing the newly formed Laboratory of Cell Biology, also in Rome. In 1977, she was promoted to professor emeritus and began spending all her time in Italy. She retired as director of the Laboratory of Cell Biology in 1979 but continued to do research there.

Cohen and Levi-Montalcini shared the 1986 Nobel Prize in Physiology or Medicine for their work with NGF. In 1987, Levi-Montalcini was awarded the National Medal of Science from President Ronald Reagan.

Bibliography
By Levi-Montalcini
"The Nerve-Growth Factor," *Scientific American*, 1979 (with Pietro Calissano)
"Reflections on a Scientific Adventure" in *Women Scientists: The Road to Liberation*, 1982 (Derek Richter, ed.)
Molecular Aspects of Neurobiology, 1986 (as editor, with Calissano)
"The Nerve Growth Factor Thirty-Five Years Later," *Science*, 1987
Elogio dell'imperfezione, 1987 (*In Praise of Imperfection*, 1988)

About Levi-Montalcini
Nobel Prize Women in Science. Sharon Bertsch McGrayne. New York: Carol, 1993.
"Rita Levi-Montalcini." In *The Nobel Prize Winners: Physiology or Medicine*, edited by Frank N. Magill. Pasadena, Calif.: Salem Press, 1991.
The Triumph of Discovery. Joan Dash. New York: Simon & Schuster, 1991.
The Who's Who of Nobel Prize Winners, 1901-1990. Bernard S. Schlessinger and Jane H. Schlessinger, eds. Phoenix: Oryx Press, 1991.

(Rose Secrest)

Gilbert N. Lewis

Area of Achievement: Chemistry
Contribution: Lewis, a leader in chemical thermodynamics and an early exponent of relativity theory, laid the foundation for the electron theory of valence, extended the concept of acids and bases, and was the first to isolate heavy hydrogen.

Oct. 25, 1875	Born in Weymouth, Massachusetts
1899	Earns a Ph.D. in chemistry at Harvard under T. W. Richards
1900	Studies under Wilhelm Ostwald at the University of Leipzig and Walther Nernst at the University of Göttingen
1901-1904	Teaches at Harvard
1904	Serves as Superintendent of Weights and Measures and as a chemist in the Bureau of Science in the Philippines
1905	Conducts research at the Massachusetts Institute of Technology with Arthur A. Noyes
1912	Named dean of the college of chemistry and chair of the chemistry department at the University of California, Berkeley
1916	Publishes his theory of the cubic atom
1922	Awarded the Distinguished Service Medal
1923	Begins to study the theory of radiation and relativity
1933-1938	Conducts research on isotopes and their preparation
1938	Performs theoretical and experimental studies in photochemistry
Mar. 23, 1946	Dies in Berkeley, California

Early Life

Gilbert Newton Lewis was born near Boston in 1875. He received his primary education at home from his father, an independent-minded lawyer, and his mother, who was educated in a Massachusetts seminary. Lewis' formal education began in 1889 at the University of Nebraska preparatory school.

Lewis transferred to Harvard in 1893 and was graduated with a B.S. in 1896. After teaching for a year at Phillips Academy at Andover, he returned to Harvard for a M.A. degree in 1898 and a Ph.D. under the chemist T. W. Richards in 1899. Lewis taught chemistry at Harvard for one year before going abroad on a traveling fellowship to study under Wilhelm Ostwald at the University of Leipzig and Walther Nernst at the University of Göttingen.

Lewis returned to Harvard in 1901 and taught thermodynamics and electrochemistry until 1904. Several of his longtime interests date from this early period, the most important of which were thermodynamics, valence theory, and photochemistry.

Lewis spent 1904 as Superintendent of Weights and Measures in the Philippines and as a chemist in the Bureau of Science in Manila. He returned to the United States in 1905 and joined the group of physical chemists assembled by Arthur A. Noyes at the Massachusetts Institute of Technology (MIT). Noyes's laboratory became the first center for physical chemists in the United States.

Thermodynamics and MIT

Lewis remained at MIT for seven years, publishing more than thirty papers, including "Outlines of a New System of Thermodynamic Chemistry" in 1907 and "The Free Energy of Chemical Substances" in 1913. They were among the most important in a long series of papers on the experimental determination of free energy and led in 1923 to the publication of Lewis' monumental work *Thermodynamics and the Free Energy of Chemical Substances*.

During his years at MIT, Lewis met Albert Einstein and became a supporter of the then-unpopular theory of relativity. This move into a new field of investigation resulted in his publications on relativity with R. C. Tolman and E. B. Wilson.

Chemical Education and Atomic Studies

In 1912, Lewis left MIT to become dean of the college of chemistry and chair of the chemistry department at the University of California, Berkeley (UCB). His recruitment of an exceptional faculty and curricular reforms made UCB the model for American chemical education. Berkeley's production of first-rate chemists soon rivaled that of leading German universities.

Lewis' work on thermodynamics became more intense at UCB, as he transformed an essentially theoretical science into a practical tool for chemists. His other interests, such as atomic structure and valence, continued to develop, and in 1916 he published "The Atom and the Molecule." In this paper, Lewis defined the chemical bond as a shared pair of electrons and introduced the electron dot formulas, or Lewis formulas, to represent a chemical bond. His most extensive treatment of valence appeared in 1923 as *Valence and the Structure of Atoms and Molecules*.

World War I Service

World War I and his commission as a major in the Chemical Warfare Service interrupted Lewis' work at UCB. As chief of the service's defense division, he instructed American army officers on the effects of poison gas and how to defend against poison gas attacks. Lewis received the Distinguished Service Medal in 1922 for his valuable contribution.

Other Interests

Lewis returned to UCB after World War I and concluded his work in thermodynamics and chemical valence with major publications in

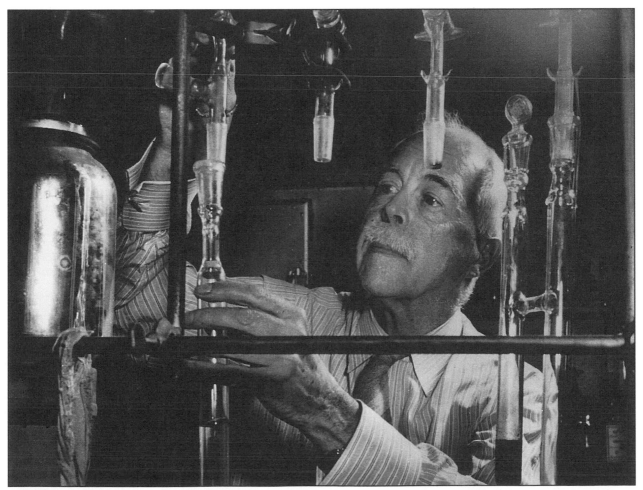

(Lawrence Berkeley National Laboratory)

both areas in 1923. He devoted the next decade to the theories of quantum radiation and relativity, before turning in 1933 to research on the separation of deuterium from ordinary water. Lewis was the first to concentrate nearly pure deuterium in quantities sufficient for experimentation and spent two years focused on the chemistry and physics of deuterium, heavy water, and other deuterium compounds.

In the late 1930's, Lewis resumed his earlier studies on photochemistry, particularly the relation of electron structure to phosphorescence, fluorescence, and color in compounds.

His last publications dealt with the relation between phosphorescence and the triplet electronic state of organic molecules.

Lewis died suddenly of heart failure on March 23, 1946, while performing an experiment on phosphorescence; he was seventy years old.

Bibliography
By Lewis
"A Review of Recent Progress in Physical Chemistry," *Journal of the American Chemical Society*, 1906

Atomic Structure

Lewis made significant contributions to the study of atomic structure with his theories of the cubic atom and shared-pair electron bond.

Lewis developed the idea of electrons in an atom arranged in concentric cubes in 1902 while trying to explain the periodic law to an elementary chemistry class. He proposed that a polar (ionic) compound results whenever two or more atoms complete their outermost cubes by gaining or losing electrons and form a stable octet (group of eight). Electrostatic attraction produces the polar bond between them.

Despite the cubic atom's success in accounting for the formulas of simple polar compounds of inorganic chemistry, Lewis' model left unexplained the vast number of nonpolar or organic compounds that do not consist of ions. He solved this problem in 1916 by postulating that the cubes or atomic shells are interpenetrable. Because of shell interpenetrability, an electron or

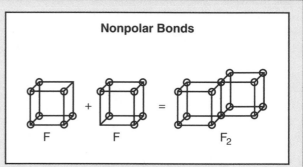

Nonpolar Bonds

F   F   F₂

The circles represent bonds. F is fluorine.

electrons from one atom can form part of another atom's shell but not belong exclusively to either atom. Hence, neither atom has lost or gained electrons. This arrangement is the mechanism for electron pair sharing or chemical bond formation. Only in purely polar compounds is the electron transfer complete.

In order to represent clearly the shared electron pair bond, Lewis in 1916 introduced electron dot formulas. Each pair of dots or colon (:) symbolizes the electron pair constituting the chemical bond. Although the cubic atom became obsolete—in his 1916 paper, Lewis replaced the eight electrons at the cube's corners with four pairs at the corners of a tetrahedron—his shared electron pair bond became the starting point for the new quantum chemistry.

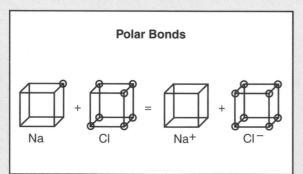

Polar Bonds

Na   Cl   Na⁺   Cl⁻

The circles represent bonds. Na is sodium and Cl is chlorine.

Bibliography
Electrons and Valence: Development of the Theory, 1900-1925. Anthony N. Stranges. College Station: Texas A&M University Press, 1982.

Thermodynamics

Lewis' rationalization of and contributions to chemical thermodynamics transformed it from an abstract science into a valuable tool for chemists.

Lewis' earliest paper of 1900-1901 attempted to establish a fundamental principle from which chemists could derive all thermodynamic relations. He proposed the idea of an "escaping tendency" or "fugacity" to express the tendency of a substance to pass from one chemical phase to another and thereby provide information on the extent and direction of the chemical reaction.

Lewis never found a fundamental fugacity, but he did demonstrate that measurements of free energy and entropy provide an exact chemical thermodynamics. Previously, chemists had relied on calorimetric measurements of enthalpy (a body's internal energy added to the product of its volume and the pressure) and heat of formation to calculate chemical affinity (attraction) and thereby predict the direction of any chemical reaction. By 1907, he had made clear that a system's free energy and entropy (unavailable energy) were key concepts, and he and his coworkers began free energy calculations from measurements of equilibria, electromotive force, and entropy.

Lewis summarized and brought up to date the theory and methods for calculating free energy in 1913 and in 1923 published his classic book on thermodynamics. This work made the techniques and fruits of thermodynamics, once the luxury of specialists, available to every chemist. Lewis' main contribution to thermodynamics was not in his elaboration of theory but in his expansion of its practical applications.

Bibliography

Elementary Chemical Thermodynamics. Bruce H. Mahan. New York: W. A. Benjamin, 1964.

"Gilbert N. Lewis and the Thermodynamics of Strong Electrolytes." *Journal of Chemical Education* 61 (1984).

"Outlines of a New System of Thermodynamic Chemistry," *Proceedings of the American Academy of Arts and Sciences,* 1907

"The Principle of Relativity and Non-Newtonian Mechanics," *Proceedings of the American Academy of Arts and Sciences,* 1909 (with R. C. Tolman)

"The Space-Time Manifold of Relativity: The Non-Euclidean Geometry of Mechanics and Electromagnetics," *Proceedings of the American Academy of Arts and Sciences,* 1912 (with E. B. Wilson)

"The Free Energy of Chemical Substances," *Journal of the American Chemical Society,* 1913

"The Atom and the Molecule," *Journal of the American Chemical Society,* 1916

Thermodynamics and the Free Energy of Chemical Substances, 1923 (with M. Randall)

Valence and the Structure of Atoms and Molecules, 1923

"The Nature of Light," *Proceedings of the National Academy of Sciences,* 1926

"The Quantum Laws and the Uncertainty Principle of Heisenberg," *Proceedings of the National Academy of Sciences,* 1929 (with Joseph E. Mayer)

"The Isotope of Hydrogen," *Journal of the American Chemical Society,* 1933

"The Color of Organic Substances," *Chemical Reviews,* 1939 (with M. Calvin)

About Lewis

Borderland of the Unknown. Arthur Lachman. New York: Pageant Press, 1995.

From Retorts to Lasers. William Jolly. Berkeley: University of California Press, 1987.

"Gilbert Newton Lewis." Joel H. Hildebrand. *National Academy of Sciences Biographical Memoirs* 31 (1958).

"Lewis, Gilbert Newton." In *Dictionary of Scientific Biography,* edited by Charles Coulston Gillispie. New York: Charles Scribner's Sons, 1973.

"Reflections on the Electron Theory of the Chemical Bond: 1900-1925." Anthony N. Stranges. *Journal of Chemical Education* 61 (1984).

(Anthony N. Stranges and Steve Kirkpatrick)

Willard F. Libby

Areas of Achievement: Astronomy, chemistry, earth science, and science (general)

Contribution: Libby is best known for developing carbon dating, a process through which organisms up to seventy thousand years old can be dated with reasonable accuracy.

Dec. 17, 1908	Born in Grand Valley, Colorado
1931	Receives a B.A. in chemistry from the University of California, Berkeley (UCB)
1933	Receives a Ph.D. in chemistry from UCB
1933-1941	Teaches at UCB
1941	Awarded a Guggenheim Fellowship and spends an academic year at Princeton University
1942-1945	Works for the Manhattan Project at Columbia University
1945	Named a professor of chemistry at the University of Chicago
1945	Joins the Enrico Fermi Institute
1954	Appointed to the Atomic Energy Commission
1959	Appointed a professor of chemistry at the University of California, Los Angeles (UCLA)
1960	Awarded the Nobel Prize in Chemistry
1962	Appointed director of UCLA's Institute of Geophysics and Planetary Physics
1976	Retires from UCLA
Sept. 8, 1980	Dies in Los Angeles, California

Early Life

The son of Eva May Libby and Edward Ora Libby, a farmer, Willard Frank Libby was born in Grand Valley, Colorado, in 1908. When he was five, Libby's family moved to Santa Rosa, California, where he grew up.

After his graduation from high school in Sebastapol, California, Libby entered the University of California, Berkeley (UCB), and in six years received both the bachelor's degree and doctorate in chemistry, completing his formal training in 1933.

Libby married Leonor Hickey in 1940, and the next year, after eight years of teaching at UCB, he and his wife moved to Princeton, New Jersey, to take advantage of Libby's recently awarded Guggenheim Fellowship. In less than four months, however, the United States had entered World War II, and Libby was drawn into the Manhattan Project, whose mission was to develop a nuclear bomb.

Uranium Isotopes and Carbon Dating

Libby's work in the Manhattan Project focused on devising a gaseous-diffusion process

(The Nobel Foundation)

Radiocarbon Dating

As a result of Libby's discovery of radiocarbon dating, organic matter as old as 70,000 years can be dated with reasonable accuracy.

In 1934, it was discovered that when the atomic nuclei of uranium are bombarded with neutrons, rather than becoming heavier, the nuclei split, producing an unimaginable burst of energy. The nuclei of radioactive isotopes are unstable. When they decay, they send out alpha, beta, and gamma rays. Walther Bothe had earlier developed an instrument to measure such discharges. Libby improved on Bothe's device by building a coincidence counter that virtually eliminated background radioactivity, making feasible a highly precise measurement.

Earlier researchers had discovered that cosmic rays striking atoms in the top atmosphere shed cascades of neutrons that are absorbed by nitrogen, causing it to decay into radioactive carbon, designated carbon 14 by scientists. Libby surmised that when carbon in the upper atmosphere is converted to radioactive carbon, it bonds with oxygen, a necessary ingredient in photosynthesis, and becomes carbon dioxide.

He concluded that organisms nourished by plants contain radioactive carbon, whose half-life is 5,730 years. He further concluded that when organisms die, their level of radioactivity decreases in predictable amounts based on the half-life of radioactive carbon.

Using this information, Libby used Bothe's coincident counter, which he had altered and improved, to measure accurately the amount of radioactivity in organic matter. Knowing the half-life of radioactive carbon, he was able thereby to date organic matter that was less than 70,000 years old with considerable reliability.

Bibliography
Carbon-14, and Other Science Methods That Date the Past. Lynn Poole. New York: Whittlesey House, 1961.
Radioactive Dating: An Archaeological Perspective. R. E. Taylor. Orlando, Fla.: Academic Press, 1987.
Radiocarbon Dating. Sheridan Bowman. Berkeley: University of California Press, 1990.

through which uranium isotopes could be separated from other materials, a feat required to produce a nuclear warhead. Although this work does not seem to be directly related to the process of carbon dating for which Libby received his greatest celebrity, it proved fundamental to it.

Using carbon dating, scientists are able to determine the age of organic matter that is less than seventy thousand years old with considerable reliability. For this pioneering work, which has had a profound effect on the research of scientists in such fields as anthropology, archeology, geology, astronomy, and history, Libby received the Nobel Prize in Chemistry in 1960.

Academic Career
Libby taught chemistry at the University of Chicago in 1945 before joining the Enrico Fermi Institute. In 1954, he was appointed to the Atomic Energy Commission, and in 1959 he took a position as professor of chemistry at the University of California, Los Angeles (UCLA). While teaching at UCLA, Libby was named the director of the Institute of Geophysics and Planetary Physics in 1962. He retired from UCLA in 1976 and died in 1980 at the age of seventy-one.

Bibliography
By Libby
Radioactivity of Ordinary Elements, 1933
Radiocarbon Dating, 1952
Isotopes in Industry and Medicine, 1957
Science and Administration, 1961
Collected Papers, 1981 (7 vols.; Rainer Berger and Leona Marshall Libby, eds.)

About Libby
Le Prix Nobel en 1960. Oslo, Norway: Nobel Prize Committee, 1961.
"Willard Frank Libby." In *The Nobel Prize Winners: Chemistry*, edited by Frank N. Magill. Pasadena, Calif.: Salem Press, 1990.

(R. Baird Shuman)

Carolus Linnaeus

Areas of Achievement: Biology, botany, and zoology

Contribution: Linnaeus devised a system of classification and nomenclature with which he organized and named the known living things. Modern classification systems trace their origins to Linnaeus, although they differ philosophically, and binomial nomenclature is still used in the form that he devised.

May 23, 1707	Born in Sodra Råshult, Småland, Sweden
1727	Studies medicine at the University of Lund
1728	Transfers to the University of Uppsala
1729	Begins working with Petrus Artedi
1732	Conducts a research expedition to Lapland
1734	Conducts a research expedition to central Sweden
1735	Obtains a medical degree from the University of Harderwijk, the Netherlands
1735	Publishes *Systema Naturae* (*A General System of Nature*, 1800-1801)
1738-1741	Practices medicine in Stockholm
1741	Becomes a professor of medicine at Uppsala
1742	Becomes a professor of botany at Uppsala
1753	Publishes *Species Plantarum*
Jan. 10, 1778	Dies in Uppsala, Sweden
1784	His collections are sold to James Smith, an Englishman
1829	His botany collections are sold to the Linnaean Society of London

(Library of Congress)

Early Life

Carl von Linné, who was known by his Latin name Carolus Linnaeus (pronounced "luh-NEE-uhs"), developed a love for and knowledge of plants in the gardens tended by his father, a Lutheran clergyman. His interest in nature, especially plants, led him to enter the University of Lund as a medical student. At the time, medical studies involved considerable botany because many medications were prepared from plants.

Linnaeus transferred to the University of Uppsala in 1728 because it had a better academic reputation than Lund. Neither university was a strong teaching institution at the time, and Linnaeus was essentially self-taught. He thrived in that environment, beginning his lifetime quest to organize all living things into a single classification system.

Petrus Artedi was the premier student of natural history at Uppsala when Linnaeus arrived. He too was interested in classification, and they worked together on a system for categorizing all living things, Linnaeus concentrated on plants, Artedi on fish. Working with

Artedi is thought to have had a profound influence on Linnaeus and his classification system.

Entrepreneurial Ability

Although Linnaeus had financial problems throughout his early career, especially during his student days, his abilities, interests, persistence, and personal charisma often drew support to his causes. At Uppsala, he lived first with Olaf Celsius, a theologian and dean, and later with Olof Rudbeck, a professor of medicine and curator of the botanical garden. Rudbeck also employed Linnaeus in the botanical garden.

In 1732, Linnaeus obtained funding from the university for an expedition through Lapland, where he gathered specimens and biological and cultural information. In 1734, he undertook a more elaborate expedition through central Sweden. That trip was financed by the gov-

The Binomial Name and Classification System

Linnaeus developed a scheme for organizing and naming living things. It allowed for the rapid assimilation of the multitude of new species being discovered at the time in explorations of the Americas, Africa, and the Orient and is the basis for modern classification systems.

Linnaeus developed a "sexual system" for all flower-producing plants. Each was classified according to the number of stamens (pollen- and sperm-producing parts of the flower) and number of carpels (egg-producing parts of the flower). Even Linnaeus recognized that the system was highly oversimplified, however, and he used other plant characteristics in his actual classification. Nevertheless, his oversimplified scheme was effectively used by the many different botanists required to categorize the plants that were being discovered as exploration of the world accelerated. Linnaeus extended the system to animals. Although less successful in that context, it had the same effect on animal classification and nomenclature.

During the development of his classification scheme, Linnaeus found the system used to name organisms cumbersome. The genus, which included a group of similar species, was given a name consisting of a single word, but each species, a single kind of organism, was named using a descriptive phrase. Thus, the organism's name consisted of the single word for its genus and the phrase that described its specific characteristics.

Linnaeus began using a single word for the species as well as the genus. The simplicity of this two-word, or two-name (binomial), system proved to have great advantages over the old system. He also used Latin and Greek words and word roots, as did the old system, for the most part. These classical languages were known by the biologists of the day, and, as dead languages (languages no longer in use), they were unchanging. Those characteristics made possible a universal nomenclature that would be constant through time.

Naturalists before Linnaeus had set up classification schemes, such as John Ray and Joseph Tournefort, and used binomial names, such as Gaspard Bauhin. Linnaeus' oversimplified scheme, however, was just what was needed at the time, and he was the first to use binomial names consistently. As a result, the large number of animals and plants being discovered could be readily named and made to fit into his system.

The Linnaean system was the basis for the classification and nomenclatural systems that developed subsequently. These systems allow biologists to organize the world's vast array of species. Such organization is necessary to understand how the complex of living things functions, as well as to learn how to use and conserve the species involved.

Bibliography

The Growth of Biological Thought: Diversity, Evolution, and Inheritance. Ernst Mayr. Cambridge, Mass.: The Belknap Press of Harvard University Press, 1982.

Interpreting Nature: The Science of Living Form from Linnaeus to Kant. James L. Larson. Baltimore: The Johns Hopkins University Press, 1994.

Reason and Experience: The Representation of Natural Order in the Work of Carl von Linne. James L. Larson, Berkeley: University of California Press, 1971.

ernor of Falun, a city in the region, further demonstrating Linnaeus' ability to excite confidence and enthusiasm in potential supporters. These and similar activities established his botanical reputation while he was still a student.

Professional Development

Linnaeus obtained a degree in medicine from the University of Harderwijk, in the Netherlands, in 1735. Artedi joined him there but fell into a canal and drowned shortly after his arrival. With financial assistance from friends in the Netherlands, Linnaeus went to considerable trouble to edit and publish Artedi's work on fish. Although published in Artedi's name, it established Linnaeus' position in the history of ichthyology. He also published many of his own most important works, including the first edition of *Systema Naturae* (*A General System of Nature*, 1800-1801) while in the Netherlands.

In 1738, he returned to Stockholm and practiced medicine until 1741, when he became a professor at the University of Uppsala, where he spent the rest of his professional career. Under him, the university's botanical garden and herbarium collection became one of the world's best.

From 1741 until 1770, Linnaeus and his students refined the ideas that he had developed during his early years. They traveled widely in Sweden, Europe, and other parts of the world, collecting new specimens and fitting them into the Linnaean scheme of classification. Johann Christian Fabricius, who applied Linnaeus' system to insects, and Pehr Kalm, who collected widely in North America, were two of his many productive students.

Principal Contributions

As his career progressed, Linnaeus made increasing use of binomial nomenclature. In 1753, *Species Plantarum* was published. It became the starting point for the scientific classification and nomenclature of plants, in part because it used binomial names consistently. In 1758, the tenth edition of *Systema Naturae* was published, using binomial names for animals throughout. It became the starting point for animal classification. Both publications, and Linnaeus himself, were immortalized as a result.

Linnaeus' health began to fail in the early 1770's, and he died in 1778. In 1784, his wife sold his collections to James Smith, who shipped them to England just ahead of the Swedish king's attempt to recover them for Sweden. This mercenary act of Linnaeus' widow was not as unfortunate as it seemed. In 1829, Smith's widow sold the botanical collections to the Linnaean Society of London, validating a second center of Linnaean immortality.

Bibliography
By Linnaeus
Iter Lapponicum Dei gratia institutum, 1732 (*Lachesis Lapponica: A Tour in Lapland*, 1811)
Systema Naturae, 1735 (*A General System of Nature Through the Three Grand Kingdoms of Animals, Vegetables, and Minerals*, 1800-1801)
Fundamenta botanica, 1736 (fundamental botany)
Genera Plantarum, 1737 (the genera of plants)
Flora Lapponica, 1737 (The plants of Lapland)
Hortus Cliffortianus, 1737 (horticulture of Cliffort's garden)
Classes Plantarum, 1738 (the classes of plants)
Ölandska och gothländska resa, 1745 (*Linnaeus's Oland and Gotland Journey, 1741*, 1973)
Flora Suecica, 1745 (the plants of Sweden)
Fauna Suecica, 1746 (the animals of Sweden)
Philosophia Botanica, 1751 (*The Elements of Botany*, 1775)
Species Plantarum, 1753 (the species of plants)
Systema Naturae, 1758-1759 (10th ed.)
A Generic and Specific Description of British Plants, 1775 (from *Genera Plantarum* and *Species Plantarum*)
Nemesis Divina, 1878 (divine retribution)

About Linnaeus
The Compleat Naturalist: A Life of Linnaeus. Wilfrid Blunt. New York: Viking Press, 1971.
Contemporary Perspectives on Linnaeus. John Weinstock, ed. Lanham. Md.: University Press of America, 1985.
Linnaeus: The Man and His Work. Tore Frängsmyr, ed. Berkeley: University of California Press, 1983.
"Order Replaces Chaos: Carl Linnaeus: 1707-1778." Alexander B. Adams. In *Eternal Quest: The Story of the Great Naturalists*. New York: G. P. Putnam's Sons, 1969.

(Carl W. Hoagstrom)

Fritz Albert Lipmann

Areas of Achievement: Biology, chemistry, and physiology

Contribution: Lipmann, a visionary biochemist, proposed the central role of high-energy phosphate compounds in metabolism and discovered coenzyme A.

June 12, 1899	Born in Königsberg, East Prussia (now Kaliningrad, Russia)
1924	Earns an M.D. from the University of Berlin
1927	Earns a Ph.D. in chemistry from Berlin
1927-1930	Studies in Berlin and Heidelberg with Otto Meyerhof
1931	Travels to the United States for a fellowship at the Rockefeller Institute
1932-1939	Takes a position with the Carlsberg Foundation in Copenhagen, Denmark
1939-1941	Emigrates to the United States to work at Cornell University
1941-1953	Heads the Biochemical Research Laboratory at Massachusetts General Hospital
1946-1957	Appointed to the faculty of Harvard Medical School
1953	Awarded the Nobel Prize in Physiology or Medicine jointly with Hans Adolf Krebs
1957-1986	Conducts research on protein biosynthesis at Rockefeller
1966	Awarded the National Medal of Science
July 24, 1986	Dies in Poughkeepsie, New York

(The Nobel Foundation)

Early Life

Fritz Albert Lipmann was born in Königsberg, the capital of Prussia, in 1899. His father was a Jewish lawyer. After a classical education at a gymnasium where he was not an honors student, Lipmann began to study medicine at the University of Königsberg in 1917. His medical education was interrupted for a period in which he served as a medic in the German army during World War I.

When he returned to his studies in early 1919, Lipmann spent a semester at the University of Munich, where his older brother, Heinz, was studying literature. The younger Lipmann then studied for half a year at the University of Berlin. He then returned to the University of Königsberg and was graduated in 1920.

A Change in Direction

Toward the end of his medical studies, Lipmann took a three-month course in modern biochemistry with Peter Rona in Berlin. After his graduation, however, Lipmann worked for six months at the University of Amsterdam in pharmacology. It was this experience that turned his career toward biochemistry.

Lipmann returned to Königsberg and spent three years studying chemistry with Hans Meerwein. For his thesis, he worked in Otto Meyerhof's laboratory at the Kaiser Wilhelm Institute in Berlin-Dahlem. He obtained a Ph.D. in chemistry in 1927.

Leaving Germany

The threat of Adolf Hitler's influence in Germany was increasing at the time that Lipmann

---

The Discovery of Coenzyme A

Lipmann discovered and characterized coenzyme A (CoA), a compound that controls the transfer of two carbon (acetyl) groups in the metabolism of carbohydrates and fats.

In the early 1940's, Lipmann was interested in energy transfer in living systems and suspected from his studies of pyruvate oxidation that acetyl phosphate was a key compound in two carbon transfers. Indeed, in certain bacteria, this compound was converted to active acetate. In animal tissues, however, it was inactive.

In the course of his research, Lipmann found in pigeon livers an acetylating enzyme that is dependent on adenosine triphosphate (ATP). This enzyme lost its activity, however, when subject to dialysis, a process whereby small molecules are removed. Furthermore, if boiled liver extracts were added to the inactive enzyme, activity was restored. Lipmann concluded that the enzyme required a heat-stable coenzyme, a helper. He called the coenzyme "A" because it activated acetate.

This coenzyme contains pantothenic acid, vitamin B_2. The acetyl group is joined to the sulfur to form a thioester. The structure of coenzyme A (CoA) is shown in the accompanying figure.

Coenzyme A is central to metabolism. All carbon groups produced in the breakdown of sugars enter the Krebs or citric acid cycle via CoA. Acetyl CoA reacts with the four-carbon unit oxalacetate to give six-carbon citric acid. Similarly, fatty or long chain acids are attached to CoA during the steps of their breakdown or oxidation. Acetyl CoA is also the ultimate product in the degradation of eleven of the amino acids.

The Structure of Coenzyme A

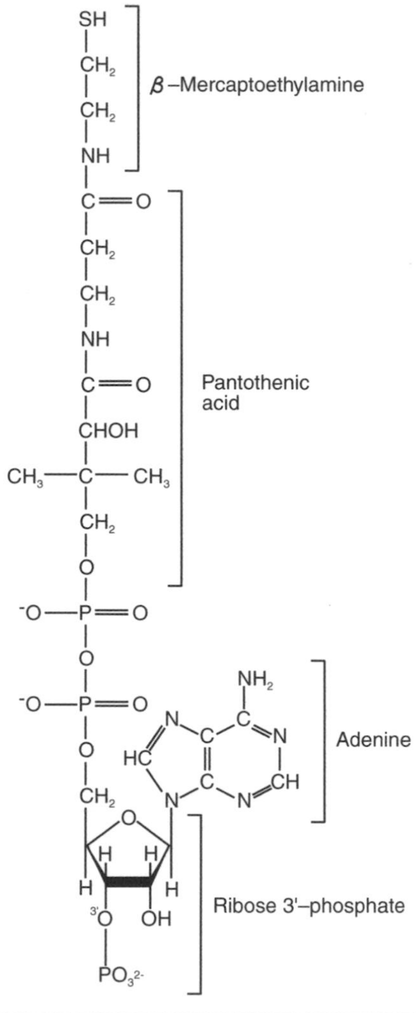

Bibliography

"Coenzyme for Acetylation: A Pantothenic Acid Derivative." Fritz Albert Lipmann et al. *Journal of Biological Chemistry* 167 (1947).

"Development of the Acetylation Problem: A Personal Account." Fritz Albert Lipmann. *Science* 120 (1954).

"The Metabolic Function of Pantothenic Acid." Fritz Albert Lipmann. In *Vitamins*. Vol. 2. New York: Academic Press, 1954.

accepted a fellowship at the Rockefeller Institute in New York in 1931. His new bride, Freda Hall, traveled to the United States with him.

In 1932, Lipmann returned to Europe to the new Carlsberg Foundation in the neutral country of Denmark, where he was first assistant to Albert Fischer, an expert in tissue culture. In Denmark, Lipmann's main studies were on the Pasteur effect, the breakdown of sugar without the production of alcohol. He also made the discovery that pyruvate acid oxidation requires inorganic phosphate and yields adenosine triphosphate (ATP). This study and discovery prompted him to realize that metabolism is intimately connected with supplying energy.

High-Energy Phosphates and Coenzyme A

The threat of war in Europe caused Lipmann to emigrate to the United States in 1939. Initially, he secured a research fellowship at the Cornell Medical School. During this time, Lipmann proposed ATP as a general energy carrier and also introduced the squiggle (~) for an energy rich phosphate bond, ~P.

His 1941 paper "Metabolic Generation and Utilization of Phosphate Bond Energy" greatly influenced the development of biochemistry and was a turning point in his own career. In 1941, Lipmann received a Ciba Fellowship in the department of surgery at Massachusetts General Hospital, which is connected to Harvard University. It was there that he discovered a new coenzyme, the acetyl-carrying coenzyme A. Lipmann won the 1953 Nobel Prize in Physiology or Medicine, sharing the award with Hans Adolf Krebs, for his work in showing the role of this important molecule.

Protein Biosynthesis

In 1957, Lipmann returned to the Rockefeller Institute, where he had first worked in the United States. During the next thirty years, he devoted considerable time to the investigation of protein biosynthesis. He died in 1986 at the age of eighty-seven.

Bibliography

By Lipmann

"Metabolic Generation and Utilization of Phosphate Bond Energy," *Advances in Enzymology*, 1941

"Coenzyme for Acetylation: A Pantothenic Acid Derivative," *Journal of Biological Chemistry*, 1947 (with N. O. Kaplan, G. D. Novelli, L. G. Tuttle, and B. M. Guirard)

"Development of the Acetylation Problem: A Personal Account," *Science*, 1954

"The Metabolic Function of Pantothenic Acid," *The Vitamins*, 1954

The Wanderings of a Biochemist, 1971

"A Long Life in Times of Great Upheaval," *Annual Review of Biochemistry*, 1984

About Lipmann

"Fritz Albert Lipmann." In *The Nobel Prize Winners: Physiology or Medicine*, edited by Frank N. Magill. Pasadena, Calif.: Salem Press, 1991.

Nobel Laureates in Medicine or Physiology: A Biographical Dictionary. Daniel M. Fox, Marcia Meldrum, and Ira Rezak, eds. New York: Garland, 1990.

Notable Twentieth-Century Scientists. Emily J. McMurray, ed. New York: Gale Research, 1995

(Helen M. Burke)

William N. Lipscomb

Area of Achievement: Chemistry
Contribution: An authority on chemical physics, X-ray crystallography, and chemical biology, Lipscomb won the Nobel Prize in Chemistry for his studies of chemical bonding.

July 16, 1919	Born in Cleveland, Ohio
1941	Earns a B.S. in chemistry from the University of Kentucky
1946	Earns a Ph.D. in chemistry from the California Institute of Technology
1946-1959	Serves on the faculty of the University of Minnesota
1947	Conducts X-ray studies of single crystals at low temperatures
1954-1955	Serves as a Guggenheim Fellow at Oxford University
1955	Named president of the American Crystallographic Association
1959-1971	Serves as professor of chemistry at Harvard University
1961	Elected to the National Academy of Sciences
1962-1965	Serves as chair of the chemistry department at Harvard
1971-1990	Named Abbott and James Lawrence Professor of Chemistry at Harvard
1973	Serves as a Guggenheim Fellow at Cambridge University
1976	Awarded the Nobel Prize in Chemistry
1986-1996	Given the National Institutes of Health's MERIT Award
1990	Named an emeritus professor at Harvard

Early Life

William Nunn Lipscomb, Jr., whose father was a physician and whose mother was a music voice teacher, grew up near Lexington, Kentucky. Beginning with a chemistry set at the age of eleven, he acquired enough chemicals and apparatus to equip a home laboratory. At his father's request, the high school instituted a chemistry course for him.

At the University of Kentucky, which he attended on a music scholarship, Lipscomb majored in chemistry and physics and also studied quantum mechanics, which was not taught there, on his own. After receiving a B.S. in chemistry in 1941, he went to the California Institute of Technology (Caltech) to study physics.

Influenced by future Nobel chemistry laureate Linus Pauling, who introduced him to X-ray crystallography, Lipscomb switched to chemistry and earned a Ph.D. under Pauling's supervision. During World War II and for more than three of his five years at Caltech, he worked as a physical chemist for the Office of

(The Nobel Foundation)

Bonding in Boranes

The chemical bonding displayed in boranes (binary compounds of boron and hydrogen) has posed challenging problems in both experimental and theoretical chemistry.

Because the lighter boranes are volatile, sensitive to air and moisture, toxic, and pyrophoric (burning spontaneously in air), their preparation and characterization are very difficult, requiring complicated equipment and time-consuming techniques. Therefore, they remained laboratory curiosities until World War II, when the U.S. government supported research to find volatile uranium compounds (borohydrides) for isotope separation in the Manhattan Project to build the atomic bomb, and the 1950's, when it supported programs to develop high- energy fuels for rockets and jet aircraft. Their study, in which Lipscomb served as a leading participant, soon became one of the most rapidly expanding areas of inorganic chemistry.

Aside from these practical applications, chemists have been interested in boranes because they possess structures different from any other class of compounds. Because boron has only three valence electrons rather than four valence electrons like carbon and because ordinary covalent bonds between two atoms usually involve a pair of electrons, boranes have been called electron-deficient compounds.

Through skillful calculations involving electron pair multicenter bonds, Lipscomb clarified their structures and developed rules permitting the prediction of stability of new compounds and the conditions for their synthesis.

Bibliography
"Boranes and Carboranes." George B. Kauffman. In *Encyclopædia Britannica*. Vol. 15. Chicago: Encyclopædia Britannica, 1995.

Hydrides of Boron and Silicon. Alfred Stock. Ithaca, N.Y.: Cornell University Press, 1957.

Inorganic Chemistry. Keith F. Purcell and John C. Kotz. Philadelphia: W. B. Saunders, 1977.

"The 1976 Nobel Prize for Chemistry." Russell N. Grimes. *Science* 194 (1976).

Scientific Research and Development on war-related projects such as rocket propellants.

The University of Minnesota
From 1946 to 1959, Lipscomb was a faculty member at the University of Minnesota, serving as assistant professor, associate professor, and professor of physical chemistry, as well as acting chief and chief of the physical chemistry division. There, in order to improve the reliability of molecular structures as studied by gas phase electron diffraction methods, he developed techniques to grow single crystals at low temperatures for use in X-ray diffraction methods.

After several studies of problems of residual entropy (the measure of disorder of a system), Lipscomb began a series of studies of the structures of the lower boron hydrides (boranes) B_5H_9, B_4H_{10}, B_5H_{11}, and B_6H_{10}. These surprisingly compact structures required the postulation of electron pair bonds that sometimes joined together three or more atoms. Numerous further studies supported the bonding descriptions in these boranes as well as in larger, more complex boranes, carboranes (cage compounds of boron, carbon, and hydrogen), and related molecules.

Harvard University
At Harvard, Lipscomb expanded his theoretical and experimental studies of boranes. Advances in computing led him to a systematic general method to obtain molecular orbitals that were even more delocalized (with electron density regarded as spread out over several atoms or the entire molecule) as a description of bonding. He also introduced L. L. Lohr, Jr., and future Nobel chemistry laureate Roald Hoffmann to the general three-dimensional extended Hückel molecular orbitals method.

Lipscomb extended his X-ray crystallographic studies to proteins, highlighting structures of enzymes such as those containing zinc (carboxypeptidase A, leucine aminopeptidase) and allosteric enzymes (aspartate transcarbamylase, fructose-1,6-bisphosphatase, and chorismate mutase). He emphasized the mechanism at the active site, and, in the case of allosteric enzymes, the transformation of conformational information from regulatory sites to the active sites of an allosteric enzyme with several subunits.

As an associate editor of two journals and the recipient of numerous awards, including many honorary degrees, by the mid-1990's Lipscomb had delivered more than 250 lectures and published more than 600 articles. He expressed his interest in reading and tennis, and he played the clarinet in classical chamber music concerts in various countries.

Bibliography
By Lipscomb
"The Valence Structure of the Boron Hydrides," *Journal of Chemical Physics*, 1954 (with W. H. Eberhardt and Bryce Crawford, Jr.)
The Boron Hydrides, 1963
NMR Studies of Boron Hydrides and Related Compounds, 1969 (with Gareth Eaton)
"Structure and Mechanism in the Enzymatic Activity of Carboxypeptidase A and Relations to Chemical Sequence," *Accounts of Chemical Research*, 1970
"The Boranes and Their Relatives" in *Science*, 1977
"Recent Advances in Zinc Enzymology," *Chemical Reviews*, 1996 (with Norbert Sträter)

About Lipscomb
"Interview: William N. Lipscomb." István Hargittai. *The Chemical Intelligencer* 2, no. 3 (July, 1996).
"William N. Lipscomb, Jr." Peter V. Bonnesen. In *Nobel Laureates in Chemistry, 1901-1992*, edited by Laylin K. James. Washington, D.C.: American Chemical Society, 1993.

(George B. Kauffman)

Joseph Lister

Areas of Achievement: Bacteriology and medicine
Contribution: Lister, a British surgeon, developed the sterile procedures that resulted in antiseptic surgery. As one of the first scientists to grow bacteria in pure culture, he was also among the early pioneers of bacteriology.

Apr. 5, 1827	Born in Upton Park, Essex, England
1847-1852	Studies for a medical degree at University College, London
1853	Serves as house physician and surgeon at University College Hospital
1854	Studies under James Syme, professor of clinical surgery at Edinburgh
1855	Installed as assistant surgeon to the Edinburgh Royal Infirmary
1860	Appointed to the Regius Chair of Surgery at Glasgow University
1860	Elected a Fellow of the Royal Society of London
1865	Tests his procedure of antiseptic surgery for the first time
1867	Publishes his works on antiseptic surgery in journal *The Lancet*
1869	Succeeds Syme in the Chair of Clinical Surgery at Edinburgh
1877-1892	Serves as Chair of Surgery at King's College, London
1883	Knighted by Queen Victoria
1895-1900	Elected president of the Royal Society of London
1897	Elevated to the peerage as Joseph, Baron Lister
Feb. 10, 1912	Dies in Walmer, Kent, England

Early Life

Joseph Lister was born in a small village east of London in 1822. His father, Joseph Jackson Lister, was a wealthy wine merchant and a self-educated man versed in both mathematics and optics. The love of science was passed on to the younger Joseph, the second son in the household.

Even at a young age, Lister demonstrated a general interest in nature. Having completed his early education in the Quaker school at Tottenham, Lister enrolled at University College in London at the age of sixteen. In December, 1846, as a nineteen-year-old undergraduate student, he was present when Robert Liston, a professor of surgery at University College, carried out the first surgical operation under ether in Europe.

Following his graduation in 1847, Lister entered the medical program at University Col-

Development of Aseptic Surgery

Lister determined that the source of infection during surgical procedures are microorganisms in the air. By maintaining sterile procedures, one can eliminate such wound contamination.

The prevailing theory concerning the source of surgical infection prior to Lister's time was addressed at oxygen in the air. It was believed that tissue became oxidized, breaking down and forming pus. Lister believed that the evidence made such a theory untenable, since tissue is routinely exposed to oxygen in the blood.

Louis Pasteur's discovery in the 1850's of the role played by microbes in putrefaction and fermentation provided the necessary answer for Lister: It is not the oxygen in the air that causes contamination but microbes. Wound infection in humans was a counterpart to the contamination of beer and wine from microorganisms in the air. Lister thought that if one could prevent such contamination, the danger of wound sepsis would be reduced.

He was shortly able to put his theory into practice. On August 12, 1865, Lister operated on a boy with a compound fracture of the tibia, with an exposed wound of several inches. After cleaning the wound, he applied a bandage soaked in carbolic acid. When fresh dressings were placed on the wound, they too were soaked in the solution. No infection developed.

Lister refined his technique in other operations. He began a thorough disinfection of the skin itself with carbolic acid. All instruments were likewise sterilized. Severe wounds with deep cavities were drained and the cavities washed and filled with the disinfectant solution. In addition, the surgeon's hands were thoroughly cleaned in the solution prior to the beginning of surgery.

The operating room itself was to be maintained in a condition as close to sterile as possible. For a time, a carbolic acid mist was sprayed in the air; this technique was unpopular and did not appear to be particularly effective anyway, and so it was stopped. Lister would not compromise, however, on the importance of sterile dressings and bandages. The preparations and procedures were complicated, but one could not dispute the results.

Lister published a complete summary of his work in an 1870 issue of the British journal *The Lancet*. The mortality rate associated with amputation had been reduced by two-thirds. The number of wounds that did not require amputation, since no infection developed, could not be calculated.

Although it was some years before Lister's practice of antiseptic surgery became universally accepted, it would eventually become a standard procedure. The danger of wound contamination will always remain, but such contamination during surgery is now the exception rather than a common problem.

Bibliography
"Germ Theory and Its Influence." L. S. King. *Journal of the American Medical Association* 249 (1983).

Joseph Lister and Antisepsis. A. H. Rains. Hove, England: Priory Press, 1977.

The Scientific Revolution in Victorian Medicine. A. J. Youngson. New York: Holmes and Meier, 1979.

Three Centuries of Microbiology. Hubert Lechevalier and Morris Solotorovsky. New York: Dover, 1974.

lege. While still a student, he presented two papers, "Gangrene," and "Use of the Microscope in Medicine," in front of the Hospital Medical Society. Lister was graduated with honors in 1852.

Medical Career

In 1852, Lister served a term as house physician, followed by nine months of service as a house surgeon. His interest in surgery as a career led Lister to move to Edinburgh in 1853, where he developed both a professional and a personal relationship with James Syme, one of the outstanding technical surgeons in England.

The outbreak of the Crimean War in 1855 led Lister to apply for a vacant position as staff surgeon at Edinburgh, and, in April, 1855, he was appointed assistant surgeon to the Edinburgh Royal Infirmary and lecturer in surgery to the Royal College of Surgeons. It was at this time that he began courting Syme's daughter, Agnes, whom he married in 1856.

Lister's reputation as both a teacher and a researcher continued to grow, and, when the position of professor of surgery at the University of Glasgow became available in 1859, he was recommended for the appointment. In 1860, he received the appointment to the Regius Chair of Surgery at Glasgow.

Antiseptic Surgery

With the introduction of general anesthesia to surgery in 1846, much of the reluctance on behalf of physicians to carry out surgical procedures disappeared. The numbers of practicing surgeons significantly increased, accompanied by a jump in the number of surgical procedures.

With surgery, however, came the danger of sepsis, or infection. Gangrene, often called "hospital fever," was a common occurrence, with the mortality associated with amputation as high as 60 percent in some hospitals. Rarely was any surgical procedure unaccompanied by infection. Most scientists believed that the cause was oxygen from the air.

In 1865, the French scientist Louis Pasteur had published his work on putrefaction and fermentation, associating each with microorganisms in the air. Pasteur's articles were read by Lister, who quickly realized their significance. Lister thought that by limiting contact of

(Library of Congress)

such organisms with the surgical incision, infection might be prevented.

On August 12, 1865, Lister attempted his first experiment in antiseptic surgery, operating on an eleven-year-old boy who had suffered a compound fracture. Following the surgery, Lister dressed the wound with bandages soaked in carbolic acid (phenol). All dressings were treated the same way, and no infection developed.

Over subsequent weeks, Lister continued to test his procedure of "carbolic acid antisepsis." The procedure was modified by treating the area around the incision in a similar manner. Attempts to spray the air with carbolic acid proved less successful. By 1867, Lister was sufficiently satisfied with the procedure to publish his successful results in the British journal *The Lancet*.

Later Career

In 1869, an ailing Syme resigned his position at Edinburgh, and Lister was appointed his successor as chair of clinical surgery at the young age of forty-two.

It is ironic that despite the success of the antiseptic procedure and its acceptance in both France and Germany, Lister's techniques did not receive widespread recognition in England. In part, this was attributable to a reluctance to accept the germ theory of disease.

In 1877, Lister accepted an offer for the chair of surgery at the Medical School of King's College in London. It was his hope that antiseptic surgery would receive wider acceptance. Although his fellow surgeons would initially be hesitant to accept the truth of Lister's views on antisepsis, the results could not be ignored. Although infection remained a common occurrence in many surgical wards, rarely was it a problem when Lister's procedures were followed. By the 1880's, the acceptance of the germ theory was becoming universal.

Lister spent his last years researching a variety of subjects. He published work on inflammation and blood coagulation. He was among the first to grow microorganisms in pure culture for study. Lister became a baronet in 1883 and was anointed a peer in 1897. He continued to publish until well into his eightieth year and died in 1912.

Bibliography
By Lister
"Observations of the Contractile Tissue of the Iris," *Quarterly Journal of Microscopical Science*, 1853

"Observations on the Muscular Tissue of the Skin," *Quarterly Journal of Microscopical Science*, 1853

"Report of Some Cases of Maxillary Tumour," *Monthly Journal of Medical Science*, 1854

"On the Early Stages of Inflammation," *Proceedings of the Royal Society*, 1857

"Some Observations on the Structure of Nerve Fibres," *Quarterly Journal of Microscopical Science*, 1860 (with William Turner)

"On the Coagulation of the Blood," *Proceedings of the Royal Society*, 1863

"On a New Method of Treating Compound Fracture, Abscess, etc., with Observations on the Conditions of Suppuration," *The Lancet* 1867

"On the Antiseptic Principle in the Practice of Surgery," *The Lancet*, 1867

"Observations in Ligature of Arteries on the Antiseptic System, *The Lancet*, 1869

"Further Evidence Regarding the Effects of the Antiseptic Treatment upon the Salubrity of a Surgical Hospital," *The Lancet*, 1870

"A Method of Antiseptic Treatment Applicable to Wounded Soldiers in the Present War," *British Medical Journal*, 1870

"On the Relation of Microorganisms to Disease," *Quarterly Journal of Microscopical Science*, 1881

"On Recent Researches with Regard to the Parasitology of Malaria," *British Medical Journal*, 1907

"On Sulpho-chromic Catgut," *British Medical Journal*, 1909

About Lister
Joseph Lister, 1827-1912. Richard Fisher. New York: Stein & Day, 1977.

A List of the Original Writings of Joseph, Lord Lister. William Le Fanu. Edinburgh, Scotland: Livingstone, 1965.

Lord Lister: His Life and Doctrine. Douglas Guthrie. Baltimore: Williams & Wilkins, 1949.

Master Surgeon: A Biography of Joseph Lister. Laurence Farmer. New York: Harper, 1962.

(Richard Adler)

Hendrik Antoon Lorentz

Area of Achievement: Physics

Contribution: Lorentz did considerable work in electromagnetic theory, which laid the groundwork for relativity theory and quantum mechanics. He was acknowledged as a leader and mentor of the new generation of physicists arising in the early twentieth century.

July 18, 1853	Born in Arnhem, the Netherlands
1871	Earns a degree in mathematics and physics at the University of Leiden
1875	Receives a Ph.D. from Leiden
1878	Awarded the Netherlands first chair in theoretical physics
1892	Proposes that charged particles in matter oscillate when struck by light waves
1896	Applies his electron theory to explain the Zeeman effect
1902	Receives the Nobel Prize in Physics jointly with Pieter Zeeman
1904	Publishes a comprehensive theory describing electromagnetic phenomena in systems moving at less than the speed of light
1909-1921	Elected president of the physics section of the Royal Netherlands Academy of Sciences and Letters
1911-1927	Serves as chair of the Solvay conferences in physics
1912	Named curator of the Teylers Stichtum Museum in Haarlem
1923	Appointed to the International Commission on Intellectual Cooperation of the League of Nations
Feb. 4, 1928	Dies in Haarlem, the Netherlands

Early Life

Hendrik Antoon Lorentz (pronounced "LOHR-ehnts") was born in Arnhem, the Netherlands, on July 18, 1853. His father, Gerrit Frederik, owned a nursery; his mother, Geertruida, died when Lorentz was only four. Lorentz attended primary and secondary schools in Arnhem and excelled at the physical sciences and languages. He was allowed to attend a special evening school, where he was able to work on his own, in many cases teaching himself what he thought he needed to know.

In 1870, Lorentz went to the University of Leiden, where he studied mathematics and physics, receiving his bachelor's degree in only a year and a half. For his Ph.D., he wanted to work in the area of electromagnetism, studying the implications of James Clerk Maxwell's electromagnetic theory.

Unfortunately, no one at Leiden was familiar with Maxwell's theories, so Lorentz returned home to Arnhem to study. He lived at home for seven years, studying on his own, working on his dissertation, and teaching in the evening high school. He passed his doctoral examination summa cum laude in 1873 and received his doctorate in 1875.

Early Research

Upon completing his Ph.D., Lorentz was unsure whether to pursue a career in mathematics or in physics. Theoretical physics was in its infancy as an independent discipline within physics, and the prospects of a career were not promising. In 1877, the University of Leiden offered Lorentz the new chair of theoretical physics, the first such position in the Netherlands and one of the first in Europe. In this position, he became an important factor in shaping the field.

In 1881, Lorentz married Aletta Vaiser, the niece of his former astronomy teacher. In 1892, he began publishing his electron theory in a series of three to four articles a year through 1904. This theory opened the door to a wide range of new experimental and theoretical avenues.

Lorentz was not an eccentric, bookish genius. Although he was a disciplined scholar, he also found time to be social, revealing a good sense of humor and a gift for conversation. He enjoyed a good cigar and a glass of wine with his friends.

The personal impression that he made on the young physicists who came to Leiden was as influential as his physics. He kept an active interest in the work of these physicists, including Albert Einstein, without trying to influence the direction of their research. They valued his

Moving Charges

Lorentz described the interaction of light with a medium: Light waves in the "ether" cause electric particles in matter to vibrate; the vibrating particles in turn produce light waves in the ether.

The debate of the nature of light was one that had its roots in Sir Isaac Newton's day. Newton had proposed that light was made of particles, while Robert Hooke proposed that light was a wave. No conclusive experimental results had been produced; most scientists believed that light was made of particles because Newton was right about so many other things.

Around 1800, Thomas Young performed experiments in which he passed light through several closely placed apertures. The observed interference patterns proved that light was a wave. Although many other people observed wave phenomena in light, no one was able to describe the medium through which these light waves propagated. A wave must have some medium through which to travel, and thus light must have a medium, dubbed the "ether." Considerable work was done at the end of the nineteenth century to determine the exact nature of this medium.In the same era, considerable work was going on in the areas of electrical and magnetic fields. By the mid-1800's, the situation was quite confusing, with a large number of "laws" having been observed with no apparent connection. One person involved in this controversy was James Clerk Maxwell. Maxwell at first tried to explain the behavior of electric and magnetic fields in terms of a complicated mechanical system in which space is willed with an elastic medium, the elusive ether.

When Maxwell discarded this mechanical model and looked at the electric and magnetic fields as physical entities without any underlying medium, he met success. In 1873, he published *Treatise on Electricity and Magnetism*, in which he described four basic equations that could describe all electromagnetic phenomena. One interesting result of these equations is that combining them results in the equation of a wave traveling with the speed of light. Maxwell's equations implied that light is a wave propagating through the electromagnetic fields.

Lorentz began investigating this new theory proposed by Maxwell, and he was able to apply it to several optical phenomena. He emphasized the distinction between matter and the ether. Lorentz named the electric particles composing all matter "electrons" and wrote a comprehensive theory on the interactions between these particles and electromagnetic fields. He was able to summarize these effects in what is known as the Lorentz force.

Lorentz was particularly interested in the effects of the earth's motion through the stationary ether. An experiment by Albert Abraham Michelson and Edward Morley attempted to detect this motion, with no success. Lorentz derived a set of transformations for the spatial coordinates and a "local time" which showed that the equations describing an electric system in motion are identical to those for an electric system at rest. These Lorentz transformations formed the basis of Albert Einstein's special theory of relativity.

Bibliography

Electromagnetic Fields and Waves. Dale R. Corson and Paul Lorrain. San Francisco: W. H. Freeman, 1970.

The Feynman Lectures on Physics. Richard P. Feynman, R. B. Leighton, and M. Sands. Reading, Mass.: Addison-Wesley, 1963.

Foundations of Electromagnetic Theory. John R. Reitz, Frederick J. Milford, and Robert W. Christy. Reading, Mass.: Addison-Wesley, 1980.

"The Fundaments of Theoretical Physics." Albert Einstein. *Science* 9, no. 1 (1940).

intellectual creativity and his thorough mastery of physics as much as his nonmanipulative leadership.

An International Leader

In 1898, on an invitation from Ludwig Boltzmann, Lorentz addressed the Düsseldorf meeting of the German Society of Natural Scientists and Physicians. Lorentz recognized the importance of interacting with his colleagues internationally, which was a fairly new idea at the time. His most important international activity was acting as president of the Solvay congresses in physics from 1911 until 1927.

Lorentz was recognized as a leader of the physics community internationally. His ability to explain physics in a clear and concise manner, his tact, and his fluency in several languages made him highly sought out as an invited lecturer.

In 1912, Lorentz resigned his position at the University of Leiden to become the curator of the Teylers Stichting Museum. This position required Lorentz to give popular physics lectures, which he greatly enjoyed, and also afforded him the freedom to pursue his research and international lectures. He also became involved in the government board of education, in 1921 becoming president of the department of higher education. In 1920, he even took charge of the calculations for the height of the dike required for the closing of the Zuider Zee.

After World War I, Lorentz fought the exclusion of the Central Powers from the international scientific community. He encouraged his countrymen to become involved in international scientific organizations. In 1923, he was appointed to the International Commission on Intellectual Cooperation of the League of Nations and eventually served as its president.

Honors

In 1902, Lorentz shared the Nobel Prize in Physics with Pieter Zeeman for his explanation of the splitting of atomic spectra when the atoms are placed in a magnetic field, known as Zeeman effect. Lorentz also received many other honors, including the Royal Society of London's Rumford and Copley medals.

On his death in 1928, he was considered to be the greatest contemporary cultural figure produced by the Netherlands. On the day of his funeral, Dutch telegraph and telephone services were suspended for three minutes in tribute. Representatives of Dutch royalty and scientific academies from around the world attended his funeral. His graveside eulogy was delivered by Albert Einstein, who called him the "greatest and noblest man of our times."

(The Nobel Foundation)

Bibliography

By Lorentz

H. A. Lorentz: Collected Papers, 1935-1939 (9 vols.; P. Zeeman and A. D. Fokker, eds.)

Leerboeck der differntiaalen integraalrekening en van de eerste beginselen der analytische meetkunde, 1882

Beginselen der Natuurkunde, 1888

Theory of Electrons and Its Applications to the Phenomena of Light and Radiant Heat, 1909

Sichtbare und unsichtbare Bewegungen, 1902

Les Théories statistiques en thermodynamique, 1912

The Einstein Theory of Relativity: A Concise Statement, 1920

Problems of Modern Physics: Lectures at the Institute of Technology at Pasadena, 1927

About Lorentz

"H. A. Lorentz and the Electromagnetic View of Nature." Russell McCormmach. *Isis* 6, no. 1 (Winter, 1970).

H. A. Lorentz: Impressions of His Life and Work. Geertruida De Haas-Lorentz, ed. Amsterdam: North Holland, 1957.

"Lorentz' Non-Newtonian Aether-Field." Nancy J. Nersessian. In *Faraday to Einstein: Constructing Meaning in Scientific Theories.* Dordrecht, the Netherlands: Martinus Nijhoff, 1984.

(Linda L. McDonald)

Konrad Lorenz

Areas of Achievement: Biology, genetics, physiology, and zoology

Contribution: Lorenz, one of the founders of comparative ethology, discovered the process of imprinting in young animals. He studied the governing of instinctive behavior by internal genetic factors.

Nov. 7, 1903	Born in Vienna, Austro-Hungarian Empire (now Austria)
1922	Studies medicine at Columbia University, New York, continuing at the University of Vienna
1927	Publishes his observations of jackdaw behavior
1928	Receives an M.D. from Vienna
1933	Earns a Ph.D. in zoology at Vienna
1935-1938	Describes imprinting behavior in young ducks and goslings
1937	Becomes coeditor in chief of *Zeitschrift für Tiersyschologie*, a leading journal in ethology
1940-1942	Named professor and head of general psychology at Albertus University in Königsberg
1942-1944	Serves as a physician in the German army and becomes a prisoner of war in the Soviet Union
1950	Helps establish the comparative ethology department at the Max Planck Institute
1961-1973	Directs the Max Planck Institute of Behavior Physiology
1963	Publishes the controversial *Das sogenannte Böse* (*On Aggression*, 1966)
1973	Awarded the Nobel Prize in Physiology or Medicine
Feb. 27, 1989	Dies in Altenberg, Austria

Nature or Nurture?

Ethologists continue to debate whether an animal's learning is innate and internal or determined primarily by external and environmental conditions. Lorenz's research on the source of learning provided critical information about this issue.

Charles Whitman, at the University of Chicago, and Oskar Heinroth, at the Berlin Zoo, first discovered the idea of imprinting, the tendency of some animals to bond with the first moving object seen after birth. Lorenz continued research on imprinting and then tried to determine how animals learn to cope with environmental conditions. He labeled the stereotyped behavior of animals as a fixed action pattern. Action-specific energy within the animal predisposes the behavioral pattern that an animal usually shows in response to a given set of conditions.

A complicated set of terms have evolved to describe these behaviors because there is no simple answer to the question of whether actions are either inherited or learned. Two categories of behavior levels are recognized. Appetitive behavior is the first part of an action and is usually more variable in its performance; searching for food is an example of appetitive behavior. Consummatory behavior is the second portion of the behavioral act and is more predictable in its performance; the actual process of eating a food item after it is found and captured is a good example of consummatory behavior. Consummatory behavior is often highly stereotyped and species-specific and therefore is probably most determined by internal genetic factors. Appetitive behavior is more likely to be determined and modified by external environmental conditions.

The interaction between endogenous and exogenous factors in the control of behavior is well illustrated by the cyclic or circadian biological rhythms seen in the life histories of many animals. Lorenz stressed that it was necessary to see an animal's entire behavior in its natural context before forming hypotheses about the functional significance and value to the animal's survival of a single behavior.

Some ethologists argue that no phenotypic (observed) trait is independent of either hereditary or environmental agents. Therefore, an attempt to divide the interrelationship of two agents, neither of which alone can produce a phenotype, is futile. Lorenz's research on the source of learning has helped establish a compromise view between the two extremes. Both genetic and environmental conditions interact to determine the behavioral pattern that occurs in response to stimuli received by the animal.

Bibliography
Animal Behavior: An Evolutionary Approach. John Alcock. Sunderland, Mass.: Sinauer Associates, 1975.

Ethology: The Biology of Behavior. Irenaus Eibl-Eibesfeldt. 2nd ed. New York: Holt, Rinehart and Winston, 1975.

Foundations of Comparative Ethology. Gordon M. Burghardt. New York: Van Nostrand Reinhold, 1985.

Introduction to Ethology. Klaus Immelmann. New York: Plenum Press, 1980.

Mechanisms of Animal Behavior. Peter R. Marler and William J. Hamilton III. New York: John Wiley & Sons, 1966.

Early Life
Konrad Zacharias Lorenz (pronounced "LOHR-ehnts") was born in Vienna in 1903. He was the younger of two sons born to Emma (Lecher) Lorenz and Adolf Lorenz. His father, the son of a harness maker, rose from poverty to become a wealthy orthopedic surgeon.

Throughout his childhood, Lorenz was extremely interested in animals. He had many pets, kept detailed diaries of his observations on animal behavior, and nursed sick animals at the Schöbrunner Zoo in Vienna. Lorenz's early education was at a private school conducted by his aunt; afterward, he entered the prestigious and rigorous Schottengymnasium. When he finished high school, Lorenz wished to study zoology and paleontology, but he obeyed his father, who wanted him to study medicine.

Lorenz studied medicine for a year at Columbia University, in New York City, and then returned to the University of Vienna to finish his medical studies. He recognized the relationship between areas of his medical studies and that of animal behavior, which remained his preferred research focus throughout his life. One of earliest papers described the behavior of the jackdaw, a crowlike bird, and was published in the prestigious *German Journal of Ornithology*.

In 1927, Lorenz married Margarethe (Gretl) Gebhardt. In 1928, he received his medical degree and continued his studies for the Ph.D. in zoology at the University of Vienna. Lorenz completed his Ph.D. work in 1933.

The Discovery of Imprinting

Lorenz was a pioneer in the study of animal behavior, often known as ethology, and of how animals communicate. He studied wild animals under natural conditions in order to discover how these behavioral actions worked and helped animals survive. One of his most important achievements in the field of animal behavior was the discovery of imprinting.

Lorenz established colonies of birds for his studies and did much of his work on jackdaws and greylag geese. From 1935 to 1938, he observed their behavior, especially that of newly hatched and very young birds. He and his colleague Oskar Heinroth discovered that immediately after hatching from its egg, the young mallard duckling would follow whatever moving object it first saw. This foster parent could be Lorenz, quacking like a mother duck, or even a moving balloon. The duckling would follow him everywhere.

Instinctive Behavior

People who study animal behavior argue about whether behavior is "learned" from external, environmental conditions or is "instinctive" and internally or genetically determined. Lorenz studied how behavioral patterns evolved in various groups of animals and tried to determine the source of the nervous energy for their performance. He also studied what happens when two or more basic behaviors occur together. If faced with a choice of either fighting another animal or eating food, what would the animal do? Often a third behavior called a displacement activity, such as grooming, occurred.

Lorenz theorized that the central nervous system of an animal builds up a specific type of "desire." If no appropriate environment exists to help release the behavior pattern corresponding to that desire, then tensions gradually increase and eventually the instincts take control, even if the correct stimulus is lacking. For example, a pregnant ewe acts in a maternal manner toward another ewe's newborn lamb even though it has not yet given birth to its own lamb.

In other studies, Lorenz and Nikolaas Tinbergen showed that the reactions of many birds to birds of prey, such as hawks, depended on attitudes or gestures made by the predator and often the general shape of the predator. In one experiment, the prey responded to the shortness of the neck of hawks. Lorenz and Tinbergen found that the sight of any bird with a short neck, or even a dummy with this feature, caused other birds to fly away.

(The Nobel Foundation)

Lorenz shared the 1973 Nobel Prize in Physiology or Medicine with Tinbergen and Karl von Frisch for his work in ethology. He continued to study animal behavior until his death in 1989.

Bibliography
By Lorenz
Er redete mit den Vieh, den Vögeln, und den Fischen, 1949 (*King Solomon's Ring: New Light on Animal Ways*, 1952)

So kan der Mensch auf den Hund, 1950 (*Man Meets Dog*, 1954)

"Phylogenetische Anpassung und adaptive Modifikation des Verhaltens," *Zeitschrift für Tierpsychologie*, 1961 (*Evolution and Modification of Behavior*, 1965)

Das sogenannte Böse, 1963 (*On Aggression*, 1963)

Über tierisches und menschliches Verhalten, 1965 (*Studies in Animal and Human Behavior*, 2 vols., 1970-1971)

Mensch und Tier, 1972 (*Man and Animal*, 1972)

Antriebe tierischen menschlichen Verhaltens: Gesammelte Abhandlungen, 1968 (*Motivation of Human and Animal Behavior: An Ethological View*, 1973)

Die Rückseite des Spiegels: Versuch einer Naturgeschichte menschlichen Evkenners, 1973 (*Behind the Mirror: A Search for a Natural History of Human Knowledge*, 1973)

Die acht Todsunden der zivilsierten Menschheit, 1973 (*Civilized Man's Eight Deadly Sins*, 1973)

This Land of Europe, 1976

Verleichende Verhaltensforschung, 1978 (*The Foundations of Ethology*, 1981)

Das Jahr des Graugans, 1979 (*The Year of the Greylag Goose*, 1979)

Der Abbau den Menschlichen, 1983 (*The Waning of Humaneness*, 1987)

Rettet die Hoffnung: Konrad Lorenz im Gesprach mit Kurt Mundl, 1988 (*On Life and Living: Konrad Lorenz in Conversation with Kurt Mundl*, 1990)

Hier bin ich—wo bist du?: Ethologie der Graugans, 1988 (*Here Am I—Where Are You?: The Behavior of the Greylag Goose*, 1991)

Naturwissenschaft vom Menschen: Eine Einfuhrung in die verglichende Verhaltensforschung, das "russische Manuskript" (1944-1948), 1992 [*The Natural Science of the Human Species: An Introduction to Comparative Behavioral Research; the "Russian Manuscript"* (1944-1948), 1996]

About Lorenz
Konrad Lorenz: A Bibliography. Alec Nisbett. New York: Harcourt Brace Jovanovich, 1976.

Konrad Lorenz: The Man and His Ideas. Richard I. Evans. New York: Harcourt Brace Jovanovich, 1975.

(David L. Chesemore)

Richard Lower

Areas of Achievement: Biology, medicine, and physiology

Contribution: One of the greatest anatomists and experimental physiologists of his age, Lower demonstrated that the difference in color between arterial blood and venous blood results when the blood absorbs air as it passes through the lungs. He was also the first to transfuse blood from one animal into another.

c. 1631	Born in Tremeer, near Bodmin, Cornwall, England
1643-1649	Attends Westminster School in London
1649	Enrolls at Oxford University
1653	Graduates with a bachelor's degree
1655	Earns a master's degree from Oxford
1665	Receives a medical degree from Oxford
1665	Carries out the first transfusion of blood from one animal into another, using dogs
1666	Moves to London
1666	Marries the widow Elizabeth Billing
1667	Elected a Fellow of the Royal Society of London
1669	Publishes *Tractatus de Corde* (*A Treatise on the Heart*, 1932)
1675	Elected a Fellow of the Royal College of Physicians
Jan. 17, 1691	Dies in London, England

Early Life

Richard Lower was born into an affluent family residing in Cornwall, England. His birthday is uncertain, but he was baptized on January 29, 1632. He attended Westminster School in London from around 1643 to 1649 before enrolling at Oxford University. Lower earned a B.A. in 1653, an M.A. in 1655, and an M.D. in 1665, all from Oxford.

Oxford University

Lower remained at Oxford for seventeen years. In the early 1660's, he assisted Thomas Willis, a professor of natural philosophy at Oxford, in his anatomical investigations. In the preface to his celebrated treatise on the brain, *Cerebri anatomi* (1664), Willis acknowledged his enormous debt to Lower and his skills as an anatomist.

Lower's first publication, *Diatribae Thomae Willisii Doct. Med. et Prof. Oxon. De Febribus Vindicatio Adversus Edmundum De Meara Ormoniensem Hibernum M.D.* (1665; *A Justification of the "Discourse on Fevers" by Thomas Willis, Doctor of Medicine and Professor at Oxford, Against Edmund O'Meara, M.D., of Ormond, Irishman,*

(National Library of Medicine)

1983), was a defense of Willis' theory of fevers against the criticisms of the physician Edmund O'Meara. This work also defended the experimental methods of investigation favored by Willis, Lower, and the other Oxford physiologists since the days of William Harvey.

While still at Oxford in 1665, Lower carried out the first transfusion of blood from one animal into another, using dogs as subjects. Two years later, in June, 1667, the French scientist Jean-Baptiste Denis performed the first transfusion of blood into a human, using Lower's techniques. Lower accomplished the same feat in November, 1667, at the urging of the Royal Society of London.

London

Lower moved to London in 1666. There, he continued to practice medicine and carry out research in anatomy and physiology. He was elected to the Royal Society of London in 1667 and the Royal College of Physicians in 1675.

In 1669, Lower published his most important work, *Tractatus de Corde* (*A Treatise on the Heart*, 1932). In this book, he described his experiments discrediting the theory, held by René Descartes and many others, that body heat and the motion of the heart are caused by a fermentation or effervescence of the blood within the ventricles.

Lower also showed in this treatise that venous blood takes on a redder appearance not while passing through the heart, as Willis had claimed, but while passing through the lungs. This change in color, Lower concluded, occurs when the blood absorbs some portion of the air. *Tractatus de Corde* is also famous for its remarkably accurate description of the structure of the heart.

Final Years

Following Willis' death in 1675, Lower was appointed the physician to King Charles II. He very quickly became the most prominent physician in London. With the accession of James II, however, Lower lost his court appointment because of his political and anti-Catholic religious views, and his practice fell off dramatically. His activities after 1685 are uncertain. He died on January 17, 1691, in London.

Bibliography
By Lower
Diatribae Thomae Willisii Doct. Med. et Prof. Oxon. De Febribus Vindicatio Adversus Edmundum De Meara Ormoniensem Hibernum M.D.,

The Color of Blood

Lower conducted a number of experiments and observations to prove that blood changes in color from dark to a bright red as a result of exposure to air.

In the 1660's, it was widely believed that dark venous blood is transformed into bright red arterial blood as a consequence of being heated or fermented in the heart. In order to refute this idea, Lower performed a number of brilliantly conceived and deftly executed vivisections showing that blood becomes bright red not when passing through the heart, but when passing through the lungs.

As part of his explanation of why this color change occurs, Lower pointed out that if blood is let from a vein into a dish, the exposed surface will turn bright red, while the rest retains its darker hue. Moreover, if the upper layer of blood is scraped off, the layer just below it will change from dark to bright red.

Lower also observed that if a cake of dark, coagulated blood is turned over, the newly exposed under surface will take on a bright red appearance. In addition, he noted that if venous blood is received into a container and shaken, it becomes florid throughout.

Lower concluded from these experiments that the difference in color between venous and arterial blood is the result not of heating or fermentation as it passes through the heart but of exposure to the air as it passes through the lungs.

Bibliography
Circulation Physiology and Medical Chemistry in England, 1650-1680. Audrey Davis. Lawrence, Kans.: Coronado Press, 1973.
Harvey and the Oxford Physiologists. Robert Frank. Berkeley: University of California Press, 1980.

1665 (*A Justification of the "Discourse on Fevers" by Thomas Willis, Doctor of Medicine and Professor at Oxford, Against Edmund O'Meara, M.D., of Ormond, Irishman*, 1983)
"The Method Observed in Transfusing the Blood out of One Live Animal into Another," *Philosophical Transactions*, 1666
"An Account of the Experiment of Transfusion, Practiced upon a Man in London," *Philosophical Transactions*, 1667
Tractatus de Corde: Item De Motu et Colore Sanguinis et Chyli in eum Transitu, 1669 (*A Treatise on the Heart: On the Movement and Colour of the Blood and on the Passage of the Chyle into the Blood*, 1932)

About Lower
Early Science in Oxford. Introduction by K. J. Franklin. R. T. Gunther, ed. Vol. 9. Oxford, England: Oxford University Press, 1932.
History of General Physiology. Thomas S. Hall. Chicago: University of Chicago Press, 1969.
Richard Lower's "Vindicatio": A Defence of the Experimental Method. Kenneth Dewhurst. Oxford, England: Sandford, 1983.

(*William Tammone*)

Salvador Edward Luria

Areas of Achievement: Bacteriology, biology, cell biology, genetics, and virology
Contribution: Luria's main contribution to molecular biology was in explaining viral replication and gene structure, thus relating virology and biochemistry.

Aug. 13, 1912	Born in Turin, Italy
1929-1935	Attends the University of Turin Medical School
1936-1938	Serves as an officer in the Italian Army Medical Corps
1940	Emigrates to the United States and obtains a position as an assistant at Columbia University Medical School
1943	Named an instructor at Indiana University's bacteriology department
1943	Publishes "Mutations of Bacteria from Virus Sensitivity to Virus Resistance" with Max Delbrück
1950	Appointed full professor at the University of Illinois, Champaigne-Urbana
1953	Publishes *General Virology* with J. E. Darnell
1959	Becomes chair of the microbiology department at the Massachusetts Institute of Technology (MIT)
1966	Publishes "The Comparative Anatomy of a Gene"
1969	Awarded the Nobel Prize in Physiology or Medicine
1974	Becomes the director of the MIT Center for Cancer Research
1984	Publishes the autobiography *A Slot Machine, a Broken Test Tube*
Feb. 6, 1991	Dies in Lexington, Massachusetts

(The Nobel Foundation)

Early Life
Salvador Edward Luria was born in 1912 in Turin, Italy, as the second son of Jewish businessman David Luria and Esther Sacerdote Luria. He received his primary and secondary education in the Turin pubic schools. In 1929, Luria was graduated from Liceo d'Azeglio, entered the University of Turin Medical School, and conducted tissue culture research that developed his interest in research science.

In 1935, Luria was graduated summa cum laude and became an officer in the Army Medical Corps for three years. He began using mathematics and physics in biological research. On leaving the army, he moved to Paris to avoid Nazi persecution, studied biophysics at the Curie Laboratory, and explored the X-ray mutation of bacteriophages (or phages), viruses that infect bacteria.

Phages and Fluctuation
In 1940, Luria left France for the United States. Arriving in New York City on September 12, he became an assistant at Columbia University Medical School and continued his bacteriophage research. In 1941, he met biophysicist Max Delbrück of the California Institute of Technology (Caltech). Luria, Delbrück, and Alfred Day Hershey of Carnegie Institute became a "phage group." They showed that a phage is made of deoxyribonucleic acid (DNA) surrounded by a protein coat and that when phages infect bacteria, the DNA turns them into phage factories.

Luria studied phages as a simple way to test gene alteration. An important discovery arose from the study of bacterial phage resistance. Fluctuation analysis, using Delbrück's mathematical model, was described in the paper "Mutations of Bacteria from Virus Sensitivity to Virus Resistance" (1943). This analysis showed that if virus-sensitive bacteria were grown with phages, the production of resistance fluctuated widely; therefore, it had to occur prior to exposure. Luria's concept of fluctuation analysis reportedly arose on watching a slot machine while he was a bacteriology instructor at the University of Indiana. He identified an analogy between machine payoff and resistant bacteria formation, if random. At Indiana, he married Zella Hurwitz and had a son, Daniel. In 1951, again via Delbrückian mathematics, he showed that during phage growth, mutants arise randomly and spontaneously.

A Nobel Prize and Social Conscience
In 1950, as a full professor at the University of Illinois, Champaign-Urbana, Luria proved that viral genes mutate. In 1959, as microbiology chair at the Massachusetts Institute of Technology (MIT), Luria showed how colicin antibiotics could disrupt cell membrane function by making membrane channels. He, Delbrück, and Hershey shared the 1969 Nobel Prize in Physiology or Medicine for their work on viral replication and gene structure. From 1974, Luria directed MIT's Cancer Research Center.

Socially conscious, he asked Americans to direct technology to the national good. Critical of defense and space program costs, he noted the money for medical research and housing lost to such programs. He gave much of his Nobel Prize award money to opposing the Vi-

Bacteriophages

Using fluctuation analysis, Luria showed that resistance to phages occurred prior to the exposure of sensitive bacteria to these bacteria-killing viruses.

Luria studied aspects of the replication and genetic structure of viruses, disease-causing microbes that live and multiply only in the infected cells on which they prey. He worked with viruses called bacteriophages (or phages) that kill bacteria. Whenever a chosen number of "sensitive" bacteria (those that a phage can kill) are grown (cultured) together with phages, the phages soon destroy all the bacteria present.

This occurs because when phages infect bacteria, they turn each infected cell into a virus factory that makes many progeny phages in a short time. The new phages destroy the cell, are released, and infect numerous other bacteria. The cycle of infection and bacterial destruction repeats continually. After several cycles, enough phages are made to destroy all the bacteria in a test culture.

Bacteria unsusceptible to a given phage can be isolated from cultures of sensitive bacteria. An important part of understanding bacterial sensitivity and resistance came from Luria's study of whether resistance to phages arose in a spontaneous fashion or was caused by the action of the phages on unchanged bacteria grown in their presence.

Exploration of this phenomenon was carried out in two steps. First, a large number of bacterial cultures of equal size were prepared. Then, the number of resistant bacteria in each one was counted after adding a fixed number of phages and allowing enough time to pass to kill all sensitive bacteria. Luria found that the number of bacterial survivors (resistant cells) varied greatly from culture to culture (see figure).

This fluctuation in the number of survivors indicated that resistant cells arose from events preceding phage exposure. It is now known that its source was spontaneous mutation. Had resistance been the result of the action of the phages on the bacteria, then the number of resistant cells in each culture would have been fairly constant.

The fluctuation test—the observation of variation of the number of resistant cells from culture to culture and its mathematical analysis—has been used to investigate phenomena such as the development of antibiotic resistance in bacteria and the resistance of cancer cells to antitumor drugs. In such cases, resistance has often been shown to develop prior to interaction with these agents. Hence, the procedure has been invaluable to the development of molecular virology, the study of carcinogenesis (the origin of cancer), and an understanding of genetics.

Bibliography

The Genetics of Bacteria and Their Viruses. William Hayes. New York: John Wiley & Sons, 1964.

Molecular Biology of Bacterial Viruses. Gunther Stent. San Francisco: W. H. Freeman, 1963.

A Slot Machine, a Broken Test Tube. Salvador E. Luria. New York: Harper & Row, 1984.

The Fluctuation Test

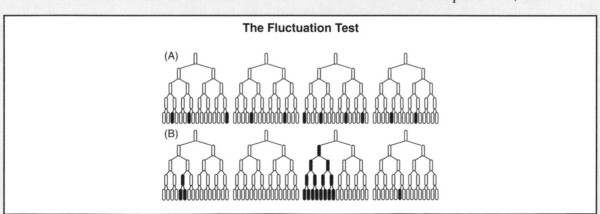

(A). Bacteria become resistant through contact with phages and their numbers per culture are fairly constant. (B). They arise spontaneously and their numbers fluctuate greatly between cultures. (from *A Slot Machine, a Broken Test Tube*, by Luria)

etnam War. His honors included the presidency of the American Society of Microbiologists and a National Academy of Science membership. Luria died on February 6, 1991.

Bibliography

By Luria
"Mutations of Bacteria from Virus Sensitivity to Virus Resistance," *Genetics*, 1943 (with Max Delbrück)

"Mutations of Bacterial Viruses Affecting Their Host Range," *Genetics*, 1945

"Reactivation of Irradiated Bacteriophage by Transfer of Self-Reproducing Units," *Proceedings of the National Academy of Sciences*, 1947

"Recent Advances in Bacterial Genetics," *Bacteriological Reviews*, 1947

"Ultraviolet Irradiation During Intracellular Growth," *Journal of Bacteriology*, 1947 (with R. Latarjet)

"Genetic Recombination Leading to Production of Active Bacteriophage from Ultraviolet Inactivated Particles," *Genetics*, 1949 (with Renato Dulbecco)

"The Frequency of Distribution of Spontaneous Bacteriophage Mutants as Evidence for the Exponential Rate of Phage Reproduction," *Cold Spring Harbor Symposia on Quantitative Biology*, 1951

"Host-Induced Modifications of Bacterial Viruses," *Cold Spring Harbor Symposia on Quantitative Biology*, 1953

General Virology, 1953 (with J. E. Darnell)

"Lysogenization, Transduction, and Genetic Recombination in Bacteria," *Cold Spring Harbor Symposia on Quantitative Biology*, 1958 (with D. Fraser, J. Adams, and J. Burrows)

"Transduction of Lactose-Utilising Ability Among Strains of *E. coli* and *S. dysenteriae* and the Properties of Transducing Phage Particles," *Virology*, 1960 (with Adams and R. C. Ting)

"The Comparative Anatomy of a Gene," *Harvey Lectures*, 1966

"Phage, Colicins, and Macroregulatory Phenomena," *Science*, 1970

Life, the Unfinished Experiment, 1973

Thirty-six Lectures in Biology, 1975

A View of Life, 1981 (with Stephen Jay Gould and Sam Singer)

A Slot Machine, a Broken Test Tube: An Autobiography, 1984

"Genetic Study of the Functional Organization of the Colicin E_1 Molecule," *Journal of Bacteriology*, 1985 (with Joan L. Suit, M. L. Fan, and C. Kaylar)

"Expression of the *kil* Gene of ColE$_1$ Plasmid in *Escheria coli* kil^r Mutants Causes Release of Periplasmic Enzymes and Colicin Without Cell Death," *Journal of Bacteriology*, 1988 (with Suit)

About Luria
The Genetics of Bacteria and Their Viruses. William Hayes. New York: John Wiley & Sons, 1964.

Molecular Biology of Bacterial Viruses. Gunther Stent. San Francisco: W. H. Freeman, 1963.

A Slot Machine, a Broken Test Tube. Salvador E. Luria. New York: Harper & Row, 1984.

(Sanford S. Singer)

Jane X. Luu

Areas of Achievement: Astronomy and physics

Contribution: Luu discovered and studied objects in the region of the outer solar system known as the Kuiper belt, leading to a greater understanding of the origin of comets.

July 15, 1963	Born in Saigon, South Vietnam
1975	Emigrates to the United States
1980-1984	Attends Stanford University
1984	Earns a bachelor's degree in physics from Stanford
1984	Employed at the Jet Propulsion Laboratory
1986-1990	Participates in graduate studies at the Massachusetts Institute of Technology (MIT)
1986	Begins a collaboration with David C. Jewitt
1990	Earns a Ph.D. in planetary astronomy from MIT
1991	Awarded the Annie Jump Cannon Prize
1990-1992	Receives a postdoctorate fellowship to the Harvard-Smithsonian Center for Astrophysics
1992	Discovers the first known object in the Kuiper belt
1992-1993	Receives a Hubble Fellowship to Stanford
1993-1994	Receives a Hubble Fellowship to the University of California, Berkeley
1994	Becomes an assistant professor at Harvard University

Early Life

Jane X. Luu was born Luu Le Hang in Saigon, South Vietnam, on July 15, 1963. Luu and her family fled to the United States when the North Vietnamese army entered Saigon on April 30, 1975. After living in a refugee camp and in Paducah, Kentucky, in 1975 and 1976, Luu's family settled in Southern California. Her name was changed to Jane Luu at this time. (The "X" in Luu's name does not stand for a middle name. She selected it as a middle initial for convenience.)

After her graduation from high school as valedictorian in 1980, Luu attended Stanford University in Palo Alto, California; she earned a bachelor's degree in physics there in 1984. During the summer of 1984, she was employed as a computer operator at the Jet Propulsion Laboratory (JPL) at the California Institute of Technology (Caltech) in Pasadena, California. Her experience at JPL, where the studies of the *Voyager* space probes were conducted, inspired Luu to study astronomy.

Luu began graduate studies at the Massachusetts Institute of Technology (MIT) in Cambridge, Massachusetts, in 1986. Her thesis adviser was astronomer David C. Jewitt, with whom Luu began a long and productive collaboration. They continued to work together when Jewitt transferred to the University of Hawaii in 1988. Luu earned a Ph.D. in planetary astronomy from MIT in 1990.

The Discovery of 1992 QB1

In 1987, Luu and Jewitt began searching for objects in the region of the outer solar system known as the Kuiper belt. Most of this work was done using a 2.2-meter telescope on the peak of Mauna Kea on the island of Hawaii. Electronic detectors known as charge-coupled devices (CCDs) were used to search for small, distant objects too dim to be detected by photographic plates.

The search continued while Luu completed her doctorate studies. She received a postdoctorate fellowship to the Harvard-Smithsonian Center for Astrophysics in Cambridge, Massachusetts, from 1990 to 1992. In 1991, she was awarded the Annie Jump Cannon Prize from the American Astronomical Society.

Luu and Jewitt discovered the first known

The Kuiper Belt

The Kuiper belt is a region of the outer solar system containing numerous small objects believed to be the source of certain comets.

In 1951, the Dutch-American astronomer Gerard Peter Kuiper suggested that there exists a region of space beyond the orbit of Neptune that contains material left over from the formation of the solar system. The small objects found there could be drawn closer to the sun by the gravitational pull of the large planets, transforming them into comets.

The existence of the Kuiper belt was confirmed in the 1990's when Luu and other astronomers discovered several small objects in this region. The Kuiper belt is believed to be the source of a group of objects known as Centaurs that cross the orbits of the planets of the outer solar system. The Centaurs are thought to have been pulled away from the Kuiper belt by the gravitational force of the planets. Their orbits are unstable, and

The Orbit of 1992 QB₁

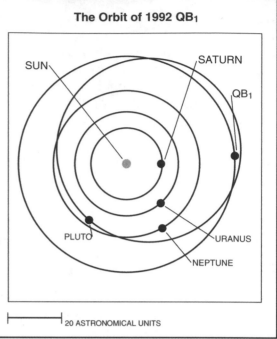

20 ASTRONOMICAL UNITS

In 1992, Luu and David C. Jewitt identified QB₁, an object in the Kuiper belt, and they were able to determine its orbit. (from Peter Samek's illustration for Luu and Jewitt's "The Kuiper Belt," *Scientific American*, May, 1996)

astronomers believe that they may be pulled into the inner solar system to become comets.

Luu has suggested that the planet Pluto, its moon Charon, and Triton, one of the moons of Neptune, may be large Kuiper belt objects that were pulled into their present orbits by the gravity of Neptune. These three objects are all much denser than the other planets and moons of the outer solar system and have unusual orbits that suggest such an origin.

The Kuiper Belt

Sun
Neptune

100 ASTRONOMICAL UNITS

Objects that could be detected by the observatory on Mauna Kea in Hawaii are shown clustered near the inner border of the Kuiper belt, according to this computer simulation. (from Peter Samek's illustration for Luu and David C. Jewitt's "The Kuiper Belt," *Scientific American*, May, 1996)

Bibliography

The New Solar System. J. Kelly Beatty and Andrew Chaikin, eds. Cambridge, Mass.: Sky, 1990.

The Quest for Comets: An Explosive Trail of Beauty and Danger. David H. Levy. New York: Plenum Press, 1994.

Wanderers in Space: Exploration and Discovery in the Solar System. Kenneth R. Lang and Charles A. Whitney. Cambridge, England: Cambridge University Press, 1991.

object in the Kuiper belt on August 30, 1992. The object, officially known as 1992 QB1, was nicknamed "Smiley" after a character in the novels of John Le Carré. 1992 QB1 was seen to be a reddish object with a diameter of about 280 kilometers orbiting the sun at a distance of about 6.6 billion kilometers.

More Fellowships, More Discoveries

Luu received Hubble Fellowships to Stanford from 1992 to 1993 and to the University of California, Berkeley, from 1993 to 1994. She became an assistant professor at Harvard University in Cambridge, Massachusetts, in 1994.

Meanwhile, Luu and other astronomers dis-

(AP/Wide World Photos)

covered new objects in the Kuiper belt. Five objects were found in 1993, and about a dozen objects were identified each year from 1994 to 1996. Luu was directly involved in the majority of these discoveries.

Bibliography

By Luu

"The Kuiper Belt" in *Asteroids, Comets, and Meteors, 1993*, 1994

"The Solar System Beyond Neptune," *Astronomical Journal*, 1995 (with David C. Jewitt)

"The Kuiper Belt," *Scientific American*, 1996 (with Jewitt)

About Luu

"The Authors." *Scientific American* 274 (May, 1996).

"The Remarkable Odyssey of Jane Luu." Marcia Bartusiak. *Astronomy* 24 (February, 1996).

Who's Who in Science and Engineering. New Providence, N.J.: Marquis, 1996.

(Rose Secrest)

André Lwoff

Areas of Achievement: Biology, genetics, and virology

Contribution: Lwoff's study of lysogenic viruses played a significant role in the understanding of the genetic mechanisms of bacterial replication and viral infection.

May 8, 1902	Born in Ainay-le-Château, France
1921	Receives a bachelor's degree from the Sorbonne
1927	Receives medical degree while working at the Institut Pasteur
1932	Earns a doctorate in the natural sciences
1932	Receives a Rockefeller Fellowship to work at the Kaiser Wilhelm Institute in Heidelberg, Germany
1936	With Marguerite Lwoff, establishes the role of vitamins as coenzymes
1938	Becomes head of the Service de Physiologie Microbienne at the Institut Pasteur
1941	Publishes *L'Evolution physiologique*
1950	Demonstrates the perpetuation of viral deoxyribonucleic acid (DNA) in lysogenic bacteria
1959	Appointed professor of microbiology at the Sorbonne
1964	Awarded the Medaille de la Résistance for service during World War II
1965	Awarded the Nobel Prize in Physiology or Medicine
1968	Retires from the Institut Pasteur
1968-1972	Serves as director of the Cancer Research Institute at Villjuif, near Paris
Sept. 30, 1994	Dies in Paris, France

Early Life

André Lwoff (pronounced "lwahf") was born at Ainay-le-Château, France, the son of Russian Jewish immigrants. His father was head physician in a psychiatric hospital and often brought André with him. Lwoff later believed that his inclination toward science resulted from such exposure.

Lwoff developed an interest in biology at the age of thirteen following a visit with Élie Metchnikoff at the Institut Pasteur. Metchnikoff, the founder of the cellular school of immunology, allowed Lwoff to observe bacteria in his laboratory, and Lwoff decided that his career should be one in medical research.

During the summers of 1920 and 1921, Lwoff spent his time at the Marine Biological Laboratory in Brittany, in addition to studying biology, chemistry, and physics in the Faculté des Sciences in Paris. He received his bache-

The Induction of Bacteriophages from Lysogenic Bacteria

Bacterial viruses (bacteriophages) are maintained in a noninfectious form in lysogenic bacteria. Exposure of these bacteria to ultraviolet light can induce the viruses to grow.

Lysogeny, the maintenance of bacteriophages in a noninfectious form, was discovered in 1921 by Jules Bordet and others, who observed that certain strains of bacteria could not be isolated free of the virus. Eugene and Elisabeth Wollman later proposed that these viruses alternate between infectious and noninfectious stages. They also suggested that during the noninfectious stage, the virus is part of the hereditary structure of the bacterium.

In 1949, Lwoff resumed the work started by the Wollmans, both of whom died during World War II. Lwoff believed that the real significance of the lysogenic question was how these lysogenic bacteria maintained the capacity to produce phages in the absence of free virus.

He began his work using a strain of a soil bacterium, *Bacillus megaterium*. He also thought that mass culture of the bacteria could not provide a proper answer. He would have to isolate and cultivate individual cells in order to make his observations.

Lwoff was able to manipulate individual bacteria within a microdrop of growth medium and to transfer these single cells to fresh medium. When the isolated cell had replicated itself into two bacteria, Lwoff would again transfer a single cell to fresh medium. He continued this procedure over the course of nineteen cell divisions.

He found that each isolated cell, even in the absence of free phages, maintained the capacity to produce the virus. Maintenance of lysogeny could not have been the result of phages sticking to the bacterial surface, since an impossibly large number of virus particles would have had to be present in order to survive nineteen divisions.

Lwoff also observed the occasional spontaneous lysis (disintegration) of single bacteria. When he assayed the culture fluid following such lysis, he observed the presence of numerous free bacteriophages. He determined that lysogenic bacteria liberate their phages through lysis. Lwoff's conclusion was that lysogenic bacteria maintain the virus in a noninfectious state, called a prophage.

He also believed that induction of the virus is under the control of environmental factors. He and his students Louis Siminovitch and Niels Kjelgaard began a search of factors that can be used to induce the prophage.

They discovered that irradiation with small doses of ultraviolet light could induce virus production. They also observed similar induction using hydrogen peroxide, X rays, or certain organic chemicals. Since many of these chemicals have carcinogenic activity, Lwoff at first believed that the induction of such viruses may also play a role in human cancer. Research would later prove this assumption to be incorrect.

Bibliography

Molecular Biology of Bacterial Viruses. Gunther Stent. San Francisco: W. H. Freeman, 1963.
Molecular Cell Biology. James Darnell, Harvey Lodish, and David Baltimore. New York: W. H. Freeman, 1990.
Phage and the Origins of Molecular Biology. John Cairns, Gunther Stent, and James Watson, eds. New York: Cold Spring Harbor, 1966.

lor's degree in natural sciences from the University of Paris (the Sorbonne) in 1921.

During this time, Lwoff had the opportunity to study with protozoologist Edouard Chatton. It was Chatton who, in 1928, first used the terms "prokaryotic" and "eukaryotic" to describe the two basic forms of cells. Lwoff and Chatton would collaborate until Chatton's death in 1947.

In 1921, Lwoff received a fellowship for the study of protozoa. He continued his research on morphogenesis and development while working for his medical degree. Studying respiration in flagellates, Lwoff was later able to establish the role of hematin as a necessary growth factor, the first example of the role played by vitamins as coenzymes.

During this period, Lwoff developed a friendship with Eugene and Elisabeth Wollman, pioneers in the study of lysogenic bacteria. The Wollmans had established that bacterial viruses (bacteriophages) were introduced into the genetic material of bacteria, a phenomenon called lysogeny. In 1938, Lwoff became chair of microbial physiology at the Institut Pasteur.

The War Years and After

Lwoff remained in France during the war, becoming a member of the Resistance. In addition to gathering intelligence for the Allies, he hid American pilots who had been shot down over France. He was later awarded the Medaille de la Résistance for his work. The Wollmans were less fortunate; arrested in 1943, they died in a concentration camp.

In 1949, Lwoff decided to continue the work started by the Wollmans. He demonstrated that single bacteria would carry bacteriophages in an inactive form. The phage, which was incorporated as part of the cell's genetic material, could be induced upon exposure to chemicals or ultraviolet light. This work would result in Lwoff's being awarded the Nobel Prize in Physiology or Medicine in 1965.

Lwoff entered a third phase of his career following his attendance at a Cold Spring Harbor symposium on viruses, held in New York in 1953. At the time, testing of polio vaccines had just begun, and Lwoff became interested in the temperature-sensitive characteristic of certain strains of the virus. He would study polio for most of the remainder of his life.

In 1968, Lwoff retired from the Institut Pasteur, becoming the director of the Cancer Research Institute at Villejuif. He retired in 1972 and died in 1994 at the age of ninety-two.

(The Nobel Foundation)

Bibliography

By Lwoff

"Studies on Codehydrogenases: I. Nature of Growth Factor 'V'," *Proceedings of the Royal Society of London*, 1937 (with M. Lwoff)

L'Evolution physiologique: Étude des pertes de fonctions chez les microorganismes, 1944 (physiological evolution: study of the loss of functions among microorganisms)

Problems of Morphogenesis in Ciliates, 1950

"Induction de la lyse bactériophagique de la totalité d'une population microbienne lysogène" (induction of lytic bacteriophage from a single population of lysogenic bacteria), *Comptes rendus hebdomadaires des séances de l'Académie des Sciences*, 1950 (with L. Simi-

novitch and N. Kjeldgaard)
Biochemistry and Physiology of Protozoa, 1951-1964 (3 vols.; as editor)
"Conditions de l'efficacité inductrice du rayonnement ultra-violet chez une bactérie lysogène" (conditions for induction of bacterial lysogen using ultraviolet light), *Annales de l'Institut Pasteur*, 1951
"Lysogeny," *Bacteriological Reviews*, 1953
"The Concept of Virus," *Journal of General Microbiology*, 1957
Biological Order, 1962
"The Thermosensitive Critical Event of the Viral Cycle," *Cold Spring Harbor Symposia on Quantitative Biology*, 1962
"Death and Transfiguration of a Problem," *Bacteriological Reviews*, 1969
"Inhibition of Poliovirus RNA Synthesis by Supraoptimal Temperatures," *Journal of General Virology*, 1970
"From Protozoa to Bacteria and Viruses: Fifty Years with Microbes," *Annual Review of Microbiology*, 1971
Origins of Molecular Biology: A Tribute to Jacques Monod, 1979 (as editor, with Agnes Ullmann)

About Lwoff
"André Lwoff." In *The Nobel Prize Winners: Physiology or Medicine*, edited by Frank N. Magill. Pasadena, Calif.: Salem Press, 1991.
Notable Twentieth-Century Scientists. Emily J. McMurray, ed. Detroit: Gale Research, 1995.
Of Microbes and Life. Jacques Monod and Ernest Borek, eds. New York: Columbia University Press, 1971.

(Richard Adler)

Sir Charles Lyell

Area of Achievement: Earth science
Contribution: Lyell established geology as a science and helped lay the foundation for the modern interpretation of Earth's history.

Nov. 14, 1797	Born in Kinnordy, Kirriemuir, Scotland
1819	Graduated from Oxford University and is elected to the Geological Society of London
1823	Visits Europe, meeting leading scientists
1826	Elected a Fellow of the Royal Society of London
1828	Travels to Europe with Roderick Murchison to study geology
1830-1833	Publishes *Principles of Geology*
1831	Appointed a professor of geology at King's College, London
1834	Awarded the Copley Medal of the Royal Society of London
1841	Sails to America and lectures at several universities
1845	Publishes *Travels in North America*
1848	Knighted by Queen Victoria
1856	Urges Charles Darwin to publish his ideas about evolution
1863	Publishes *The Geological Evidences of the Antiquity of Man*
1864	Elected president of the British Association for the Advancement of Science
1864	Created a baronet
1869	His health fails
1873	His wife dies unexpectedly
Feb. 22, 1875	Dies in London, England

Early Life

Born in Scotland, Charles Lyell was the oldest child of a well-to-do English couple. His father was university educated and studied law. His mother was well read but, as was the custom of the time, did not pursue a university education.

The family moved to Hampshire, in southern England, when Charles was a baby, and it was there that he spent his boyhood. His father was an avid collector of rare plants and encouraged Charles's interest in botany. Charles and his brother Thomas attended boarding school in 1805. In the winter of 1808, Charles became ill with pleurisy. While convalescing he developed an interest in insects and their habits.

Academic Influences

In 1816, Lyell entered Exeter College, Oxford, and took a classical education, studying Greek, Latin, and the writings of Aristotle. While at Oxford, he attended lectures in mineralogy and geology given by William Buckland. His interest in things scientific shifted from insects (entomology) to the formation of the earth (geology).

In the summers of 1817-1818, Lyell toured Scotland and Europe, observing and recording rock formations, fossils, and various terrains. He was graduated from Exeter in 1819 with average grades, but he was elected to the Geological Society of London that same year.

In 1819, with his father's encouragement, Lyell began to study law. His summers, however, were spent traveling and observing the geology and fossils of England, France, and Scotland. He met and studied with many famous scientists of the period, including naturalists Alexandre Brongniart, Baron Georges Cuvier, and Alexander von Humboldt.

Lyell began to practice law in 1825 and continued for two years. Although this profession would seem to keep him away from geology, he was assigned to the western circuit and used his travels to observe and map the geology of southwest England.

First Book and Life's Work

In 1826, Lyell published an article in the *Quarterly Review* entitled "Transactions of the Geo-

(Library of Congress)

The Foundation for Modern Earth Science

In his work Principles of Geology *(1830-1833), Lyell championed a new paradigm for interpreting the history of the earth, uniformitarianism.*

Another Scottish geologist, James Hutton, had introduced the idea of uniformitarianism fifty years earlier, but it was Lyell who clarified and illuminated it with field data. Simply, this theory states that forces observed today such as erosion, sedimentation, and uplift, although subtle and slow by human standards, are the same that have occurred in the past. Further, the structure and topography of the earth can be created with these forces if its history is measured in millions or billions of years. *Principles of Geology* became the standard text of geology and went through twelve editions, the last appearing after his death.

When Charles Darwin returned from his long voyage on H.M.S. *Beagle* in 1836, he had outlined his theory on "descent by modification" (evolution). During this five-year voyage, he had studied Lyell's *Principles of Geology* and incorporated many of its ideas into his own geologic interpretations. In 1838, Darwin presented a paper of his geological observations in South America to the London Geological Society in which he supported Lyell's position on uniformitarianism. Between the years 1836 and 1841, the two men saw each other on a regular basis until Darwin moved from London. Thereafter, they corresponded frequently and met occasionally.

On November 26, 1855, Lyell read an article by Alfred Russell Wallace entitled "On the Law Which Has Regulated the Introduction of New Species" in which Wallace expressed evolutionary ideas similar to Darwin's. On April 13, 1856, Lyell visited Darwin and urged him to express his ideas on evolution formally and to publish them immediately. Darwin was reluctant but began writing. In 1858, Wallace sent Darwin his full manuscript and asked for a critique. Darwin was shocked to see his ideas in Wallace's handwriting. Lyell helped Darwin resolve the question of intellectual priority for the evolution theory. On July 1, 1858, he and Joseph Hooker read both Darwin's and Wallace's papers into the minutes of the Linnean Society's meeting. Both would share authorship of the theory.

The question of evolution and new fossil discoveries in Europe intrigued Lyell. He spent the next few years researching the question of the origin of the human species. In 1862, he wrote the book *The Geological Evidences of the Antiquity of Man*, in which he organized the knowledge about humankind's prehistory, stone tool discoveries, and the discovery of a Neanderthal skeleton. He concluded that if all races were descended from a common ancestor, then large amounts of time were needed for small gradual changes to develop the various races observed in modern times. In the tenth edition of *Principles of Geology*, Lyell fully supported Darwin's theory. The question of geologic time would not be resolved quantitatively, however, until the discovery of radioactivity in 1895 and the use of radioactive dating methods developed in the 1920's.

Bibliography

Early Science in Oxford. Richard T. Gunther. Oxford, England: Oxford University Press, 1937.

The Founders of Geology. Sir Archibald Geikie. New York: Macmillan, 1905.

Principles of Geology. Charles Lyell. 3 vols. London: John Murray, 1830-1833.

logical Society of London." This was in actuality a description of the state of geological knowledge and major questions of the period. This paper caused him to rethink his own views concerning geological processes.

Catastrophism, the idea that geological history was characterized by sudden and violent changes, was the current explanation for the shape of the earth. Lyell reasoned that these mysterious and capricious forces were unnecessary, and that, given enough time, the shape and structure of the earth could be explained by currently known physical processes.

The question of the age of the earth was at the heart of the debate. Catastrophists held that Earth was created in a short time (the biblical six days) with large, violent forces no longer in effect. The Uniformitarianists thought that the slow and gradual forces that they currently observed had acted in the past and that the past was measured in millions of years, not a few thousand.

Lyell made geological tours of Europe during the summers of 1827, in which he visited France, and 1828, when he was joined by leading geologist Roderick Murchison and his wife. They toured France, Germany, and Italy, where Lyell observed situations which convinced him that understanding the present was the key to unraveling the past.

Returning to England in 1829, he set to work on the book *Principles of Geology*, which was first published between 1830 and 1833 but the revision of which would become his life's work. In this book, he set the modern foundations for the science of geology.

England Honors Her Best

Many honors and awards came to Lyell, both scientific and social. He was awarded knighthood by Queen Victoria in 1848 and the title of baronet in 1864. He won many scientific honors and chaired many societies. Two are notable: In 1834, he was awarded the Copley Medal of the Royal Society of London and the Wollaston Medal of the Geological Society of London.

After 1869, his health failed steadily. In April, 1973, his wife died unexpectedly, and Lyell never recovered from the loss. He died on February 22, 1875. He was buried in Westminster Abbey.

Bibliography
By Lyell
Principles of Geology, Being an Attempt to Explain the Former Changes of the Earth's Surface by Reference to Causes Now in Operation, 1830-1833 (3 vols.; numerous subsequent editions)

Elements of Geology, 1838

Travels in North America in the Years 1841-2: With Geological Observations on the United States, Canada, and Nova Scotia, 1845 (2 vols.)

The Geological Evidences of the Antiquity of Man with Remarks on Theories of the Origin of Species, 1863 (commonly known as *The Antiquity of Man*)

About Lyell
Dictionary of Scientific Biography. Charles Coulston Gillispie, ed. New York: Charles Scribner's Sons, 1973.

The Founders of Geology. Sir Archibald Geikie. New York: Macmillan, 1905.

Giants of Geology. Carroll Fenton and Mildred Fenton. Garden City, N.Y.: Doubleday, 1952.

(*Richard C. Jones*)

Barbara McClintock

Areas of Achievement: Botany, cell biology, and genetics

Contribution: A pioneer in genetics, McClintock proved that genetic recombination involved an exchange of chromosomal material and discovered the existence of mobile genetic elements, called jumping genes.

June 16, 1902	Born in Hartford, Connecticut
1927	Receives a Ph.D. in botany from Cornell University
1931-1933	Given a National Research Council Fellowship
1933	Travels to Germany on a Guggenheim Fellowship
1941	Takes a position at Cold Spring Harbor Laboratory
1944	Elected president of the Genetics Society of America
1944	Named to the National Academy of Sciences
1965-1975	Named Andrew White Professor-at-Large
1967	Wins the Kimber Genetics Award
1970	Awarded the National Medal of Science
1981	Wins the Albert Lasker Basic Medical Research Award
1981	Wins the Wolfe Prize in Medicine
1981	Receives a MacArthur Foundation lifetime annual fellowship
1982	Wins the Horowitz Prize at Columbia University
1983	Wins the Nobel Prize in Physiology or Medicine
Sept. 2, 1992	Dies in Huntington, Long Island, New York

Early Life

Barbara McClintock was the daughter of Thomas McClintock, a physician, and Sara Hardy. Barbara spent considerable time with her paternal aunt and uncle in rural Massachusetts. There, she gained a love for the outdoors. When she was eight years old, her family moved to the Flatbush section of Brooklyn, New York. She enjoyed reading and outdoor sports, including ice skating and bicycle riding. She was graduated from the Brooklyn school system in 1918.

McClintock enrolled in Cornell University in Ithaca, New York, in 1919 to study biology in the College of Agriculture. She was elected president of the women's freshman class. At Cornell, she studied genetics under C. B. Hutchison and cytology under Lester Sharp. McClintock became interested in the behavior of chromosomes during cell division. She worked with Rollins Emerson, who was studying the genetics of maize (Indian corn). She received her B.S. degree in 1923.

McClintock continued as a graduate student at Cornell, with a major in cytology (the study of cells) and a minor in genetics and zoology. As a graduate student in 1924, she revolutionized the study of maize genetics when she developed a technique to visualize maize chromosomes microscopically. She received her M.A. in 1925 and her Ph.D. in 1927.

Early Research

McClintock continued to study maize while she worked as an instructor of botany at Cornell from 1927 to 1931. She worked with graduate students Marcus Rhoades and George Wells Beadle and became interested in the morphology of maize chromosomes and the correlation of chromosomal morphology with phenotypic traits. It was during this time that she and Harriet Creighton proved that genetic recombination results from an exchange of chromosomal material during the process of meiosis (gamete formation). McClintock and Creighton published their work in 1931, four months before Curt Stern, a German biologist, published similar findings for *Drosophilia* (the fruit fly).

In 1931, McClintock received a National Research Council Fellowship for two years to study maize. Since Cornell refused to give her

Transposable Genetic Elements and Crossing-Over

McClintock theorized that some segments of deoxyribonucleic acid (DNA) can move from site to site within a chromosome or between chromosomes. She also offered cytological proof that during the formation of gametes, segments of homologous chromosomes can exchange (cross-over), resulting in genetic recombination.

In the 1940's, McClintock noticed that maize (Indian corn) plants often contain kernels that are unevenly colored. She discovered that these variegated kernels contain genetic elements that she named dissociation (*Ds*) and activator (*Ac*) that could move (transpose) from one part of the chromosome to another and from one chromosome to another.

Provided that *Ac* is present in the genome, *Ds* can induce chromosome breaks adjacent to its location and move to another location. At its new location, *Ds* may cause a mutation by suppressing genetic activity at that site. *Ds* may then move again, relieving the suppression. Although *Ds* requires *Ac* for movement, *Ac* is capable of autonomous movement.

McClintock realized the implications of her discovery. She thought that the *Ac* and *Ds* genes were controlling genes that could dictate the action of other genes during development. She also realized that mobile genetic elements could be important in evolution, leading to the rapid development of species.

Studies by molecular biologists in the 1980's and 1990's demonstrated that *Ac* is a code for an enzyme called transposase, which is essential for transposition. *Ds* has a similar structure but cannot code for transposase. This is why *Ac* is capable of autonomous transposition but *Ds* requires the presence of *Ac*.

After molecular biologists discovered mobile genetic elements in bacteria in the late 1960's and in *Drosophila* (the fruit fly) and other animals in the 1970's, it became apparent that mobile genetic elements were not an isolated phenomenon specific to maize.

Her work is now known to be of great biological and medical importance, since mobile genetic elements have been shown to cause human disease. The roles of mobile genetic elements in evolution and cell regulation are being determined.

With Harriet Creighton at Cornell University, McClintock also demonstrated that genetic recombination correlates with the exchange of chromosomal material. They designed plants with an unusual ninth chromosome. This unusual chromosome, with a knob at one end and a piece added on the other, carried the dominant gene for colored aleurone and the recessive gene for waxy endosperm. The other ninth chromosome had a normal morphology and carried the recessive gene for colorless aleurone and the dominant gene for starchy endosperm.

These plants were crossed to plants with two normal chromosomes, one carrying the colorless and starchy genes and the other carrying the colorless and waxy genes. If no genetic recombination occurred, the progeny plants would be colorless and starchy, colored and starchy, and colored and waxy. Among the progeny, however, was the genetic recombinant colorless and waxy.

An examination of the ninth chromosome of these recombinant plants revealed a chromosome with only the elongated piece and not the knob, proving that genetic recombination resulted from a physical exchange of chromosome parts.

The cytological proof of genetic recombination is one of the major factors resulting in genetic variation and diversity.

Bibliography

"Barbara McClintock's Controlling Elements: Now at the DNA Level." H.-P. Doering and P. Starlinger. *Cell* 39 (1984).

Mobile DNA. D. E. Berg and M. M. Howe. Washington, D.C.: American Society of Microbiology, 1989.

Mobile Genetic Elements: J. A. Shapiro, ed. New York: Academic Press, 1983.

"Transposable Genetic Elements." S. N. Cohen and J. A. Shapiro. *Scientific American* 242 (1980).

"Transposable Genetic Elements in Eukaryotes." D. J. Finnegan. *International Review of Cytology* 93 (1985).

"Transposable Genetic Elements in Maize." N. V. Federoff. *Scientific American* 250, (1984).

an appointment—the university hired women only to teach home economics—she accepted a position as a research fellow at Thomas Hunt Morgan's laboratory at the California Institute of Technology (Caltech).

Between traveling from New York to California, she often spent time at the University of Missouri in Columbia, studying the effects of X rays on the chromosomes of maize with Lewis Stadler. There, she discovered that when X rays break chromosomes, the broken ends have a tendency to "find" one another and fuse. When the chromosomes attempt to separate during meiosis, they break again. She described these events as a breakage-fusion-bridge cycle.

In 1933, McClintock traveled to Germany to work with Richard Goldschmidt on a Guggenheim Fellowship. Adolf Hitler had just become chancellor of Germany, and Nazism was on the rise. After a brief stay with Goldschmidt, she returned to New York to work in Rollins Emerson's maize genetics laboratory at Cornell.

In 1936, the University of Missouri offered McClintock an assistant professorship. She remained there until 1941, when she left because the university would not offer her a permanent position because she was a woman.

Cold Spring Harbor Laboratory
In the summer of 1941, McClintock accepted a temporary appointment to study at Cold Spring Harbor Laboratory with Rhoades. Later that fall, she accepted a staff position there, a position that she would hold the rest of her life. In 1944, she was elected president of the Genetics Society of America; she had been elected vice president in 1931. In 1944, she also became only the third woman to be elected to the National Academy of Sciences, the most prestigious science society in the United States. From 1958 to 1961, she trained Latin American cytologists in maize genetics.

Building on observations made a decade earlier, she spent her early years at the Cold Spring Harbor Laboratory gathering data that suggested the existence of mobile genetic elements. From the early 1940's through the 1950's, she developed her theories on mobile genetic elements, which are now called transposable elements and sometimes referred to as jumping genes.

(The Nobel Foundation)

As soon as it was recognized that McClintock's discoveries had broad application, she received numerous awards for her scientific achievements. These awards included the Kimber Genetics Award in 1967, the National Medal of Science in 1970, the Wolf Prize in Medicine in 1981, the Albert Lasker Basic Medical Research Award in 1981, a MacArthur Foundation Fellowship in 1981, the Horowitz Prize of Columbia University in 1982 (shared with Susumu Tonegawa), and the Nobel Prize in Physiology or Medicine in 1983. At the time she was awarded the Nobel Prize, she was only the seventh woman to receive such an award in science and the only sole female recipient in physiology or medicine.

Bibliography
By McClintock
"A Correlation of Cytological and Genetical Crossing-over in *Zea mays*," *Proceedings of the National Academy of Sciences*, 1931 (with Harriet B. Creighton)

"Chromosome Organization and Genic Expression," *Cold Spring Harbor Symposia on Quantitative Biology*, 1951

About McClintock
"Barbara McClintock." Sue V. Rosser. In *The Nobel Prize Winners: Physiology or Medicine*, edited by Frank N. Magill. Pasadena, Calif.: Salem Press, 1991.
"Barbara McClintock: The Overlooked Genius of Genetics." Evelyn Fox Keller. In *A Passion to Know: Twenty Profiles in Science*. Allen L. Hammond, ed. New York: Charles Scribner's Sons, 1984.
Feeling for the Organism: The Life and Work of Barbara McClintock. Evelyn Fox Keller. San Francisco: W. H. Freeman, 1983.
"A Naturalist of the Genome." Roger Lewin. *Science* 222 (1983).
"Nobel Prize to Barbara McClintock." John Maddux. *Nature* 305 (1983).
Nobel Prize Winners. Tyler Wasson, ed. New York: H. W. Wilson, 1987.
Nobel Prize Women in Science. Sharon Bertsch McGrayne. New York: Birch Lane Press, 1993.

(Charles L. Vigue)

Cyrus Hall McCormick

Areas of Achievement: Invention and technology

Contribution: McCormick invented, developed, and manufactured a reaper that revolutionized nineteenth century American agriculture and allowed rapid land development during westward migration.

Feb. 15, 1809	Born in Rockbridge County, Virginia
1831	Patents a hillside plow
1831	Designs and builds a reaping machine for harvesting crops
1834	Patents the Virginia reaper
1835	Moves to a farm on South River given to him by his father
1836	Constructs an iron furnace and enters into a partnership with his father to manufacture iron
1840	Begins to manufacture and sell the Virginia reaper
1841	Sells his iron furnace, plunging the family into debt
1841	Improves the cutting apparatus of the reaper by reversing the direction of the serration to eliminate clogging
1847	Founds the McCormick Harvesting Machine Company in Chicago
1856	Patents a mower
1858	Marries Nancy Maria Fowler
1864	Runs as a Democrat for the House of Representatives and loses
1878	Elected to the French Legion of Honor and made a member of the Académie des Sciences
May 13, 1884	Dies in Chicago, Illinois

Early Life

Cyrus Hall McCormick, the son of a farmer and mechanic, was born in rural Virginia. His formal education was limited to reading, writing, and arithmetic at a country school. A surveyor living with his family also taught him higher mathematics. McCormick grew up watching his father invent devices and machines, including an ineffectual reaper. He learned his mechanical skills from his father and was not aware that others, such as Obed Hussey, were working on mechanical reapers.

McCormick's mechanical skill manifested itself early. By the age of fifteen, he had designed a lighter cradle (an implement used to harvest grain by hand slowly) so that he could compete with grown men at harvest time. At eighteen, he built surveying instruments. He also patented a hillside plow at the age of twenty-two.

The Development of the Reaper

In 1831, after his father's final attempt at inventing a reaper, McCormick invented a working reaper. Rather than practicing trial and error with full-size machines, as his father had done, he first built small models and drew up

(Library of Congress)

An Effective Reaper

McCormick was the first to combine the basic elements that made the reaper a practical grain-harvesting device.

Several elements made McCormick's Virginia reaper an effective design: a straight knife with a serrated edge and reciprocal or vibrating motion to cut grain; fingers or guards extending from the platform to prevent grain from slipping sideways while being cut; a revolving reel to hold grain against the knife and to lay cut stalks on the attached platform; a master wheel to carry the weight of the machine and furnish power to operate the reel and knife through ground traction; a forward draft from the right or stubble side; and a divider on the left to separate grain to be cut from grain left standing.

The reaper effectively solved a bottleneck. Slow harvesting techniques, such as cradles, limited the amount of grain that a farmer could grow because the grain had to be harvested immediately upon ripening. With the reaper, farmers could harvest grain more quickly and thus grow larger amounts.

The invention of the reaper stimulated the invention and adoption of other improved agricultural tools. The reaper also allowed men to leave agricultural work—to fight in wars or move to cities—because even with the loss of labor, farms still produced enough to feed the nation. By the 1870's, one farmer with machines could harvest as much as an entire village had before the reaper.

Bibliography

American Agricultural Implements. Robert L. Ardrey. 1894. Reprint. New York: Arno Press, 1972.

The Farmer's Age. Paul W. Gates. New York: Holt, Rinehart and Winston, 1960.

Machines of Plenty. Stewart H. Holbrook. New York: Macmillan, 1955.

plans. He had developed these skills while working with a surveyor.

Even when he had a full-size working machine, McCormick wanted to perfect this device before he patented it or put it on the market. This delay later caused legal fights between McCormick, Hussey, and others over who owned the rights to the reaper. McCormick's original design, called the Virginia reaper, included the basic elements that remained essential parts of harvesters for the next hundred years.

McCormick tried to raise money to build reapers to sell. First, he started an iron furnace business, which failed. Next, he licensed the design of the Virginia reaper to manufacturers in New York, Ohio, and Illinois. Unfortunately, some of these manufacturers produced inferior reapers. Eventually, McCormick decided to manufacture reapers himself so that they would be of high quality. He went into business with two of his brothers and a manufacturer in Chicago.

A Business in Chicago

In 1847, he founded the McCormick Harvesting Machine Company in Chicago to manufacture his reapers. He made improvements on the reapers by adding self-raking, mowing, and binding features. Originally, the McCormicks ran their factory like a family blacksmith shop, a setting with which the brothers were familiar from their youth. Around 1880, the factory switched to mass production methods and was able to produce larger numbers of reapers.

McCormick's inventions also included business techniques. His company was one of the first to offer customer services that would become standard for consumer products in the twentieth century: warranties, service/repair, and credit. These services made the Virginia reaper the most popular in the nineteenth century.

McCormick died in Chicago in 1884 at the age of seventy-five.

Bibliography
By McCormick
The Century of the Reaper: An Account of Cyrus Hall McCormick, the Inventor of the Reaper; of the McCormick Harvesting Machine Company, the Business He Created; and of the International Harvester Company, His Heir and Chief Memorial, 1931

About McCormick
Cyrus Hall McCormick. William T. Hutchinson. New York: Da Capo Press, 1968.
One Hundred Fifty Years of International Harvester. Charles H. Wendel. Sarasota, Fla.: Crestline, 1981.
Reaper Man: The Story of Cyrus Hall McCormick. Clara Ingram Judson. Boston: Houghton Mifflin, 1948.

(Linda Eikmeier Endersby)

BIOGRAPHICAL ENCYCLOPEDIA of SCIENTISTS

Index

In the following index, volume numbers appear in **bold face** type and page numbers appear in normal type. The names of scientists who are profiled in the encyclopedia are shown in **bold face**.

Index